A WORLD SO SMALL

CAMERON DREAMSHARE

There is no greater agony than bearing an untold story inside you.
-Maya Angelou

I remember fantasizing as a child about Jane Austen secretly writing novels in the drawing room, hiding her forbidden work by pretending she was writing letters to her cousin. I was inspired by Helen Keller, without sight or hearing, driven to write prolifically, surpassing the limitations of conventional communication to share her profound messages with the world. I think about my PhD supervisor typing up her thesis on a typewriter, starting the page over for each mistake, while my trusty robot servant whisks away my errors and even helps me format my citations. I have every opportunity and technology at my disposal to write what my heart wants. First, I am so grateful for that. Second, technology may be changing the world, but for me, it was my own will to finish my book that was the limitation. Despite the odds against them, these people and so many more followed their dreams of singing their heartsongs. Come with me, dear friend; let me tell you of two people just like us... the year is 2034...

CONTENTS

PART ONE: A WORLD SO SMALL

CHAPTER ONE

Jordan closed his eyes, his hair whipping around his face in the breeze as he glided down the street. He enjoyed the sound of the wheels of his longboard grinding against the pavement as he went. The sun shone down on him, fat and warm, and he drank it in while he had the chance. He would miss the rest of the day at work.

He rolled up to Bridgehead, the coffee shop by his house. He flipped the longboard under his arm and swept his hair out of his eyes with his hand. Jordan was handsome and he knew it, and he felt eyes on him as he entered the shop. There was a certain kind of girl who was not deterred by his sloppy zip-up hoodies, ripped jeans and longish, usually somewhat greasy hair. He was a gig rat, to be sure—a millennial working for pitiful wages in late capitalism—but with his good looks he didn't have trouble keeping lovers around.

He walked up to the counter, getting in line. He pulled a device out of his pocket. Wealthy people used Virtual Reality Connect but he was still using smartphone technology like most gig rats. He opened the app for note-taking.

To Do:
-apply for sound tech job
-look for sound editing jobs
-edit recorded songs
-book Canada Day gig for the Waves
-groceries
-

"What can I get you?" asked the barista at the counter, a woman in her thirties with several piercings in her lip and an armful of tattoos.

"A latte," said Jordan. The $6 premium was the biggest useless expense in his budget, but he needed this one luxury to stay sane. He moved down to the bar, looking at his phone, switching apps to Tinder.

As he waited for his drink, he swiped through profiles of women.

No.

No.

No.

He paused as a picture of a woman appeared on the screen with long black hair and a huge smile. He scrolled through her pictures. Bikini. Palm trees. Laughing with her friends. He swiped yes, even though her life looked kind of intimidating. Was she 'the one'? Of course not. Tinder was as much about consuming profiles, the constant gratification of possibility—possibility that never needed any follow-through—as it was about going on a real date.

No.

No.

Another woman appeared who intrigued him, this one short with brown curls, cute glasses and a tattoo.

Yes.

As soon as he swiped yes, a message appeared on the screen: *It's a Match!*

That meant that she had also swiped yes to his profile.

A chat box opened where he was supposed to type something. The empty space filled only with the blinking type cursor made him feel heavy. He quickly closed the app. He switched to social media, looking furtively around the café, and then hitting the search bar.

S-A-R-A-H he typed. Sarah Singh popped up in his recent search history. He clicked on her, going to her profile to see what new things she'd posted.

A picture of her and her best friend. His gut clenched seeing her laughing face. An article about the lineup for Bluesfest. Before the breakup they planned to go to that festival together this summer.

Against his own better judgement, he clicked to expand her profile picture. It was her and her boyfriend holding ice cream cones and snuggling a dog.

He grabbed his coffee and went to the condiment stand, adding sugar to his latte. He took a few sips, looking at the picture, sinking deeper into the feeling in his stomach of half nausea, half punch.

The tattooed barista popped up over his shoulder, holding milk to top up the condiment stand.

"That's your ex, right? I remember her coming in here with you. Still thinking about her, eh?" She sounded sympathetic.

Jordan flushed red.

"I just wanted to see Snark," he said sheepishly.

She looked confused.

"The dog."

"Her dog?"

"Our dog," he said.

The barista gave him a look. "It's her dog now. Exes can't share pets. It doesn't work."

"I know. But I miss him."

"Well how come she got to keep him?"

"I couldn't walk him as often as he needs with my schedule, so it made more sense this way."

The barista looked down at the profile picture. "Is that her new boyfriend? He's hot."

Jordan sighed.

"Yea." He scrolled through pictures. Beach vacation. An image popped up of the guy cuddling Snark.

"Snark you little cheater," he murmured, closing the app.

The barista finished topping up the milk.

"Have a nice day," she said.

Jordan left the café.

Valkyrie Snow lay in bed later than usual. She was having her period, a rare occurrence these years, and time was slower when she bled. She needed more sleep, her body moved differently, and her thoughts came more sporadically. She was propped up on pillows in a massive wood bed, deep in feather duvets, holding a notebook and jotting her thoughts. This was her most creative time, when memories and ideas smashed together in ways they never did when she was being methodical. She had been spending a lot of time lately drawing up designs for her latest arcology project, but right now she was letting her dreams flow onto the page, both the nonsensical and the genius. Her architecture company, Hammer & Bone, produced romantic gothic-inspired condominiums throughout the 2020's, but in 2032 she went in a new direction. Valkyrie was building arcologies, or self-sustained, carbon-neutral oases for living. She moved out of the condo market and into a new framework where one complex building combined residential, industrial and agricultural in an efficient, integrated system. The building had automated gardens and natural air filtration systems. All waste materials were recycled, eaten by the building itself.

Val was always looking to the future. She hit the market at the perfect time; she was in talks with all the major space companies, and it looked like Snow Arcologies would replace the ugly cubic buildings already falling apart on the moon. The first fully automated living unit on Mars would be a Snow Arcology.

Valkyrie scribbled in her notebook.

There are 3D printer plans for every mechanism in the arcology
The community itself able to replace and repair
3D Printers on every floor for residential use. Everyone will be trained to use them

Val's brain surged into overdrive.

3D Printers for foods as well. Printed from nutrient-dense bio matter, flavoured and textured like gourmet foods…

Val lingered in bed, doodling diagrams and working out ideas, filling several pages of her book. Finally, her growling stomach drove her to get up. She pulled on a cozy oversized sweater and went downstairs. She went to the kitchen and pulled an espresso. She closed her eyes, drinking in the aroma of the crema, enjoying the splutter of the liquid pour into her china cup. Every sense, particularly smell, was heightened when she menstruated.

Valkyrie carried the cup close to her face over to the floor-to-ceiling windows of the main room of her open concept condo. She peered out at the people in the street, hurrying in the rain. Drops clung to the windows, gathering and dripping down slowly, while the sound of distant cascades rising and falling joined the soft patter of rain on the balcony as cars drove through the wet streets below. Val leaned against the window frame, sipping her espresso.

The apartment was only a one bedroom, but the soaring ceilings made it feel deceptively large. The kitchen was silver and wood with quartz counter tops, and the main room was sparsely and tastefully decorated with hand-curated items that suited Val's personality. The walls displayed antique prints of gothic architecture. The creamy thick-piled sheepskin rug on the floor looked cozy enough to sleep on. Val had several odd sculpture pieces carved from wood, matching her mid-century leather couch and chairs. A desk sat by the window covered with pens, pencils and drafting paper. The coffee table was a thick slab of glass on what appeared to be an ancient child-sized coffin. This macabre element was counterbalanced by messy racks of plants and colourful flowers on the balcony. Life and death.

There was a knock at the door.

"Come in," called Val.

A man entered. He was here to clean. She smiled and he nodded as he got to work tidying her dishes and refilling her barista machine with fresh beans. Most wealthy people nowadays were using biodegradable disposable plates and cutlery, made from cassava and mushroom, but Val preferred china, like the peasants. This man was lucky to keep his job. Disposable, automated culture was widespread and soon china would be in museums only.

Val slipped into her desk, comparing her jotted notes to the precise schematics of her latest arcology. Something was missing.

A dish clattered in the sink.

"Careful," she murmured. The servant mumbled apologetically. He went upstairs to change her sheets.

Jordan's feet ached and his hands were raw from the hot water. It had reached that point in the evening where he felt like he almost couldn't take it anymore, which meant that he had about an hour left. He stretched his arms as far back as he could in the tight space behind the kitchen, feeling his back pop, and then pushed himself to go hard for the last hour. He scrubbed the pots and pans, willing his mind to think about what he would do after he was done.

"Just finishing the dinner rush," called the kitchen manager, poking his shiny head into the windowless room. He eyed Jordan, elbow deep in greasy water.

"You're still faster than the machines," he laughed.

"Not for long," muttered Shanice, scrubbing beside him.

Earl O'Brien, the kitchen manager, lingered in the doorway, breathing hard and watching them work. He took pleasure in watching them washing the dishes. It wasn't a sexual pleasure, exactly, but it titillated him in a way he couldn't explain. He was married to a woman and he knew he was straight, but he especially liked watching Jordan, his hand moving up and down in the soapy water, red from the steam, the muscles and veins rippling up his arm. The sweat dripping off his nose. He loved telling Jordan, and Shanice too, to do things for him.

Jordan felt an uncomfortable prickle up his spine at Earl's gaze. He kept scrubbing and didn't turn around, but he knew that if he did, Earl would be watching him closely, his mouth open and his tongue slightly visible. Jordan could feel his shirt riding up and wanted to pull it down, but he didn't want to stop working or Earl would bark at him.

Eventually Earl left, and the shift wrapped up.

"Good night," said Jordan as he dried his hands.

"Night," called Shanice as she hurried off to pick up her kids at the babysitter's. Even though they spent hours together, they barely knew one another because it was loud in the back and hard to carry on a conversation while they washed the dishes.

"Night Scrubs," said Earl as they left.

Jordan burst out into the alley behind the restaurant, breathing in the cool night air. He ran his hand through his wet curls, letting the breeze dry out the steam still clinging to his whole body. He shifted his backpack up onto his shoulders and walked off briskly toward home. He didn't have much time but he needed a shower.

Jordan soon reached his crumbling brick walk-up. He typed in the access code and waited for the elevator. The doors groaned open and he stepped in, careful not to breathe through his nose because it usually smelled like vomit. He hit the 5 button. The floor was littered with trash and the walls inside the elevator were scrawled with messages like the inside of a men's washroom.

The elevator creaked up to the fifth floor. Jordan walked past the sounds of domestic life through the shitty thin walls of the old building, down to his unit. He unlocked the door and went in. No one was home because they were probably at the venue already.

Jordan lived with three other guys. They were all gig rats, picking up shifts and contracts where they could to make ends meet. Matt and Jerome and Jordan were in a band together called the Waves. Alex, who they usually called Bubba, wasn't in the band but he lived with them and went to all their shows anyway.

Jordan peeled off his clothes and threw them on the floor outside the bathroom, jumping in the shower. He lathered up his body quickly, feeling the sweat and grime melt off, willing Earl's sticky gaze to wash away too. The tub was lined with black mould, and the cracked tiles smelled like mildew and piss. The floor around the toilet was sticky and yellowish brown.

Jordan rinsed off and shut off the tap. He hopped out and grabbed one of several damp towels on the floor. He walked down the hall to his room, tousling his hair in the towel, and grabbing a T-shirt, jeans and a sweater from the clothes in his bed. He checked his phone: a text message from Jerome.

Where are you?
Jerome:

on my way
Jordan:

He rummaged around looking for socks, but he could only find one. He gave up, shoving his bare feet into high-tops and tying the laces. He grabbed a bag of corn chips off the counter and poured the crumbs into his mouth on his way out the door. He checked his phone again.

kk
Jerome:

He would be there soon. He sped up his pace, almost jogging. Chinatown was within walking distance of his apartment but he had to hurry to be on time for their set. He was the lead singer and they couldn't go on without him. He could just hear Matt's voice in his head: *It's like you don't even take the Waves serious.*

Matthew Doyle's father was a school teacher and his mother was an accountant in a small town. Teacher's college was a waste of time and money nowadays—no jobs. But Matt should have gone to college for accounting, and just maybe he could have gotten in at his mum's work. Instead he took History. His dad always wanted him to take History, but his dad grew up in a time before the internet, before peak oil, before space travel and head transplants and Virtual Reality Connect. Matt was taking History at the university, so reality wouldn't kick in for him for another year, when he had to start making his student loan payments.

Then he'll get it, thought Jordan.

Jordan arrived at Presse, the café where the Waves were performing, only ten minutes late.

"There's my man," said Jerome, giving Jordan a half hug and a slap on the back.

"Good crowd tonight," said Bubba, grinning. The café was packed, and there were a lot of girls.

"I hate it when you're late," said Matt. Jordan winked at him and slapped his butt. Matt didn't smile but Jordan could tell he wasn't mad. He was just glad Jordan had made it. The first band was just finished packing up.

"C'mon guys."

Jordan ran his hands through his hair and jumped up on stage. The lights were warm on his face. The microphone was greasy with sweat, but it felt good in his hands. He squeezed it so hard his fingers tingled. The crowd cheered.

"How's everybody tonight?" he said softly into the mic. Bubba crowed in the front, holding up beers in both hands. Jordan grinned.

"This one's for Bubba," he said with a wink. Matt kicked off the set on the drums with a bang.

The Waves played a few of their classics, tunes the locals were getting to know. The vibe was high. The first band must have really pumped them up, and brought some new faces. Jordan looked around the café. The tables were full of people having drinks, and there were quite a few people standing up front. A couple of girls were dancing. One looked familiar.

"This crowd is really special tonight," said Jordan, a thick wave of hair falling over his eye. "We weren't going to debut this one yet, but I think it's time."

He turned to Jerome on guitar, a question in his eyes. Jerome nodded. Matt sat back, tossing his drumsticks. He would sit this one out.

"This one's for my own special lady, when I find her," said Jordan. The girls cheered. Jerome played the opening notes. Sombre tones floated above the room like a strange dream. The people on the dance floor swayed slowly.

Val felt fresh and clean after a long hot shower. She didn't feel like wearing underwear so she popped in her Diva Cup instead. She slipped into a simple black silk dress and went to the kitchen to fix herself a bowl of fresh fruit and yogurt. The moon was full and light poured into the condo. She felt the urge to go for a night walk. She loved looking up at the moon, and although the rain had stopped, the streets were still glistening. She wrapped a dark red scarf around her long neck and slid her feet into sandals on her way out the door. She considered bringing her purse, but she wanted her hands and body free for her walk. She didn't need keys. There was a punch code on the exterior door of the building and she rarely locked her apartment.

Valkyrie walked along a side street, avoiding the main drag. The air smelled like chlorophyll and slightly moldy leaves. She drank it in.

The night air was unusually warm and heavy with moisture after the rain. She felt her skin soaking it in, her hair curling. The moon was eerily bright. She was always amazed that no matter how much the city changed, the moon stayed the same. Where she walked now, on ugly pavement, a few hundred years ago Anishinabek people lived in a city of wood and hide, green with life rather than grey with concrete.

Snow Arcologies will never be grey, thought Val. *They will be green…*

Val walked on through the night, enjoying the sound of dripping as she passed a park where the trees glistened with the afternoon's rain. Suddenly, between the night sounds of passing cars and people walking home from late dinners, she heard a sound she couldn't place. It was like the song of a bird, or a musical instrument she had never heard before.

What is that? she thought. Her curiosity was piqued, and she walked faster, following the sound.

Val approached Chinatown. She wasn't intending to walk this way because the lights were brighter and the moon would be harder to see here, but the song was her quest now. She came out on the corner of Wellington Street, and ahead she could see warm light pouring from the windows of a café where young people stood around outside smoking cigarettes. It was a voice. A human voice. She thought it must be a man's, but the sound was sweet and bright, and also mournful, and it was difficult to tell. She approached the café, peering inside. It wasn't the kind of place she had been to in a long time. A woman opened the door for her with a smile. The sound of the voice flooded out the open door, and the call was irresistible. Val smiled back at the girl, stepping into the café and slipping over to a table with an empty seat.

"May I join you?" she asked. Two young women in polyester dresses with gemstone stickers on their faces turned to her.

"Of course," said one, moving her purse from the seat. Valkyrie sat down.

The man on stage was sitting on a stool, his eyes closed, and big dark waves of hair falling around his chin. Val felt her heart beat faster. She felt intoxicated, lightheaded. She couldn't look away. She didn't understand the words he was singing; she could only hear the vibration of his voice in her whole body. She held the sticky table with her hands, watching him sing. A warm golden light pulsed around his head and shoulders like a halo. She couldn't make out his features.

"Was it you who wanted the coffee?" asked a waitress. Val tore away her gaze.

"Excuse me?" She eyed the mug of steaming liquid, the Pabst Blue Ribbon and the spotty glasses on the server's tray. It was hard to tell if they were supposed to be clean.

"Sorry no, I don't think so."

"Can I get you something?"

"Not yet, thank you." The waitress bustled away. Val turned her attention back to the stage.

Jordan was singing his heart out. Matt, who was usually frowning, had a big grin. The new song was great and the crowd was loving it. Most of their songs were cheesy and lame, but they had a couple hits. Jordan's voice was good, but every once in a while, he would take a song to the next level. This new song was melancholy, sometimes shaky, sometimes rich and strong. There were a few heart-wrenching moments. Jordan was casting a spell on the audience, who could feel the longing in his voice, manifesting a deep and intense love.

Val itched to get closer and see the details of this man's face, but she didn't want to be in the press of sweating bodies by the stage. The sound of his voice was like a siren calling her to the rocks. She stayed put. The notes floated from his lips, filling the air in the café. He was like some kind of beautiful creature sitting there amongst the faded decaying furniture and chipped mugs, shining like a light.

Finally, the song ended. The lights shifted and the crowd cheered. The man smiled and tossed his hair, droplets of sweat flying like crystals in the floodlights onstage. The details of his face became clear as his backlit glow faded.

Val breathed in sharply with a frown.

He's just a boy, she thought.

The stubble on his chin that had looked like a beautiful shadow was dishevelled and patchy down his neck, he was wearing a cheap hoodie, and his jeans were filthy. She almost laughed. She clapped her hands. He was a great singer.

"Thank you," she murmured to the gemstone girls as she left.

With that final song, the Waves were done their set for the night. The boys had a hug offstage.

"Great show," said Matt.

"Pure biz," said Jerome.

Jordan's smile was huge. He looked a bit dazed, like he was coming back to the world. He knew he had been great. Bubba brought them a round of Pabst. They all scanned the crowd with thirsty eyes except Jerome, who had a girlfriend. Matt gave Jordan's neck a squeeze and headed over to a pretty girl with cat eyeliner.

"You look like you're into drummers," he said. She laughed.

Jerome's girlfriend Rachel slid her hands around his waist, burying her face in his chest. He held her tight, kissing her hair.

"Great show," she said.

They kissed.

Jordan looked around. A few girls were checking him out with obvious interest. Right after a show was his biggest window to pull tail, but he didn't see anything especially enticing. Bubba sidled up beside him and elbowed him, gesturing to the ladies.

"Who you going for?"

"I don't see much..."

"What?" scoffed Bubba. "You're crazy, there's at least four really hot chicks here tonight." Onstage Jordan had felt over the moon, but now he felt like shit again.

Is this depression? he thought, not for the first time in the last year. Picking up women after a show used to give him a big rush; now it made him feel hollow inside. For months now, his sex drive had been almost nonexistent. His friends thought that the breakup with Sarah was still affecting him. It hit him hard, to be sure, but it wasn't just a broken heart. He was unhappy before they had broken up. Sometimes he felt like he wanted her back, but when he was being honest with himself he knew that he never liked spending time with her anyway. He liked how pretty they looked on Instagram, how other guys checked her out when they walked down the street, how having her felt like he was #GoodAtLife. Adulting properly. Deep inside, every day they were in a relationship, he felt worse and worse, knowing he didn't really love her and his whole life would be this way, because he would never break up with her. In the end, she had been the one to do it.

"What a bitch," the boys had said.

"Dirty skank was probably cheating on you anyway bro, you dodged a bullet," said Matt. Jordan almost convinced himself it was true. It made him feel better at first, but eventually nothing filled the grey space inside him that was utterly numb.

Sarah had checked all the boxes. Sure, one of these girls tonight might too. What difference did it make? At the tender age of twenty-four, Jordan realized that the love game was a bullshit fantasy.

"Be a brother and be my wingman," said Bubba. His chances were next to nothing without Jordan beside him.

They walked over to the ladies who had been dancing up front.

"I saw you dancing," said Jordan softly. "Thanks for bringing that energy to the show."

They chatted for a bit and then Jordan excused himself to go to the bathroom, leaving Bubba to make a move. He went into the stall to piss in peace and to check his phone. He had a message.

Hey

You look great up there :)

Charlotte:

Charlotte was a girl Jordan had met on Tinder. They went on one date and hooked up that night. Every few weeks she'd text him, and come over and they'd sleep together. She was a cool girl, and Jordan liked falling asleep with her. In the morning though, he wished she would just go and get on with her day.

He texted her back.

Charlotte felt the buzz of her phone in her hand. A text flashed across the screen.

Hey! I thought that was you out there

Jordan:

He saw me, she thought.

She smiled wide. She was sort of dating Jordan, hoping things would pick up. It seemed like he needed his space though so she was taking it slow. He invited her to all his shows, or at least he had added her to the group message on Facebook Messenger where the Waves blasted their shows. She tried to come whenever she could. She waited a few moments, looking at the screen, hoping he would say more.

In the bathroom stall, Jordan was scrolling through Instagram, looking at videos people were posting of the show tonight and tagging the band. The Waves really had been great. A notification appeared; Bubba was texting him.

Where you?

Bubba:

Shitting bro

Jordan:

Love me a good shit

Bubba:

Jordan kept watching videos. Ten minutes later, another notification popped up on his screen.

plans tonite?

Charlotte:

Jordan considered. Did he want Charlotte to come over? He hated sleeping alone, but he knew she would start expecting more from him eventually. That's why he rarely initiated the conversation.

She's the one texting me though, he thought. *So she knows what she's getting herself into.*

> What did you have in mind? ;)

Jordan:

He left the bathroom. The next band was on, and the girls were dancing up front. He looked around for his roommates. They were at a table having a drink.

"Jordan!" called Jerome. Rachel was sitting on his lap. Matt was chatting with an okay-looking girl who was not the one from earlier.

"What happened to cat eyes?" asked Jordan.

"Not into drummers," he said.

Even Bubba had found someone. Two girls stood beside him. One of them was cracking jokes and having a good laugh, and the other looked bored.

Don't underestimate the funny guy, thought Jordan. The other girl noticed him and perked up. He looked her up and down, thinking for a moment, and then decided that he liked the reliability of Charlotte more.

"I'm heading out," he said.

"What? No!" said Bubba. "Meet Melissa."

Charlotte walked up to the table. "Hey guys."

"I see," said Bubba. "See you later bro."

Jordan and Charlotte walked out.

"Is that his girlfriend?" asked Melissa.

"Yea," said Rachel.

"Uhhh sort of…" said Jerome.

"Nah," said Matt.

Charlotte and Jordan walked down the dark street in silence. She wished he would hold her hand, but he didn't.

"Are you… like, a shy guy?" she asked.

"Not really, why?"

"Sometimes you seem kind of shy, that's all."

Maybe he isn't super affectionate, she thought. She wanted a guy who was warm, but she was willing to compromise. He would be affectionate later.

Could it be that he isn't really into me? she thought. *But then why would he sleep with me? And there were exclamation marks in his text.* It seemed in his text like he was excited she had come to his show, but now he was kind of distant. She had seen that girl at the table checking him out. *When I showed up, he wanted to go home with me right away*, she thought. *That means he wasn't into that girl right?* Charlotte decided that it meant that Jordan really was into her, and it was just taking him time to warm up. Rachel told her that he went through a tough breakup last year and he might be scared to put himself out there again.

Poor Jordan, she thought. She decided that holding his hand might be too much, so she linked her arm through his, and they walked home arm in arm. Jordan gave her a squeeze, and she felt the thrill of it all over her body.

When they reached his building, he pulled out his arm and punched the code to open the door. He led her into the stinky elevator, wrapped his arms around her and kissed her. She melted into his soft lips. When the bell dinged at floor five, he led her down the hall by the hand, jerking the keys in the door because the lock was always jamming up. Finally he got it open and they went in. By this time she knew the apartment well enough and went straight to his bedroom. She pushed aside the wet towel in his bed and sat down, taking off her clothes. Jordan walked in, chucking his hoodie in the corner and pulling off his beer-stained t-shirt.

"Shut the door," she said, "the boys will be coming home soon." He turned and shut the door, and then climbed in beside her. They kissed and kissed. Jordan held her tight in his arms. He felt like going to sleep. Charlotte reached down to unbuckle his pants, struggling for a moment before he reached down and took off his belt and pants. He was completely unaroused.

"Not in the mood?" asked Charlotte.

"No it's not that…"

"Too many beers probably," she said. "That's okay, don't worry about it." She snuggled into his shoulder.

"No, no, just use your hand a bit," he said.

"I can do one better." She went down with her mouth. Eventually it worked, and they were able to get a condom on and have sex.

They fell asleep that night holding onto each other for dear life.

CHAPTER TWO

Valkyrie Snow tossed and turned all night. She was having a vivid dream that she was walking through a beautiful forest garden. Lilies-of-the-valley, trilliums and forget-me-nots carpeted the forest floor, and ferns brushed her legs as she walked barefoot beneath the trees. It was a place she visited often while she slept. She looked down at herself.

Today she was wearing a loose muslin dress with deep pockets at the front held closed by knobby wood buttons. She opened one and felt inside.

Mushrooms! she laughed. *Delicious.*

From somewhere in the forest, she heard a bird singing. The sound was light like the wind. She followed it. The song deepened, and she found its source. A nightingale, the largest one she'd ever seen, sat in the branches of a tree. Its song was both bright and mournful. She recognized it.

The song from the man in the café, she thought. She would have to find out the band's name so she could get a copy of their album. It was lovely. There was a patch of sunlight ahead, and Valkyrie spotted a thicket of raspberry bushes. She picked the berries and popped them into her mouth as she listened to the bird sing over and over, until suddenly she heard a man's voice. She turned around, and instead of a nightingale, there was the boy from the filthy café, singing his song. He came right up to her, took a berry from her hand, and ate it.

What is he doing here? she thought. She frowned. She came here to escape people. She shook her head until she woke up in her own bed in Ottawa.

Because of the dreams, Val was obsessed with finding this forest. Eventually she purchased a parcel of land just west of the city. She wanted to build a simple retreat from urban life. The land was almost a square kilometre—two hundred or so acres—of mostly forest, with some overgrown fields, and a tiny river running through it. It was even better than her dreams. She was designing a beautiful glass house to visit on weekends.

She banished the thought of the singing man from her mind, but she had a feeling that she would see him again.

The next morning, Jordan woke up before Charlotte. He had rolled over to his side of the bed, but he could hear the soft rise and fall of her breathing. He blinked awake, rubbing his eyes. He rolled over, wrapping his long arm around her, cupping his legs around the curve of her backside and squeezing slightly. She didn't wake. Her hair tickled his face, so he pushed it aside and nuzzled her neck with his nose. She wriggled slightly, waking up and realizing that the tickle on her neck was Jordan.

"Mmmm." His warmth felt good against her. He gave her one firm squeeze and released, crawling out of bed. Charlotte turned over, and saw him pulling on jeans off the floor.

"Where are you going?" she asked with a grin. "Getting me breakfast?"

"I have to go to work."

Charlotte sat up. "I thought you didn't have to work for a few hours…"

"I have some things to do," he said, putting on the clothes from yesterday.

"Seriously though, we could go for breakfast?"

"Sorry beautiful." He leaned down to kiss her face. "You can let yourself out right?" he said as he left the room.

Jordan grabbed his longboard by the door. He headed to Bridgehead to get his morning coffee. Breakfast would have been nice, but he didn't have a lot of extra cash to spend and he could eat toast for free when he got to the restaurant.

At Bridgehead, he decided to sit a while before his shift. He got his coffee for here and dashed sugar and cinnamon on top. He never put cinnamon on it when he got it in a paper cup because it always stuck to the lid. Now he would enjoy it slowly, playing with the foam with a spoon. He threw his backpack into a booth at the back, carefully setting his latte on the table. He pulled out his sketchbook and a pencil and continued the Superman drawing he was working on.

A woman walked into the shop. She was tall and elegant, dressed in high-waisted pants and a knitted high-neck crop top with a pearl pendant on a long gold chain. She wore leather sandals and carried a satchel on one side with a large notebook under her arm. Jordan looked up for a moment, noticing the way she held her arms and the way her hair fell in waves like his as she bent down to look at the sweets in the counter window.

Rich woman, he thought, looking back at his sketch.

"A latte for here," she said softly, "and one of those chocolate brownies." She usually ordered a lemon square, but today her cycle was craving chocolate.

The barista steamed the milk as the cashier rang up the order.

"Oh, and a pound of fresh beans, please. Medium roast." She paid the bill, and wandered over to the bar to get her drink. She picked up the coffee, turned to find a seat, and suddenly she saw him. *The singing man.* She almost spilled her coffee, but she walked over slowly, observing him. He seemed kind of dirty, but there was something graceful about the shape of his nose, the line of his chin, and his full bodied hair. She could see that he would clean up well, obscured as he was beneath the worst clothes. Why did she keep seeing him? Val believed in signs. What was the purpose of seeing him at his concert and then again today? He had even interrupted her dream. She sat down at a table nearby, and pulled out her notebook to chase an idea about biotech and 3D printers.

She's drawing, thought Jordan, noticing the page where Val was doodling something with labels. He couldn't tell what it was. She felt his eyes and looked up. Her gaze was direct and intense in a way he wasn't used to. He looked down quickly, focusing on Superman.

Hmmm, she thought.

When he finished his coffee, Jordan left Bridgehead to go to work.

Valkyrie liked working in coffeehouses sometimes to change the scenery from her desk at home. Hammer & Bone had an office downtown, but she rarely visited. She relayed her intentions and designs through her personal assistant. She would build a beautiful library in her glass house where she would work on weekends, but for now she visited the different Bridgehead Coffee locations around town. She liked the company because all of their packaging was biodegradable and they used local organic milk. Sometimes she would spend time in libraries, but she found them either too quiet, or noisy in the most annoying way, with one or two loud-voiced people carrying on a conversation. Coffee shops had a kind of ambient noise that didn't bother her while she worked.

"Hi. Excuse me, but I am so curious about what you're drawing."

Val looked up. The man who approached her table was tall and well-dressed.

He must work at one of the office buildings close by, she thought.

He pointed to a note in the corner of the open page of her book: *The definition of economy is shifting away from capitalism.*

"Wow. Do you really think that?"

"Excuse me?"

"Capitalism is in decline, but it'll make a comeback."

"What is your field?"

"My field?"

"Yea, you look like a civil servant. Which area?"

"Executive Risk Management, why?"

"Just curious." Val was interested in discussing this topic with an economist, but she was past the age of wasting her time soliciting the opinion of someone who read the Wikipedia page on capitalism.

"Have yourself a lovely day." Val turned her attention back to her book.

"How about you? What do you do?"

"I'm an artist," she said, not looking up. He eyed her clothing skeptically.

Must be a trust fund artist, he thought. She didn't look married.

"What is your family's business?" he asked, sitting down at her table. She frowned, setting down her pen slowly.

"What are you talking about?"

"Sorry, you just look like you come from money. I mean it in a good way."

"No offence taken."

"I'm Jeff," he said. There was a long silent pause.

"So what are you drawing?" he asked, looking at her book, reading aloud. "Splitting carbon dioxide into carbon and oxygen, integrate bioprinter with plasma vaporization machine…"

"It's actually private," said Val, closing the book.

"Sounds like science, not art."

"I'm a romantic, they aren't separate."

Jeff looked at the cover of the book. There was a white label with crisp black text:

Hammer & Bone
Suite 47
Slater Plaza
Ottawa

"Hammer & Bone… that's the company that built all those gothic condos in Centretown right? I'm guessing you're some kind of speculative engineer."

"You mean an architect?"

"Sure."

"Something like that." Val wanted to go back to her work, but her train of thought was broken now.

Jeff guessed that she was probably some kind of mid-level manager in the company or a senior designer, because of her age.

"So… is there a Mr. Architect?" Jeff was at a stage in his life where he didn't bother talking to (happily) married women for long.

"Never married."

"Really." *Red flag.* Her expectations were through the roof. "I'm divorced."

He's handsome, thought Val. *But something in his personality is annoying…* Like a sweater with rack appeal but itchy when you put it on. She slipped her book under her arm and stood up.

"Well nice to meet you, Jeff. Good afternoon," she said, leaving the coffeehouse.

The next morning Val was tempted for a moment to go to Bridgehead, but she decided against it. She got some work done the day before, but there were too many interruptions. This provided the push that she needed to really focus on the glass house plans. She spent the next several weeks at home during the day, drafting the finishing details to send off to her builders.

Val struggled with the size. She was tempted by the influence of the culture of excess to build extra rooms, more space, more unnecessary amenities. She dedicated herself to filling the glass house with many small luxuries, but tiny in scale. There would be enough space to live comfortably, but the focus was to spend time outside in nature. She had designed her own condo with these principles in mind. High ceilings and many windows made the relatively small square footage feel spacious.

The main structure of Glasshouse would be an octagon, with a river stone hearth in the centre. Val planned for a tiny kitchenette to be on one side of the fireplace, a bed floating on wooden chains on the other, and a massive copper bathtub behind the fireplace, overlooking the river. All the walls of the main room would have floor to ceiling windows. A small room off the main space had three custom built-ins for her books, and a simple writing table. There would be a small wooden porch enclosed with mesh to keep out the mosquitoes in the spring. Val designed a small desk for the porch as well for when she wanted to work outside. The path from the main road was dirt. Glasshouse was powered by solar panels, and the toilet closet used grey water from the tub and kitchenette sink. A small turret on the roof housed a rain catchment system. It was perfect, with every inch of space carefully and painstakingly arranged to suit Valkyrie's needs.

Val hired a car to take her out to her property. She didn't own a car—why would she?—everything in the city she needed was close enough to walk. With her flexible schedule, she would spend hours every day walking. She didn't know how to drive a car if she had one either. Every car made nowadays was self-driving. All the gasoline cars from 1999 onward were junk, and rapidly becoming obsolete. The only old cars on the road now were from a time before the decline of high-quality manufacturing. Collectors held onto older models for the novelty of 'driving', or for the romantic pleasure of hoarding old things from bygone days, but this generation's vehicles were automated and electric. BluRoads Inc., Val's company that recycled the stone silicate byproducts of her arcologies, accommodated these new vehicles. Val had invested in self-driving technology, and BluRoads Inc. made a substantial donation to MADD (Mothers Against Drunk Driving) to run a compelling series of advertisements.

Val called Uber, and her ride arrived swiftly at her door. A decade ago, Uber drivers were humans, but these were replaced by bots. When Uber grabbed the market in 2014, there was widespread pushback from cab drivers. The protests were violent. When Uber shifted from drivers to self-driving, there was not a whisper of dissent. Uber drivers were scattered, un-networked, un-unionized workers. Besides, the customers preferred the iron-clad statistics of self-driving bots, who never caused accidents. No one wanted to ride in a tin can of human error.

"Hello." The voice was professional with hints of seductive undertone.

"Repeat journey," said Val. The last time she had hired a car it was to her property. They rode in silence. The bot could chat with her, but the preference on her account was to forego the small talk.

It took an hour and a half to reach the property. Val walked down the dirt path to the cleared worksite by the river where construction would begin soon for Glasshouse. She closed her eyes and breathed in deep, trembling with contentment. She had watched countless buildings she designed come to life in cities around the world, but this one was something special. She had been working around the clock for years at Hammer & Bone, and finally she would be able to build a private place just for herself. She hummed a tune as she walked along the river's edge, considering building a small ornate footbridge to the other side. She would commission a stone troll to live beneath it. She smiled at the thought.

No, too tacky, she decided, eying the opposite shore. *Hmmm. Perhaps a gargoyle carved in the handrail,* she thought. *Yes.* She had lots of time to choose. It took her years to get to this point already. Agonizing over the details was half the fun for Val. She spent the afternoon walking in the bush.

Suddenly she froze. She heard an uncannily familiar voice calling out to her. It was a nightingale.

Impossible, she thought. *Nightingales are not indigenous to North America.*

She followed the sound to a large and twisted tree. There he was, perched on a lower branch, singing his heart out. His little brown chest puffed out as he sang.

"How did you survive the winter?" said Val. She felt sorry for him, not only because this climate was too harsh for such a delicate creature, but also because he would sing day and night, calling for a mate that he would never find here. Perhaps she could capture him somehow and keep him inside when the leaves changed. That would be a fun game for her out here, hunting the nightingale.

She returned to the worksite, enjoying its emptiness one last time before the earth was turned for the construction of Glasshouse. As the sun sank low in the sky, she walked back up the path to the waiting car, and rode away from the setting sun into the city.

The car drove down Elgin Street, pausing at the lights. Val's forehead was pressed against the window and she was deep in thought. Her eyes suddenly focussed, noticing a young man crossing the street.

"It's him!" she said.

"I'm sorry; what did you say?" said the robot driver politely.

Val made a snap decision.

"Let me out here please." The car pulled to the side of the road and Val exited.

"Have a nice night," said the car.

Val walked several long paces behind the young man. What would she do? She felt like tapping on his shoulder and saying something like, *do you have something to tell me?* She felt sure that he had some kind of message she needed to hear; the synchronicity of seeing him around town three times now was too much. Of course, she had probably seen him many times before, but after hearing him sing she was noticing him.

No, she decided, she would just follow along behind him until she thought of something less crazy to say.

Jordan was walking down the street on his way to a night shift at the restaurant. The Black Cherry was a popular local spot, with several locations around the city. The one he worked at was frequented by a lot of students. The food was just as shitty as takeout but cost more, but the cheap pitchers of house brewed beer kept the place full. Jordan was a dishwasher, sweating away in a windowless room in the back on his feet for hours. He had tried a few times to get moved to the front end, but the front and back managers both hated him, resenting his good looks and his dreams of a music career with the Waves. They both seemed to want to knock him down as many pegs as they could, so he was stuck in the back.

Val watched as the young man turned down a side street. She popped into the restaurant next door, getting a table at the patio overlooking the alley.

"Just a glass of red wine," she said to the server, declining the menu. "The driest you have."

She watched as the young man leaned up against the brick wall, one hand plunged into his sweater pocket, hunching his shoulders in the evening air. He pulled out a pack of smokes and lit one up.

Disgusting, she thought. *Why am I intrigued by this man?* She frowned, sipping her wine.

His voice. He was utterly unremarkable in the evening alley, but when she thought of his voice in the café she couldn't imagine why he wasn't a famous performer.

Jordan checked his phone. 7:56 pm. He had two more minutes to be out here before Earl would start shouting at him. He sucked on a cigarette, willing himself into numbness, preparing for a long night in the back of the Cherry. He closed his eyes, feeling the breeze and thinking about the Waves. They still didn't have anything lined up for Canada Day. He would ask the front of house tonight if they could perform at the Cherry. He would beg; they would love that, and probably not let him do it, but he had to try.

Val watched as the man finished his cigarette and went into the back entrance of the restaurant next door. The Black Cherry. She was been there once for a meeting, and never went back. The food was garbage and there were too many drunks. He must be a waiter, or perhaps a line cook. A few decades ago, a young white man with that face and body could walk into just about any job, and smile his way to the top of the food chain. Nowadays even the pretty great-great grandsons of Family Compact worked in the back like everybody else.

CHAPTER THREE

The next evening, after a long day of drafting, Val felt like going for a walk and having a bite to eat. She went out on the balcony and decided against grabbing a sweater; it would be a hot night. She slipped into sandals and walked out to the street. She wanted to think that she didn't know where she was going, but she knew; she was heading to the Hound and the Hare, the restaurant beside the Black Cherry where she sat to drink a glass of wine when she followed the singing man.

It was 7:15 pm when Val arrived. She asked for a seat in the dark corner of the patio. She looked over the menu.

"I'll have the beet salad," she said. "Please bring me a glass of water, no ice, and after the salad I'll have a Monte Cristo."

"Whipped cream?"

"Yes, please."

Val took her notebook out of her bag, sketching the form of her table, with the street in the background. Every once in a while she turned to look at the alley door where the man had disappeared the other night.

Val lingered until 8:55 pm, but there was no sign him. She knew it was silly, but now she was determined to catch sight of him again.

Over the next few days, Val walked in the neighbourhood of the Black Cherry, getting ice cream across the street, even reading a book in the park close by, but to no avail. She knew that you couldn't force the universe. If she was supposed to see him she would. She gave up on looking for him, and went back to her usual routine.

The phone trilled in her apartment. It was Kayla Parker, a friend from university. Val called her Kale.

"I'm coming to town for a conference next week," said Kale. "Can we please have a visit?"

"Yes! I miss you so much! When are you coming?"

"Sunday night, I think. I'll be there until Wednesday."

"Are you staying here?"

"The university will expense the hotel," said Kayla. She was a professor.

"Well stay with me at least one night!"

"Sleepover!"

The two laughed.

Kale flew in on Sunday afternoon and took the light rail downtown. Val met her at the stop and they walked to her apartment.

"I have to be at Ottawa U around 9:30 am," said Kale. "How far is that from here?"

"Not far. This city is really easy to get around."

They dropped off her bags at the house and went out for dinner. As they were browsing menus on the street, Val saw a familiar face.

"Valkyrie Snow," he said. She looked at him for a moment, trying to place how he knew her.

"It's Jeff. We met at Bridgehead the other day."

Oh. Him, she thought.

"I'm Kale," said Kale, holding out her hand. He shook it.

"This is Mario," he said, indicating the man beside him.

"What are you up to tonight?"

"Getting dinner," said Kale. She was all smiles. There was nothing she liked more than going out for double dinners, flirting all night, and never seeing the men again. Kale had a beautiful wife named Susanna, and they were very much in love, but Kale was bi-romantic and enjoyed the intrigue of going on occasional dates with strangers. Susanna didn't mind.

"How did you know my name?" asked Valkyrie.

"Well you told me you worked at Hammer & Bone, so I looked you up." He turned to Mario.

"She's the CEO," he said with a laugh. "She led me to believe she was just an architect."

"I said I was an artist."

She turned to Kale, who was obviously interested in joining up. She sighed.

"Would you like to join us for dinner?" she asked. "Kale loves meeting new people."

"Absolutely."

The four of them got a table at Ruisseau on Sparks. The place was reliably always a hit. The food was excellent, the drinks were good, and the décor was on point. Val ordered a dark & stormy and the steak tartare.

"I'm starving," said Kale. "How are the portions?"

"Get the lobster mac and cheese. You won't regret it," said Val.

"If it sucks, you're getting dinner."

"I insist on getting dinner anyway, and it's really good. I know you, and you'll like it."

The conversation was casual and light, and the dynamic was good; if Val got bored with the discussion, she could trust Kale to pick up an interesting thread and steer. Kale was a neuroscientist who studied the effects of yoga on the brain.

"Seriously? That sounds like you made it up," said Jeff.

"Maybe I did," she said, sipping her wine and laughing with her eyes. "You have absolutely no idea."

Mario was a medical doctor who had just opened a new practice in the city. Jeff was showing him around. Val still found him slightly annoying, but she had mostly warmed up to him and appreciated that her friend was having a good time.

At the end of the night, Jeff asked for her number, her Virtual Reality Connect access.

"I don't buy into that," laughed Val. "The idea of other people or companies contacting me right into my thoughts is terrible. Sorry."

"Well how about your phone then? Or email? Whatever."

"Look, Jeff, this was a lot of fun, and I'll give you my phone number to do this again when Kale's in town, or maybe to go skiing this winter or something, but I want you to know that it's not for something romantic, okay?"

She could see the disappointment in Jeff's face, like a deflating balloon. There was a pause. He was considering.

"Okay. Got it."

She gave him her information.

"Let us give you a ride home," he said.

"We're going to walk," said Kale, giving both Jeff and Mario a kiss on the cheek, and linking arms with Val.

"It was lovely. Goodnight," she said, as they walked off.

Val pointed up at a tall curved building close by.

"That's where you're going tomorrow," she said. "For your conference."

"Mmm, that's close," said Kale, the effects of alcohol apparent in her voice.

They walked down Elgin Street.

"That looks like a great patio," said Kale, pointing.

The Hound and the Hare. Val smiled.

"It is. Let's meet there after your conference. Just bring whoever along." Val knew that Kale would meet some colleagues she would want to have dinner with.

"Great."

The next evening, Kale called Valkyrie as she finished up the day's panels.

"I'll be about 30 minutes."

"I'll make a reso."

"Thanks love. 4-5 people."

Val got ready and went ahead to Hound & Hare, getting a table for six on the patio where she had a good line of sight to the back door of the Cherry. She sipped a tea, waiting only a few minutes.

"Hello love," said Kale, kissing her on the cheek. "These are the scientists I've been gabbing with all day: Raji Kam, Heather Tisdale, Padma Latha, Muhammed Amjed, and Khang Nguyen." Val smiled and nodded.

"This is Valkyrie Snow, the designer of all of these lovely new buildings replacing the suburbs."

"Oh, interesting," said Padma, sitting close.

"I knew you'd like her," said Kale with a laugh.

Val and Padma chatted about her arcologies for a while.

"Now I want to hear about your work," said Val. "I know you all just spent the day talking about it but give me the rundown." She was friends with enough academics to know that most of them hated that question.

Dinner came and the conversation flowed easily. Val was excited to ask questions about biotechnology. She told them about the new work she was doing with Snow Arcologies.

"If you have anyone in mind looking for work in the field, I would love to hire a consultant," she said.

"I can think of a grad student who would be great," said Padma.

"Let me put you in touch." They shared contact details.

The evening wound down, and the scientists were starting to look tired as they ordered dessert.

Suddenly, Valkyrie noticed a familiar figure in the alley. It was the singing man. He leaned up against the wall, holding his phone in his hands, the blue glow of its light shining on his face. The night was sticky with heat and he wore a sleeveless shirt, his long pale arms lightly lean with muscle. His sweater was tied around his waist, and it hung longer than his short shorts. He lifted his hand to push his hair out of his face. It stayed back for a moment, slightly stiff with moisture.

Val felt some emotion stir in her. She couldn't tell what it was.

The young man slid down the wall, sitting in the alley with his knees up, still on his phone.

Something about the vulnerability of his pose, the way his hair fell over his eye like that—reminded her of his voice, clear and sweet, floating through the air and straight into her heart at the Chinatown café.

She was more intrigued than ever.

"Valkyrie!" said Kale. Everyone was looking at her. Val could tell Kale had said her name more than once.

"Yes?"

"Are you ready to head home? I think we're ready."

"Ready," said Val with a smile.

"I got your dinner girl," said Kale.

"Thanks hunny."

Val stood to leave and turned one more time to look into the alley. The singing man was staring straight at her. She smiled at him, and then followed Kale out of the restaurant.

"I'll miss you," said Val as she dropped Kale off at the airport.

"I'm so glad we got to catch up. You're a babe." Kale kissed her on the cheek and gave her a big squeeze.

"I'll come see you soon."

"Yes! And I'll come see you again when Glasshouse is done. It's going to be amazing."

They hugged one more time and Kale was off through the security check. Val watched her go, waving.

One evening a few days later, Valkyrie's phone trilled.

"Hey Valkyrie. It's Jeff."

"Hello. How did you get my number? I thought I gave you my email."

"I asked around. Dinner plans?"

"Hmm. No, actually. What did you have in mind?"

"How about the Market? Prickled Pear?"

"Ehhh... I'm not a huge fan. And I'm in the mood for something more casual. How about Green Table?"

"Where's that?"

"Hintonburg."

"Sure." Jeff could tell that Val was the kind of person who always got her own way. He was fine with that. He was smart enough to understand that a relationship with the CEO of Hammer & Bone would mean that she would call the shots. As far as he was concerned, she seemed to have impeccable taste. He'd never heard of Green Table, but he had also never heard of Ruisseau, and it had been incredible.

"Meet you there in an hour?" she said.

"I can swing by and pick you up..."

"Meet me there."

"Sure."

Jeff arrived at Green Table fifteen minutes early. He had his sight set on Valkyrie Snow. Jeff was persistent, and when he wanted something, he always got it. Snagging Val would be like scoring the winning goal in overtime.

After his divorce, Jeff had done the young arm candy thing. He had gone on SugarMatch.com and the site had garnered several very fruitful arrangements. It pissed off his ex-wife, and that made the whole divorce situation harder for the lawyers but funnier for Jeff. After almost five years of Dead Bedroom—or a stagnating sex life in marriage— he felt like his ex deserved to be jealous.

Look at me now, he thought.

He was rarely unfaithful to his wife while they were married, and those times were with sex workers while he was on work trips. In his mind, that was barely cheating. It wasn't an embarrassment to his wife, in the way that porking the neighbour or their kid's teacher would be. The first time he ordered an escort, he was staying at a hotel in Washington. When he put down the phone after making the call, he was shocked at how easy it was. Leading up to the call he was rabid with lust, but while he sat in the room waiting for her to show up, he had not even a twitch of a boner and he felt a bit nauseas. She knocked on the door and he let her in. It played out just like in the movies, except that he didn't murder her after, and her pimp didn't rush in to rob him or something. He just paid her and she left. It happened so fast; the memory was a blur. The next time, he was less nervous and he remembered it better. He remembered how right afterward, he thought that it was barely better than jerking off. All of the thrill and intrigue of pulling tail was gone. It was just a simple financial transaction for wetting his dick with something other than his own hand.

Jeff's SugarMatches, after his divorce, had been a great time. He bought them gifts, and they genuinely enjoyed his company. The sex was glorious. He was a decent looking guy who looked great in a suit, so the arrangement was pretty pleasant for both parties. Now, six years after the divorce papers were signed, he could see how tacky that was. It was what he needed at the time, and for that he was grateful, but at this point in his life it would be a waste of his time to continue on SugarMatch. Jeff was ready to sink his teeth into something different.

Amy was a kindly, doting wife. She was a public servant as well, working the same hours he did during the day. Her evenings were spent taking care of the house, and when they'd had a son, she took on the majority of that responsibility as well. By the end of their marriage, she was exhausted, lonely, and bitter.

The SugarMatches were immature girls looking for tuition support for school. One who was slightly older had actually been looking for a long-term relationship, but Jeff grew bored with her. He was ready to look for something special. A real catch. He wasn't going to go for what was easy, like he had with Amy.

Jeff imagined strolling into a charity dinner at the golf club with Valkyrie Snow on his arm. She was hot in the way that Beyoncé was hot, in the terrifying and intimidating way. She was cool and formidable. Everything she wore hung off her like it was made for her body. She was rich, and she looked like money. She was a bit cold, but that kind of turned Jeff on; if she was a bitch to his friends, so much the better because it would take them down a peg and they could say nothing that she wouldn't have an answer for. And then he would kiss her, and they'd know that she was his. It was a scene he played over and over in his mind before bed since the day he met her, imagining the fine details, sometimes jerking off to the fantasy before falling asleep.

Valkyrie showed up at Green Table right on time. Jeff watched her like a hawk as she walked in, scrutinizing his potential future wife with a more critical eye. She wore a navy pencil skirt, with small gold buttons from top to bottom. Her cream silk blouse was tucked in, billowing perfectly as she walked. A wide black leather bracelet balanced her look, matching her shoes and bag. She took off an expensive looking pair of sunglasses as she entered the restaurant, scanning the room for him.

For me, he thought. *Valkyrie Snow is looking for me.*

He'd had her so many times in his fantasy that it seemed only a matter of time before it happened in real life. He would enjoy the challenge of making it happen. He smiled as she approached his table.

"You look great," he said, careful to look in her eyes as he said it so it didn't come off as unscrupulous. It worked.

"Thank you," she said, without a trace of annoyance.

"You don't wear a stroke of makeup, do you?" he asked with admiration.

"No..."

Too much, thought Jeff. There was that trace of annoyance. *Dial it back*, he coached himself.

"So. You'll have to tell me what's good here," he said, keeping his tone friendly.

"There is so much! It's a buffet," she said. "You fill your own plate, and they weigh it."

They walked up to the food counters, and she pointed out her favourite dishes.

"No meat, it seems," said Jeff.

"Oh yea. It's vegetarian." She smiled wide. "I forgot to tell you."

Jeff made a face. "I'm usually not into rabbit food…"

"Trust me, it's delicious. One of the best restaurants in town."

"Okay, I'm trusting you…"

They filled their plates and paid at the counter. They sat down and chatted as they enjoyed their meal.

"As usual, you have great taste. This is great." Jeff meant it. His dinner was incredible.

"What kind of music do you like?" she asked.

"I like the oldies. 90's rock reminds me of my youth."

He couldn't figure out what she was thinking. Her steely gaze was unreadable. He didn't ask what music she liked. He didn't even think of it, because he didn't really care. He was trying to figure out how old she was.

"The good old days."

Jeff wondered what her net worth was. He would look it up online later.

"So what was your favourite?" she asked, nodding to his empty plate. She was only half finished. Jeff was a fast eater.

"I liked the lasagna. That cheese felt like meat my mouth," he said with a laugh. Val smiled and continued eating.

"So we never got to finish that conversation about capitalism," said Jeff.

Val groaned.

I really don't want to listen to your idiotic and 2-dimensional views on finance, she thought.

"How about you tell me about your work instead."

"Well, I work for the government, so I deal with some of the most pressing issues of our times. Safety and security are my number one concerns, but the government deals with all the most important aspects of our lives, from the military, to healthcare and education. I'm federal. Education, for example, is managed by the provincial government…"

"That's shocking." Val's face and tone betrayed no sarcasm, but for some reason Jeff had a feeling that Val was not, in fact, shocked.

"Umm…"

"Go on."

As Val finished her meal, Jeff explained how important his job was. Most of the details of why were classified, top secret information, but he assured her that he was, indeed, very important.

"Well Jeff, it's been real. I've got a project to work on bright and early tomorrow, so I'd better get home and get some sleep."

"What kind of project?" he asked. It was the first question he asked her all evening, except for *you don't wear a stroke of makeup, do you?* She had a feeling that he asked about her project because he wanted to keep her there longer, not because he was interested.

"It's top secret," she said with a wink as she stood up to head off.

As Jeff grabbed a ride home for the evening, he had a bounce in his step.

That went well, he thought. There were a few moments when she had teased him a bit, so that meant she liked him, right? And he got to tell her all about his job, which was damned impressive. He was the king of the public sector, and she was the queen of the private sector. That made them well matched. He didn't feel like that date had sealed the deal, but he was confident they would get there. Women like that didn't jump into bed right away anyway.

I'm dating a classy lady, he thought. He hopped into his Uber.

"My man!" he said to the driver, forgetting for a moment that it was a robot. Sometimes he missed the days when he could tell the cabbie how his date had gone.

Jordan was lying in bed, headphones in, listening to the latest hit from Death Row Dollies. They were a band of four women releasing songs from a Chinese prison. Jordan had heard a lot of theories about the DRDs; some said they were Chinese ladies looking to make a quick buck in tough times and they weren't really in prison. Others insisted that they were an anti-Chinese propaganda scam of the Americans. Some thought that Death Row Dollies were produced by the actual Chinese government. Anonymous said that the DRDs were legit. Whatever the case, Jordan liked their songs. The lyrics were cryptic and intense; he liked that. The tunes were catchy. What more could you ask for?

I'm a material girl, tick tock tick tock
Drowning in shoes
Swimming in a sea of, tick tock tick tock
Everything you ever wanted.

Give me a chance, tick tock tick tock
I'll show you what the world is made of
Bounded by feet, tick tock tick tock
On a line that never ends…

A message popped up on Jordan's phone.

Charlotte:
> **Hey**

Jordan:
> Hey :)

Charlotte:
> **What you up to?**

Jordan:
> Just chillin what's up?

Charlotte:
> **Wanna hang out?**

Jordan looked around his dark room. He was feeling pretty relaxed, but some company could be good.

Jordan:
> Ya sure

Charlotte:
> **We could go for a drink, or a walk or something :)**

Jordan:
> I'm kind of tired… you want to just come over? :) :)

Charlotte's face glowed blue in the light of her phone screen. "What is it?" asked Audrey, her roommate.

"What?"

Audrey paused the movie they were watching. "You have that look on your face. Like you're kind of pissed off."

"I'm not pissed off."

"Who are you texting?"

Charlotte smiled. Audrey was sharp as a nail. "It's Jordan."

"Mmm hm."

Audrey gave her a knowing look. They both laughed.

"Gimme," said Audrey, snatching at the phone.

Charlotte didn't resist. Audrey scanned through the recent message history.

"Aww, girl... why are you putting up with this shit?"

"What do you mean? I told you we're taking it slow."

"Doesn't look slow to me. Looks like a booty call."

"You think so? I feel like we're getting closer."

"When was the last time you went on a date before you went back to his place?"

"We only went on one date, ever," she said quietly.

"So you're saying that your whole relationship is you going over there to sleep with him, and you don't go on dates, or talk about real stuff... just fucking."

Charlotte was silent.

"You deserve better than that."

"But he's so... cute and talented and amazing... I can't help it..."

"Sorry to be brutal, but he's not nice. No matter how much you like him, you can't make him nice. What do you think is going to happen? Do you think down the road he will magically change?"

"He's... nice..." Charlotte knew it wasn't true. He was nice to his friends, but that was even worse, because it meant he could be nice to people he actually cared about. And she wasn't one of them.

"He's just shy."

"I doubt that."

She had a point. He was a singer, after all. "So... what should I do?" she asked.

"Move on girl."

"I don't know if I can..." Charlotte thought of the last time she and Jordan hooked up, how he had kissed her in the elevator, how he had held her tight. "No Audrey, I know he cares about me."

"Then ask him."

"What do you mean?"

"Just ask him. Ask him out, ask him on a date, to be your boyfriend, ask him how he feels."

"I couldn't! What if I scare him off!"

"Nah. If he's really into you, that would excite him. If he were shy, it was be a relief for him. If you ask him and he ghosts on you, it means that he was just an asshole all along and you dodged a bullet."

Charlotte exhaled loudly. How would he react? She was afraid to find out.

"Sorry to be brutal Char, but you gotta know that if you set your expectations low that's all you're ever going to get."

"You're right. Something has to change…"

"What are you going to do?"

"I guess start by saying no. We'll see what he says…"

Audrey watched her type. "Sounds good hun."

They hugged.

"Let's just finish our movie in bed. You can cuddle me instead."

They giggled and took the laptop into Audrey's room to finish the movie. Charlotte put her phone in her room so she wouldn't be tempted to check it. As she set it on her desk, she realized that she was obsessively checking her phone lately to see if he had responded to her messages and usually he hadn't. She was tempted to check again right now. She clicked the screen-on button. Nope.

Obviously, she thought. *Why am I doing this to myself?*

She went to Audrey's room to enjoy the movie phone free.

I'm not texting him again unless he reaches out, she decided.

Jordan waited for Charlotte to respond to his text. It was taking longer than usual. He watched the typing signal blink, waiting for her to say she'd be right over.

> Oh I was hoping more to actually hang out. So I'll go for a drink with Audrey or something. Goodnight. :)

Charlotte:

What? Charlotte was usually so reliable. What would he do now? He thought of some of the other girls in his phone he could call. But Charlotte was so chill. She was the one he preferred. He was a bit annoyed.

> Goodnight :(

Jordan:

Jordan lay there in bed, trying to sleep. His mind was overactive and he was totally awake. He was sweating. It was really hot outside. He kicked off the sheet, lying on the bed naked. He wriggled closer to the fan beside the bed to catch more air. The fan clicked with each revolution, blowing warm air on his body. The top corner of the bottom sheet had popped up off the mattress and was curled up underneath him. The bunched fabric felt annoying under his shoulder and he pulled his pillow over to cover the bare mattress.

Pull the sheet back on the mattress, he thought. *That's what you should do.* But he just couldn't. He squirmed uncomfortably in the bed. He sniffed the air—it was getting a bit skunky in here. He should do laundry soon.

I wish I had Air Conditioning, he thought. He could pick up a used unit on Sellit.ca and figure out how to install it himself. Even a used AC was like a hundred bucks though. He just didn't have the extra cash.

You're such a loser. The thought slithered into his mind like a snake, lurking in the shadows of his consciousness, flicking its little tongue, challenging him to deny it.

At least I have the band, he thought.

Your songs suck. You've got maybe two good tunes and the rest are garbage, said the snakey voice.

We've got fans, thought Jordan. *We've got over four thousand followers on Instagram.*

But how many have you gotten in the last year? said Snake. *You're washed up at twenty-four. You're going to wash dishes for people who can afford to go out for dinner for the rest of your life.*

"I'm gonna be okay," whispered Jordan.

Face it, you're miserable.

Jordan popped his headphones back in and dialed up the volume. The Death Row Dollies drowned out his thoughts.

Do you really think that's what I need? Tick tock tick tock
It's a cheap imitation of the real thing.
Don't you think I deserve better? Tick tock tick tock
I don't even know if I do.

Jordan felt himself calm down.

Thanks Dollies, he thought.

He'd like to actually do something to thank them. He imagined that he was a famous rock star. In the fantasy, he was on tour in China, and he made a stop at the prison where the Death Row Dollies lived.

"I talked to the Chinese government," he told them, "but I couldn't negotiate your release. They're tough, those Chinese bureaucrats. I'm sorry girls."

"We understand," they said. "We're just glad you're our fan." Then they exchanged autographs. It played out in Jordan's mind like a video clip on social media; they signed each others' arms, laughing and smiling. They were focused on each other, but it looked great on camera too.

Stupid, he thought. Jordan couldn't thank the Death Row Dollies at all. He couldn't even afford to pay for their music; this was an illegal download he was listening to.

> *I'm an exceptional girl, tick tock tick tock*
> *Trapped in a prison of*
> *The cruel design of the Invisible Hand, tick tock tick tock*
> *Won't you take me out to play?*

You'll never make music as good as this, hissed Snake.

Jordan pulled out the headphones. He felt the sting of tears in the corners of his eyes. He needed a distraction, fast. He grabbed his phone, texting Charlotte.

> I miss you...
>
> Come cheer me up ;)

Jordan:

Audrey and Charlotte finished their movie, wiping their tears with tissues as the ending credits played. A well-dressed white couple smiled as they walked along the beach, snapping pictures of a little brown boy playing with a scruffy dog. They all faded into the sunset as sentimental music played. The screen faded to black.

"Such an intense film!" said Audrey. "I can't believe the government just shot all those children, and no one did anything to stop them."

"And the dogs," said Charlotte.

The movie, *Olympic Dreams,* was about a little boy who lived on the streets of Los Angeles during the 2024 Olympics where the city 'cleaned up the streets' by shooting children and dogs to prepare for the influx of tourists. In the end, the little street boy escaped and was adopted by some Europeans.

Y2K Cinderella, thought Charlotte. She imagined him growing up in Scandinavia, sleeping in his little IKEA bed, running around the streets of Copenhagen or Stockholm with the other little children.

"Time for bed," said Audrey. "You gunna to be okay?"

"Ya I'm fine. Thanks for the talk hun." She kissed Audrey's cheek and went to her room. She grabbed her phone from the desk, slipping into her bed.

Surprise! A text from Jordan.

> I miss you...

> Come cheer me up ;)

Jordan:

Charlotte's heart beat a little faster. *I miss you*, it said. Jordan missed her. Audrey was right, she just needed to stand up for herself.

> Hey. You still up?

Charlotte:

Miraculously, he texted back right away.

> Yea :)

Jordan:

> How about you come over here? 237 MacLarish. Text when you get here and I'll let you in.

Charlotte:

> Okay see you in 10

Jordan:

See you in 10? That was easy, she thought.

Twelve minutes later, Jordan was at her door. She tiptoed down and opened it. She felt her heart warm at the sight of his silhouette outlined against the streetlight, his long hair, his longboard tucked under his arm.

"C'm'ere," he said, leaning the longboard against the wall and pulling her in for hug. She relaxed into his arms, pleasantly surprised.

"Mmm," he sighed, giving her a squeeze.

"Come in," she said, leading him by the hand. "Shh, Audrey's asleep."

She took him up to her room. He peeled off his sweater and jeans and threw them on the floor. They made out a little in the dark, and fell asleep holding one another.

CHAPTER FOUR

In the morning, Jordan woke up early in Charlotte's room. Someone was puttering around with pots and pans in the kitchen. *Must be Audrey,* he thought.

Charlotte was fast asleep. Jordan looked around the room, taking in what he hadn't seen in the dark last night. Charlotte had a matching bed and dressers. The lavender bedspread matched her lamps, and she had pictures of smiling people in matching lavender frames around the room. Charlotte's dirty clothes were tucked away in a laundry basket in the corner, and the room smelled like a cinnamon candle. Light poured in from East-facing windows. The room was somewhat small and narrow, but there was a door leading onto a balcony, making it feel bigger. The whole place felt comfy and clean, except for Jordan's small pile of dirty clothes on the floor. He relaxed into the soft duvet. Charlotte stirred beside him.

"Good morning," he murmured, kissing her ear.

She giggled. It tickled.

Jordan felt a surge of pleasure; he was horny for the first time in a long time. He rubbed up against Charlotte, kissing her harder, more intensely.

"Wait," she said. "I have my period."

Jordan backed off a bit, still kissing her, still horny. "I don't mind," he said. He'd never had sex with a chick on her period, but it couldn't be that bad, right?

"Are you sure? It's going to be kind of messy," she said.

"Well it's your bed, so it's up to you."

"Okay," she said. "Just a sec."

Charlotte got up and went to the bathroom. She pulled out her tampon and cleaned herself up before grabbing a towel. She came back to the room, putting the towel down on the bed.

"No time for foreplay," she said. "Just go for it. And no need for a condom, unless you want one."

Jordan slid in. It felt fine—a little more wet than usual, but it didn't feel gross.

They kissed. Charlotte seemed a little stiff. She was worried about leakage—she knew how blood could get everywhere. Jordan slipped around a bit and she grabbed his ass, holding him down to keep from getting too messy. The added pressure felt really good, and she felt like she might orgasm, but her mind was just a little too preoccupied to get herself there.

"I'm coming," said Jordan. Then he did.

Afterward he relaxed onto her for minute, breathing hard. Then he started to get up.

"Careful," said Charlotte, easing him out slowly. She felt a rush of hot liquid trickling down her thighs. She grabbed the pillow quickly, pulling off the pillow case, trying not to move too much.

"Here," she said, thrusting the pillow case into Jordan's hand. He wrapped it around his dick. She pulled up the edges of the towel, hoping the blood hadn't leaked through. It would suck if she stained the mattress. She shimmied off the bed awkwardly, squeezing the towel between her thighs and throwing on her bathrobe to go to the bathroom. It wasn't too bad. She washed up, put in a fresh tampon, and went back to her room.

Jordan was lying on her bed, relaxed. There was a thin skid of blood on the bed.

"Oops," he said with a grin.

Charlotte went to the closet to get fresh sheets.

"Don't worry about it," said Jordan. "These sheets are still clean."

Charlotte eyed the blood on the sheets, thinking about how as it slowly dried it was staining the fabric. What did he mean they were still clean?

What Jordan meant was that they weren't yellow with sweat. A little spill wasn't enough to make him do laundry.

Charlotte wondered how long—how many days, weeks— Jordan would sleep on bloody sheets before he changed them. She stood there holding the clean linens, looking at him. He didn't move. She didn't want to ruin the moment by telling him to get up, so she put them down on the desk. She would change them when he left. She got into bed beside him, trying not to think about the blood. Jordan gave her a big squeeze, and then got out of bed to clean himself up. While he was up, she changed the sheets.

When he came back, he pulled on his clothes.

"I'm off to work," he said.

"Want to do something later?"

"Maybe." He gave her a kiss. "Bye."

After he left, Charlotte took her dirty laundry out to the machine.

"Jordan was here, wasn't he?" said Audrey.

"Yea…"

"I saw his longboard by the door," she laughed. "What happened?"

"He said he missed me," groaned Charlotte, shutting the machine and joining Audrey at the table.

"Haha, you sucker…"

"I know."

"So? Did you talk?"

"Not really. He had to go to work."

Audrey looked at her, unimpressed.

"Next time I see him, I promise."

Construction began on Glasshouse as scheduled. Val was vibrating with excitement. The designer she'd hired, Mika Nakamura, was a promising junior engineer at Hammer & Bone. Val had personally vetted everyone who would be working on the property, even though the project was so small. She was not usually this bad of a perfectionist, but Glasshouse was special to her.

Mika grabbed her bag and put on sturdy boots, calling a car to take her to the project site. A few curious eyes followed her down the hall.

"What are you doing today?" asked Arjit, another junior at the company.

"A special project. For Dr. Snow," she said.

"You mean her house?" he said, a touch of sneer in his voice. It was a tiny project.

"Yes," she said, boarding the elevator.

Mika was smart enough to know that working on Dr. Snow's private property was not only an honour, but an opportunity. There would be no room for creativity or error here; she had to produce Dr. Snow's house exactly as specified, and on schedule. This was her chance to prove that she was competent, proficient and that she could deliver a tight project. She would not cut corners, and she would personally oversee every detail. If she played this right, it could fast-track her career. At the very least, it would give her valuable one-on-one time with the big boss. She trembled with excitement just thinking about it.

What an opportunity. She wondered if Arjit was actually that foolish, or if he was just jealous. She wasn't sure.

As Mika was standing outside waiting for her car, a man came up to her. He was very tall, with a chiselled jaw and wide shoulders. His suit was freshly pressed and his hair was freshly cut. He was handsome, and probably about 25 years older than she was.

"Hi," he said with a smile, and an air of authority.

Mika looked from side to side. Yes, he was talking to her. "Hello."

"It looks like you work at Hammer & Bone."

She frowned slightly. "Does it," she said dismissively.

The man laughed as though she had made a joke. "Jeff Harper," he said, jutting out his hand for a shake.

"Dr. Nakamura," she murmured, shaking his hand.

He held on a beat longer than usual, looking into her eyes, giving her hand an extra squeeze. He let go, stepping a bit closer. "Can I take you for lunch today Dr. Nakamura?" he said. He wanted to ask her about Valkyrie.

"No," said Mika, stepping into the car that pulled up to take her to the project site.

Jeff frowned.

What a bitch, he thought. Giving them the hand and then the deep gaze always secured him a lunch date.

Am I getting old? he thought.

Nah. Some of his SugarMatches had been younger than that bitch.

Jeff talked to every woman as though she were already head over heels in love with him. Chicks loved it. He'd seen a special about it on Virtual Reality Connect. It was called the Red Score movement. (Feminists called it the Rotten Core movement. Once they had a protest about it—*Red Score, Rotten Core! Red Score, Rotten Core!* They had shouted in the streets.) The key was to understand that you were entitled to a woman's time. It was your right as a man. At the end of the day, women loved being degraded and even though sometimes it felt like too much, it was just nature. That's why he was sure he would eventually get Valkyrie Snow. She was so tough that she must be in deep need of some degradation.

Jeff's lunch break was over, and he headed back to his department.

When Mika pulled up thirty minutes earlier than the designated time, Val had already been at the project site for hours.

"Am I late?" she asked, as Val emerged from the forest, her feet bare and covered in black mud.

"Absolutely not. I'm early." She looked down at Mika's boots.

"Good to see that you're dressed for the job." She walked to a picnic table and grabbed a towel to wipe her feet and put on her work boots.

"That's the boulder you want to keep, correct?" said Mika, pointing to a large triangular stone covered in moss.

"That's right. I want minimal impact."

Val had taken a trip to China where she encountered Daoist monks whose respect for nature was so deep that they built their homes and temples around the landscape, disturbing as little as possible. They even curved around beautiful ancient trees, drawing architectural inspiration from the shape of the land. Seeing these temples was a life-changing event for Valkyrie, marking her transition from sleek gothic condos to green arcologies. Daoist architecture was ancient and low-tech; Val would incorporate the ethics of Daoism into her high-tech modern structures. She was working on two new prototypes at Hammer & Bone; one she simply called Snow Arcologies, the massive green fortresses where 100 residents could live in luxurious, affordable community, and the other she called Futurustic. These were tiny off-grid living units for humans in nature with no toxic impact. Futurustic was a portmanteau of the words 'future' and 'rustic'.

Val knew that the reality was that environmental crisis was global. As the northern ice fields melted, the continent was filling up with water, but as large tracts of land were deforested and eaten by suburbia, the water table of the landscape could not absorb the excess water. Here in Ottawa, there would be summers where it would rain every day, and across Canada the floods filled the streets. The runoff was full of salt and pollution. Val was determined to find solutions to this faulty design. She directed the creative minds employed in her many companies toward this new purpose.

The builders arrived, and a large truck full of materials was unloaded. Val watched Mika closely. By afternoon, she was satisfied that she had made the right choice. Mika knew exactly what she was doing. She called a car to take her back into the city.

"Carry on," she said. "You're doing a great job."

For the first time all day, Mika smiled.

That evening, Val's phone rang. It was Jeff.

"Dinner?" he asked.

"I had a long day. I'm going to order in tonight I think."

Jeff felt a little swell of arousal. She was inviting him to her place.

"Well Val that sounds just fine." There was a heavy edge to his voice.

"Er, no. I meant I'd prefer to spend the evening alone."

"Come on. I'll bring the wine."

"Sorry Jeff. I'm just not interested."

Jeff felt his semi shrink. He was not having good luck today. "Okay. Another night."

"Good night." Val hung up the phone.

She stared at it for moment. What would she order? She decided that perhaps instead she would visit the Hound & Hare. She slung her purse over her shoulder and headed out.

Something's not working, thought Jeff. He'd have to step up his game. Tomorrow he would send her flowers at work. That's something a classy woman would like.

Business associates sent flowers to Hammer & Bone to mark partnerships or occasions. No man had ever made the bourgeois gesture of sending Valkyrie flowers directly at work with romantic intention before.

Hammer & Bone as a corporate being had developed into its own distinct entity. In the beginning, it was a self-created nickname, a play on her own moniker, Valkyrie Snow. Hammer honoured the Norse gods of her namesake and Bone was white as snow, like Val's uncanny paleness and her love of the Canadian winter landscape. When business started to take off, Hammer & Bone slipped easily into incorporation, channeling Val's dreams but taking on a life of its own.

Jordan was working the day shift today. He liked the day shift in the spring and summer because when he got off around six there was still some daylight left to enjoy. In the winter, it was miserable. He never saw the sun.

He would be off soon. What would he do tonight? Maybe lay in a park, taking in the end of a beautiful day.

Jordan scrubbed hard for the last hour, getting things in order for the night shifters. His hands were raw, and sweat was pouring down his back. He wiped his hair out of his face. He would have to get his hair cut soon, or start wearing it in a bun.

The night shifters showed up, ready to jump in as the dinner rush brought a constant flow of dishes and pans. He stepped away, wiping his hands on a towel and stepping out into the back alley to cool off. The temperature outside was not much better. The sun beat down, not as hot as the afternoon but still surprisingly intense. He peeled off his shirt, shaking it out in the small breeze, enjoying the air on his bare skin.

From the balcony of Hound & Hare, Val sipped a Caesar, staring intently into the street below. There he was—the young singing man. He stood in a sliver of shade outside the Black Cherry, the skin of his chest glowing white against the darker shade of his arms. He raised an arm, scratching his head, his curls wet with sweat. His chest was thin and bony on top with a layer of softness around his stomach, but his forearms and biceps rippled with muscle from scrubbing the heavy pans.

Val looked long and hard at him, pulling an olive from her drink and enjoying its salty taste in her mouth.

Jordan felt the hair on his arms rise lightly, the sensation of being watched coming over him slowly. He looked from side to side, and suddenly turned up to the patio above. A woman was looking at him. They locked eyes, and to his surprise, she didn't look away. Even from this distance, her gaze seemed curious, interested, and confident. She looked very familiar, but he couldn't think of why. She was older, but classically beautiful, like a marble statue with a long pale neck. Where would he have met such a woman before? She kept staring at him, sipping her drink.

Suddenly, he felt conscious of his nakedness, and he pulled on his shirt. When he turned back to look at her, she was gone.

He reached into his pocket and pulled out his phone. There was nothing he specifically needed to check or to know, but reaching for his phone had become an instinctive gesture, like looking both ways before crossing the street. He opened each app, flicked through it, and then closed it, one after the other.

No notifications, no surprise... whispered Snake.

A couple people had 'liked' his repost of the concert last week. That was good.

But not enough for it to mean anything.

Against his own better judgement, Jordan looked up Sarah Singh—another instinctive gesture. Same profile picture as last time. Predictably, he felt terrible.

Loser.

He swallowed hard. Time to go inside.

Workers in the Industrial Revolution had been addicted to escaping reality with alcohol; today's workers were addicted to the digital worlds of social media. It was almost satisfying, like a kind of social masturbation. They avoided the crushing realities of environmental degradation, the decline of democracy, and the critical failure of capitalism by pretending that everything was fine, that these bright and shining flashes of their best experiences captured on social media were somehow the essence of their lives, and not ephemera. The placebo was powerful.

Val regarded social networking apps as business tools. She was a creator, not a consumer. She never took pictures of herself, crying out to the masses to see her, to acknowledge her existence and her humanity. She grew up before this kind of attention was something people desired, and she expressed her vanity privately. She preferred to be hidden and the internet already told more people than she wanted more than she wanted to share.

Jordan walked around to the front entrance of the restaurant. He was going to ask the front end manager if the Waves could play Canada Day. He figured they owed him that much, after he had slaved away on the dishes for over two years now, taking any shitty shift they gave him. He only whined a little bit when he had to work back-to-back shifts. They paid him cash for those because it was illegal.

He hated asking for things. But the boys were counting on him. He took a deep breath and stepped forward.

"Stew? Can I talk to you?"

"Not if you take more than a minute."

"I wanted to ask you something… maybe we could go into the hall?"

"Really? During the dinner rush?" Stewart looked pissed.

Bad start, thought Jordan.

Why are you doing this to yourself? hissed Snake. *Just go home.*

"I was wondering if the Waves could play at the Cherry for Canada Day."

"Who?" Stew knew exactly who the Waves were.

"My band, the Waves."

"That's a big night for us, Jordan. A huge night."

"I know. We'd put on a really good show."

"Sorry but we're not some rinky-dink little café for you to practice at. The Black Cherry is a serious restaurant, with a serious reputation."

Jordan saw then that this was probably going nowhere. He fought to contain himself.

Piece of shit slimy student bar with shit food and shit cocktails and watery beer, he thought.

"Please Stew. It would mean a lot to me."

"Look, it would be a big deal if I let you play any night, let alone Canada Day in Ottawa. It's just not happening. And you've got some guts on you, asking me for a favour like that."

Suddenly Earl appeared behind him, joining the conversation.

"The Cherry isn't here to build you a music career, Scrub," he said with a smile.

They smirked at each other as Jordan walked out, fists clenched. He was so angry that he didn't notice that the statuesque woman who had been staring at him from the patio of the Hound and the Hare was standing in the lobby at the Cherry, and heard the whole exchange.

Jordan felt the steam coming from his ears. He wanted to quit his job, to smash Earl and Stew's faces, to kick something really hard. He walked quickly down the street, his heart pounding in his throat, his eyes burning. What he really wanted was to cry, but that would never happen.

I hate my life, he thought. Snake just laughed. He was right all along.

Charlotte sat at her desk, trying to study. She looked at the page of her textbook, her eyes losing focus as her mind wandered. She was thinking about Jordan.

Nope, she told herself sternly. *You are not texting him. Focus on your homework.*

Charlotte was in Health Sciences at the university. She had gotten a Massage Therapy diploma at Algonquin College, and she worked on commission at a clinic in Centretown. She was hoping to get a more permanent gig with the university degree.

Charlotte had resolved to stick to her promise not to text Jordan anymore unless he reached out first. She took a deep breath and went back to typing her notes.

The hours passed as afternoon turned to evening. Charlotte felt her stomach grumble. It was almost time for a break. She sat up and stretched, looking at her word count. She was pleased with her progress. She had gotten a lot of work done today.

Ding! Her phone signalled. She picked it up.

Jordan:

> Hey :) I'm off work

Charlotte smiled. She thought for moment and then typed.

> Awesome :)

Charlotte:

There, she thought. *That way I am acknowledging his text, but still leaving it up to him to invite me somewhere.*

She turned back to her book, but there was no way she would be able to study now. She opened Vimeo and started watching a music video.

Jordan:

> Still want to hang out?

Charlotte:

Yea :) Want to go for dinner?
I'm hungry

Jordan:

Nah I ate at work

Well what could she say to that? She wanted to see him, but she wanted to actually hang out. She wasn't inviting him for a booty call. Hmm.

Charlotte:

Where do you want to go?

Jordan's face glowed dimly in the light of his phone screen. He wanted to go to Charlotte's house. It was so clean, and quiet and nice. He wanted to lie in her fluffy bed and forget about today.

Jordan:

I can come over and we'll
figure something out

Charlotte:

Sounds good :) Give me like
an hour, I need to make dinner

An hour? Jordan didn't know if he could wait that long. His thoughts were tormenting him and he needed a distraction fast.

Jordan:

Sure

He would hop in the shower and then go over. That should keep him occupied.

"Showering," he shouted in the apartment in case anyone needed to take a dump before he went in. There was no response. Jerome was at his girlfriend's place, and Matt and Alex were playing video games in their rooms. Jordan pulled off his clothes and turned on the water.

The faint smell of mould wafted up into his nose. The crevices in the tiles were filled with it. Jordan splashed water on it, hoping it would wash away. No effect. Oh well.

You live in a shit hole, said Snake.

Jordan cranked up the cold water, and started humming a song. Snake slithered away.

Charlotte tidied up her room, put on a touch of lipstick, and whipped up a stir-fry for dinner. It was just a quick meal with the vegetables she had in the fridge, but it turned out pretty well. She took a plate to Audrey.

"I know you're studying hard, but here's dinner," she said, setting it on the desk.

"Thanks girl it looks great," said Audrey, blowing her a kiss and pushing up her glasses on her nose.

Charlotte and Audrey usually ate dinner together at the table in the kitchen, but they were both taking condensed summer classes and studying right now. She took her plate to her room and ate it with chopsticks sitting in the chair at her desk. She browsed the internet while she waited for Jordan.

Her phone buzzed.

Here

Jordan:

Jordan was fifteen minutes early. Charlotte went down to the door to let him in.

"Hey," he said. His face looked ghostly.

"Are you okay?"

"Yea I'm fine!" Jordan smiled, shaking off his funk. He followed Charlotte to her room. Charlotte closed the door behind them.

Jordan jumped onto the bed. "Whatcha watching?" he asked.

Charlotte came over and lay beside him. "Just virals. I studied all day and I needed a break."

"Sure you did."

"Hey!"

They kissed.

"So where did you want to go?" asked Charlotte.

"Well we could stay here," he said, as though he just thought of it. "It's so cozy." He looked into her eyes.

He had a good point. "We could watch a movie or something."

"Yea I'm down for that." Jordan took off his pants and crawled under the covers.

Charlotte noticed that his hair was wet. He smelled clean.

He showered for me, she thought. She smiled and went to the computer to put on a movie. She picked Iron Man, because she figured Jordan would like that. She snuggled into bed beside him, nestling her neck on his shoulder. He put his arm around her.

This is nice, she thought. *Is this a date?* It was probably the earliest in the day that she had ever seen him.

"Hey do you have any weed?" he asked.

"No, sorry. I don't smoke."

Bummer, he thought. He liked to toke a bit before he watched a movie.

Jordan fell asleep in five minutes, and Charlotte watched the movie all the way to the end.

When Charlotte woke up in the morning, Jordan was gone.

CHAPTER FIVE

Valkyrie Snow went down to the Black Cherry to confront the singing man. She had overheard a conversation he had with his boss. It was painful to hear. When she turned to leave, she noticed a poster on the message board just inside the door. It was a picture of the Waves. *Like us on Facebook. Follow us on Instagram.*

She pulled out her small Ricoh GR and snapped a photo of the poster.

When she got home, Val went to her desktop computer and looked up the Waves. She scrolled through their Insta feed. She saw close-ups and wide shots of shitty venues around Ottawa, portraits of the band members, and various candids of the guys drinking and smoking. She saw a solemn portrait of the singing man, handsome even without a smile, one eye slightly larger than the other. He was photoshopped onto a tropical beach paradise background; Val could see the fine digital lines of his silhouette.

Contact us.

Val clicked the chatbox.

> Hi. I would like to book you to play on Canada Day.

> Best

> V. Snow

Val stood up and walked to the kitchen. She was still a little buzzed from the Caesar. She pulled a bowl of cherries from the fridge, poured herself a glass of scotch, and opened the book she was reading. It was a volume highlighting the life's work of postmodern architect Rem Koolhaas. The book was beautifully put together and Val was considering commissioning something about her gothic work, now that she was moving in a new direction.

When she was done the cherries, Val dialled up a friend of hers in Montréal who owned several bars.

"Âllo?"

"Âllo Lucette, c'est Valkyrie."

"Val! Ça va bien?"

"Oui ça va merci."

"What can I do for you?"

"I have a band of very talented young men, I'd like to set them up with something for Canada Day."

"What kind of musique?"

"They're sort of pop-rock I'd say."

"This is very short notice... I won't be able to do anything big, but I do have a small bar in Plateau where I'm sure we could put them in. It's small though, you understand."

"Yes Lucette. Just do your best. Email me the details."

And she knew Lucette would.

On his way to work, Jordan noticed that he had a message on the band Instagram account: jordanbarkerthewaves. He opened the private chat.

> Hi. I would like to book you to
> play on Canada Day.
>
> Best
>
> V. Snow

Jordan stared at the black text on the white background of his screen. Was this real? He was in shock. No one had ever invited them to play for a real event. They had done house parties, and they played all the local spots where bands charged cover and the bar made their money from the drinks, but this was a message from someone who saw them play, liked what they saw, and reached out.

This is it, thought Jordan. *We're gonna be famous.*

Don't get your hopes up, hissed Snake.

> Hi! Yes we are available.
>
> Where? What time should we
> be there?

Someone wanted to book them for a Canada Day gig! Jordan felt a wave of excitement wash over him. He hadn't told the boys yet that the Black Cherry had said no. This was even better than the Cherry.

V. Snow. Who could that be? He clicked the account that had messaged him.

Hammerandbone 613?

He scrolled through the photos. Buildings. It was a construction company.

Jordan wanted to tell the boys right away, but he would wait to find out the details.

He walked to work with a bounce in his step. When he got to the Cherry, he didn't even need a cigarette. He walked in the back door, hung his backpack up on the hook, and took off his sweater to start his shift. Earl popped his head in.

"Hiya Scrub," he said. Jordan just smiled at him. Today, he didn't even care.

Valkyrie checked her company Instagram account. The Waves had responded. She smiled and typed.

> Don't you want to know how much? :)

> I was thinking $2500. The bar is in Montréal. Please call me. 613-580-2940

She turned away from the computer and opened her drawing book. She looked out the massive windows. They were dripping with rain. It was pouring buckets outside. Val went over to the balcony and opened the sliding doors. She loved the smell of rain and the sound it made pounding the patio. Rain was lovely when you had floor-to-ceiling windows. Val returned to her desk.

At work, Jordan itched to check his phone, but there was never a quiet moment to take a peek. Earl watched him like a hawk, and Jordan was sure that the moment he dried his hand and fished out his phone, Earl would be right there to catch him and holler. The hours grinded on slower than ever before. Jordan would not receive a break. There used to be labour laws about mandatory breaks, but that was when there was plenty of work. If anyone said anything nowadays they would just schedule you for a four-hour shift.

Most jobs were automated and the work was done by machines anyway. There were simply not enough hours of work to keep everyone employed five days a week. Companies no longer hired employees, they made them sign temporary contracts. That way they could make their own rules. Jordan was not an employee of the Black Cherry, he was a 'freelance dishwasher'. He could be fired at any time.

Finally the pressure was too much. Jordan had to check his messages and see if V. Snow had responded. He waited for his moment. The next time Earl popped his head in, Jordan would check right after.

Fifteen minutes later, Jordan's moment came. He whipped his hand out of the sink, gave it a shake, and wiped it on his pants. Then he thrust it in his pocket, pulled out his phone, and clicked on Instagram.

> Don't you want to know how much? :)

> I was thinking $2500. The bar is in Montréal. Please call me.
> 613-580-2940

His heart jumped. *$2500!!* It was their lucky day. He typed his response as fast as possible with his thumb.

> Call you at 6:30 when I'm off work

"SCRUB!" screamed Earl. Jordan jumped, almost dropping his phone. He jammed it back in his pocket as fast as possible.

"You're having quite a week. First you ask Stew for a favour—not me, mind you, not me your boss—but the front-end manager—and now I catch you stealing time from me, playing around on your phone when you should be working!"

Jordan plunged his hands in the hot steaming water. He scrubbed furiously.

"Sorry boss!" Jordan could not afford to lose this job.

That evening after work, Jordan ran out the door as fast as he could. He needed to call V. Snow and hit the shower before his gig tonight. The Waves were playing at Maverick's. He wanted to avoid a chat with Earl. He escaped in the nick of time. He burst out the back alley door, flying down the street on his longboard.

As he rolled up to the crumbling walk-up where he lived, Jordan pulled out his phone to make the call.

He paused. He hated talking on the phone. The last time he called someone it had been his mother over six months ago. A queasy feeling churned in his stomach and his palms felt sweaty. He just couldn't do it.

I could text, he thought. He typed in the phone number.

No... V. Snow specifically said to call.

Don't fuck this up, said Snake, serious for once.

Jordan took a few deep breaths. Then he hit 'Call'.

As the phone trilled he was terrified. What should he say? *Hi, I'm Jordan. From the Waves.*

"Hello?" said a soft voice from the other end.

"Hi! I'm Jordan."

"Sorry, who?"

Shit, he thought. "Jordan Barker. The lead singer for the Waves."

"Oh yes. Jordan." She said his name slowly, enunciating the 'D', feeling the word on the roof of her mouth.

"We will take the gig."

"Excellent. Can you come by to discuss the details? I'll give you the address."

"Umm, actually I can't because we have a show tonight. Can I come by tomorrow? I get off around six."

"Yes. Do you have a pen?"

"A pen?"

"To write down the address."

"Oh, sure." Jordan put her on speaker phone, typing the address in a memo app as she told him.

"How about 6:30 pm?" she said.

"Sure."

"Very good. I'll see you tomorrow then."

"Wait!" said Jordan. He didn't catch her name. But it was too late; the connection was closed.

Jordan burst in the door of the apartment with a huge grin on his face. No one was in the living room. The 'living room' was basically just a corner of the kitchen with a ratty couch thrown into it that they'd picked out of the trash in Sandy Hill and carried home. The boys usually hung out in their rooms.

"Guys!" he shouted. "Guys come out! I have great news!"

"Whaa?" said Bubba, poking his head out of his room. He was wearing just boxers, his big hairy belly hanging over the front.

"C'mere! Jerome and Matt home?"

"Yea. Matt is probably having a nap."

"Hey Jerome!" he shouted. They heard a muffled sound from behind his closed door. Jordan popped it open, leaning in. Jerome was playing a video game.

"What?" he said, distracted. ""Give me like ten minutes."

Jordan went straight into Matt's room and jumped on the bed.

"Hey buddy," he said, giving Matt a big smooch on the cheek. "Wakey wakey! I've got news!"

"Fuck off," said Matt, his voice groggy with sleep.

"Seriously! Wake up!"

Bubba stood at the door laughing. He pulled out his phone to take a picture.

"Fuck off with that Bubba, not in the apartment," said Jordan, waving him away. "It's a shithole in here."

Jordan was very careful about curating his digital life. As pathetic as it was, he didn't want the fans to see how the Waves lived.

Fake it til you make it. Dress for the job you want. If you believe it, you can achieve it. That sort of thing poor people were always saying.

"Boys, I have an announcement. The Waves have a Canada Day gig."

Bubba hooted. Matt turned over in bed, sleepy but pleased.

"Wait, I'm almost done!" called Jerome from the other room. "Guys!"

"Get the fuck over here then."

"Yea it's just a game, get in here."

Jerome made a frustration noise but didn't get up.

"The Cherry? Your boss isn't as bad as you thought," said Matt.

"Or maybe Jordan gave him the ole this and that," said Bubba, pantomiming a blow job.

"You dirty fucker."

"Guys, it's not the Cherry," said Jordan. He yelled louder so Jerome could hear. "It's not the Cherry!"

"Wait for me!" Jerome was clicking furiously, in a sort of trance-like state, vaguely aware that something important was going on in the real world but he was hypnotized by the rush in his game.

"I got a message on our Insta from a chick in Montréal. We're playing a bar."

"Cool," said Matt. "That's sweet."

"Road trip!" shouted Bubba.

"And that's not even the best part."

"GUYS!" squealed Jerome. "Two fucking minutes!"

"It's a paying gig. 2500 bucks."

"All right!"

"Awesome!" Bubba gave Jordan's shoulders a squeeze. Matt was nodding.

They heard fists slam on the desk. Jerome came in. "I lost, assholes," he said. "What I miss?"

"Everything man. We've got a paid gig for Canada Day. $2500 in Montréal."

They all jumped on top of Matt in bed, having a kind of wrestle hug.

"We should take the train," said Bubba.

"Nah, we can't afford the train," said Matt. "We can get a rideshare real cheap and spend the extra on something for the band."

It didn't matter how they got there. It was a paid gig. They were real musicians.

"I'm meeting up with the chick tomorrow to get all the details."

"Get her to pay you in advance," said Matt.

"Yea good idea."

"Okay dickheads, time to get ready for the show tonight."

"Can I take a picture now at least?" asked Bubba. "To announce our Montréal show?"

"We can take a group pic at the show later."

That night the Waves were on fire. The energy was high, the crowd was great, and they had an enthusiasm and intensity like never before. They felt like rock stars tonight with the news of their upcoming gig.

"The boys and I have an announcement," said Jordan softly into the mic, brushing his hair out of his eyes. Matt banged out a little beat on the drums.

"The Waves will be playing Canada Day in Montréal."

The crowd cheered.

"Check our social media for details, and you are invited to join us on our sweet roadtrip."

Matt counted them in on sticks and they launched into the next song.

From the front of the dance floor, Charlotte smiled up at Jordan. She was so happy for him.

When the show was over, Charlotte found Jordan.

"I'm so proud of you," she said.

"I'm pumped. 2500 bucks. It's gunna be amazing." He was grinning from ear to ear. Charlotte had never seen him this happy before.

"You coming over tonight?' she asked.

"Uhhh…" he considered it. "Nah, I want to celebrate with the guys tonight."

"Sure no problem," said Charlotte. She reached up on her tiptoes to kiss him. He stepped away a little, looking from side to side. He didn't want anyone to see him kissing her. She wanted everyone to see him kissing her. She reached out and touched his arm. He smiled and turned to walk away to find the guys.

Matt and Bubba were on the other side of the stage. They had picked up girls. Jordan could tell they were coming over tonight. Rachel was there; she'd be coming home with Jerome too. He would be the awkward one out.

He pulled out his phone, finding Charlotte's name.

> Hey so want to come to my place instead? :)

Jordan:

Charlotte was so confused. *Well I guess he wants to celebrate with the guys but also see me…*

Charlotte:

> Sure

> We're going to head out soon. Meet me outside the door in ten?

Jordan:

Charlotte waited at the door for thirty minutes, and then the band and entourage came out. They all headed back to the walk-up to continue the party there. They cheered and sang as they walked in a group down the street, drunk and happy.

"Shut up!" shouted a tired man from his balcony.

"Move to the suburbs!" shouted Matt back.

They tumbled in the apartment door. Bubba threw on some tunes, and he and Matt and the two girls they brought back from the bar squeezed onto the ratchet couch. Jerome and his girlfriend disappeared into his room right away.

"Want to just go to my room?" said Jordan. "There's no space in our shitty living room."

"Okay."

They went down to the dark end of the hall, disappearing into Jordan's dank bedroom. Jordan left the light off. Charlotte could feel clothes and crumbs under her feet. She really really liked him, but she was starting to feel weird about this. Was he waiting for the right moment to ask her to be his girlfriend? Or was she just his fuck buddy? She frowned in the dark.

Jordan's lips found hers and he kissed her softly. All her doubts melted away as she let herself get swept into the kiss. She wrapped her arms around his body. He felt so good.

They heard a crash in the other room.

Jordan laughed. "Fucking idiots," he said.

He jumped onto the bed. "Come here babe," he whispered. He took off his pants.

Charlotte stripped down and climbed into bed with him. The filthy apartment dissolved around her as Jordan made love to her slowly.

"Let's go have a drink with the boys," he said afterward.

They put their clothes back on and went out to the main room. Bubba and his girl had rosy faces; they were finished too. Matt and Jerome were still in their rooms. Jordan and Bubba chatted about the Montréal gig and the girls talked together about school. Everyone had a drink, and eventually Bubba's girl went home and Charlotte and Jordan went back to bed.

The next morning, Jordan woke up to the sound of his alarm. Charlotte was already awake, watching him sleep.

"Good morning," he said, hitting snooze and stretching his arms.

She smiled, leaning over to kiss him. "Good morning."

Charlotte knew Jordan would have to get up to go to work soon. She had something to ask him and now was the time.

"Jordan? Can we talk about something?"

Here it is, he thought. He rolled his face into the pillow and made a goofy noise.

"I'm not sure what that noise means…" said Charlotte gently.

He popped his face out, looking at her with a guilty expression. "What?" he asked.

Charlotte was suddenly shy. As she looked at his face she knew that all the signs pointed to this conversation ending with Jordan disappearing from her life. But she was hopeful. Her eyes lingered on his beautiful long lashes, his lips, the way his hair fell on the pillow. She could love him, if he would let her. She swallowed hard.

"Are you into me?" she asked softly.

Jordan looked at her sweet face looking at him so earnestly. He knew what she wanted to hear. He felt a surge of satisfaction at the love and adoration so obvious in her eyes, drinking it in like a vampire, and at the same time he felt nauseas with self-loathing.

You sick fuck, hissed Snake.

For a flicker of a moment he thought, *I think I love her too,* then he felt overwhelming disgust and disdain for her, and hated her for making him hate her. He sighed. Truly, he knew that he didn't really care that much one way or another about Charlotte.

"I guess, well, ya, this is nice," he said, reaching out with his foot to rub her foot. "I mean, I enjoy this."

Charlotte was quiet.

"I mean, you're enjoying this, right?" he added.

"Umm, yea, I'm enjoying this..."

Jordan leaned forward and kissed her, willing her to relax and drop the conversation.

"I was thinking, maybe this weekend, if you're free, or next weekend, or whatever, I could rent a car, and we could go somewhere. Like camping or something."

"I work all the time. And the Waves play weekends."

"Okay. Well how about some evening when you're free we can camp out on the beach. One night."

Jordan made a noncommittal noise. "Maybe..."

"Or you pick. Something you want to do together."

Jordan put his face back in the pillow.

"When do you have a free night?" Charlotte asked.

Jordan could see that she wasn't letting this go. "I don't know," he said. There was an edge to his voice.

"If you were really into me you'd want to plan something to spend some alone time together, to get to know each other," she said, very softly. He said nothing.

Charlotte felt tears in her eyes. She didn't want to cry, and she didn't expect herself to, but there they were, salty droplets sliding down her face.

Jordan looked ashamed, and a little bored. Charlotte got up and started putting on her clothes.

"Aww, Char, don't go like this," he said. She turned to look at him, sad and hopeful.

"It's just… I hate sleeping alone."

She exhaled with disgust.

"Really?? You are such an asshole."

Jordan was flabbergasted.

Me? An asshole?! No way! What the fuck is her problem? he thought.

"I have only ever been nice to you," he said. She could hear genuine surprise in his voice.

"What!?!"

"You got what you wanted out of this, right? *You* texted *me*. You chased me. Half the time I wasn't even horny."

"You should have said no! You should have said, 'let's be friends'!"

"Chill, I was doing you a favour," he mumbled.

"That is complete bullshit! You could have found a one night stand at any of your shows. You brought *me* home with you at the end of the night. For you. Don't pretend it was for my own good! You led me on!"

Jordan said nothing. He kept his eyes down.

"You're *not* nice. It's obvious that I'm into you, Jordan. There are lots of other girls out there who might be into a casual relationship. You should have been honest with me from the start about what you want."

His eyes scrolled up to her face. He couldn't say anything. He looked stunned. He had never thought of that. Blood rushed to his cheeks. He tried to imagine what it would be like to be honest with her. Jordan didn't want to sleep with a girl who was into casual relationships. That was disgusting. (Jordan was a hypocrite.)

"You're crazy!" he yelled.

Charlotte walked out of his room, wiping her eyes. Mercifully, no one was up yet so there was no one to see her cry. She went straight out the door, closing it gently behind her.

Jordan pulled the sheet up over his head, rolling over to face the wall. He reached up and grabbed Charlotte's pillow, hugging it tight against his body, burying his face down into it. He felt like shit.

CHAPTER SIX

The next day, Val went out to see what progress had been made on Glasshouse. It rained on and off all day, but that was every day this summer. The work continued. She wore her rain boots and a long waterproof coat. Her hair curled up around her face from the moisture in the air.

Mika Nakamura was unfazed by the weather. She was determined to complete Glasshouse right on schedule, or perhaps slightly sooner.

"The foundation is finished, including the river stone chimney, and we've erected the frame. There was a problem with the sizing on a flat of glass panes, but that's been solved. We're coming along nicely," she reported.

"Everything looks great," said Val dreamily. She couldn't believe that after so many years of scheming about this place it was finally becoming a reality. She loved seeing every part of the building process of her projects, from the ground to the finer architectural points and the finishing details. She couldn't wait to see how her polished antique copper tub, hand-selected on a trip to France, would look in the space. The design was simple and luxurious, like all of her designs. She hummed as she walked around the worksite, watching her dreams constructed before her very eyes.

The hours flew by. Val was thoroughly soaked with rain by dinner time.

"I have a meeting," she said to Mika. "I'll ring up some supper to be delivered to you and the workers. And some extras for them to take home."

"That's kind, thank you."

There were still a few hours of workable sunlight left in the day, despite the clouds and drizzle.

Val called a car. On the way home, she had the robot order trays of shawarma and salads to be sent to the worksite.

Valkyrie's car pulled up to her building. She hopped out and walked up to the entrance. A man approached her, his head buried in a large black umbrella. He was wearing a sharp suit and very convincing patent leather knockoffs on his feet.

"Hi, Val," he said. It was Jeff.

"Umm, hello." Val looked up and down the street. "What are you doing here?"

"I just thought I'd swing by after work and see if our paths crossed. We're in luck!"

"How do you know where I live?" Val stepped up to the front door, pulling it halfway open, stepping inside and speaking through the half-closed space.

"Oh well you mentioned it at dinner with Kale."

A shiver tingled up Val's spine. She had certainly not mentioned her address at dinner.

"Alright well good night."

"Wait," said Jeff, stepping forward, wedging his foot against the open door. "How about dinner? Or a drink?"

Valkyrie's grey eyes flashed with anger. She kicked his foot firmly off of the door.

"I have a meeting. Please don't invite yourself to my house." She pulled the door shut behind her before he could say anything else, or push himself further into her space.

Val stomped up the stairs. Jeff had left her flustered.

How rude, she thought. *Can he not take a hint?* She valued her privacy above all else. When she entered her apartment, she locked the door behind her. At one time, Valkyrie would have let Jeff in, or talk her into dinner, even though she wasn't interested. *Good girls obey,* her subconscious upbringing would have told her. At some point in the last few years, she got over that.

At forty-one years old, Valkyrie went back to school to get her doctorate, despite all the people who told her it was a waste of time. Ever since then she did what she wanted and stopped asking for permission.

A tall grandfather clock stood in the foyer. *6:00,* it read. *Almost time for the singing man.*

Jordan had a hard time crawling out of bed for work after Charlotte left, but scrubbing dishes in the back of the Cherry actually helped take his mind off things. He willed himself to 'dull out'.

'Dull out' was Jordan's term for shutting off his feelings when they got too intense. He first started doing it when he was little kid. His dad was a loser, and his mom was always away trying to hustle up some food or money to feed Jordan and his older brother Michael. They would go for days without seeing her. If the food ran out, Jordan's dad would just take off somewhere. When that happened, the old lady in the apartment next door would leave boxes of cookies or saltines outside their door. When his mom came home, Jordan would cling to her and cry with relief. She was exhausted and it kind of annoyed her, which made him even more afraid that she would leave and never come back. Eventually he learned to dull out instead.

Michael had died of a fentanyl overdose over ten years ago. Jordan barely remembered his face; sometimes he would close his eyes and an idealized image of a handsome boy would float up into his consciousness, but Jordan knew that Michael probably didn't even look like that. He had no pictures because all his social media accounts eventually deleted old pictures and he hadn't noticed until it was too late.

What did Charlotte think was going to happen? he thought. *Did she think we would get married? Have a happy little family?* Jordan snorted at the thought. Marriage and children were the furthest thing from his mind.

I just want to work somewhere decent that pays me decent and I can live comfortably and not worry about money all the fucking time.

Jordan played this track over in his mind so many times that by now he knew it by heart. But he did it anyway.

I need to apply for more jobs.

But that's not going anywhere.

I need to write more songs. I need to try harder. If I try harder my music will take off.

But what if it never does.

I could start a business.

But I would need some start-up cash for that.

Do I even want to run a business?

No. I want to make music.

Jordan felt the anxiety catch fire inside him and burn up like a magnesium strip, *Poof!*

Time to dull out.

He scrubbed harder, willing his mind into silence, telling himself that none of it mattered.

"Chill the fuck out man," he whispered to himself. He shot a glance to his left; Cyn, his shiftmate, had not noticed.

After an hour or two of concentrated muting, Jordan let himself start to think again.

At least I've got the meeting tonight with V. Snow, he thought. *That's something to look forward to.*

Charlotte cancelled her massage appointment that day and she and Audrey went out for dessert in the Market.

"I need a mental health day," she said to the client on the phone. "I'm sorry."

"I totally understand," said the woman, a wealthy retiree who rescheduled for the following afternoon.

Audrey held her hand as they walked into Oh So Tasty.

"The reservation is Audrey, table for two," she said to the host, a cute little robot named Louis.

"Right this way," said Louis, rolling over to their table. "Just push the red button if you need anything."

They both smiled at him. There were restaurants all over town with robots now it seemed. All of the hotels had robot concierges. The first models had rubber skins to imitate the look of a human. These had deeply disturbed too many people, so the second gen of robots were intentionally synthetic and miniature, like future-chic elves, or a child in an R2D2 costume. These had the opposite effect on people, who oo'ed and aww'd at the cute preset smiles and large blinking light eyes.

Terminator's baby, thought Audrey.

"Thanks for this," said Charlotte. "I really needed a date."

"Of course! Get your mind off things with chocolate."

They opened the menu.

"I don't know what I want," said Charlotte, looking at all the options. "I used to know what I wanted..." she trailed off, her eyes tearing up.

"Oh my goodness girl... you're a mess eh? You pick two. We can share both."

"But what do you want?"

"I like everything. You go ahead. This is your day."

Charlotte picked an apricot mousse cake and death by chocolate. Audrey pushed the red button on the table and a human server came over to take their order.

"With heaps of ice cream on the side," Audrey added with a smile.

When the server left, Charlotte let out a long sigh.

"I don't know why I'm so upset. I mean Jordan and I were never really together. I guess I just feel stupid, y'know?"

"I know. You're so nice, and trusting, and you just didn't expect him to do you like that. That's his problem, not yours."

"The thing is, he didn't even think he'd done anything wrong. It was so weird. It was a terrible conversation..."

"Oh honey, he knows what he did wrong."

Jordan finished up at work. He grabbed his backpack and headed out the door. He reached in his pocket: no smokes.

Fuck, he thought. He'd really been looking forward to a drag. He scowled and walked faster. Up ahead, there was a crowd of people. They were carrying signs.

RAISE MINIMUM WAGE OUT OF THE GUTTER

LIVING WAGE

I WORK HARD AND LIVE IN POVERTY!

BROKEN SYSTEM

Jordan's scowl deepened. These people blocking the street were in his way. He heard a woman on a loudspeaker.

"I have two children," she said. "I can't afford to feed them." Jordan felt a shiver down his spine. "Put the politicians on minimum wage, see how fast things change!"

The crowd roared. Police in riot gear shifted on their feet, standing ready. The tension was growing.

Stupid protesters, thought Jordan angrily. *What do they hope to get from this? Nothing's going to change.* Jordan didn't want minimum wage to go up. Then all the new people at work would make the same as him and he'd been there two years.

And I live in poverty too, dipshits. He kicked a Tim Hortons cup into the gutter.

A surprising number of people were at the protest. It wasn't just angry students. There were pensioners, mothers suckling their babies, and people of all ages with flags of many different communities. Jordan pushed his way through.

Ahead there was a massive plywood board painted white, with a message scrawled on it in black permanent marker.

WORKERS OF THE WORLD UNITE

They know that the laws are for the strong, that they protect the class that owns everything.
The oft-repeated charge that the Industrial Workers of the World is organized to hinder industry is false. It is organized in order to keep industries going. By organizing industrially they are forming the structure of the new society in the shell of the old.

Now, don't you see, it is impossible to maintain an economic order that keeps wages practically at a standstill, while the cost of living mounts higher and even higher? Remember, the day will come when the tremendous activities of the war will subside. Capitalism will inevitably find itself face to face with a starving multitude of unemployed workers demanding food or destruction of the social order that has starved them and robbed them of their jobs.

In such a crisis the capitalist class cannot save itself or its institutions. Its police and armies will be powerless to put down the last revolt. For man at last will take his own, not considering the cost. When that day dawns, if the workers are not thoroughly organized, they may easily become a blind force of destruction, unable to check their own momentum, their cry for justice drowned in a howl of rage. Whatever is good and beneficent in our civilization can be saved only by the workers. And the Industrial Workers of the World is formed with the object of carrying on the business of the world when capitalism is overthrown. Whether the IWW increases in power or is crushed out of existence, the spirit that animates it is the spirit that must animate the labor movement if it is to have a revolutionary function.

Helen Keller, 1918

Jordan read every word to the end.

What revolution? These people are whack.

He wasn't sure he understood the whole thing, but he went back to re-read this part:

"It is impossible to maintain an economic order that keeps wages practically at a standstill, while the cost of living mounts higher and even higher... the day will come when the tremendous activities of the war will subside. Capitalism will inevitably find itself face to face with a starving multitude of unemployed workers demanding food or destruction of the social order that has starved them and robbed them of their jobs."

Jordan and all the other gig rats hated living on the edge of satisfaction. They would love for a new way of thinking and of living to rise up and replace the one where they had to fight each other for shitty jobs they didn't enjoy. The problem was that none of these people knew what this new world would look like.

Valkyrie Snow knew what the new world would look like. She was designing it. She sat at her desk, pressing the carbon tip of her pencil against the page along the edge of a ruler, her lines sharp and pristine. She was constantly producing designs. Some of these just went into storage at Hammer & Bone, too outlandish or unfashionable to be actioned. Sometimes though she would stay up all night working on a sketch, and call her assistant in the morning to bring it to the office to go into committee straight away. Once in a while Val went down into the stacks in the windowless belly of Hammer & Bone and fingered through her old drawings to pull out something intriguing that perhaps the world was ready for. It rarely happened, but it was possible. That was why she kept everything. Val drew her first arcology when she was just twelve years old. She abandoned them for decades because people weren't ready, but now was the time.

Right now, she was quickly drawing up an idea that had been drifting in and out of her mind since her recent weekend in Toronto. As she was sitting in a hyperloop pod it dawned on her that instead of merely boarding a pod to travel across a large distance quickly, she could design a community of pods that were mobile, and travelled via a hyperloop matrix. That way, you could custom design your living space to perfectly suit you, and then instead of moving or travelling, you could just go in your pod. You could connect your pod to a community of like-minded people in their pods, or your family, or you could move far away and be amongst strangers if you wanted.

This idea was in the realm of outlandish, she knew. The entire social system of earthling communities would have to be re-structured for it to work. The freedom of LoopCity, as she called it, would be a policing nightmare for governments. In fact, government would have to be completely re-thought. LoopCity's philosophy hearkened back to a nomadic style of living that the modern nation-state system, with its border control, passports, and trade agreements had fought hard to squash and eradicate.

No, this project was not one that Hammer & Bone, or Snow Arcologies, or any of Valkyrie's other subsidiary companies would be actioning. Not on Earth, anyway. This project might work on Mars, though. She would file away this dossier to look at with the fresh eyes of a future day.

Val was deep in thought, her grey eyes moving quickly across the page, when the buzzer rang. She jolted, startled.

The singing man.

She walked to her door, pressing the intercom.

"Hello?"

Jordan heard the woman's soft voice on the intercom. He stepped over to it, pushing the talk button.

"It's me, Jordan. Waves Jordan."

"Come up," she said, pushing the buzzer to let him in.

Jordan swung open the large wooden door, letting it thud closed behind him as he entered the lobby. The light was low, but warm. The tiles were wide grey stone, and Jordan could hear trickling water. There was a river in the floor to the right.

Bougie[1], he thought.

There were no fixtures in the ceiling; the walls were lit by sconces on the floor, casting soft pools of light on the ceiling from below.

He walked to a wide staircase, taking it up to the fifth floor where V. Snow lived. He walked down the carpeted hallway, stopping at a tall black door. No bell. He grabbed the massive iron lion's head knocker and gave it a go.

Tap tap tap. He had only seen these in movies.

In moments, he heard the grind of locks and the door pivoted open. A woman stood there in a plain white raw silk dress. Unruly hair curled around her ears and her long white neck. His eyes locked with hers, and he felt his throat go suddenly dry. It was the woman who had been staring at him from the patio of Hound & Hare the other night.

"Valkyrie Snow," she said, extending a long, pale arm. "Pleased to meet you."

---

[1] Pronounced boo-gee with a soft 'g'; short for bourgeois.

Jordan stared at her hand, feeling like an idiot. He reached and took it. She shook it. It was the first time he had ever shaken someone's hand before. Also just like the movies. He suddenly remembered that he was supposed to say his name.

"Jordan Barker."

Val stepped aside, motioning for him to come in. He moved forward, shutting the door behind him. Val went over to the island.

"What will you drink?" she asked.

"Oh, umm… what do you have?"

"I have a nice rosé open, tangy, not too sweet, but I also have scotch, or vodka if you prefer."

"Well I guess I'll have what you're having."

Val pulled out the rosé, and two glasses.

"Please, have a seat," she said.

Jordan went over to the sofa and sat down. As Val prepared the drinks, he looked around the apartment. The wall of windows was stunning, like no apartment Jordan had ever seen before. It looked like a building at the university.

"Killer place," he said.

"Thank you."

Val came over and handed him his wine, sitting across from him. He looked down, noticing the coffee table.

"Is that… a coffin?" he asked.

"Yes. Seventeenth century."

"A child's coffin?"

"It looks like it's for a child, but adult Europeans used to be that small. Incest disease and malnourishment."

They sipped their drinks. Val was staring at him intently, like the day he saw her looking down into the alley. From this close he could see that her eyes were grey. She had that same expression on her face—intrigued, curious.

"So, how did you hear about the Waves?" he asked.

"I was walking in the rain, and I passed a café where I heard you singing. It was lovely."

"Thanks," he said.

That's how it happens, he thought excitedly.

"So tell me about the show."

"It's a bar in Montréal called le divan orange. Do you speak French?"

"Yea."

"Great. I'd suggest you put something together in French for your show—as I recall from your poster, all your songs were in English."

"Okay, yea I can do that." Jordan lacked direction, but when he was given a task, he enjoyed rising to the challenge.

"You guys show up around 8 pm to set up, there is another band at 11. I will forward you an email with the details."

"Sounds great."

"Do you have any questions?" Her face was serious, like his question was important.

"Uhh, nah, I can't think of anything right now, but give me a minute."

Val downed her drink. She got up to pour another. Jordan was already finished and handed her his glass.

"Still rosé, or something stronger?" she asked.

"Well I'm not driving," he said. She poured vodka in two tumblers.

"Ice?"

"Umm, no it's okay."

Val plunked two cubes of ice in her glass, and brought both over. She handed the neat glass to Jordan.

"So. What do you do at the Black Cherry?" she asked.

"I... work in the back," he said. *So it was her watching him from the patio of Hound & Hare. And she just acknowledged it.* Jordan felt his heart beat faster.

"The back?"

"Yea, I wash dishes."

"And you sing."

"Yea, I've always been into singing."

"Who writes the music?" she asked.

She was leaning forward, her grey eyes fully focused on him. Through the pucker of her dress, Jordan could see down her front. She didn't appear to be wearing a bra. Jordan didn't think he'd ever seen a woman not wearing a bra under her clothes before.

"I write all the music."

Val leaned back into the cushions of the couch.

"I had a feeling," she said. "You're very good." She sipped her vodka.

"I like to think so."

"Don't you know it?"

"Sometimes," he laughed.

Val surveyed Jordan from head to toe.

Nature's first green is gold, she thought. He was naturally appealing, his lips and skin soft with youth, his body firm and supple before age stopped hiding his bad habits. She guessed that in a few short years, his face and body would start showing the grey of cigarettes, the wear of labour and drink, the bad teeth of a gig rat who couldn't afford dental. She, on the other hand, would go on glowing for many more decades. The disparity in life expectancy between rich and poor, once measured by good old-fashioned lifestyle was gaping ever wider, especially in the last twenty years, due to science and technology. Valkyrie Snow took care to buy only the best treatments and therapies.

But for now, nature is on Jordan's side, she thought. Jordan raised his hand to brush a lock of hair behind his ear. Val's eyes followed the movement greedily. Jordan had beautiful shining hair.

"How old are you?" she asked.

"Twenty-four."

Jordan sipped his vodka. He wished now that he asked for ice. It was strong. He tried to relax, but he felt nervous, on edge, like he was at a job interview. He tried to lean back into the pillows, shifting awkwardly.

There were shouts outside. Val stood up and walked over to the window, peering down into the street. She saw nothing.

"It's a protest," said Jordan. "For minimum wage."

Val turned to him. "I'm sorry to keep you," she said. "You must be wanting to be down there."

"Me?" he scoffed. "No."

Val looked amused. "Oh. Why not?"

"I don't protest."

"I see."

"Even if I did... doesn't raising minimum wage kill small businesses?"

"Ha, no. Most small businesses pay their workers a living wage already, because they employ friends and family. It's a different business model... Small businesses don't make their money off the backs of their workers by gouging their wages. Massive franchises and retailers do. That's who the increase is targeting. If a company must exploit people to make a profit, then it's a bad company. It deserves to fail." She made this bold statement casually, still looking out the window, ice cubes clinking in her drink.

"People say that if minimum wage goes up then more people will lose their jobs. I don't want to lose my job to pay for someone else's pay increase."

Val walked back to the couch and sat down.

"That's a rhetorical tactic used by large companies to pit their workers against one another. It doesn't really make sense. The large company needs the workers to perform the actual labour, and the less money they take for it the more CEOs make from that labour. They aren't going to fire the very people who hold up the company on their backs; who would perform the labour? The CEOs cry and threaten to fire workers when minimum wage increases, because it is their own massive fortune that must pay for it." Val knew this because she owned many companies and she made choices about the costs of labour every day.

Jordan thought about it. It was true. Earl would never fire him, as long as he worked so hard. If the government made him pay Jordan more, he would have to do it. At least until the robots became cheaper.

"If minimum wage goes too high, they'll automate my job. The dishwasher robot costs thirty grand. Once I make over that, I'm gone."

"Paying you so little you can barely live comfortably is just avoiding the problem. Pretending it will go away. Like government after government ignoring environmental degradation. You're right; a robot will replace you. A robot may one day replace me."

Val smiled, amused at the thought of a robot sitting in her desk, issuing orders at Hammer & Bone.

"Destroying all the robots, or trying to stall innovation won't solve the problem. We need to conceive of an entirely new social contract, one without wage labour, without the five-day-work-week. Machines are performing all the labour. We are running out of manual tasks for humans to keep busy performing forty hours a week. So without labouring to fill your days, what will you do instead?"

"How would I live though? How would I pay my rent?"

"That's what we have to figure out."

Jordan would love to spend his days writing music.

It'll never happen, hissed Snake.

A few generations ago, you could get a job, and work your way up into higher pay and less intensive labour as you got older. You could put in the time and earn days off, and feel like your quality of life was going up. Nowadays you bounced around between gigs, hoping to squeak by. Years of this would wear you down. Suicide among middle-aged people was at an all-time high.

"What do you do? What is your work, I mean." asked Jordan.

"I'm an architect."

"I'm surprised your job hasn't already been automated..." Jordan was starting to loosen up. The vodka was relaxing him.

"Computers help me a lot," laughed Val. "But I've managed to keep myself relevant."

Nowadays there was new technology invented by computers that only computers understood how to use. Val kept drawing her designs by hand. She knew that her brain couldn't learn the constantly new technologies fast enough anyway, so why bother?

"Would you like to see some of my work?"

"Yes," said Jordan. He actually did want to see it.

"Come here." She went over to the desk.

Jordan stood beside her as she lifted sheets of drafting paper, showing him what she was working on.

"This is insane," he said. "In a good way." Jordan loved drawing, but he rarely had time to do it. He eyed the pencil shavings and ruler. "You did these by hand?"

"I did."

His arm brushed hers. He pulled it away quickly, suddenly aware of how close they were standing. She straightened up, downing the last of her drink. He stood as well, looking into her steely grey eyes. She was slightly taller than him. He had no idea what she was thinking.

Val took her glass to the sink. Jordan walked back to the couch.

"It's getting late," she said. "How about I write you your cheque?"

"Sure," said Jordan. He had never seen a cheque before. He had only been paid by direct deposit, e-transfer and cash.

Val went upstairs.

Jordan got up and walked to the balcony. The view was incredible. He felt like a bird in a nest up here, safe and comfortable. He looked around the room. This apartment was unbelievable. He could imagine the drums set up right where Val's desk was, guitars, a mic stand. He daydreamed further, picturing a recording setup, maybe even a table to write ideas by hand. He sighed, turning to look at the kitchen. It was so clean and modern, with everything in its place. Val came down the stairs, her feet silent on the stone slabs.

"Would you like an espresso?" she asked.

"Oh, no." He had been staring into nothingness with a look on his face that Val liked.

"Are you sure?" She smiled. "You can have whatever you want."

Jordan considered for a moment. Did he want an espresso? He spent so much time repressing what he really wanted that he wasn't sure. He decided that yes, he wanted one.

"Sure, I'll have one," he said. "Thanks."

Val put the cheque on the island counter, turning to make an espresso. Jordan heard the familiar sound of beans grinding in the machine, then the splutter of liquid. He walked to the island, leaning on the marble countertop, looking at the cheque.

Jordan Barker, it said. *$2500.* He felt his heart skip with a momentary injection of pleasure.

Val saucered the little cup, placing it on the island and pushing it toward him. Then she made one for herself. When it was ready, she held out her demitasse.

"Cheers," she said. They clinked cups.
"I love good espresso."
"Me too."

They finished their coffee and Val put the cups in the sink. Jordan took the cheque off the counter with a trembling hand. He would take it straight to a bank.
"Thanks," he said, sliding it into his backpack.
"Thank you."
"Will I see you at the show?"
"Not likely. Maybe."
"Okay, well thanks."
Val saw him to the door.
"Goodnight," she said.
"Goodnight."

CHAPTER SEVEN

As Jordan walked home in the night, the cheque for $2500 safely deposited in his bank account, he realized that going to Valkyrie Snow's house had been kind of fun.

Free booze and coffee, he thought. But beyond that, she was an interesting person. He enjoyed their conversation, and her apartment was beautiful.

She sees me as a true artist, he dared to think to himself. *She sees my potential.*

This thought smouldered like warm coals deep in his belly. True, it took validation from another person to give him this feeling of satisfaction, but it helped prove to himself what he knew but was afraid to acknowledge:

I am a musician.
I am a good musician.

Val wasn't sure if she would go to the Canada Day concert in Montréal or not. She had checked hotels twice now, noticing that they were booking up. She decided to book a room, just in case. With that done, she could relax, knowing that she was free to decide the day of the concert if she would go or not.

The phone rang in Valkyrie's apartment.

"Hello?"

"Hi Val." It was Sukhwant Thaila, her personal assistant. "Athershore is requesting a meeting."

Athershore was one of Val's major manufacturing partners.

"When?"

"I cross-checked their schedule with ours, and it looks like July 1st would be best."

Canada Day, thought Val.

"Nothing else is possible?"

"Did you want me to try to move it?"

Val thought a moment.

"No. Go ahead and book it. 10 am."

"I'll go ahead and schedule that."

"Thanks, Sukhwant."

Click.

Well that settles that, she thought.

Val turned her attention back to the file she was reading. It was the latest research and development update from the team of scientists at the University of British Columbia who were working on a special project funded by Snow Arcologies. The heart of Val's arcology design was a plasma vaporization machine. All the building's waste entered a palladium glass chamber. A plasma torch disassociated the molecules of the organic matter, and the resulting gasses were captured to power the arcology. The particulate that couldn't vaporize came out of the machine in small gemstone-like baubles encased in stone silicate. The baubles would be sold to be made into road building materials for now—BluRoads Inc., another of Val's companies—but in the future she would innovate a way to use all arcology by-products within the arcology itself.

Valkyrie had met the UBC scientist at a conference, and was immediately impressed. She researched further, and when she was satisfied with Sonam Devgan's work history, asked her to take on the vaporizers. The team was afforded a very generous budget, and in exchange Valkyrie's company retained all the rights to their research.

Val loved receiving their briefings.

I should send a gift to whatever grad student is writing them, she thought. *They're doing a wonderful job.*

A great deal of cutting edge research and development on green energy was being done by China, but Valkyrie liked to support Canadian universities when she could. She would love to sit down with the researchers themselves to hear about how the project was going. She rang up her assistant.

"Hi Sukhwant."

"Hi Val. The meeting is confirmed."

"Great. I wanted to add something—could you please arrange a visit to UBC? Tell the team I'd like to get a briefing in person."

"Absolutely. When were you thinking?"

"Well if they're free this weekend, I'd like to make something happen."

"I will ask. Just a moment."

"Thanks."

Sukhwant put her on hold. Val continued flipping through the file. Fifteen minutes later, Sukhwant was back.

"Sorry for the wait."

"No problem. What's the verdict?"

"They're on for this weekend. I can make a reservation somewhere quiet for you meet and have a few drinks? Or would you prefer a more formal setting?"

"Quiet with drinks would be perfect. I'd like to tour their facility as well, but I'm sure they suspect that."

"I'll make all the arrangements and send you an email confirmation."

"Thank you, Sukhwant, you're a gem."

"You're welcome. Enjoy your weekend."

Val went upstairs to pack her bag. She had a few comfortable suits and a black dress she thought fitted the occasion. She put them in a garment bag, along with her toiletries and a book to take notes in.

Ding! The notification sound rang throughout the apartment. That must be Sukhwant's confirmation. Very few people had access to Val's Virtual Reality Connect.

"House," she said softly. "Is that from Sukhwant?"

"Yes," said a voice from the house intercom.

"Read it, please."

The house read the message. Val would be leaving for Vancouver the day after tomorrow via hyperloop.

Canada Day was approaching quickly. The boys were practicing hard. Jordan wrote them a new song in French. Normally the thought of writing a song in French would terrify him. His father was French but wasn't around enough for Jordan to learn to speak fluently so he felt insecure. Val's suggestion had empowered him to stick with it, and he was happy with the result.

"Great idea," said Matt. "I hope our Montréal song is a hit."

"It was Valkyrie's idea," said Jordan.

"That's the chick who booked the gig right?"

"Yea."

"Is she, like, an agent? You should go get some tips from her. Like I was thinking of maybe investing some of that gig money into advertising for the Waves... you should ask her if that's a good idea."

"Okay." The thought of calling up Valkyrie Snow again felt daunting to Jordan, but it was a good idea.

Val woke up the morning of her trip without the urge to lie in bed longer. She hadn't been to the west coast in a long time and she was excited. She got ready quickly, getting together her things and heading out to catch her lift. Hyperloop got her there in 3 hours.

When she arrived at the station in Vancouver, a student from the research team was there to meet her.

"Ms. Snow?" said a tall young man with brown eyes and a clean-shaven face.

"Call me Val." She smiled and extended a hand.

"I'm James," he said, shaking her hand.

"James Ahote, right?"

"Yes," he smiled, surprised.

"From the file." Her grey eyes were unreadable.

"Let me take your things," he said, reaching for her bag.

"Please, no. It's more than enough that you've come to get me at the station."

"When the generous sponsor of your life's work comes to visit, you pick her up at the station," laughed James. Val hadn't thought of it that way.

He led her off the platform and over to their ride to the hotel.

Vancouver underwent a structural paradigm shift in the last few years, replacing all roads within the city and automotive transit with solar trains and bicycle thoroughfares. The ground level of the city was completely pedestrian oriented, and the city had eliminated a significant amount of air pollution. Val was inspired.

James could see her eyes lighting up, so he pointed things out as they whizzed past.

"All these new buildings here produce all the energy they need to consume. And over there, the fences have built-in wind turbines."

The wheels in Val's head were turning fast. Her eyes were taking mental pictures to file away and draw ideas from later.

"Thank you James."

They arrived at the Georgia and Val checked in.

"I'm famished. Would you join me for lunch?"

"Sure, I'd love to."

James followed her up to her room. Val pushed open the door. The suite was lovely, and too large for one person. The bed was massive. Val walked over to doors leading out onto a rooftop terrace. There was a gas fireplace and seating for at least ten guests.

"We might as well have our meeting here," she said.

"This is gorgeous. I've never been up here before."

Val flicked on the fireplace.

"Let's just order something to be sent up here," she said.

"Sure," said James. *Probably really expensive...* he thought.

"What will you have?" she asked.

"I'll call for a menu."

"I'm sure the kitchen makes everything," she laughed. "I feel like having salmon."

Vancouver was on the coast and had a reputation for great salmon. Ottawa was an inland city so Val was excited for the local flavour.

James called reception. He ordered the day's special, a clam chowder soup and beet sandwich.

"Make mine a spinach salad with grilled salmon on the side," she called. "And a bottle of dry red."

James came and joined her on the patio.

"Concierge," she said softly. Nothing. The hotel did not have Virtual Reality Connect.

"What is it?" asked James.

"I was going to tell them to bring it right out onto the terrace."

"I'll do it," he said, getting up.

"Thank you."

"So you must be the chemist," she said when he came back.

"Yea. Did you look me up?"

"I noticed in the reports that you were the one noted in the work on carbon. Fascinating stuff."

"It's so refreshing to talk to someone outside my research group who understands the work…"

"Is that original research you've done with molecular disassociation? Or just work you're drawing on?"

James' ears blushed slightly crimson. "It's my own work."

Val smiled wide. She was irresistibly drawn to talent, and she could see it in this young man.

"Well that is very interesting."

James met her penetrating gaze. She was a beautiful woman, soft and lovely, but there was something hard and steely in her eyes. He guessed she must be at least ten or fifteen years older than he was, and she was probably older still than she appeared. Her smile dazzled him.

There was a knock on the door, and a robot came in with their lunch, wheeling a silver tray out onto the terrace.

"Is everything to your liking?" it asked.

"Looks lovely," said Val. The robot had remembered to bring water.

"Can I help you with anything else?" It asked.

"Actually, yes. Could you show me how to turn on the hot tub?"

"Absolutely." The robot led her over to the tub perched on the edge of her garden. James followed. The robot turned it on, and showed them how to turn it off.

"Thank you, that's perfect." She turned to James. "You're welcome to have a soak too. If you're free this afternoon."

James felt heat rise in his chest. This was not how he imagined he would spend this afternoon.

"I… sure," he said. *What underwear am I wearing?* he thought.

"Do you have swim shorts he can wear?" she asked the robot, as if reading his mind.

"I will bring them up," it said, rolling over to measure his waist.

"Wonderful."

Val walked back to their lunch. James followed, his eyes outlining the curve of her shoulder and the round shape of her backside under her dress.

The robot poured two glasses of wine on its way out.

"Cheers, Mr. Ahote."

"Cheers."

They ate their lunch, chatting about the project. Val asked James many questions about the progress of the work, the team members, and the details of his own chemistry contributions.

She is really into the project, he thought, noticing her excitement. *Is she flirting with me? Or just curious about the work?* He couldn't tell. Val was smiling at him, pressing him for more information, but anytime she seemed to be actually hitting on him, she pulled it back quickly and he had his doubts. *But she invited me into the hot tub. Come on… she must be flirting.* He still wasn't sure.

They finished lunch. James started to feel nervous.

"Ready for a dip?" she said with a smile.

"Sure," he said.

She got up and went to the bathroom, where she took off all of her clothes. She wrapped a towel around herself and went back out onto the terrace. James was not there. He had gone to the bathroom in the adjoining room of the suite to change into the swim trunks the hotel offered. Val slipped into the bubbling water of the hot tub. She nestled into the corner, leaning back with a long sigh.

James changed into the swim trunks. He caught himself in the mirror.

What is happening? he asked himself silently. *Is this actually turning into a date with Valkyrie Snow?* He tousled his hair a bit—not too much though—and flexed his arms.

I look okay, right? He was a decently handsome guy. Better than decent. His skin usually turned a lovely dark bronze in the summer, but all the time in the lab had left his body looking a bit pale. Only his hands and face showed their usual summer colours. He felt a bit self-conscious about it. He strolled out to the terrace.

There was Val, in the tub. It appeared that she had no top on, but he couldn't tell because she was mostly submerged in the bubbles.

"Bring the bottle," she said, holding out her empty wine glass. He smiled and grabbed his glass and the bottle and brought them over. He slid into the tub, and she moved closer so he could fill her glass. He topped it up, and his own too.

Definitely not wearing a top, he thought.

She shimmied back to her spot on the other side of the tub.

James wanted something to happen. He wasn't going to make a move though. He would leave that to Valkyrie. He had a feeling she was used to taking the lead anyway.

"So James."

"Mmhm?"

"I think this will have to be my last glass of wine. Otherwise I won't make it to dinner tonight."

"That's fair."

She was looking over at him with those unreadable eyes.

"What are your plans after the project is complete?" she asked.

"I'm not sure. I'll probably apply to hundreds of research positions, and hopefully I'll get one."

"I could use a mind like yours for some of the things I'm working on. You might have to relocate closer, though."

"If you were offering me a job I would totally move for it. Once this project wraps up."

"Excellent." She sipped her wine. "No promises, but I have some things coming up I'd like to send your way to look at, once you have more time."

"That sounds... amazing," he said, leaning closer.

"Even though you'd have to leave this gorgeous city?"

"Yea, I don't mind."

"I really should visit the west coast more often. When I was growing up, it was way more work to travel across Canada. It took a long time by fossil car and flights were expensive. With hyperloop, there's really no reason why I don't come more often."

"Yea?" said James. He was sure she would make a move any moment now.

Val set her wine glass at the edge of the tub. She stood up and walked toward him. He didn't move, just gazed up at her body, dripping with water. He felt the beginnings of an erection.

She picked up her towel and stepped out of the tub, patting herself down.

"It's getting late, I'd like to take a little nap before dinner," she said. "Please feel free to use the bathroom or bedroom in the other side of the suite if you'd like." She twisted the towel up around her hair. James watched her walk away, noticing how the two dimples in her bare backside looked like quotation marks.

Val went to shower off. She turned the water on cold, gasping as it poured down her chest. She was starting to get turned on in the hot tub, but thought better of the temptation, getting out before she made any rash decisions.

Especially a bad idea if I want to hire him for future projects, she thought.

When she had rinsed off the salt from the tub, she slipped under the covers in her bed, setting an alarm for forty minutes.

James went into the other bedroom and showered. He got dressed and lay on the bed, pulling out a device to play on to pass the time. As a student, he was poised at the edge of plebeian distractions like social media apps and the pursuits of the wealthier folks he might possibly one day join the ranks of. The odds of landing one of those career jobs were shrinking every year though. You really needed to get set up by someone with power.

Someone like Valkyrie Snow, he thought.

What had happened between them? He was thoroughly confused, and glad he hadn't embarrassed himself by making an unwanted move.

Val's alarm woke her up, and she rose to dress and fix her hair. When she was ready, she went to take some air on the patio, ordering an espresso to be sent up. She ordered an extra one for James.

He heard her moving around the suite and he came out to see what she was doing. The robot came by to deliver the drinks.

"I ordered you one too," she said softly.

They drank their coffees in companionable silence. James was relieved to see that there was no awkwardness between them. Val stood close to him, and he felt the vibration of a connection between them.

They chatted on the terrace a bit longer and then headed downstairs to make their way to the restaurant where Valkyrie would be meeting the team. The place that Sukhwant chose was an upscale sushi *resutoran*, with Edo-style booths sunk into the floor around a low table and wood and paper walls creating an intimate setting.

"Lovely," said Val, her eyes sparkling. She loved trying new places with great food. Sukhwant knew her tastes and sometimes she found some really great gems.

Several people were guided to the table by their server. James stood up.

"These are my colleagues, Emily, Arjuna and Wen-pei." Val shook hands with each of them.

"So pleased to meet you," she said with a smile. One person was missing. James checked the time. It was still a little early.

Sonam Devgan, the lead scientist on the UBC research team, arrived just in time for dinner.

"Dr. Devgan," said Val, sliding further down the bench, "please come and sit by me."

"Everyone's here!" she laughed. "I feel late."

"Nonsense, we're early."

The server brought them a round of nihonshu.

"To the Heart Project," said Val.

"Cheers!"

"The Heart Project. You called it that on the phone as well. What did you mean?" asked Dr. Devgan.

"The machine is the heart of the arcology. Realistically, it's more like the digestive system… but I think of it as the Heart Project because I think of my arcology as an organism, a functional independent installation where all the parts are working together efficiently. The buildings of the past were hollow shells to be filled and emptied by people. Snow Arcologies take care of their humans, converting their waste into energy, growing food, filtering the air…"

"It's a beautiful vision," said Wen-Pei. "We're glad to be a part of it."

"Val—Dr. Snow—loves the turbine fences the city's putting in." James looked at her with admiration. She smiled politely.

"Such a great initiative."

"Not everyone thinks so…" said Emily. They all laughed. They filled her in on the local political squabbles over development.

"It's so interesting these people who have no problems forcing development on other countries are so resistant to implementing necessary change in their own communities. I try to keep my work as local as possible," said Val.

The conversation flowed easily as plates of sushi filled the table.

"Great choice. This place is incredible."

"Thank you Dr. Devgan but I have to give the credit to my assistant. She picked it. She knows how much I love edomae nigirizushi."

"Please, call me Sonam."

"Then call me Val."

Sonam pressed her shoulder up against Val's.

"I'm so glad I came out. I felt like I was getting to know each of you through the reports and I just had to see you in person."

"We're excited to show you the lab tomorrow," said Arjuna. His last name was also Devgan, and Val assumed that perhaps he was Sonam's husband. She could see now that he was probably a nephew she was able to land in this research contract.

"We hustled to get it ready for your visit."

"I'm so sorry about the short notice, I hope it wasn't too much trouble." Valkyrie could tell they were all trying to please her. Research funding streams were hard to secure, and she was paying for their entire lab.

"No trouble at all," said Sonam. "A pleasure."

Rounds of food came to the table as they talked.

"I thought my lunch was good, but this is just incredible," said Val.

"Where did you go?"

"We ordered in at my hotel," said Val, looking at James. He looked back at her, his heart beating faster.

"It was pretty good. I got a peek at the restaurant downstairs—it looks lovely. Maybe we could all go back there after the tour tomorrow. My suite has a terrace and a hot tub."

James blushed, the tips of his ears turning red.

"You should all bring your bathing suits," said Val. "It should be fun."

The students looked excited. They had never been in a suite at the Georgia before.

"Can I bring my husband?" asked Wen-Pei.

"Of course!"

James' heart sank. *I guess she wasn't flirting after all.*

The next day they showed Val around the facility where a majority of their work was done. They displayed a miniature model of what the finished product would look like.

"We would have liked to offer you a more impressive life-sized mock-up, but with the time constraints…"

"Don't worry," interjected Val. "I'm more interested in watching some testing of completed components."

"I thought so," smiled Sonam.

"Out of curiosity, where did you have this model done?" asked Val.

"A friend of Arjuna put together a quick schematic and we 3D printed it."

Val considered having some of her more interesting building designs 3D printed. Then she smiled at her own vanity. She was not ashamed to say that she was damn proud of her life's work.

The team showed her their stations, their latest work, and the testing models completed so far. She was up to date on all of this already, but it was great to actually see it in person. After they took her through all of their work from start to finish, they went back to the Georgia for the evening. Wen-Pei brought her husband and they all relaxed on the patio, dipping into the tub, and enjoying cocktails and conversation.

Val was mesmerized by Sonam. She was just as formidable in person as she seemed from the lecture at the conference. Her knowledge was broad, beyond science. They drank scotch in the hot tub, sitting close because the sound of the bubbles was noisy.

"Now Val. I feel we've reached a point where I can ask you the serious questions."

Val's interest was piqued and she moved in close.

"Yes."

"Are you ever concerned that your arcologies are too perfect in design, that it will drive people to madness?"

Val grinned. "You mean like le Corbusier."

"Yes, precisely like le Corbusier."

"You know him!" Val was tickled that this scientist had such a diverse breadth of knowledge. Le Corbusier was a Swiss-French architect who in the 1920's envisioned la Ville Contemporaine. It was a perfect city of three million inhabitants working in a congruent grid of sixty-story concrete buildings, surrounded by a series of lower residential buildings and a massive parkland. Le Corbusier even fantasized about flattening Paris and building this 'purist' city on top.

"A house is a machine to live in'," said Sonam, quoting one of le Corbusier's more notorious lines.

"You are more than a scientist, Sonam, you're a public intellectual."

"Like yourself," she replied, her eyes lingering on Val's lips for a moment.

Val couldn't believe that she was back in this hot tub flirting with someone new. She laughed, her tone warm and inviting. Sonam moved closer, her arm touching Val's. It was a nice feeling, somewhat sisterly, with a touch of erotic undertone. They both felt the thrill of mutual appreciation that is intense and excited but not necessarily sexual.

"I've thought about this before. Le Corbusier was inspired by industry and the grind of machines. I don't want to think of the house as a machine. I prefer to think of it as an organism, a gentle and efficient mother."

"But what of standardization? People who lived in his housing projects felt alienated and disoriented..."

"Le Corbusier created homes with minimums, and I want each unit to be luxurious. Luxury is reasonable in small scale. The excess killing the world is the mansions with ten bathrooms for a family of four. I want people to live well. Ten bathrooms is not living well, it is goiterous gluttony."

"I take your point."

"Le Corbusier loved concrete, he was obsessed with it. He believed that it gave a building what he called 'Pompeian tranquility'. I watched all of those poorly constructed concrete buildings fall apart in the 2000's, and I can see that it was all artificial. That's why I spent so many years making gothic buildings—stones don't lie."

"What about your arcologies?"

"I'm building them to last. Le Corbusier loved the idea of cheap manufacturing, of being able to throw away everything when you get bored with it and get the newest style. Fast forward, and here we are dealing with heaps of cheap plastic goods that won't decompose for thousands of years, of things not built to last. The Heart Project, our machine to break down waste and rebirth it at will is the key to my arcology."

"I see. So that means I am very important to you." Sonam raised an eyebrow, sipping her wine.

"Keeping you happy is my number one priority."

"Is it?"

"How am I doing so far?"

"Pretty well, I'll let you know when I need something."

"I'm sure you will." Val laughed. "Now, may I interest you in a lovely dinner downstairs?"

"Mm yes, I'm getting hungry."

They got out of the tub, showered off and dressed for dinner. Together they all went down to the hotel's restaurant, where Val had booked them a table.

The dining room was a beautiful 1920's ballroom.

"It's been such a wonderful day," said Val. "I'm so happy I came."

"We were nervous for you to see the lab, honestly," said Emily.

Val laughed. "Well no need, I'm having a great time."

"Now I'll be able to put a face to the name when I send you the reports."

"So you're the one putting them together. I wanted to thank you personally. They're so organized."

"Thank you," said Emily proudly. "I'm glad you're actually reading them."

Val made a mental note to send Emily a gift—perhaps a weekend at the Georgia would be nice.

"Of course she's reading them," said Sonam. "This is her Heart Project." She winked at Val, and they both laughed.

They chatted and enjoyed their dinner. Wen-Pei's husband got up and played the piano for them.

At the end of the night, it was time to go. Dr. Devgan stood as the last dessert plates were cleared.

"Thank you for a beautiful day, Dr. Snow, and a wonderful visit. We hope to see you back with us soon."

"After such hospitality," said Val looking around at each of them with a smile, "I will absolutely be coming back." Her eyes rested on James, who was looking back at her with a kind of crush of adoration.

The party walked off, some to the lobby to leave, others to the bathroom. James went out to the ballroom patio for air. Val watched him go, and then followed.

"James," she said softly, touching his arm.

"Hey," he said, turning around, his full attention on Valkyrie. "What are you doing out here?"

"Just getting some air," he said with a grin, leaning against the railing.

"Would you like to come back upstairs with me?"

The question was direct and caught him off guard.

"Umm, sure, yea."

"Alright. Well I'm going to go ahead, so you get your air and come up when you feel like it."

"Okay, sure," he said, swallowing hard.

Val disappeared back into the ballroom.

James was convinced that their afternoon in the hot tub was just a misunderstanding, and now he was confused again. *Is she inviting me up for a drink? A chat? Something more?* He squeezed his fingers into his palm, took a breath, and walked slowly to the elevator.

Up in her suite, Val peeled off her clothes and tied a silvery silk bathrobe at the waist. Her breasts moved freely beneath the soft material and her leg was exposed up to the thigh as she walked. There was a quiet knock on the door. She padded over and opened it a crack. It was James.

"Come in," she said. The room lights were turned off and lamps around the room cast a soft glow. James came in, closing the door behind him. Valkyrie looked him up and down, her eyes resting on his face. It was difficult to tell what she was thinking.

"Did you... were you thinking of maybe having another soak in the hot tub?" he asked, trying to sound casual. This time, he would brush her foot with his, or sit close, inviting further contact.

"I don't think so," she said. "Come here." She turned and walked to the bedroom. As she turned, James saw the line of her bare calf, stretching up into her thigh. From behind, the robe hugged the curves of her body. James felt a wave of arousal. He followed.

Val walked over to the nightstand. She bent over, opening the drawer. She pulled out the file, and came to the edge of the bed, sitting down. She opened the file, looking up at James, who was looking back at her, confused. She crossed her legs, the robe sliding back and open, exposing most of her bottom half. Val patted the spot on the bed beside her. James came over and sat down.

"Right here," she said, pointing to the page. "There's a notation about temperatures I wanted to ask you about, I forgot all about it on the tour."

James looked at the page, willing his boner to go away, trying to focus on the words swimming before his eyes.

"Yes. One of the problems the team is facing is dealing with the high temperature of vaporizing such a large or continuous quantity of biomaterial. See, we've figured out ways to handle it in our isolated experiments, but the scale is so huge for your arcology... we're still working it out."

Val was distracted by his lips. Sitting here on the bed, she felt the heat rising. It didn't help that she could feel his attraction to her, his energy reaching out to her.

Focus, she thought.

"Would it help if I sent you a cooling specialist? Maybe someone working on nuclear reactor systems?" She was looking into his eyes, feeling herself drawing closer.

"That could work," he said.

"I'll look into it."

They looked at each other for a moment longer, and then Val leaned in, giving in to the impulse, her lips touching his. He kissed her back, bringing his hand to her cheek, touching her long neck lightly with his fingertips.

"Is this okay?" she asked softly, her grey eyes concerned.

"Yes," he said, kissing her face between her nose and cheek. She heard the enthusiasm in his tone.

"Good." She smiled, kissing his neck, reaching down to loosen the knot of her robe. It fell open, her skin pale and bright against his hands as he clasped her thigh, kissing her harder.

"Not here," she said, pulling away and walking out of the bedroom. She let the robe slide down to the floor. James followed, loosening his clothes and letting them also fall to the floor.

Val walked out to the balcony, a warm breeze blowing her curls as she lay down on a sun bed, her legs open and inviting. James joined her, and they made love in the moonlight flooding the garden terrace.

Afterward, Val went to the bathroom to wash up. When she came back outside, James way lying on a couch by the fire, relaxing naked.

"I'm going to bed," she said softly. "You're welcome to spend the night in the other bedroom of the suite." She walked back to her room and went to sleep.

The next morning, Val woke up feeling incredibly satisfied. She forgot how nice sex was for having a good deep sleep. She brushed her teeth, and then packed up her things for the journey home.

She knocked on James Ahote's open door. He was awake and dressed, playing on his phone on the bed.

"Breakfast in the ballroom?" she asked. She almost suggested breakfast on the terrace, but that might make her think too much about last night and she didn't want any distractions making her late for her hyperloop.

"Sounds good," he said with a smile.

They ate breakfast and then James escorted her to the station.

"Thank you for a beautiful weekend in Vancouver," she said, leaning forward and kissing him softly. He wrapped his arms around her for a goodbye hug.

"Don't be a stranger," he said.

Off she went.

CHAPTER EIGHT

Jordan was having trouble sleeping at night. He would look at the time and think to himself, *I should go to bed now,* and then he would stay up just a little bit longer, watching an episode of some internet show, one more viral video, or listen to a few more songs. Some nights he would stay up until the early hours of morning, finally forcing himself to lie down in bed and close his eyes, exhausted and miserable. He would wake up feeling like he was hungover. On the worst days, he really wanted to message Charlotte. When she was over, he could always fall asleep. One night he sent her a text:

Hey :)

Jordan:

The message went viewed and unanswered.

Why couldn't he sleep?

Maybe I was in love with Charlotte, he thought. *And now I'm heartbroken.*

Grow up, hissed Snake.

Jordan knew that he didn't give a shit about Charlotte. He was just lonely for a warm body.

Maybe I'm nervous for the show, he thought. *What if I fuck up the whole thing? What if I don't get enough sleep before the show and that fucks up the whole thing?*

His mind tortured him when he lay in bed trying to sleep. That's why he stayed up so late putting it off. He had been feeling so good about things—their new song, the gig—and now he was back in this strange place in his head.

The next day after work Jordan texted Valkyrie Snow.

> Hi, I was just wondering if you would be able to meet up to talk about our gig? I wanted to run my new French song by you

Jordan:
He received a strange reply:

> You have texted a landline. Your message has not been received.

Jordan had never met anyone with a landline before. That was something out of vintage movies and sitcoms. She had insisted before that he call her. This must be why.

How does she live without a cell phone? he thought.

He couldn't imagine a world where everybody didn't have one. He wondered when they were invented. Valkyrie must have been around before that.

I should call her, he thought. It made him feel sick to his stomach.

Maybe later.

Canada Day finally arrived. Val woke up early, the morning rays of sunlight streaming in through her condo's massive windows.

Time for my meeting, she thought.

She sighed, squeezing an armful of blankets tight. After a few minutes, she let go, pulling the blankets down and slipping out of bed. She couldn't linger too long in bed after she woke up. If she waited too long she would get horny and start touching herself, and this could make her late for the meeting. Val padded over to the bathroom for a quick shower.

She towelled dry, picking a grey tie dress to slide on. She picked out Oxfords and, inspired by Canada Day, she rifled around her jewellery case looking for something special.

It must be here, she thought.

Then she found it. She had only worn it a few times, because it was so heavy. She unclasped the hooks, letting the cool weight press down on her throat, joining it again at the back of her neck, with a soft *click*. Five polished Indian rubies were set in dark bronze, glowing red and brilliant on her slender neck. She looked at her face in the mirror, turning her head from side to side, admiring the craftsmanship of the necklace.

Why not.

Valkyrie went to her desk to pick up her latest sketch. She saw the desktop computer sitting there. She clicked it on. The soft whir of the motors started up. The screen blinked on. She clicked the Instagram app to check her messages.

There was one.

> I wrote the French song! See
> you tonight.

Val frowned. She clicked off the screen and went down to catch her car.

"Hammer & Bone," she told the driver, distracted.

The office came into view. It was a tall, sleek building full of gothic elements, complete with gargoyles. Instead of being dark and grey they were carved from white marble. The street level of the building was accented with raw marble that was white as snow.

Val made a decision. She strode in, signalling the receptionist.

"Book me a hyperloop to Montréal, please. To arrive before 5 pm. And a car to Le Crystal when I arrive."

"Yes, right away."

Val took the elevator up to her meeting. She checked the clock on the wall as the doors closed. *Right on time.*

Jordan, Matt, Jerome, Rachel and Bubba were on their way to Montréal for the show. Rachel had scored her parents' car for the weekend.

"I knew we liked you," said Bubba when she rolled up to get them. They cranked up the tunes, singing along to the radio. The car itself was electric and made barely any noise as they drove down the highway. It was fully charged with enough juice to get them there and back again. There were no gas stations since fossil cars were almost extinct, but they stopped at a little restaurant on the way for a bite to eat. Jordan paid the bill. The food was cheap, but he still got a little thrill from spending so much money at once, something he very rarely did. He was using the gig money, but it still went on his chip.

The energy was high. None of the boys had been on a trip in a long time. Jordan hadn't been in a vehicle like this in at least two years. He had only been to Montréal once before in his life. He went there on a school trip when he was fourteen or fifteen. He remembered beautiful cobblestone streets, little shops, and going to the musée des beaux-arts. This would be his first time going as an adult.

Am I an adult? he thought. He supposed he was. When he was a child, twenty-four was the age of a man. In many ways though, Jordan still felt like a boy.

"Hey guys, are we adults?" he asked quietly. The noise in the car dulled for a moment.

"What the fuck, Jordan."

"Seriously. Do you feel like an adult?"

"What, like are we getting old?" said Jerome. "Nah, we're just getting started."

"I'm a mannnnn," said Bubba.

Jerome was right. Jordan felt like he was just getting started. Sometimes though, he felt like he was getting old.

Jerome wanted to ask Jordan if he was okay. He seemed a little off lately. But Jerome was up in the front seat beside Rachel, who was driving. He would find a better moment to ask, later.

Rachel pulled up to their hostel and let the boys out while she parked. They waited for her at the front desk, because she had also been the one to make the reservation. She booked a private room for her and Jerome, and a bunk room for the others. They put their things in their rooms and relaxed a bit before heading to the venue to set up.

After her meeting wrapped up, Val went straight to the station to catch her hyperloop to Montréal. It had been a long time since she had done anything to celebrate the holiday and she was looking forward to the show. She checked into le Crystal, a hotel she often stayed in when she visited the city.

"Welcome back, Dr. Snow," said the robot concierge. She ordered a glass of scotch to her room.

"Make it two," she amended. Just in case the bar had terrible drinks.

The robot arrived with her drinks. The problem with the robot in general was that it replaced the kind of job a young person could be promoted into. Young people did the work that was not worth buying a robot for, and the higher level jobs, the ones they would usually pay someone more to do, were filled by robots. The highest level jobs, the management kind, were humans who were hired laterally. That meant that the establishment did not promote employees into these positions, but hired professionals from other establishments. If you wanted one of those jobs, you had to know someone, or pay someone, to get it. To make matters worse, older people were not retiring the way they used to. They would stay on and on in their well-paid positions, leaving the young people to scrounge for jobs unfit for robots. Val could see how it was creating economic havoc, creating a subclass of underemployed youth. With the internet and freedom of information, these youth were well-educated and had access to this information. She was surprised that they had put up with it for this long.

Not a problem in my business though, she thought, taking a swig of scotch. *Not yet, at least.*

The boys walked into le divan orange, looking for a manager to tell them where they could haul in the gear.

"Holy shit," said Bubba, with a whistle. "This place is swanky."

The bar was middling to semi-formal, certainly more upscale than anywhere else they'd ever performed.

"Let's be sure to get lots of pictures of this, for the Insta," said Matt. He looked sideways at Rachel, who was better at taking pictures than Bubba. They noticed a small jump in followers since she'd started posting. She winked at him.

Jordan went to the bar to ask. The bartender directed him to the manager.

"You're the opening band from Ottawa?" she said, obviously busy.

"Yep. The Waves."

"Great. Come this way and I'll show you where you guys can put your stuff and where to set up and take down." Jordan signalled the guys to come over as he followed her backstage. He felt a thrill of excitement all over his body. She spoke to him like he was a real musician, like this was just a regular gig for the Waves, the band from Ottawa. Would it always feel this way, like something new and fresh and incredible? And kind of scary? He hoped that one day he could just stroll into a place like this and be that man who knew exactly what he was doing.

"Pinch me, pinch me," said Bubba quietly as the manager showed them the sound board. Jordan grinned and pinched him.

"Ouch!" he said, grabbing his arm.

The manager gave them a withering look. Matt looked furious.

"Did you get all that?" she said.

"Got it!" said Bubba.

"We're good," said Jerome. "I was listening."

The manager walked off, leaving them to deal with their gear.

Val got a car to le divan orange. The show would be starting soon. This time she would actually get to sit in a decent lounge, and listen to the show from start to finish. She hoped it would be as good as she remembered. The night was warm. She put down the window, letting the air blow through her hair as they drove down St. Laurent Boulevard. Val felt the light tingle of alcohol in her fingertips; she had just finished both glasses of scotch. The rubies of her necklace pressed down on her neck, sticky with sweat.

When she arrived at the venue, she bypassed the line. The bouncer didn't recognize her, but something about the way she was dressed told him that she wasn't here on a whim. She went straight to the bar and asked for Lucette.

"She's not here tonight," said the bartender, a woman with thick eyeliner, bleached hair and tattoos on her wrists. "But she said you would be here, and told me to pour you a glass of this."

Val was about to protest, but the woman was already pouring, and Val couldn't resist. It was Highland Park Valkyrie, a single malt that was peatier than she usually liked, but she did enjoy the spice, and of course, the name Valkyrie helped.

"Thank you," she said, raising the glass. "What's your name?"

The bartender smiled, and poured herself a glass. "I'm Antoinette. Valkyrie, right?"

"Call me Val."

"Cheers Val." They clinked glasses and took a sip.

From across the bar, Jordan saw a flash of red crowning a plunging neckline. He turned his head and saw a woman who was unmistakably Valkyrie Snow. She was perched up high on a stool at the bar, knees crossed, one long leg stretched out as she sipped something dark and clear from a tumbler. She was wearing a simple grey dress, but like everything else she wore, it looked great on her. Her cheeks were flushed, as though she had been out for a walk on a breezy day, and her hair was soft and wild. She looked a bit too elegant for this bar.

"What is it?" asked Jerome from behind him.

"That's V. Snow," he said, gesturing to Val.

"She's older than I thought she would be."

"Yea?" To Jordan, she had no age. She was like some kind of immortal creature who had lived a thousand years and would look just like she did tonight, her eyes grey and penetrating, her hands long and graceful, long after he was dead. "How old do you think she is?"

"Man, I can't say. Fifty? Sixty? Nah, forty... I have no idea."

"She can't be that old. But she's got money..." They watched her for a moment. The bartender was leaning over, touching her hand. They were both laughing. Jerome turned to Jordan.

"Are you okay bro? You seem a little off lately, like I'm not worried about you or anything, but you just seem like in another world or something."

Jordan laughed. "Thanks, man, I'm okay. Just sick of my job I think."

Sick of my life.

"Okay. Well you know I got your back, right?"

"I know."

"She's hot," said Bubba from behind them.

"Who?" asked Jerome.

"That old lady you're looking at. She looks like a saucy minx."

"That's V. Snow, Bubba."

"Yea I could tell. Go get her to buy us a drink Jord."

It wasn't a terrible idea. Jordan was pretty good at getting free drinks. He grinned at the boys, ran his hands through his hair and walked over.

Valkyrie turned just as Jordan came up behind her stool. She smiled as their eyes met, but as she looked him up and down the smile disappeared into her intense impassive gaze. This was not the reaction Jordan expected. His saunter melted as he plunged his hands into the pockets of his hoodie.

What is he wearing? thought Val. *Does he only own this sweater and jeans?* She was surprised that he had not made more of an effort when she had given him this great opportunity. It meant that either he was careless or clueless. *Maybe both,* she thought.

"Hello Mr. Barker. Are you ready for your set?"

The last time someone had called Jordan Mr. Barker was in high school.

Yea, he thought. *She's a bit like a school teacher...*

"We're all ready to go. Just waiting for show time."

"Antoinette, this is Jordan, Jordan, Antoinette," said Val. "Pour him a glass of what we're having."

Antoinette looked from Val to Jordan and back again. She poured him a glass of Highland Park Valkyrie.

"To your first gig in Montréal." Val's words were slightly slurred. Jordan realized that she was a little drunk. They clinked glasses.

Your first gig in Montréal. The words started to sink in. Jordan smiled, the first genuinely happy smile he'd had in a long time.

"Do you want to meet the boys?" he asked. He regretted it instantly, and he wasn't sure why.

"Maybe after the show," she said. She put her hand on his forearm, giving it a squeeze.

"You're going to be great." Jordan could see she meant it. He felt a wave of relief. He knew the show would be great too. He leaned up against her thigh, comforted by her kindness.

"Thank you," he said.

Val could see he also truly meant it. Maybe he wasn't completely careless.

It was 9 pm and time for their set to begin. The boys stepped up to the stage. It was cleaner, the crowd was bigger, and their hearts were beating fast, but it was familiar all the same and they were ready. Jordan stepped up to the microphone.

"Hi everyone." The people in front turned to see what was happening on stage but the general noise of the bar did not shift as people continued their conversations. Jordan spoke louder. "Salut tout le monde, we're the Waves!" There were no cheers or hoots of encouragement, like there would have been in Ottawa. Jordan cleared his throat. He felt a wave of nausea as he looked around the room. He wondered what all these people were thinking. His palms were sweating.

His eyes settled on Val. She was sitting on her stool, legs crossed, leaning back against the bar, holding her scotch. She was looking at him with a smile.

I can do this, he thought. He was too nervous to make small talk with the crowd. *Just sing,* he thought. *Just get right to it.*

"Five, six, five-six-seven-eight…"

Matt slammed in on the drums, Jerome came right in on time on guitar and they were off.

Jordan raised his hands to the microphone. He looked down at it, comforted by its familiarity. They had practiced and performed this song so many times that his voice joined in automatically, no need to overthink. By the time they reached the chorus, Jordan chilled out enough to open his eyes and take in the crowd. People were listening. No one was dancing, but Jordan could see that the Waves weren't boring them. He felt his voice strengthen, and the crowd responded. He felt their energy pouring into him as his voice called them to listen. Jordan threw himself into the second chorus, relaxing his shoulders and running his hands through his hair. He felt incredible.

This is it, he thought. *This is what I want to be doing with my life.*

The first song crashed to a close and the crowd cheered.

"Wooo!" he shouted into the mic with a laugh. "Hello Montréal!" The audience cheered more, drawn into his excitement. All his fear was gone. Jordan felt drunk off the thrill of performing on stage. His eyes met Valkyrie's and he smiled wide.

Val smiled back, enjoying the performance. She was worried for Jordan for a moment but he was fine now. She loved his voice. There was something about it that pulled her in. As the evening went on, she could hear his tone becoming more rich and intense. He had something special, and she could tell that there was so much potential waiting to be developed in his voice.

The Waves surged into their next song.

"Can I get you another drink?" asked Antoinette.

"No, I'm done drinking for the evening, I think."

"Is that your boyfriend?" she asked. "Or, your lover," she added, seeing the confused look on Val's face.

"No, he's just a friend." *I've seen him enough times to call him my friend now, right?* she thought. And he had been in her apartment. She did not invite people over often.

"I see. So you're single?"

"Always," said Val with a smile.

After the show, the boys packed up the stage for the next set. They ordered a round of beers.

"On the house," said Antoinette, "for the performers."

"Best night of our lives so far, definitely," said Matt.

Jordan grinned. He felt the same.

They drank their victory beers and chatted excitedly about the set, recapping highlights the way card players go over the last hand. Everything had been perfect.

"I don't know if I can go back to our regular shows in Ottawa after this," said Jerome.

"Those café shows were practice for us. It's time to do gigs like this where we get paid. All the time," said Matt.

The thought of trying to hustle up big gigs made Jordan feel anxiety, but he pushed those feelings away as hard as he could. *Not tonight,* he thought. He focused instead on what it would feel like when they landed the gig, getting up on stage, and singing his heart out. He smiled, holding onto the feeling he'd had on stage tonight. He'd be holding onto that feeling for a long time, holding onto it for dear life.

The next band started up their set. The boys cheered.

"Let's go," said Bubba, and they headed over to enjoy the show by the stage.

Jordan stayed with them a few minutes and then he went back to the bar.

"What did you think?" he asked Val with a smile.

"You were as good as I knew you would be."

Jordan still wasn't sure what Val's role was in this. Did she own the bar? Was she some kind of music rep on the side? Or had she just taken a really keen interest in the band? He swallowed hard.

"So you think the Waves have potential?" he asked her earnestly.

"The Waves are good," she said. "You are special. Jordan Barker has some exceptional talent."

"What about Jerome? He's pretty amazing." Jordan knew that Matt wasn't really the best drummer.

"Honestly Jordan, your friends are blinks to me."

"Blinks?"

"You know, normies. People who come and go on earth and you never know. I don't mean it in a bad way… what I mean to say is that you have something special."

Jordan knew he should be annoyed, but it felt really, really good to hear her say that.

"Can I ask your advice?" he said.

"Sure."

"Do you have any tips for like moving forward? Matt thinks we should invest in advertising…"

"Again, I'm going to be honest with you." Val looked at him with her critical gaze.

"Okay."

"It's time you stepped up your game." She paused, looking at his outfit. "You're handsome, Jordan, but it's not enough. Dress like you care about this."

Jordan looked down at his dirty jeans. He looked over at the stage, where the headlining band looked super put together. Each member had their own unique style, but they looked cohesive as a group. Their sound was incredible too. Jordan felt anxiety creep up the back of his throat as his insecurities grew.

Valkyrie felt his energy shift. She reached out and took his hand, bringing his focus back.

"They're the main act. That's where you want to be, right?" Jordan said nothing. He felt a bit stunned. Val had seen right through him. She knew what he was thinking just as if he actually vocalized it. He pulled away his hand and felt the walls inside him stiffen.

Val continued. "Use bands like that as your models. If they're where you want to be, learn from them," she said.

"Thanks," he said, without emotion.

"Go celebrate with your friends. But call me if you want me to take you shopping some time."

Jordan softened. "Thanks, seriously."

He felt like giving her a hug, but it seemed too awkward so he just left.

"So where are you staying?" asked Antoinette, after Jordan left.

"Le Crystal."

"Oooh, I've never stayed there before."

"Really." Val looked at her with a smile.

"Really."

"What time are you working til?"

"3 am."

"Okay, well I am definitely going to need another drink then," said Val, getting out her credit card.

The next morning, Val woke up in her suite in le Crystal, Antoinette cuddled up beside her. She rose and went to the bathroom to brush her teeth. She looked in the mirror at her reflection. Val always looked good the next day. It was one of the benefits of wearing no makeup. She remembered the crusty feeling of mascara around her eyes in the morning from long ago with distaste. She put some chapstick on her lips and slipped back into bed. She put her hand softly on Antoinette's thigh, spooning her. Antoinette stirred, snuggling deeper into Val behind her, reaching up to pull her arm around her. Val held her tight, and then kissed the back of her shoulders softly. Antoinette made a quiet pleasure sound, turning around to face her. They kissed, Val slipping her leg between Antoinette's, pulling her close. They kissed and kissed, their bodies warming inside and out as they rubbed up against one another. Val pulled Antoinette on top of her, spreading open her lips to expose her clitoris, and they held each other tight as first Val, then Antoinette climaxed. They relaxed, Antoinette sliding off, and they kissed more, exploring each other's necks, arms, and the softness of breasts and belly. They spent the next hour touching each other, enjoying the pleasures of discovering someone new, sometimes kissing slowly and softly, and sometimes bringing each other to orgasm.

Finally, Val's clit couldn't handle anymore.

"I'm totally satisfied," she said. "How about you?"

"That last one was a struggle," laughed Antoinette. "I don't think I have any more in me."

Val took her for brunch before heading back to Ottawa.

CHAPTER NINE

The boys had a bounce in their step after the Montréal gig. The video Rachel took of their show had been shared over a hundred times, and they were thinking about getting a bass player.

"Maybe I could take lessons," said Bubba, his mouth full of cereal and milk. He and Jordan were standing in the kitchen eating dinner.

Jordan ate a spoonful of cereal and didn't say anything. Matt had said they wanted to find a really good-looking guy to attract more fans.

"Do you think we should spend some of the gig money on advertising?" he asked.

"I don't know. Seems like a good idea but what if the ads are shitty? It might be just a waste."

"What about new outfits?"

"What?" Laughed Bubba.

"Well that band in Montréal had a good look, y'know? Maybe we need to work on our look."

"I guess..." they munched their cereal.

"V. Snow offered to take me shopping..." said Jordan.

"What? No way!"

"Yea, but she seems like she's got expensive taste, so the cash wouldn't go very far..."

"Dude, it sounds like she's going to pay for it."

"I don't think so..."

"She will totally pay for it. You should hit on her," said Bubba.

"What? I thought you said she was old," said Jordan.

"Who cares? I was just talking shit. Think of all the shit she'll buy you if you bang her."

"I don't think it's like that."

"Maybe I should hit on her then..." Bubba grinned.

Jordan laughed.

"Idiot," he said. He thought of Valkyrie's long legs, her red lips, her wild hair. She was a beautiful woman, but so different from Jordan that she seemed like she was from another planet.

"Call her up man," said Bubba. "Let her take you shopping."

She probably already forgot about that conversation, he thought.

Val was back to work on her arcology designs. Montréal had been great, and she was still thinking about it. As she wrote notes in tiny lettering with a needle-sharp pencil on her work, her mind wandered to Antoinette's soft skin and great smile. She loved tall women, and Antoinette was just the kind of statuesque femme that Val found really beautiful.

Maybe I'll invite her up to Ottawa, she thought. She doodled some more, tracing lines against the edge of her ruler. She changed her mind. *No... Maybe that was a one-time thing.* Her thoughts turned to the Waves and their show. She had told Jordan about blinks — her word for people who occupy the world without changing it. She had heard other terms, like "sleepers", or "fillers", her artist friend called them, but essentially they were the vast sea of people who let capitalism wash over them like a rising tide. The others she called Truehearts. Every once in a while as her life followed its journey, Val would meet a Trueheart, or a person who was wise to the energies of earth and their collective connections. She had a feeling that Jordan could be a Trueheart, but it was difficult to tell. If he was, she could tell that there was something blocking his potential. When she had mentioned blinks, she could tell that Jordan knew what she was talking about. That alone was a pretty good sign that he was a Trueheart. The strangest part was that sometimes Jordan knew that his purpose was to make music, but sometimes he didn't know.

Truehearts know... she thought.

Val took a break for lunch. She made a plate of fruits and vegetables, little pieces of cheese and naan bread, and went out on the balcony. The sun was bright and warm now, but it rained earlier in the day. Val dumped water out of her lounging chair and plunked down into it to enjoy her lunch. She closed her eyes and let the sun warm her face as she munched on grapes, popping them into her mouth one at a time and enjoying the explosion of sweetness as she bit down on them. Rainwater seeped into the back of her dress, cold against her inner thighs. She felt like listening to music.

The Nightingale song, she thought suddenly. *The song from the night in the café. Jordan didn't sing it.* At this moment, that's all she wanted to hear.

Jordan and the boys were looking for new opportunities to perform their music.

"We need more paying gigs," said Matt.

"True, but I think we should get into festivals too. The crowds are huge, we could really build up our fan base," said Jordan.

"What about Folkfest?" said Jerome, half-following the conversation, focused on his video game.

"We're not really folk though..." said Jordan.

"Neither is Kanye West. The bigger question is, are we good enough?" said Bubba, carefully eating a Jamaican patty steaming hot from the microwave.

"Festivals are kind of lame," said Matt. "We can fill a bar at our own shows."

"Folkfest isn't lame. It's a big fucking deal. If we got in at Folkfest that would be crazy."

Jordan felt his phone vibrating in his pocket. It kept vibrating, like a sustained pulse. It was a phone call. He felt a wave of panic.

"I don't know…" said Matt, looking skeptical.

Jordan swallowed, trying to ignore the phone. He knew he should answer, or at least check and see who it was, but he couldn't make himself do it.

"Are you okay?" asked Bubba.

Jerome turned his head quickly to look at Jordan and then back at the game on his screen. "What's up Jor?" he said, clicking furiously.

"Nothing, just had a phone call."

"Okay well go take it, we'll keep looking," said Matt, scrolling through Google search results.

"It's okay."

"What? What if it's someone booking a show? Go check it man."

Jordan looked at Bubba for a moment, and then stepped into his room. He reached in his pocket and pulled out the phone. Unknown number.

Fuuuck, he thought. What if it was important?

Ding. Whoever it was left a message.

The thought of checking the message also made Jordan nervous, but he knew that the boys would ask who it was, and if he said it was an unknown number Matt would be pissed. He forced himself to dial his voicemail. Miraculously, his password worked. He was always forgetting it.

"Press 1 for English. To check your messages, press 4."

Maybe it's V. Snow. That thought relaxed him slightly. V. Snow would understand that he didn't answer right away.

Maybe it's work, he thought. His anxiety shot through the roof again.

The message began and Jordan could hear heavy breathing.

"Uh, hi, Jordan? Hey, it's your mum… just calling you about something, call me back." *Click.* The message was slow and slurred. Where was she calling from? He didn't recognize the number.

Jordan flicked through his contacts.

Mom. He hit 'call'.

"The number you are trying to reach is out of service. Please hang up and try your call again…" said the robotic voice in the phone. Why was her number disconnected?

Jordan clicked through to the 'missed calls' screen, found the unknown number and called it. The ringer trilled in his ear. Each ring heightened Jordan's nerves and he struggled not to hang up.

"Hello?" said a voice on the other end.

"Mum?" It was her, but something was off, like her head was in a fish bowl.

"Hi baby," she said.

"Where are you?"

"Huh?"

"Your phone got disconnected?"

"Oh, I got a new phone sweetie."

That explained it.

She didn't tell me, thought Jordan.

"What's up?" he said. There was a hard edge in his tone. He was trying not to sound upset, but his mother could hear it in his voice.

"Don't be mad at me, Jor, I'm doing my best." She sounded emotional. Jordan knew that if he said the right thing she would yell at him. He decided not to.

"Okay mum, what is it?" He softened his voice.

"Your cousin is getting married. Mélanie. It's next month, and she wants you to come."

Mélanie was French, but since Jordan's father wasn't around much Jordan felt disconnected from that side of the family. It was one of the many things he resented about his father. Jordan felt like if his father had taught him to speak French more fluently, he would have a decent job by now.

"Oh ya?" The edge was back in his voice. He couldn't help it.

"Will you come? We'd like to see you."

You'd like to see me, but not enough to give me your new phone number, he thought. Not that he would have called her anyway.

"Sure. Will you come pick me up?"

There was a long pause.

"Jordan, I'm exhausted. I can't drive all the way to Ottawa to get you… can't you rent a car?"

"I can't afford to rent a car."

"Not even for a family wedding?"

"I'm not cheap, ma, I'm fucking poor."

"Don't yell at me…" she said, emotional again. He hadn't yelled.

"Are you drunk?" he asked.

Another long pause.

"Jordan I'm not taking this shit from you."

Yes, she was drunk. It was obvious now.

"Just come and get me," he said.

"You know I can't. I wish you would just figure it out."

Jordan felt the sting of her words in his chest. *You're 24 years old,* he thought. *Why are you such a loser?*

"I'm busy right now ma. I have to go. Send me the info and maybe I can make it."

"Really?"

"Yea."

"Okay honey."

"Bye."

He ended the call. He stared at his phone, lying flat in his hand.

I should update her contact in my phone, he thought.

No. Fuck her. He slipped it into his pocket and walked back to the door.

"Who was it?" asked Matt, back in the living room.

"My mom. Cousin's getting married."

"Cool. We're filling out the application for Folkfest."

"Awesome."

The phone call with his mother left him feeling terrible, but looking at this application gave Jordan a tingle of excitement in the back of his neck. This felt right. He was also relieved that Matt was filling it out, because Jordan felt like he was always the one trying to pull gigs and it was hard for him. He went back to sit beside Bubba on the couch before Matt tried to pass it over to him.

"They have a mandate to feature local artists, so we might actually have a shot at this," said Matt.

Jordan was glad he was getting into it.

Suddenly, he felt his pocket buzz. She was calling him back. He pulled out his phone and hit 'respond'.

"Yea?" he said, getting up to go back to his room.

"Excuse me? Is this Jordan?" said a woman. It wasn't his mother.

"Oh, hey. Yes."

"It's Valkyrie Snow."

"Yea, sorry, I thought it was my mother."

"Your mother?" She sounded amused.

"Not that you sound like my mother," said Jordan quickly, blood rushing to his face. "It's just... she just called me."

"Oh?"

"Yea, my cousin is getting married."

"Congratulations," said Val.

"Thanks." Suddenly Jordan wished he could go.

"So..." started Val. Jordan detected a trace of awkwardness. Was V. Snow nervous? He felt a thrill and smiled.

"What is it?" he asked. His tone was warm.

"Oh, well, I was just thinking that at your show in Montréal, I really wanted to hear the Nightingale song, but you didn't sing it."

"The Nightingale song?"

"Mmhm, the ballad. The acoustic piece."

"The one you heard at the Grind Café show."

"That's the one."

"We didn't put it in the set because it's not totally ready yet. And it's kind of slow... we stuck to up-tempo."

"I thought as much. But I really wanted to hear it."

"Sorry," said Jordan with a smile.

"Can you sing it for me?"

"What? Like right now?"

"Yes. It's stuck in my head and I couldn't find it recorded anywhere online."

"We haven't recorded it yet."

"So sing it for me."

"Umm, I can't just... really?" Jordan babbled. He felt nervous, but it wasn't his old familiar anxiety. This feeling was new. He was agitated, but he felt it in a different part of his body. It was fear, to be sure, but it energized him instead of sucked the life out of him.

"Please," said Val.

Jordan exhaled. "How about this. I'll call you in a few hours and sing for you." He was embarrassed to sing on the phone where the boys could hear it.

Val considered.

"Okay. Promise you won't forget." Her tone was absolutely serious.

"I promise." Jordan hated making promises, but this one slipped out easily.

"Okay. Talk to you later."

"Bye."

Val hung up the phone. Jordan felt a little strange about calling Val later to sing to her, but it was cool that she had asked.

He paused before returning to the living room. He scrolled through the missed calls on his phone, and added his mother's new number to his contacts.

After Val hung up the phone, she felt relieved. She could tell that the nightingale song would have haunted her until she called him. Now she could work for the rest of the afternoon.

The boys finished up their application for Folkfest and submitted it. Jordan was excited to tell Val. As the sun went down, he started to feel his anxiety kick in. He wanted to call her, and he knew he had to, but for some reason he didn't want the boys to hear him singing to her on the phone. He decided to see if he could go over and sing to her in person. That would be okay.

He found her in his contacts. Forcing himself not to overthink, he hit 'call'.

"Hello?"

"Hi. It's Jordan."

There was a pause. Jordan panicked. What if she was kidding about him singing to her later?

"Are you going to sing for me?"

"Um, well my roommates are busy right now and I don't want to disturb them..."

"You promised though."

Jordan smiled. "Yea I promised."

"I've been waiting hours," said Val.

"Yea. I was thinking that I could maybe come to your place to sing for you. Since you don't have roommates."

Val laughed. "Fine."

"Kay. On my way."

"Bye."

"Bye."

Jordan didn't usually end a conversation with goodbye. He always hung up the phone as soon as he could because he found goodbyes awkward. With Valkyrie it wasn't awkward because it felt like she was following some kind of system of conversation etiquette and it was a relief to just follow her rules.

He grabbed his longboard and headed to the door. No one asked where he was going.

Jordan was coming over. Val looked down at her outfit. She was dressed in a soft bamboo maxi dress with no bra or panties. It was her go-to work from home clothing. She wondered if she should change. If it were Jeff, or some other man coming over, she would definitely change. She wouldn't want them to get the wrong idea. She felt like Jordan wouldn't mind. When she talked to him, she got no predator vibe whatsoever. She decided to stay dressed as she was. She walked instinctively to the bar to get out a bottle of bourbon. As her hand landed on the bottle, she decided against it.

No, I'm okay, she thought. She felt pretty relaxed and didn't feel like she needed to take the edge off.

Jordan arrived at the building. Here he was, back at V. Snow's condo. This time, it felt familiar.

Valkyrie, he thought. He buzzed up, and when she let him in he walked into the waterfall lobby and up to her apartment.

Val heard a knock at the door.

"Hi," she said, leaning on the frame.

"Hey." Jordan was holding his longboard under his arm, wearing his usual ratty sweater. Val looked him up and down, struck by the strange circumstances of their friendship. He was so different from her. She let him in.

She went over to the couch, pulling a loose-weave cotton blanket over her legs as she curled up.

"Sing for me," she said, leaning back and closing her eyes.

She looked really cozy, laying there on the couch. Jordan sat in the chair across from her.

"What, no booze?" he said.

"Did you want something to drink?" she asked, opening her eyes.

"No, no, you just seem to drink a lot."

"Do I?"

"Well not like, too much, I mean, I wasn't saying…"

"It's okay," she laughed. "Sometimes I drink to calm my nerves… it used to be a problem, but I've got it under control."

"Really?" Jordan knew a lot of people who had a problem with alcohol, but he had never heard someone admit it before.

"That warm feeling makes me relax, but I'm feeling pretty relaxed."

"Good," he said. "I… I get worked up sometimes too."

"Do you?" she asked, inviting him to say more.

"A little bit."

Val could tell that he didn't feel like talking about it so she didn't ask him anything more.

"Why do you call it the nightingale song?" he asked.

"I don't know. The name just popped in my head."

Jordan was excited to sing it, because he had added a verse about a nightingale, just for Val.

"Okay. You ready?" He looked mildly self-conscious.

"Mmm. Yes." Val closed her eyes again.

Jordan stood up and cleared his throat. He hated singing sitting down.

A single bloom in a jar in the window
Pictures of all of the places you've been
A song for each memory, playing forever
Makes me come over again and again.

My heart song for you is a simple one
It's the stories I love that you tell
I still can't believe that you love me
When you know me so well.
When you know me so well.

I picture us happy, that's new for me
You're more than I deserve as I stumble through now
You're a lighthouse to tomorrow, if I make it out alive
This ship's still afloat anyhow.

My heart song for you is a simple one
It's the stories I love that you tell
I still can't believe that you love me
When you know me so well.
When you know me so well.

You glide into my life without warning
I forget how I got to this place with a smile
Like a nightingale song in the morning
I still don't know who you are...

My heart song for you is a simple one
It's the stories I love that you tell
I still can't believe that you love me
When you know me so well.
When you know me so well.

As Jordan began the last part of the song, Val opened her eyes with surprise. He had added a verse about a nightingale. She smiled as he sang. His eyes met hers and he smiled too, happy that she liked it.

He sang the last notes slow and soft. He could feel Val hanging on every word. His heart swelled with joy. She truly appreciated his music.

When he finished, she clapped with delight.

"You added a verse!" she said. "It's lovely."

"Yea I hoped you'd like it."

"The song feels complete now."

"It does. There was something missing."

They both smiled.

Jordan felt suddenly awkward, noticing that Val looked ready for bed, curled up in a blanket, wearing a dress with no bra.

"Well thanks for coming," she said.

He breathed a sigh of relief. She always knew what to say.

"No problem. I'm glad you liked the song."

Val got up and walked him to the door.

As Jordan turned to go, they both reached for each other at the same time. Jordan put his arms around her and laid his head against her shoulder. She pressed her forehead against his soft hair. They both closed their eyes, enjoying the embrace. After a minute, Val pulled away.

"Goodnight," she said with a friendly smile.

"Goodnight," said Jordan, grabbing his longboard and heading out the door. Val locked it behind him.

That night, Jordan slept better than he had in weeks.

CHAPTER TEN

On the weekend, the Waves had a show in the Market. It was a landmark occasion, because it was the first time ever that they would be paying their rent with gig money. As Jordan threw on clothes after a quick shower after his shift at Black Cherry, he sniffed himself, realizing that he hadn't washed his clothes in a really long time. When he put his hands in the pockets, he also realized that the holes in there were getting pretty big. He would need to buy a new sweater soon.

Well at least we're making money now, he thought. *Maybe I can afford to spoil myself soon.* The thought gave him pleasure and he didn't feel the usual anxiety that accompanied thinking about money.

The show was a success. They drew a good crowd, and they were the headlining talent. They had only ever opened at this bar before, and played for tips. This was a victory and they could all feel it.

The girls looked great too. There were lots to choose from. Matt and Bubba started their usual prowl.

"We're heading out guys," said Jerome, holding Rachel's hand. He had been sleeping at her place most nights for about a month now.

"I'm gonna take off with you," said Jordan.

"What?" Bubba and Matt protested.

"I'm exhausted. Have fun," he said, eyeing the ladies who were looking in their direction.

"Okay man, goodnight," said Bubba, giving him a half hug.

"Night losers," said Matt.

Rachel, Jerome and Jordan left the bar.

"Want a ride home?" asked Rachel, jangling her keys. Her parents had given her their old car to keep.

"Nah I'm good," he said.

"You sure man?" asked Jerome.

"Yea, I'm going to walk, enjoy the night air. Goodnight love birds," he smiled.

Jerome realized that Jordan was smiling a lot more lately. He was glad.

"Night bro."

Jerome and Rachel took off.

Jordan walked slow. He really was enjoying the night air.

He breathed in deep, thinking about songs he was going to write. A lyric floated into his head.

Songs about angels in broken down bars
And devils in fancy hotels...

He reached in his pocket and got out his phone. He wanted to transcribe it. He opened the recording app and laid out a melody.

Songs about angels in broken down bars
And devils in fancy hotels
Dreaming in rainbows and staring at stars
When he told her that only sex sells.
Sense dulls and bell tolls and you're deep in a hole,
And he told her that only sex sells.

The app recorded both his voice and voice-to-text. He looked at the words on the screen, glowing in the night as he walked. He felt a thrill, pulling his hood up over his head and imagining that he was a famous musician, and this was a regular evening for him, walking and brainstorming new songs.

My process, he thought. That's what he would say at a late night interview about his work. *I have a few drinks and I walk around the city at night, thinking up lyrics.*

Ssss... Ssss... Snake laughed at him. *Loser.*

There you are, thought Jordan. *Haven't heard from you in a while.*

The moment was gone. Jordan looked down at the lines. They were a good start. He closed the app. Instinctively he opened social media and started scrolling.

Ugh, no, he thought, closing it again. He opened the text app compulsively. Who would he message? He thought of texting Valkyrie. She didn't text. He looked at his recent messages. He clicked on 'Charlotte' and typed.

> Hey. Thinking of you.

Jordan:

The moment he hit send, Jordan felt terrible. He regretted it. *Too late now,* he thought. *So stupid.*

Jordan had strange feelings about Charlotte. They had left things on a bad note and he felt guilty. He felt like he had been right during their final conversation, but she was right about some things too. They never really talked about what happened.

Jordan kept walking.

What the fuck is wrong with me? he thought. *Why did I text her?*

If she didn't message him back he would feel terrible, and if she did he would feel even worse for the way he had treated her. All the old memories dragged up out of his subconscious along with the pain and anxiety.

The good feelings were gone. He had ruined it. There was a big rock on the edge of the sidewalk ahead. When he reached it, he kicked it as hard as he could.

I fuck everything up, he thought. He felt so alone.

He pulled out his phone, and went to his call history. He clicked on *Mom,* and hit 'call'.

The phone rang at least ten times, and then she picked up.

"Hello?" The voice was scratchy and groggy, like she had been sleeping.

"Mom?"

"Jordan. What is it?"

"I just wanted to talk."

"About what?"

"I don't know… the wedding."

"For fuck's sakes Jordan, it's the middle of the night. I'm sleeping."

"Ma…" his voice cracked.

"I told Mel you're not coming. She's okay, don't worry."

"Oh. Okay."

"It's fine Jordan. Go to sleep."

"Ma... do you ever think about Michael?" Michael was Jordan's older brother who had overdosed on fentanyl.

There was a long silence. Then Jordan could hear muffled sobs.

"Sorry..."

"Leave me alone," she said. "Go to fucking sleep." *Click.*

She hung up on me. Jordan wanted to scream and cry. He kept walking. He walked and walked, past the hooting drunks and the glowing bars in the night. Past Chinatown. He felt the corners of his eyes burning, but there were no tears.

His mind was reeling. He thought about terrible things, like going for a swim in the Ottawa River, drowning in the night, his body being found the next day, a frown on his face. His mother would feel bad that she had hung up on him. He thought about breaking into Parliament and jumping off the Peace Tower. That would sure make the news. He zigzagged across streets, not caring about cars. They honked. He didn't give a fuck.

Boom. He felt dazed, flat on his back on the road. His hand hurt. He looked at his palm—it was bleeding. The driver opened the door of the vehicle. It was an old antique gasoline car, converted to electric and manual drive.

"You okay buddy?" he said, looking at Jordan lying on the road. Jordan scrambled to his feet.

"What happened? What's going on?" He was stunned.

"Well I bumped you... you ran into the road... but you seem okay, right?" His brow was furrowed with worry.

"Umm, ya, I think so," said Jordan.

"Is there anyone I can call?" asked the driver. "I mean, please don't call the police... they'll take my car away for sure... But I mean like friends or family or something."

"No. No one gives a fuck about me."

Jordan's eyes had a faraway look, like he wasn't even there.

"Come on, there has to be somebody. Let me give you a ride. Anywhere you need to go."

Jordan felt his legs get weak and he stumbled forward. His knees hit the pavement. The man driving the old classic darted forward, pulling Jordan up and helping him into the passenger seat of the car. He pulled over to the side of the roadway.

"Come on now. We've got to call somebody."

Jordan pulled out his phone. He was too messed up to argue. He looked at his call history. *Valkyrie.* He hit 'call'. It rang and rang. No answer. There was no voicemail. The phone just kept ringing.

Finally, she picked up.

"Mr. Barker, it's 2 am," she said softly. She had asked her Virtual Reality Connect who it was and decided to answer.

"I... I'm sorry Val. I know."

"Well?"

"I'm sorry, I shouldn't have called." He sounded close to tears.

"Whether you should have called or not doesn't really matter because I took the call. What is it?"

"I'm having a bad night," he said quietly.

"He got hit by a car," said the driver loudly.

"What?!"

The driver gestured to Jordan and took the phone from his hand.

"He got in a little car accident, nothing too serious," he said into the receiver. "He's just got some bumps and bruises."

"Bring him here," she said. She told him her address.

The driver was happy to oblige. He dropped Jordan off at the front door of the condo building.

"Are you okay to get up there?" asked the driver.

"Yea."

He waited until Jordan buzzed up and was inside before driving off into the night.

Jordan trudged up the stairs. *What am I doing here?* But the thought of going home filled him with such sadness that he walked faster up to Val's floor.

He didn't need to knock. She was waiting for him with the door open. He looked a mess.

"Come inside," she said, closing the door behind him.

She went over to the bar and poured him a drink.

"Here," she said. He reached up to take it, and she saw his

blood-crusted palm. She frowned.

Jordan took the drink and downed it in one big gulp. He handed back the empty glass.

"I guess if you wanted to talk about it, you'd be saying something," she said, annoyed.

She folded her arms across her chest, her hair wild around her head. She was wearing her silver silk bathrobe, and that was all.

Jordan looked at her. His eyes were wide and dark and sad all at once. They were red, like he had been crying, and shining with emotion. With that one look, and his trembling lower lip, her irritation melted away. She put her arms around him and held him, soft and warm. He leaned against her. His arms didn't move.

Val breathed in his smell. She could tell that he hadn't washed for days. He stank of body odor and stale cigarettes. She led him gently upstairs and pushed him into the bathroom.

"Take a shower," she said. "Leave your clothes outside the door." She went to her bedroom to find him something clean to wear.

Jordan peeled off his filthy clothes, now stained with blood. He kicked them into the hallway and then turned on the taps. He didn't bother shutting the door. He stepped into the shower, turning up the heat and letting the scalding water burn away his misery. He sat down on the bottom of the shower, letting the water pour onto the back of his head.

After ten minutes of steaming, Jordan felt a little better. He looked around him. Val's shower was so clean. It was pristine. There were little jars and pots of expensive looking products. He rummaged through them, looking for soap and shampoo. He scrubbed his body, willing the night to wash away down the drain with the blood and dirt.

Val took his clothes to the laundry chute, pulling out his phone, and shoving them in. *Disgusting.* She put one of her soft bamboo maxi dresses on a hanger and hooked it on the inside of the bathroom door. She looked at Jordan from the corner of her eye. Through the steam in the shower, she could see the dark of his forearms tanned by the sun, and rippled with muscles. His upper arms were slim and pale, and his back looked soft and inviting. He started to turn around and she slipped out.

Valkyrie walked downstairs to put on a kettle for tea. She had Jordan's phone in her hand and she was about to put it down on the counter when it buzzed. A message flashed on the screen.

Charlotte:

Hope the show was good.

Val put it down and got the teapot ready. She suspected that Charlotte was a girl that Jordan was seeing, and then admonished herself for making assumptions. Jordan might not even be interested in girls. Or maybe Charlotte was his sister. She had no idea. She realized that she barely knew him.

The kettle boiled and Val put on tea. She made herself a steaming mug and went to the couch to curl up in a blanket.

Jordan came down the stairs wearing the maxi dress she had laid out for him. His hair was long and dripping wet. He looked handsome.

"This is the most comfortable thing I've ever worn," he said. His face was sombre, but he seemed much more himself after the shower.

"There's tea," said Val.

Jordan walked over to the counter, and poured a cup. He added milk. "Am I doing this right?" he asked. "I've never had tea before."

"What?" Val looked shocked. Jordan had to laugh.

"Well?" Jordan had seen people preparing tea in movies.

"Yes that's right. Come over here."

Jordan took his tea and came over. Val lifted her legs and he sat on the other side of the couch and pulled her legs onto his lap. He tucked the blanket back over her feet. They sat in companionable silence, blowing on their tea and sipping.

"How do you like it?" asked Val.

"It's okay. The taste is not, like, great, but it's comforting."

"Mmm, yea, that's true."

"Sorry I woke you up," he said.

"I don't mind."

"No?"

"Jordan you got hit by a car. Of course I don't mind."

"Well. It was more than that. It was... I was feeling like

hell."

Val sipped her tea. She said nothing.

"I was really sad…" his voice was emotional again.

"You can call me any time," she said.

"You just tell me when you want me to go," he said quietly.

Val reached over and squeezed his arm. She slid her legs off his lap and stood up.

"You're not going anywhere tonight." She finished her tea and walked over to the sink to put in her mug.

"I'll grab you a toothbrush so you can brush your teeth, and you can sleep here." She disappeared upstairs. She had a spare toothbrush in the bathroom. She looked at her reflection in the mirror.

It would be really nice if he could sleep in my bed, on the other side, she thought. *It would be nice to wake up beside someone.* But she knew that would be strange and complicated. She went downstairs.

"Here you go," she said.

Jordan reached up to take the toothbrush. That did it. With the brutal night, the hot shower, the exhaustion, and the tea, he finally broke down. He let out a sob that shook his whole body, breathing hard, tears coming down his cheeks. He was shocked at himself, but he couldn't stop. His body felt completely out his control. Val sat down beside him and he lay his head on her shoulder, balling his eyes out.

"That's… so… nice," he said finally, when the worst of it was over.

"What, this toothbrush?" said Val. She couldn't help but laugh. Jordan laughed too, his eyes bloodshot. They smiled at one another.

"I really appreciate this," he said.

"Go brush your teeth," she said gently. "I'm exhausted. I'm sure you are too. Everything will be better in the morning."

Jordan went upstairs to get ready for bed. Val got out blankets and pillows for the couch. As he came back down the stairs, he almost started crying again seeing her making the couch up for him.

He needed to sleep.

Jordan gave Val a big hug.

"Goodnight," he said.

"Goodnight." She gave him a kiss on his forehead and went up to bed.

CHAPTER ELEVEN

In the morning, Jordan woke up to soft light flooding the open-concept space. The windows had northern exposure, but it was still really bright. Val purposely situated her unit this way so that when she stood on the balcony she could see the sunrise in the morning and the sunset in the evening.

Jordan gathered the blankets around him, hugging them. He felt so soft and comfortable. He felt safe up here in Val's nest. He reached one arm over his head, propping himself up a bit and letting himself wake up slowly.

Time to face the day, he thought.

From upstairs, he heard movement. Val was getting up too. He heard the shower turn on. The sound was comforting. He was really glad that she had let him spend the night.

After her shower, Val got dressed for the day. As she rubbed rose oil on her face and neck, she went over last night's events in her mind.

Jordan is not okay, she thought. He probably needed medical attention, counselling, something. She knew he wouldn't seek it though. She also knew it was none of her business to try and make him do it. He would have to come to that realization on his own.

You can't make people change, she thought. She had figured that out long ago. That's why she lived alone.

Val came downstairs. Jordan turned to watch her approach.

"Morning," he said.

"Good morning."

"So… where are my clothes?"

Val went over to the kitchen to pull out a plate for croissants and cheese.

"Those clothes were in pretty bad shape to begin with… now they're even worse. They should probably get thrown out, but I put them in the wash," she said.

"I can't throw those out. That's my favourite sweater, and basically the best jeans I have."

"What are your plans for the day?"

"I work at 4."

"Okay. Well then let me take you out to get something new to wear."

"Val... it's okay. Really."

"I insist. Let's go. I'll make sure you're at work by 4."

Jordan wasn't going to refuse again.

"Thanks."

Val called the car and they headed out. Jordan had to wear the maxi dress, which wasn't something he was used to, but he didn't mind. He was a bit self-conscious without underwear though. He felt like his crotch was really visible under the soft, pliant fabric.

Val took him to some of her favourite stores. She refused to shop anywhere that used fossil fuels, slave labour or unrecycled materials. Nowadays, that was a lot easier to manage than it had been just ten years ago.

"Try this," she said, holding up a jacket. It was a lot nicer than anything she had seen Jordan wear, but it had a hood so she knew he'd like it.

"This is too much," he said, fingering the high-quality material of the sleeve.

"What do you mean? Do you like it?"

"It's awesome," he said. "I mean, it's too expensive."

"I'm sure it's less than you think. This store is profitless. They produce clothing ethically, pay their workers a living income, and there is no capital gain."

"Really?" He looked at the price. He was surprised.

"This is part of the future I am investing in," she said. "If everyone invested ethically, then we could have that future a lot sooner."

"It's really nice," he said.

"Try it on."

Jordan slid his arms into the jacket. His shoulders fit perfectly. He stretched out his arms. The sleeves were just right too. He turned to look in a mirror. He parted his lips slightly, running his hands through his hair, enjoying his obviously handsome silhouette.

"Looks good," Val smiled, putting her hands on his shoulders.

Jordan grinned.

"Mmkay. Now you need pants. And shirts."

"Seriously Val, this is too much."

"Look at it this way; every dollar I spend in this store is supporting a paradigm I believe in. Ethical purchasing. So let's get you dressed."

Jordan picked out two pairs of pants, a few t-shirts, and some underwear.

"Every pair of underwear I own has holes in it," he laughed. Jordan had stopped wearing underwear most days. Val rarely wore underwear herself, but for different reasons.

Val chose a powder blue button-up shirt with a pale purple floral overlay pattern.

"Try this one."

"I couldn't pull that off."

"Just try it. Those colours are perfect for you."

Jordan tried on the shirt, buttoning it all the way up. He turned sideways and back.

"Looks pretty good," he admitted.

"I can just see you singing in that."

Jordan looked at Val in the mirror. She had an expression on her face that he couldn't quite place. The closest thing he could compare it to was erotic, but it wasn't. She was getting pleasure from dressing him up. Not sexual pleasure, but something.

"Can you?" he said, a soft, deep edge to his voice.

Val's eyes caught Jordan's in the mirror. She looked away, the tiniest blush in her cheek.

"Yes. It's going to look great with your new pants at your next show."

She took two steps away.

"Let's find you a scarf and I think you're all set."

Jordan picked out a light brown scarf. He tried on a white raw silk one, but he knew it would get ruined in two seconds flat at his apartment. It looked beautiful on him though.

Val paid at the register and they walked out of the store, Jordan carrying his parcels protectively.

"I'll drop you at work," she said.

"I have to go home first. I don't want to ruin my new clothes scrubbing pans in the Cherry."

"What's your address?"

Jordan told the robot driver and they went together.

"So this is where you live," said Val.

"I'd invite you up, but the place is a dump."

"That's okay, I have a lot of work to catch up on this afternoon anyway."

"Sorry I hijacked your day."

"I had a great time Jordan."

"Me too."

They squeezed hands as he stepped out of the car and shut the door.

Val drove off.

Jordan stepped into the filthy elevator at his apartment building. It smelled worse than usual; he recoiled with disdain as he realized that the floor mat was soaked in fresh piss. He stepped off at his floor, wiping his feet as he walked down the hall. He rattled his keys in the door, forcing the lock until it opened.

"Damn busted lock," he mumbled.

Jordan walked into the dark entryway of his apartment. Dust and dirt lined the area where the walls met the floor, cleared in the middle where feet walked. Nobody had ever swept here since Jordan moved in. The walls were yellow with marks of discolouration—brown from water damage and smudges of fingerprints and scrapes along the wall. The hall opened into the main room, where a fluorescent overhead bulb buzzed, casting cold light. The stove was covered in grime, the counters full of takeout containers crawling with fruit flies. The bottom of the fridge was streaked with rust and the tiles on the counter were cracked and filthy. Their two-seater couch was against one wall, and a few mismatched chairs sat around the room, one turned upside-down. There were empty cans from the last time they drank in here, and cigarette butts covering the coffee table. There were no windows. Each bedroom had a window, except Bubba's. Bubba's bedroom was off the kitchen, Jerome's was down the hall, and Matt and Jordan's rooms were opposite.

Jordan kicked a can, walking down to his room to drop off his new things and change for work. He opened the door and looked around the room. The walls were covered with pictures of bands he liked. He had printed off a bunch of pictures and put them in frames from charity shops and hung them all over. The wall beneath was full of holes and dings, but the pictures covered up the worst spots. The floor was scuffed parquet littered with discarded clothes and papers. His bed was a mattress he found in Sandy Hill when the students moved out in the spring, propped up on milk crates he had nicked from a coffee shop. He dumped the bags onto a chair in the corner of the room, and lay down on the bed. It was hot up here. He turned on the fan, and it clicked faster and faster as it fired up.

Jordan sniffed the air. It stunk too. Val's maxi dress that had seemed like such a simple garment when he put it on felt too nice to be on this bed. He stood up and peeled it off. He checked his phone.

Shit. It was later than he thought. He had to get ready for work. He rifled through clothes, grabbing something to pull on. It felt scratchy and dirty against his skin. He looked at the bottom sheet on the bed, curled up off the mattress again.

Jordan pulled off the bedsheets and gathered up the mess on the floor. He shoved it all into a basket. If he ran, he could get it in the wash at the laundromat before his shift. He headed out the door.

Something was up at the Black Cherry. People were crowded around the screens, watching something unfolding on the news.

Police are facing off with gunmen today in over ten locations across America. We are receiving reports that the men call themselves the Rebels, in the largest coordinated mass shooting in American history.

The news station was calling the attackers "gunmen", but they weren't acting out solo—it was clear from the footage that each shooter was supported by a backup team. America was declaring war on itself.

In a snap decision, the President has called in the military. We are receiving news that several shootouts are wrapping up, and others are unravelling quickly. The attackers are taking over public buildings and advancing forward.

"Attackers?" said a customer, incredulous. "Shootout? It's a militia. It's a civil war."

Jordan felt his blood chill. The country to the south was armed to the teeth. The Rebels probably had an arsenal comparable to a small nation's military. That was all legal in America; it was embedded in their cultural ethos. They watched in horror as the news station broadcasted footage from their helicopter surveillance of bodies falling to the ground.

The boss flicked the channel back to a Canadian station. Several reporters were commenting on the situation to the south.

"These men are all part of extremist groups," said one. "The Americans were monitoring their activities but focused their crackdown efforts on black and Muslim communities rather than the increasingly mobilized white supremacists."

In the last ten years, over thirty thousand Jews moved out of the United States and into major Canadian cities, many going to Montréal. There was a steady influx of black, Muslim and Latino Americans moving into Canada as well. The constant and increasing gun violence to the South made life untenable for people frequently targeted.

The reporter moved on to Canadian news.

"A woman in Prince Edward Island has found a variety of heirloom potato once thought to be extinct," said the reporter. The boss flicked back to the American station.

"Rebels in Charlottesville, Virginia, have overtaken and occupied from Charlottesville City Hall to the University of Virginia campus. There are reports of at least 25 civilians dead, including the public execution of Dr. Helena Gimbutas, a prominent civil rights activist and peace advocate." The helicopter footage zoomed in from above in crisp 5k detail, showing the woman's body swinging from a rope in the rotunda.

Earl popped his head out of the kitchen angrily.

"You're on the clock," he growled.

Jordan jumped, hustling to the back to get working.

Val watched the news report with a frown. The situation had been unravelling down south for years and things were coming to a head. A series of unfortunate political and military decisions in the last fifty years crippled the nation to the point that the federation was held together by ideology alone. California seceded from the union of American states and became the independent country of New California in 2022. Silicon Valley implemented widespread progressive reform projects and the future looked bright. The other American states, both rich and poor, were agitating for secession, and the Rebels were just the latest push to topple the union.

"The Senator of the state of Maine is in talks today with officials to become a province of Canada," said the reporter.

Val shuddered. That could not happen. *Let the people of Maine stay American and work at Canadian companies. But don't enfranchise them. We can't have millions of religious-zealot foreigners obsessed with violence and guns voting in our democracy.*

Val knew that it wouldn't happen. The financial cost alone of enfranchising Mainers would outweigh the potential economic gains, not to mention the cultural fallout.

We would have to physically disarm communities used to guns. The cost of updating crumbling American infrastructure, of creating and implementing public works, of building schools and hospitals in impoverished neighbourhoods, would not be worth the economic output of acquiring new territory.

At least the 2004 proposal to adopt Turks and Caicos meant Canada would get tropical islands out of the deal.

After work, Jordan felt driven to clean his room. It was an uncommon feeling for him so he made the most of it, straightening pictures on the walls, dusting the corners of the room with an old t-shirt. He only had time to do one load of laundry, but the most important thing was that the sheets were fresh. He made the bed, put his clean clothes in the dresser, and piled the dirty clothes that were on the floor into the empty basket. He jumped onto the made bed, a grin on his face. He looked up at the ceiling, sliding on his headphones and listening to the Death Row Dollies, letting a feeling of contentment warm him from the inside out.

You like me?
Then why do you treat me this way?
What will you do to save us?
'Likes' don't count…

Jordan closed his eyes, enjoying the smooth blanket under him, the smell of clean clothes, and the Dollies wailing out their sorrows.

Snake had nothing to say.

Jordan listened to the whole album, all the way to the end. Then he got up slowly and walked to the kitchen. He opened the cupboards.

Tea would be nice, he thought. They didn't have a kettle though. He looked around the messy kitchen. Should he clean it? The thought was a bit too much for him. He walked back to his room and closed the door. He pulled a battered old laptop off his dresser, plugged it in and jumped onto the bed. He would work on some new merchandise ideas for the Waves. Someone had asked about t-shirts at the last show. The thought of someone wearing a Waves t-shirt filled him with pure joy.

Jordan opened the web browser, scrolling through pictures of merch for ideas. The internet was flooded with news of the American troubles. Jordan took the bait, clicking on a link to an article about the shooters. A young man stared out at him from the screen. He was thin with a long nose and long greasy hair tied back in a bun. He had a narrow chin and an intense expression in his eyes. He was somewhat handsome, but creepy too.

Jeremy Jennings. 34 years old. Difficult home life. Worked at a call centre.

Jordan scrolled down to the next shooter. This one had short dark hair and a terrible complexion. He was overweight and pale as moonlight.

John Wilson. 24 years old. Graduated from college and moved back home when he couldn't find a job. His parents suspected nothing. "He loved computers and video games," they said. "He had a bright future ahead of him."

Donald Courtney. 57 years old. No known relatives. Quiet gun enthusiast. "I thought his gun obsession was normal," said a former work colleague.

Jordan remembered how when Jerome first came to Canada he was surprised that people weren't as accustomed to murder or violence here.

Jordan kept reading the profiles. He couldn't stop. He opened a tab for Facebook and looked up the shooters, scrolling through photos, statuses and comments. It was amazing how normal some of these men had seemed.

Jordan noticed that a lot of them liked to dress like soldiers. Some had actually worked in the military, but many were just obsessed with it. They ordered camo pants from China, knock-off military issue rucksacks and boots, and gun paraphernalia. They worked shitty jobs and put their pennies into their collections the way that Jordan did with music.

Music gives me hope, he thought. *Music makes my life worth living...* he tried to understand how the gun obsession could give them hope. From an outsider's perspective, it seemed like it could only do the opposite, like it was a death wish or a recipe for cynicism and paranoia.

It must be empowering somehow, realized Jordan. Music empowered him. *I would have nothing without my music.*

Even with his music it sometimes felt like he was clinging to existence.

I'd feel like a loser or a sell-out if I ever joined the military, he thought. *But if I were conscripted I'd be a hero.* He would be a martyr. The thought appealed both to his sense of victimhood as a struggling artist, and to the self-righteousness that drove him to seek recognition.

Jordan imagined getting forced to join up. They would use his face on posters and ads to make other young men join up, and then if he survived he'd be a hero for life, interviewed on talk shows and given discounts at the supermarket. A living hero.

Or die trying, he thought.

Jordan looked at the faces on the screen. He wondered what their families thought about how their lives had turned out. There were a few attempts at establishing Rebel chapters in Canada, but for the most part the instigators grew frustrated and moved south.

Jordan imagined picking up a gun and shooting a crowd of smiling people. He felt a thrill shiver through him. The sensation was kind of a cold shock, like the weightlessness of a rollercoaster in the downswing. He liked the feeling of performing live a lot better.

CHAPTER TWELVE

"We have a problem," said the head contractor, standing beside the half-finished Glasshouse.

"Explain." Mika was calm. It couldn't be anything significant; she had poured over the designs with meticulous care.

"I don't feel comfortable with the weight of the rain catchment system on the roof, with those skylight panels. I just have a bad feeling about it."

"The roof design has been tested already, in Latin America. We're fine."

"I looked over those reference blueprints, and you're right, except that they don't account for the added weight of snow and ice in the winter, and the extra insulation we added to keep the water from freezing. I don't think it's going to work."

Mika frowned. She knew that the roof would probably be fine. There wouldn't be a problem for a few years at least. Down the road, the problem would begin to show. For a split second, she thought about proceeding and leaving the problem to a future engineer, but she knew that would be foolish. Dr. Snow would need to be briefed on this.

"I'll ring up the boss. Just hold on the roof for now."

"What should we do? We can't do anything until the roof is installed."

"Okay. Take the rest of the day off. I will let you know if we can resume tomorrow."

The contractor nodded and walked off to dismiss the crew.

Mika walked out to the car at the road and sat in the back seat.

"Call Dr. Snow," she said. The robot dialled. The connection crackled and then the phone rang.

"Hello?" said Val.

"Hello Dr. Snow, it's Mika Nakamura."

"How is construction going?"

"I dismissed the workers for the day."

"Oh?"

Mika took a small breath and then didn't sugarcoat it. "The contractor is concerned about the load bearing capacity of the roof, given that the design was not tested under heavy snowfall conditions."

"I see." Part of Valkyrie was annoyed at the delay, but part of her also enjoyed solving engineering problems.

Mika said nothing. She knew that 'sorry' would not address the problem.

"I'll be out there as soon as possible. Don't let the contractor leave." Val hung up the phone.

Mika was hoping that Dr. Snow would have her come back into the city to meet at the office, because it wasn't far from her apartment. Instead Valkyrie was coming all the way out here. Oh well.

Mika trudged back to the construction site to tell the contractor to stay onsite for when Dr. Snow arrived.

Val changed quickly and called her car.

"To Glasshouse," she said to the driver, getting in. The car followed the now-familiar path to the west.

Val had angled the skylight panels specifically with falling snow in mind, but it was true that she hadn't added joists or supports for added weight to the overall structure of the roof. Would this really be a problem? She would see what Mika had to say.

An hour later, Valkyrie's car made its way up the laneway to the project site. Glasshouse stood framed out, surrounded by building materials like a skeleton who had shed its skin.

"Hello, Dr. Nakamura," she said, approaching the women pouring over design schematics.

"Hello Dr. Snow."

"I'm concerned about this glass panel here," said the head contractor, pointing to the page. "The others are well supported by ceiling joists, even for the added weight of ice and snow, but for this one, above the entryway to the library at the back of the main structure, I think that lack of bearing wall will be insufficient. Maybe not this winter or the next one, but eventually this is going to give you problems." She looked at Val, her eyes wide with concern.

"What's your name again?" asked Val.

"It's Sunday Banerjee, Ma'am."

"Well Dr. Banerjee, I think you're right."

"I'm not a Doctor," she laughed, "I have a diploma in Construction Excellence though."

"I see. It's so complicated when women don't have PhDs because then you have to decide what to call them... Miss Banerjee? Mrs. Banerjee?"

"Call me Sunday."

"Okay then. Call me Val."

They both laughed. Mika tried to join but she felt terrible for not noticing the problem.

"We could give this window a frame at the bottom," said Sunday.

"No," said Val, narrowing her eyes and looking at the plans. She loved vanishing windows and she didn't want anything impeding the visual effect; it would bother her forever if that one panel looked shorter than the others. She thought for a moment. What if she made it stand out on purpose?

"Let's make that panel into a porthole instead. We can frame it up securely and make it look intentional. I will order the piece tonight and draw up the designs. I want work to resume tomorrow."

"Great idea," said Mika.

"So. Besides the potentially disastrous design flaw, how is construction going?"

"Come take a look."

Mika and Sunday showed Val the work so far. Things were looking good. Val's only concern was timing. She wanted the house finished before winter. It would be nice to spend the fall here too.

That might be wishful thinking, she thought. She contented herself thinking about how next year she would have this place to escape to any time she wanted.

That evening Val worked furiously on the new roof design. She was actually very pleased with the porthole idea. It would give the place a more whimsical look. She generally didn't like designs that involved glass on the roof because there was constantly a threat of leaking, but this house would look stunning in the forest, like an arboretum, or a human terrarium, built around a stone hearth.

The phone rang.

"Hello?"

"Hi... Valkyrie?" It was Jordan.

"Yes?"

"I was just wondering what you were doing."

"I'm working late. Are you okay?"

Jordan could hear concern in her voice.

"Yea, I'm fine."

"Good." There was an awkward silence.

"Well, I guess I'll let you get back to work then."

"Okay."

"Okay."

"Wait... Jordan, if you want to come over, I have to work on this but you could bring a book and read or something."

"Yea?"

"Sure."

"Okay. I'll be over in a bit."

Jordan was feeling lonely. He had considered calling his mum again, but decided to call Val instead.

He looked around his room for a book. He had a few books, but he had read them all. He walked down the hall to Jerome's room. He knocked on the door.

"Come in," he heard Jerome say.

"Hey man," he said, popping his head in the door. Jerome was on the computer.

"Hey," Jerome replied, not turning his head.

"Do you have a book I can read?"

"Ya dude, check my shelf."

Jordan walked over to the bookshelf in Jerome's room. Technology was developing at breakneck speed, but paper books had not disappeared. Newspapers and textbooks were all but gone, and although there were many attempts to create an alternative digital text reader, the trade paperback that slid easily into a backpack and could be passed to friends could not be replaced. Jordan scoured the shelf, running his finger along titles.

"*The Diviners*, Margaret Lawrence," he said out loud. "How's this one, Jer?"

"It's okay. I read it for Grade 9 English."

"Huh. I'll check it out." He pulled it off the shelf. "Thanks."

"Yea no prob."

Jordan left the room and closed the door behind him. He went down the hall to his room, pulling his backpack off its hook on the wall, putting the book inside, and grabbing his longboard on his way out the door.

Jordan knocked on the door.

"Let him in," said Val quietly to the house. The locks disengaged and the door swung open. Jordan came inside and the door closed behind him.

"I can't chat tonight, but please make yourself comfortable."

Jordan walked over to the couch and dropped his bag. He sat down and sunk into the leather sofa.

What am I doing here? he thought. He got out *The Diviners* and opened to the first page. It took him a few minutes to relax into the novel. He shifted to a more comfortable position on the couch and it wasn't long before he had finished the first chapter.

Of course, I picked a book about a shitty mother, he thought. The book was pretty good though. Jordan liked the stream of consciousness style and the writing was poetic. Jordan was captivated by the way the author didn't hide anything. She was real, and fictional. He liked that. He looked around the room. This was really nice, just reading at Valkyrie's house. He felt deeply content. What would he be doing now at home?

Scrolling through my phone, he thought. His hand crept to his pocket, almost involuntarily. He fingered the edges of the box-like object under the fabric of his pants.

What am I doing? he thought. He opened the book and kept reading.

Another forty minutes passed, with Val scratching away at her work and Jordan reading. He sighed, closing the book again for another break.

Jordan stood up slowly and stretched. Val looked up, noticing the way his shirt rose, revealing soft blond hairs under his belly button. Jordan walked over to the desk where Val was working.

"Can I get you anything?" he asked softly.

She smiled at him. "Thank you. How about tea?"

Jordan went over to the kitchen. The kettle was on the stove already. He filled it with water at the sink and set it to boil. He got two mugs out of the cupboard. He rifled around the press looking for tea and the teapot.

Val enjoyed the soft sounds of Jordan puttering in the kitchen. Sometimes she felt lonely in the evening, but she didn't want to invite company over. This was nice, having him here and working together quietly. She didn't feel like she needed to entertain him, and she could tell that he was content to just do his own thing in her presence.

The kettle squealed, and Jordan filled the teapot with boiling water.

"How long do I leave it for?" he asked quietly.

"A few minutes. I like it strong so I leave it a little longer."

Making tea is a long process, thought Jordan. No wonder he had never done it before. It seemed like a bit of an archaic practice, out of place in a fast-food world.

Valkyrie's not a fast-food girl, he thought. *Er, woman.*

He went to the fridge and got out cream. He poured it into the little creamer. All the little tea things looked nice on the marble countertop.

Tea and its accoutrement... he thought. It was almost a song lyric.

He lifted the lid of the teapot, letting the steam waft up. He breathed in deep. It smelled delicious. Chai with hints of rose.

"Check the colour," said Val.

Jordan tugged the teabag. The tea looked a bit watery.

"I should have told you to put in a second bag," she said softly. "I usually do for a full pot. Go ahead and put another in."

"I hope I didn't ruin it..."

"It's fine." Val smiled.

Jordan put in more tea and let it steep again, tapping the bag impatiently with a spoon. He felt a bit anxious about making bad tea. When he felt like it was ready, he poured two cups and added the cream. He brought them to the living room area, setting down his mug on the macabre coffee table. He brought Val's over to the desk. She set it down on a coaster to cool.

He looked at her anxiously.

"Is it okay? I'm sorry," he said.

"Jordan, it's fine!" Val reached out and squeezed his hand. "Don't worry, it's fine, really." She put her hands around the warm cup. "Thank you for the tea."

She looked at his expression and laughed. He smiled, relaxing.

"How's your book?"

"It's really good actually."

"What is it?"

"*The Diviners*... have you heard of it?"

"Margaret Lawrence. I've read that one... a long time ago."

"I had no idea what to expect, but she's kind of a poet, isn't she?"

"That's true, I can totally see you being into that."

"How's your work coming?"

"Almost done. If you can stay awake long enough, I'd love it if you sang me the nightingale song when I'm finished."

Jordan looked down and grinned, his hair falling over his face. He looked up at her, his eyes full of appreciation.

"Sounds good."

Val went back to work. Jordan went back to the couch and kept reading.

A phone jangled. Jordan looked confused for a moment. Val walked over to a brass contraption on a side table and lifted the receiver.

"Hello?" she said softly.

Jordan had only seen phones like that in movies. Land lines were for the rich—to have a land line you had to be a landowner, and to be a landowner nowadays you had to inherit.

"Hey Val."

"Hi Jeff. What do you want?"

Jeff heard the exasperation in her voice. Some part of him knew this just wasn't going to happen. The other part of him told him that he got everything he wanted if he tried hard enough. *Maybe it's just halftime,* he thought. *Can't give up at halftime.*

"I just can't help but feel like we should give this another chance."

"Jeff, let me be direct. I see what you would get out of a relationship with me, but I am not seeing what I would get out of it. Do you really think I need to spend my evenings having things mansplained to me? Thank you for the flowers. I am not playing hard to get, please don't misinterpret my manners for interest. Please don't call me again."

She hung up.

"Who was that?" asked Jordan.

"A man who wanted something from me, but I don't think he knew what he would really get."

"What would he really get?"

Val looked closely at Jordan, amused. She didn't answer. Her eyes were grey and shining, her lip turned up at the corner, and he had no idea what she was thinking.

Valkyrie put the finishing touches on her design. She stood up, stretching. Jordan looked up, noticing how her breasts rose with her arms, her nipples slightly visible beneath the soft fabric. He realized that he forgot to bring back her dress. He would bring it next time. He went back to reading.

Val went over to the computer. She scanned the papers, sending them to the office for Mika.

Jordan was almost finished his book. The soft whir of the computer broke the silence.

Val came over to the couch. She sat down beside Jordan, relaxing.

"I'm exhausted," she said, turning to look at him.

"Do you still want your song?" he asked.

"Yes."

Jordan started to sing. As the last soft notes of the first verse floated into the chorus, Val leaned over, putting a pillow on Jordan's lap and laying down.

By the time the song was finished, Val was fast asleep. Jordan stroked her arm softly.

"Valkyrie," he whispered. No response.

Jordan knew he should wake her up, but he didn't want to just yet. She felt so nice on his lap, the weight of her and the sound of her breathing comforting. He lay back, closing his eyes and enjoying the moment.

After a few minutes, Jordan rubbed her arm harder.

"Valkyrie," he said, a little louder. "Valkyrie…"

She stirred, moving her hand down to his knee and holding him. Jordan exhaled, leaning down until her soft wild curls were brushing his cheek.

"Valkyrie, you fell asleep…"

She sat up slowly, blinking her eyes in the dim light. Jordan took her hand and helped her up. He put his hand around her waist and walked her to the stairs.

"It's late," she said softly. "You can stay if you like." She went upstairs, going into the bathroom.

Jordan went back to the living room, putting his book into his backpack. He cleared away the tea things. He straightened the pillows on the couch and laid out the blanket. When Valkyrie was done in the bathroom he would tell her he didn't need sheets. He took off his pants, laying them beside the couch. Luckily he was wearing his new boxers today so he would have something to sleep in.

Valkyrie brushed her teeth and got ready for bed. She paused at the top of the stairs. Should she? *Why not.*

"Come upstairs," she said softly.

Jordan looked up at her, standing in the darkness, her pale hand on the railing, wearing a long oversized t-shirt. He walked over to the bottom of the stairs and said nothing as he walked up to meet her. She turned and walked down the hall to her bedroom and disappeared behind the door.

Jordan went to the bathroom, having a pee and splashing water on his face. He dried off on a towel and followed Val's footsteps to the room at the end of the hall.

Valkyrie was tucked into bed already.

"You can sleep on the other side," she said quietly.

Jordan slipped into bed, pulling the covers up over his shoulders. They were both fast asleep in minutes.

CHAPTER THIRTEEN

Valkyrie woke up early. She turned to see Jordan lying beside her, his soft hair falling over his face as he snored quietly into the pillow. Even in sleep he looked a bit anxious. From this close, Val could see fine worry lines creasing his smooth face. His right arm was pulled up under the pillow, his elbow reaching out and almost touching her. She could see the fine blond hairs sticking up along his arm. It was so lovely to wake up beside someone.

She slipped out of bed, careful not to wake him. She pulled on a day dress and padded downstairs to start her day.

Jordan woke up to the sound of the espresso machine grinding beans. He reached out beside him to where Valkyrie had slept. Under the blankets, it was still warm. He rolled over onto his back and pulled the blankets up in his arms, hugging them. This bed was like sleeping on a cloud. He hadn't slept so deep in a long time. He looked around the room.

The walls were a dark warm brown, and the headboard was carved out of rich knotty wood. A canopy hung over the bed with veils of creamy lace, like a mossy tree. There was no window. It was like sleeping in an animal's den in the roots of an ancient tree. Downstairs was ultra-modern, but up here Val had made some old fashioned choices. Beds this size were not common anymore and canopies were not in style, but she liked what she liked.

Jordan felt safe in this room, as though when he was in here, the whole outside world didn't exist. That thought was comforting.

He heard the sound of beans grinding in the machine. The thought of Val's delicious coffee in a steaming mug impelled him to get up. He crawled out of bed and started down the stairs.

"I laid out a towel for you to shower," said Val, looking at him with her impassive expression. Jordan looked at her for a moment and then turned around to go back up and take a shower.

Thank goodness, thought Val. Jordan was a bit greasy.

Val put together a plate of nutty breads and spreads, with her usual bowl of fruit. She made one up for herself, as well as a cup of coffee, and took it out to the balcony.

Now that Glasshouse was finally underway, Val felt herself turning to other projects that she was working on. All the funding, research, and procurement for Snow Arcologies was coming along nicely. Val was toying with the idea of building an expensive prototype to really drive up interest. The city of Toronto just recently completed a project a long time in the making, which was a "city within a city", or a small luxurious mecca of new urban technologies situated on the harbour front. Although it took a long time to build—they had been talking about it since the 2020's—it was wildly successful.

Valkyrie Snow's arcologies were themselves like a city within a city. She designed them to be part of a cityscape where they were integrated into the transportation grid, and ultimately oriented around launch stations for an Earth connected to the stars.

We must collectively overcome war mongering first, she thought. Val was convinced that it was the destiny of the human race to live amongst the stars. It was the only way to overcome the inevitable death of Earth.

And filthy human pollution, she thought. She would prefer it if humans lived in luxurious carbon-emission-neutral arcologies and leave most of the Earth's surface to give the biodiversity of animals and plants being killed off by human mismanagement a chance to make a comeback.

"Morning," said Jordan, coming out to the balcony with a plate of breakfast and a cup of coffee.

Val turned to him, a slight frown on her face and a faraway look in her eyes. "Morning," she said distractedly.

"You look lost in thought."

"Mmhmm…"

"What are you thinking about?"

"Oh, just more to be done…"

"Work stuff?"

Val's attention focused back on Earth, onto Jordan's face. "Work stuff."

"You designed buildings all over the city, right? I checked out your Insta feed."

"That's what Hammer & Bone does, yes."

"So what are you working on now?"

"Now I'm doing something just for me. I'm building my dream house." Val's eyes danced.

"Better than this?" Jordan gestured to the beautiful condo.

Val laughed. "I guess I'm never truly satisfied."

"I guess not!"

Val turned serious. She thought about it for a moment. "It's not the condo. It's also the lifestyle. For this apartment, I designed the best way of living in a condo, in this neighbourhood, in this city. But here I'm missing connecting to nature, the complete silence of being away from other people for days on end, the thrill of privacy... all things I don't need here in this space. But could be perfect somewhere else."

"Seems pretty private to me." Jordan thought about his apartment where he lived in intimate proximity to others. The reminders were everywhere, from the sound of Rachel and Jerome fucking in the next room, to streaks of Bubba's shit in the toilet bowl that he never cleaned when he took a dump.

"Wait until you see this place." Val grinned.

It was infectious. Jordan was smiling too.

"Sounds good."

Val drank the last of her espresso. She looked at him with that stone expression she sometimes had.

"Jordan, I won't push this, but I wanted to say it. If you need me to get you some counselling, I would be happy to."

Jordan turned serious again, his walls shooting up.

"What, like a shrink? Nah, I'm good."

"There's nothing wrong with seeing a therapist once in a while. Anyway, I'm not trying to tell you what to do, just offering a possibility. Sorry if I offended you."

Jordan thought about when he dragged himself in here dripping with blood in the middle of the night. He softened.

"I get it. I'm a little nuts. But everybody is, right? Except you." He grinned.

Val smiled. He just didn't know her well enough yet to see her demons.

"How about a gym membership? Working out can help to get your crazies out... it's not a replacement for therapy at all, but at least let me get you that."

Jordan thought about it. Having access to a gym was completely out of his realm of possibility so he hadn't considered it before. He couldn't afford such a luxury, and he couldn't afford one of those fancy apartments that came with a gym in the building either. He had learned a bit about body building in high school.

He didn't really remember the details of working out, but he remembered that he enjoyed it.

"I could try it…" he said.

Val smiled and stood up, leaving her empty cup at the balcony table. Her cleaner, John, would be here this afternoon and he would clear it. Val walked to the desk.

"House," she said quietly. "Please register a six month gym pass for Jordan Barker at my gym. Print the paperwork."

The computer whirred to life, arranging the details.

Jordan came in from the balcony. He went over to the couch where he left his pants. He pulled them on over his boxers.

"I gotta head to work. Thanks for the reading date," he said with a smile.

Val met him at the door and handed him the information for the gym. He put it in his backpack, and gave Val a great big hug. She held him tight, rubbing the soft cotton of his white t-shirt. He smelled clean.

"Mmm," she said, letting go. Jordan took off.

When Jordan got home from work that night, he rifled through his backpack and pulled out the information about his gym membership. Val had spent two thousand dollars on it. He went to the dresser and dug around for gym-looking shorts. He had an old pair of black ones that he'd held onto since high school. He sat on the bed. Should he go? He wanted to, but something held him back. It wasn't anxiety… it was something else. Like a heavy invisible arm holding him down. He forced himself to change into the shorts. He sat on the bed again.

She spent a lot of money on this, he thought. *And I said I'd go.*

Lazy fuck, hissed Snake. *Just get up and go…*

She's going to ask me if I went, he thought. *I need to go at least once.*

Jordan stood up and felt himself walking out the door.

I'm doing it, he thought.

He was proud of himself. He kept feeling it all the way down the elevator, out of the building, and down the street. He got out his phone and let it navigate him to the facility. It was about halfway between her house and his. He walked up the steps.

A wooden sign decorated with shining white letters announced Gym Nordik. Jordan walked inside the large front doors and went over to the reception desk.

"Umm, hey," he said, pulling out the receipt and sliding it over to the robot standing at the register.

"Hello," it said, scanning the paper. "Jordan Barker."

Jordan was relieved that he didn't have to talk to anyone. Maybe he would actually come back.

"Umm, where do I go?" he asked.

"One moment please." The robot signalled a personal trainer bot to take him to the change rooms. He followed along behind it, passing a weight room full of sweaty buff people in athletic wear. Jordan looked down at his ragged shoes. He hoped he wouldn't get kicked out.

"Thanks," he said. "Can I borrow a lock?"

"Yes." The robot whirred off to get him a lock.

Maybe they could lend me some shoes, too, he thought. He tossed his things into a locker. The robot returned and showed him how to open the lock. It started to leave.

"Wait," said Jordan. "Can you tell me how to use the machines?"

"Yes."

The robot led him to the cardio setup. Jordan avoided anyone else's gaze along the way. The gym was a weird semi-social space. The robot guided him through a basic workout. After an hour and twenty minutes, he was sweating heavily and ready to head out.

"Thank you," he said.

"It is my pleasure," said the robot in a cheery tone.

Jordan went to the change rooms. The walls were high and tiled with slate stone, with shiny gold hardware accents. The sinks were gold, and even the rings on the shower curtains were gold. There were shelves of fresh fluffy white towels. Jordan decided to take a shower. He peeled off his hot gym clothes and turned on the gold taps. Water gushed out of multiple nozzles and he was surrounded in a warm mist. He groaned happily, pumping soap out of the dispenser and lathering up his body and hair. This was so much better than showering at home. He was already planning on coming back. This would be a great place to get ready for a show, get him in the headspace for success.

For the next six months at least, he thought. He would have to make the most of the time he had. He couldn't believe how scared he had been to come here.

I'm glad I did, he thought with a grin.

Jordan rinsed off, and closed the gold taps. He wrapped himself up in a soft white bathrobe, and tied a fuzzy towel around his hair. He considered stuffing a bathrobe into his backpack, but then resisted the impulse. This was the only place he would wear something like this anyway. Maybe when his membership was up he would take a souvenir.

Jordan pulled on his clothes, still damp with sweat from the workout. He realized he would have to do laundry more often. These clothes stunk already. Next time, he would scrub his workout wear in the shower with him, and bring clean clothes to change into.

He left Gym Nordik with a bounce in his step, walking home in the dark.

Over the next few weeks, Valkyrie focused her intentions on Glasshouse. She took a brief hiatus from her work at Hammer & Bone to go to her property almost every day to monitor their progress. The exterior was complete and the house was looking magnificent. The stone fireplace was complete and the interior was framed out with walls and floor treatments installed. It was almost time to add the more subtle elements, like light fixtures and hardware. Val had planned out every detail of the project, ordering everything to exact specification long ago. The house was elegant and minimal. Nothing was ornate or overdone, but the space was designed to feel simple, comfortable and luxurious.

It's going to be gorgeous here in the winter," said Mika. "You can watch the snow fall from every direction."

Val smiled. She had always thought of Glasshouse as a greenhouse, filled with pots of flowers, flats of fresh herbs, small fruit trees, and deep crockery vessels holding hothouse vegetables, the sun filling every corner with light through massive windows. In her fantasy there was green everywhere, outside and in. She had not been thinking about winter, when Glasshouse would be a snow globe, a cozy oasis of warm under a stormy white sky. That would be lovely too. She would pile blankets on the bed, and read books by firelight. Her own private world.

Glasshouse was one of the prototypes she designed for her Futurustic project. She envisioned a housing development with minimal impact on the environment where residents could live in a like-minded community while maintaining relative privacy. One of the basic tenets of buy-in would be protecting biodiversity.

"Every season has its blessings," said Val. She sniffed the air. It still smelled like summer, but fall would be on its way soon.

Jordan went to the gym every chance he got, which was at least three times a week. At first, he spent the whole time consuming social media, but pretty quickly he realized that pounding out his anxieties on the treadmill calmed his mind and he didn't need the distraction. The first few minutes of his workout were always tough, but then he fell into a rhythm that made him feel powerful, like he could take on the world. Some days he thought of song ideas, and sometimes concept art for albums. Once in a while he liked to fantasize in his head about one thing or another. Once he imagined he was an ancient Greek Olympian, training for a running competition. His fans would line the practice track, cheering him on. He smiled and nodded to them as he ran past, his heels kicking up loamy dirt in the hot sun.

There were a few hot girls at the gym and sometimes he would imagine that they were looking at him, admiring his firm legs as he ran on the treadmill, or his growing biceps as he pumped iron in the weight room. Those fantasies were almost real, because the women were right there. He liked to think that they were all in love with him. One part of him knew how stupid that was, and the other part of him believed it was true. When he thought about it too much he would force himself to think about something else so that he didn't get a hard on in his gym shorts.

His favourite fantasies were of performing live at shows where the crowd was so big that he couldn't see where the people ended and the rest of the world began. The thrill of that feeling was better than sex.

After his workout, Jordan always showered at the gym. He had completely stopped showering at home. He would throw his clothes in the bottom of the shower, lather them up with soap, and let the cascade of water rinse them out as he bathed. He would wring out the water and put the clothes in a glass jar in his bag to hang dry at home.

The gym had a few amenities that Jordan eventually tried out for the first time, like a cedar dry sauna, steam rooms with different kinds of incense, and a black room where you could lay on a big heated stone slab and even fall asleep if you wanted to. On days when he was feeling anxiety, he would sit in one of those facilities, or on the floor of the shower, for an hour, breathing in the steam with his eyes closed. It actually helped to mellow him out. The gym membership was like a lifeline, giving him a space to feel like he had his shit together. It distracted and satisfied him the way sleep did, but he didn't feel guilty about it.

After just a few weeks, Jordan started to notice changes in his body. His skinny chicken legs were filling out, and his arms were getting a little bigger and more defined. His skin was rosy and elastic, losing the ashy grey dullness he never knew was there until he saw the effects of exercise on his skin.

The Waves had a show tonight. After the shower, Jordan put on his favourite new jeans and the powder blue collar shirt that Valkyrie bought for him. He looked in the full length mirror in the soft light of the change room, pursing his lips slightly. He looked good. He pulled out his phone to take a selfie for the Insta.

Click. Click. Click. Click. Click.

Jordan took ten or so pictures. He scrolled through them. To an observer they all looked the same but to Jordan each one was slightly different. He agonized for a moment and then picked the best one. He opened the app, editing the picture with filters until it was perfect and then posted it.

Ready to rock, he wrote.

He slung his backpack over his shoulder and walked out of the change room with confidence in his step.

As he walked, a woman fell in step beside him. She had long black hair and a classic hourglass figure: juicy ass, small waist, big tits propped up with some kind of tight and effective boob contraption. She looked like Barbie's little sister, complete with Barbie makeup that must have taken her a long time to apply. Her big plump lips were red, her eyes were encircled with greys and silvers and blacks, and her eyes popped blue framed with daddy-long-legs level fake eyelashes.

"Hi," she said, eying him with interest.

"Hey," said Jordan. Matt always said that girls who looked like this must be batshit crazy if they were into you. If they were sane, they would be going for a rich guy.

"I'm Raven," she said.

"I'm Jordan." He realized that she must think he was a rich guy, because of his great outfit. He smiled.

"I haven't seen you in here before," she said.

That's right, thought Jordan. *Only rich people can afford this gym.*

"I joined last month," he said.

"New in town?"

"Not exactly…"

"So where are you off to?"

Jordan felt his chest swell with joy. "I have a show tonight. I'm a musician."

"Oh, very cool."

Jordan could tell she was impressed. A musician who could afford a membership at Gym Nordik must be at least moderately successful.

"What are you doing tonight?" he asked. "You should come to my show."

Raven batted her eyes at him. "Sounds like a plan."

She gave him her number. "Text me the details," she said.

"I'm heading there now… the show's not until 9 but we could have a drink first."

She laughed. "I just worked out! I have to do my makeup and change, I'm a mess."

"You look fine to me," Jordan grinned.

"Aww what a joker. Text me!" she said, walking in the other direction.

Jordan texted her the information. He really hoped she came tonight.

Raven, he thought. She even had a cool name. He was definitely going to get a picture of them together to post on Facebook. He'd post it on the Waves page too, because Sarah Singh might see it there. His ex had deleted him as a friend from Facebook, but she was still a fan on their page. Jordan knew it because he checked periodically.

Tonight the Waves were playing Live on Elgin. They had built up a pretty good following and the bar was happy to have them. The last time they played here, it had cost them a couple hundred bucks to book the venue and they just barely made their money back in ticket sales. Now the bar booked them for a couple hundred bucks and made their own money in alcohol. The shows were becoming a decent secondary source of income for the boys.

Jordan reached the venue and put his backpack in the back. He was the first one there. He walked around the stage, looking out at the seats that would be full in a few hours, and the floor where people would be dancing. His heart beat faster with excitement. He walked over to the bar. The owner was behind the counter, fiddling and checking up on everything for the evening.

"Hi Larry."

"Hi Jordan." The owner wiped a hand on his pants and stuck it out for a handshake. Jordan grabbed it with confidence.

"You want coffee? I've got a pot on."

Jordan thought about it. "Nah, just water, man." He was thirsty after the gym.

"You going healthy on me?"

"Don't worry, I'll be drinking later."

Larry filled a clear plastic cup with tap water and ice. Jordan took a long swig and finished half the glass.

"So when do you want to book us next?" asked Jordan.

"Let's see how tonight goes. If it goes well, we can talk."

"Cool."

"You guys playing any new stuff? I'd like to hear some new stuff tonight."

Jordan shifted uncomfortably. "We're working on a few things."

"Okay good. If we book you again then I want to hear a new album."

Jordan sipped his water. Larry continued his tidying.

"Jordan, I really think you guys have something," he said after a few minutes.

"Yea?" Jordan straightened up. Larry had been booking local flavour for a long time, and he saw who went on and who crashed and flat-lined. He knew a thing or two.

"Did you bring albums to sell tonight?" he asked.

"No... we meant to get some made, but we haven't booked recording time yet."

Larry frowned. "If you want to make this work, you gunna have to work at it, son."

"I know. We've got other jobs or school and it can be hard sometimes."

"We've all got other things going on. If you want the dream, you have to make it happen yourself. No one else is going to do the work for you. You gotta work twice as hard to fight the destiny everyone else has picked out for you, understand?"

"Yea..."

"Your sound is good. Your posters are good. If I book you again, I expect to see albums for sale, and I want to hear some new material. You know how many Ottawa bands make one album and quit?"

"Yea." Jordan finished his water.

The doors jangled open.

"EEEHHHHH boys," shouted Bubba, carrying a guitar case and a cymbal stand. Jordan grinned.

Jerome and Matt followed lugging heavy equipment. They brought it up to the stage.

"You gunna help or what?" said Matt.

Jordan hopped off the bar chair and went to help set up.

"Look at you, fancy," said Jerome, giving Jordan's butt a pinch.

"Where'd you get that?" asked Matt. "You holding out on us?" The boys rarely made big purchases without one another and the shirt looked expensive.

"Nah, Valkyrie got it for me."

"Valkyrie?" said Matt.

Bubba hooted. "V. Snow is your sugar momma!"

"Seriously?" asked Matt.

"She's taken an interest in the band," said Jordan. His cheeks and the tops of his ears turned slightly pink as the words came out. All three other boys erupted with laughter.

"I knew you were fucking her after the Montreal show," said Matt.

"I'm not! We're just friends, seriously!"

"It's all good bro, we're happy for you," said Jerome.

They finished setting up as the doors opened and people started coming in. The show wasn't for over an hour, so the boys had time to take it easy and socialize.

About fifteen minutes before their set, Jordan felt his pocket buzz.

> My friend and I are on our way
> ;)

Raven:

Jordan grinned.

"Who's that?" asked Matt, looking over his shoulder. "Sugar momma?"

"Nah, this really hot girl I met today. She's bringing a friend to the show tonight."

Bubba whistled. "You're the man, look at you!"

"Wait til you see this chick, she's like supernatural hot."

The boys went backstage. It was almost show time.

Valkyrie lay in her bed, unable to sleep. It was a hot night, but she didn't want to turn on the air conditioning because she disliked the way it made her body feel clammy and tingly. She was completely naked, lying on the soft sheets staring up at the ceiling. Her eyes were half closed. She ran her hands idly over her body, feeling the softness of her chest, the rise of her breasts, down to her stomach. She reached lower, touching herself between her legs, softly at first—*am I doing this?* she thought uncommittedly for a second—and then she felt a tiny warm spike of pleasure in her abdomen and she rubbed harder. She rubbed and rubbed, not quite making it to where she wanted to be. She closed her eyes and touched her body all over, rubbing up her thighs, her arms, stimulating her nerves. The image of a man's face floated into her mind. He was young and unsure, but firm and yielding, and she felt her passion deepen as her imagination strove harder to please her.

She imagined that she was in the suite at the Georgia in Vancouver, and James Ahote was in her bed. She was riding him, harder and harder.

Valkyrie flipped onto her stomach, pulling a pillow under her. She slipped two fingers inside her and rubbed harder, gasping as she started to orgasm. The sensation crested over her like a slow wave, taking its time to manifest. When it passed, she relaxed, breathing hard and hugging her pillow in her arms.

Finally, she drifted off to sleep.

After the show, Jordan went to find Raven. He spotted her in the crowd from up on stage and he couldn't wait to show her to the boys. He grabbed a beer at the bar and wove though the crowd, searching for her. He turned around, and at that very moment bumped into Sarah Singh, his ex-girlfriend.

"Oof, hey," she said with a friendly smile. There were those big lips he knew so well, the lips that drove him crazy with lust when they first met but disgusted him by the end. In this moment, he felt an uncomfortable mixture of those two emotions, looking at her lips.

She looked him up and down. He was glad he was wearing a nice outfit. He stood a little taller.

"Hey Sar, how you doing?"

"I'm good! I love indie night at Live on Elgin. And the Waves played, awesome Jordan."

She was a sweet girl and Jordan knew she had no ill intentions with her comments but her tone felt patronizing, almost surprised that the Waves could land this spot. Jordan winced internally, his insecurities rearing up inside him like bile.

Don't blame Sarah, she knows you all too well, hissed Snake.

And why *would* she think more of him? She had constantly been pushing him to try harder with his music but he had sunk deeper and deeper into a pit of inaction the longer they were together.

Jordan didn't know how to respond. He looked at her, unsure of whether to smile or scowl. Seeing her was like looking in the mirror and having his own feelings of unworthiness looking back at him.

"Jordan!" At that moment, Raven called out his name, as she and her friend walked toward him.

She looked like a character in a vampire novel, dressed in a sparkling blue corset, with matching contact lenses and silky extensions in her already long black hair. Her breasts poured over her top like lolita pornography. She was wearing black latex pants and her face was painted like a magazine. Raven's beauty was cartoonesque. Jordan looked at Sarah's face and wanted to laugh at the prosaic poetic cliché of this moment. Raven floated toward him, planting a big kiss on his cheek.

"Sweetie, you were amazing! We loved it!" Raven's friend nodded and they both made little squealing noises—not like pigs, more like kittens.

"Thank you. You two look like living goddesses." He grinned.

He turned to Sarah. "Nice seeing you, have a great night."

He led Raven over to where the rest of the band members were hanging out.

"This is Alexa," said Raven, introducing her friend.

"You don't say," said Bubba, getting closer to her. "Alex is my real name."

"Nice to meet you," she said. "Who are you?"

Matt and Jerome laughed and swigged their drinks.

"I'm the band manager," he said.

"I see."

"You've got an incredible voice," said Raven softly in Jordan's ear. "You gave me chills."

"I'm glad you came," he said. She wove her arm through his. She was claiming him.

Matt was staring at Raven's tits from across the table. She could feel his gaze, and when she turned to look, he barely hid it. She looked back at Jordan, scanning his face. He didn't seem to notice as he chatted about his music. He was a beautiful man, but perhaps a little clueless. She could see that he had good taste in clothes, but terrible taste in friends.

She felt Matt staring again and she turned and looked annoyed. Rachel noticed, and came over.

"Is he bothering you?" she asked. "I can tell him to fuck off."

"What?" said Jordan.

"Matt's giving this girl the creepy eye."

Jordan looked at Raven. She didn't say anything but he could tell it was true.

"You want to get out of here?" he asked. *Perfect segue. Thanks Rachel.*

"Sure," she said.

"Thanks girl," she said to Rachel, standing up to leave.

"Where's your friend?" asked Jordan.

"Oh she left an hour ago. We could go to a cocktail bar..." she said, leaving it open-ended.

"I've had enough alcohol I think," said Jordan. He'd spent way more than he should have on drinks tonight.

Raven looked at him, contemplating. She leaned in, brushing her nose along his cheek, feeling the softness of his hair, kissing him lightly where his ear met his jawline. He smelled good.

Jordan felt a tremor of excitement. He looked into her eyes with his best soulful expression, letting his hair fall onto his face and sweeping it back casually with one hand, holding the back of his neck and showing off his bicep.

"Let's go to your place?" he said softly. Usually he was too lazy for that, but for this girl he would go all the way out to Orleans.

"I don't usually take boys home on the first date..."

"But..."

"But I did meet you at my gym, which means you have a healthy lifestyle, and your voice is just so incredible..."

Jordan slipped his arm around her waist.

"Let's get you home," he said.

They walked outside.

"Which way?" he asked.

"Let me call an Uber," she said, pulling out her phone.

"It's that far?"

"Yea, I live in South Keys."

Damn. Jordan would normally take the train all the way out there.

"Let me get it. I insist," he said, pulling out his phone. He didn't have any money, but he didn't want her to know that.

"I already have my address programmed in. Don't worry about it," she said.

"Are you sure?"

"Relax," she laughed. Raven hated it when guys acted like they were paying for sex, as if they were never going to see her again.

"You can take me out for dinner next weekend."

The car arrived and they hopped in. They kissed a little in the back. Jordan couldn't believe how perfect this girl looked, like she had stepped off the pages of a magazine. He suddenly remembered that he needed to take a picture for the Insta. He pulled out his phone, turned on the camera, and held his arm out to get a snap of them kissing.

"Omg don't," said Raven, holding her hand in front of her lips. "My lipstick probably looks horrible."

"What?" he held the camera closer so she could see herself on the screen.

"You look gorgeous."

"Let me take it."

He handed her the phone, and she took a series of carefully posed photos at practiced angles. She reviewed them, deleting the ones she didn't like.

"There you go," she said. "Even though I'm a mess."

"Babe, you're not a mess," he murmured. He wasn't sure if she really believed she looked bad or if she just wanted him to tell her she looked good.

"You look so good."

She kissed him lightly on the cheek.

They arrived at their destination. Raven lived in a townhouse with several other women and femmes. One was obviously MtF, and Jordan wondered if Raven had lady parts under her clothes. With all that makeup, it was difficult to tell. Not that it mattered. She was hot.

"Here is my room," she said, leading him into a dark room and flicking on a purple bedside lamp. She seemed a bit shy all of a sudden. He kissed her softly.

"Mmm, you have great lips," she said.

"So do you," he breathed.

They kissed and kissed, and after probably forty minutes Jordan started to feel a bit uncomfortable. He didn't really know this girl and he was really far in the south end. Was it even worth it? He got the picture he wanted. His passion was fading.

"Can we turn another light on?" he said. "I want to see your beautiful face." The visual would wake him up.

"Let's not," she said. "The overhead light is harsh."

Okay then, time to step it up. Jordan kissed her breasts, and the feeling of their soft firmness against his mouth made him hungry for more. He licked his lips, and tasted something strange. He went back to her lips and kissed her.

"Foundation," she said, laughing a little.

"What?"

"You taste like foundation. It's makeup," she said. She grabbed a tissue and wiped the tops of her boobs, and then wiped her lips, brushing inward carefully with the tissue.

"I don't want to stain outside my lipline," she explained. When she was done she jumped on the bed and pulled him down on top of her. He grinded up against her, kissing her. She grabbed a hair tie from the bedside table and pulled her long locks into it loosely, carefully folding and piling hair around the pillow. She didn't want to ruin her extensions.

Jordan felt the hard corset bodice, grasping for a zipper or some way to open it. He couldn't find one. He wanted to feel skin against his. He pulled off his pants. Raven peeled off her latex bottoms. She wasn't wearing anything underneath. Jordan groaned with pleasure, his penis getting erect in his boxers and pressing up against her. When he tried to kiss her anywhere but on her lips, she moved away uncomfortably.

"Are you okay?" he asked.

"Yea I just don't want to mess up my makeup," she said. He didn't tell her that the tail of one cat eye was streaking down her cheek.

"Do you need to, like, take a shower or something?" he asked.

"No silly…"

She grinded up against him and they kissed for a few more minutes.

"I'm ready," she said.

Jordan reached down and pulled off his boxers. He fished a condom out of the pocket of his jeans and put it on, and then he eased his way into her, thrusting slowly. Raven made pleasure sounds so he went a little faster. He felt his arousal grow. She grabbed his butt and pressed down, moving him to the right places to get her off. He followed her lead, thrusting into her the way she liked until she came, the dark outline of her stained lip liner and the dark around her eyes exaggerating her expression of pleasure as she opened her mouth. Pleasure overcame him and he pumped until he came. He rolled off of her, satisfied.

After a few minutes, Raven got up and went to the bathroom. Jordan lay back and relaxed. After a while he got out his phone and scrolled through the feeds on all of his apps. He resisted the urge to check Tinder, out of respect.

When Raven came back, she had removed her hair extensions and done her natural hair in a teased high ponytail. She was wearing a tight lacy bustier and panties, and her cat eye was fixed. Jordan smiled up at her.

"You look beautiful, but I don't think I have anything more in me," he said.

"Oh, this is my pajamas," she said. She climbed into bed carefully and lay on the pillow beside him. He reached over to cuddle her, but she didn't want to roll on her side and smudge her face.

"Sorry honey," she said, carefully turning off the bedside lamp. She put her arms up over her head and then she lay perfectly still.

"Is that how you sleep?!"

"When I put my arms like this, it keeps me from moving around too much."

Jordan scooched closer and pressed his leg along hers. Raven closed her eyes.

"Goodnight handsome," she said.

"Night."

Raven seemed to fall asleep quickly, but Jordan could not. Every time he looked over at her out of the corner of his eye in the darkness, the shiny makeup on her eyelids made it look like she was laying there with her eyes open, even though she was fast asleep. It creeped Jordan out, like he was sleeping beside some kind of life-sized doll, like one of those sex robots people ordered on the internet. Her uncanny position added to the effect.

He tossed and turned, careful not to disturb her, deeply uncomfortable. The thought of socializing with her and her roommates in the morning added to his anxiety. Finally, he got up and pulled on his clothes. He let himself out, and as the night started brightening into morning, he took the train back home.

What do I tell her? he thought, scratching his head. He would just leave things at that, except that he would surely see her at the gym and that would be terrible.

Fuck it, he thought, remembering Charlotte. He decided to just go for honest.

> Sorry but I couldn't sleep so I had to head out and catch some zzz in my own bed. Have a great day.

Jordan :

There. What more could he say?

He looked out the window, watching tall buildings flash by as the train passed. The sky was incredible colours like soft peach and pale blue. Jordan felt peaceful. His mellow mood grew into inspiration and he got out his phone to capture some lyrics.

When the train reached downtown, Jordan got off and walked to his building. The air was crisp.

Summer must almost be over, he thought.

He crept into his room, pulled off his fancy clothes and threw them on the bed and climbed in to get a nap in before he had to go to work.

PART TWO: GLASSHOUSE

CHAPTER FOURTEEN

Glasshouse was finally complete. Valkyrie Snow hired a car to take her and a box of her things out to her new home.

She thought back to times she had moved in the past. In her twenties she had so much stuff that she had to rent a moving van to hold it all. The more wealth she built up, the less things she owned. She had everything she needed to live comfortably at Glasshouse, and everything else she needed to do her creative work was here in this box.

When the car pulled up the lane and stopped in front of the house, she stopped for a moment to breathe and to enjoy the feeling of satisfaction and pride she felt looking at her creation. Here was her small but beautiful dream house, 100% carbon neutral, made without plastic or fossil fuels, and gloriously set in the Canadian Shield. She exhaled slowly, and then got out of the car.

"Shall I carry your box?" said the robot driver.

"No, thank you, I will take it in myself."

She walked the box up the shallow wooden stairs to the large glass door.

"Open," she said softly. The door slid open and she walked through. It slid closed by itself behind her.

The house was floored with wide dark wooden planks. The octagonal room was dominated by the massive stone hearth in the centre, whose chimney reached up to the ceiling. To the left was a small kitchen area, and to the right a bed floated on chains from the ceiling like a cloud, suspended in a greenhouse of windows on all sides. Val walked between the bed and behind the fireplace, where a large copper bathtub was installed, also surrounded by floor to ceiling windows that extended up overhead, the massive glass panes joining the back roof. She walked past it to the back room, looking up at the round porthole window above, behind the stone chimney. It was perfect. The office room was quite dark. She set her box down on the desk. The bookshelves were already full. There had been no room for books in her condo, so her collection was packed away in storage in her building. She had Mika send someone to bring them to the Glasshouse office.

Val stepped close to the shelves, running her hand along the faded spines like she was greeting old friends. It was so nice to have them close again, inspiring her as she worked. Maybe she would re-read some classics.

She opened her box, pulling out pencils, pens, drafting paper, and an Oracle. The small device was an AI computer that was constantly connected to the internet and was designed to learn and intuit Val's needs. It was the next generation of personal assistant, replacing her House system. She set it up. She arranged everything the way she wanted it on the desk, ready to work when inspiration struck. She could already feel it tingling in her fingertips. She could tell that this place would inspire many brilliant ideas.

She pulled a small linen bag out of the box. Inside was a large flat sea shell, a wand of herbs bound with string, and a box of matches. She walked out to the main room, laying them on the hearth. She decided she would take a bath in the tub to purify herself, and then she would perform a cleansing *seidr* ritual to seal and honour the house.

Valkyrie removed her clothes, folding them and laying them on the rack by the beautiful copper tub. She shivered with anticipation to bathe here for the first time as she climbed inside. She poured fragrant oils and turned on the water, laying back and closing her eyes.

When the tub was full and she turned off the water, Valkyrie could hear the sound of the river flowing by beneath the windows.

Just like I dreamed, she thought.

After the bath, she towelled off and performed the ritual naked, singing protection *galedr* as she burned the herbs on the shell throughout the house. She invited the land spirits to feel welcome in her home, and invited them to be friends with her ancestors and the spirits she brought with her to this land. She made clear her intention to respect the earth and the spirits while she lived here.

Thunk.

Valkyrie heard something hit the large window. She frowned and went outside to see what it was.

Lying in the overturned earth beside the house was a tiny bird. The nightingale.

"I'm sorry little one," she cooed, scooping him up and bringing him inside. She wrapped him in a towel and set him by the hearth. After a few minutes he twitched to life, stunned.

"It's better for you in here," she said softly. "You would never have survived Canadian winter outside."

Val realized that she must have called him in with her *galedr*. She remembered her dream, thinking with a laugh that *galedr* was the Old Norse word that developed into the Old English word for nightingale—*nœcti-galœ*.

She made a mental note to order a cage later, something wood to match the house, and food.

"You'll be a caged bird now," she said quietly. The thought was bitter sweet.

Ding ding.

What was that?

Jordan Barker is calling your home phone, said a voice. It was the Oracle.

Did she feel like talking right now? She thought for a moment. She had probably called him with the *galedr* too.

Fine.

"Respond," she said.

"Hello? Val?"

"Hello Mr. Barker."

"Hey. What are you up to?" he asked. The day after his encounter with Raven, Jordan crashed hard. Maybe it was the lack of sleep, or maybe it was just an emotional relapse, but he was feeling terrible.

"I'm in my Glasshouse," she said dreamily.

"Oh, it's all done? That's awesome."

"It's perfect."

"Yea so I was hoping maybe we could hang out, have a reading date or something."

Valkyrie thought it over. She could order a car and have him come here. But she really felt like being alone for her first night in Glasshouse.

"Sorry Jordan, not tonight. I just had a bath and I want to be alone right now." Her voice sounded husky and relaxed. Jordan had never heard her sound so mellow before.

"Okay, no problem…"

"Can I call you later to sing me to sleep?"

"Yea. Sounds good."

"Bye nightingale," she said softly.

"Bye Valkyrie."

Click. Jordan disconnected with a smile. Val had called him nightingale.

She always knows how to make me smile, he thought. He dialled the volume back up on his music and looked forward to her call.

Val watched the sun set from her porch, wrapped in her silky grey robe and sipping a mug of tea. This place was everything she wanted it to be. Next year, she would have a lovely vegetable garden. She looked at the forest around the house, drinking in the evening air.

When the sun slipped down behind the trees and the sky was dark, she went inside. Today was a long exciting day and Valkyrie was ready for bed. She slipped off her robe and hung it on the rack, and climbed up into her floating bed. It was gloriously soft, piled with the blankets she envisioned, holding her like a hug.

"Call Nightingale," she said.

"Sorry, repeat?" said the Oracle.

"Call the young man who called today, Jordan Barker. He is Nightingale."

The phone trilled.

"Hey Val," said Jordan softly. His voice drifted over from the back of the house as though he were here.

"Hi Jordan. I'm ready for bed."

"It's kind of early, isn't it?"
"I've had a busy day. Sing for me."
Jordan laughed. He cleared his throat.

A single bloom in a jar in the window
Pictures of all of the places you've been
A song for each memory, playing forever
Makes me come over again and again.

My heart song for you is a simple one
It's the stories I love that you tell
I still can't believe that you love me
When you know me so well.
When you know me so well.

I picture us happy, that's new for me
You're more than I deserve as I stumble through now
You're a lighthouse to tomorrow, if I make it out alive
This ship's still afloat anyhow.

My heart song for you is a simple one
It's the stories I love that you tell
I still can't believe that you love me
When you know me so well.
When you know me so well.

You glide into my life without warning
I forget how I got to this place with a smile
Like a nightingale song in the morning
I still don't know who you are…

My heart song for you is a simple one
It's the stories I love that you tell
I still can't believe that you love me
When you know me so well.
When you know me so well.

By the time the song was over, Val was fast asleep. Jordan wished he was there to fall asleep beside her. He could have disconnected the call, but he left it. He closed his eyes and fell asleep listening to the soft sound of Valkyrie Snow dreaming.

CHAPTER FIFTEEN

The next morning, Valkyrie decided that she would bring Jordan to Glasshouse for a vacation. That would help him to relax. She could tell when he called her yesterday that he was struggling.

"Oracle," she said, "call Jordan."

"You are already in a call with Jordan," responded the device.

"Jordan?" she said, realizing that they were on the phone together all night. Then louder, "Jordan?"

"Mmm, good morning," he said, waking up.

"Good morning."

They enjoyed the companionable silence for a moment.

"Can you take a few days off work?" she asked. "To come out here?"

Jordan thought about it.

"Yea. I'd like that." With the extra cash the Waves were pulling in, he could afford a little vacation. "How about this weekend? I'm free Friday to Sunday."

"Okay. I'll send a car to bring you."

"Thanks."

"Well I'd love to lie in bed all day and chat," she said, "but I have work to do."

"No worries, we can do that this weekend." Jordan froze, realizing the potential sexual connotation of what he just said.

"That's going to be nice," said Val.

Jordan relaxed. He would never want to jeopardize their friendship by crossing any boundaries.

"Good luck with your work."

"Thanks. Have a beautiful day."

Click.

On Thursday morning, a car arrived at Jordan's building to pick him up and take him out to Glasshouse. He was excited because he rarely got the chance to leave the city. He hadn't spent time out in nature in a while.

When he jumped into the back seat with his backpack, the robot turned around, extending an appendage.

"Dr. Snow told me to give you this." Jordan reached out his hand and the robot dropped a small jute bag. Jordan untied it, reaching inside. He pulled out shrivelled up plants.

"She told me to tell you that it's a naturally derived psychotropic substance, and that if you ingest it you will hallucinate. It is perfectly safe, and if you eat it now you will be high by the time we reach our destination. She said, and I quote, no pressure Jordan."

Jordan popped the plants into his mouth without hesitation. He smoked weed whenever he could afford it and was open to trying new things.

The car powered up and merged into morning traffic. Thankfully they were going west and everyone else was going east. Jordan wondered if Val would also be eating these plants. They had a bitter flavour. He wished he had water to wash them down.

As they left the city limits, Jordan watched the scenery flash by, wondering what Val's house looked like. She said there were lots of floor-to-ceiling windows, like in her condo. He felt no effects whatsoever from the herbs.

Maybe they're not very strong, he thought. He shook the little dry crumbs from the bag into his mouth.

The car turned off the highway and onto a feeder road. After about twenty minutes, they turned again onto a narrow country road. Jordan put the window down, resting his arm on the casement, and letting the air blow over him full force. It felt wonderful.

"How far away are we?" he asked. He still felt completely sober.

"Ten minutes," said the robot.

Jordan smiled. It was so beautiful outside. He couldn't wait to sit out under a tree and finish the rest of *The Diviners*.

Valkyrie is such a blessing, he thought. He hoped she had a nice blanket he could wrap around himself, and some snacks.

Maybe I should have brought some snacks, he thought. His mouth dropped open. Why had he never thought about that before? Why had it never even crossed his mind to bring something for Valkyrie?

"Robot, can we make a detour?" he said.

"Certainly."

"Please stop at a store. Like a snack store."

The robot performed a U-turn, and backtracked to the feeder road, where it turned the other way.

Suddenly, Jordan saw a fruit stand by the road.

"Stop robot! Let's get fruit."

The car exited the roadway, and Jordan stumbled out with his backpack. He pulled out his wallet. Eight dollars in change.

He looked over the selection, and then picked out a small basket of ripe peaches that looked delicious. He paid, and walked happily to the car with his purchase.

"Now we can go to Glasshouse," he told the robot.

"Affirmative."

Fifteen minutes later, they turned up Valkyrie's long dirt driveway that wound its way up to the house. It was beautiful in summer but it would be treacherous in winter. She would have to get it ploughed regularly.

The trees parted and the house came into view. Jordan gasped. It was like a dream. The car stopped.

Jordan got out of the vehicle, pulled on his backpack and carefully carried the basket of peaches up to the house. Val came out to greet him.

"Welcome," she said.

Jordan held out the basket proudly. "These are for you."

"Thank you, they look delicious."

"Well, for us. I really want to try one."

Val laughed.

"Is that rude? I'm sorry..." Jordan put his hand on his face. It was really hot, and his skin felt strange under his hand. "My skin... feels strange..."

"Come in the house," said Val. "Don't worry, I had some too."

She gave him the grand tour. He was suitably impressed.

"Val, this is incredible, I mean, it's like the Emerald City in here."

"The Emerald City?" she giggled.

"Yea, and you're the Wizard of Oz."

"I'm totally not... I'm definitely one of the witches."

"Really? I think you're the wizard. Who am I?"

"Who do you feel like?"

"Oh man... I feel like Dorothy. To be honest, I always feel like the hero."

"I can see it. I've never felt like Dorothy."

"Cool. What's that?"

It was the nightingale. He was in a beautiful big cage, and feeling a little better.

"He's a nightingale," she said. She looked close at Jordan. "Like you."

"Like me?" Jordan went over to peer into the cage. He was a sweet little brown bird with a grey beak and a tan belly. "He's cute. Does he sing?"

"Not yet. But I'm sure he will."

"What do you want to do now?" asked Jordan.

"I'm not sure. I'm open. Let's start with a late lunch."

"Sounds good."

Valkyrie had prepared a stew in advance. It was bubbling merrily on the counter in a crockpot. She stirred it and filled two pottery bowls. She handed one to Jordan with a fluffy bread roll, and then turned off the crockpot. The stew was steaming and chunky and delicious.

Before his last few bites, Jordan felt his consciousness alter quickly as the food pushed the hallucinogens around in his stomach.

"You want to play outside?"

"Yes."

They took off their shoes and took off into the forest.

"Tag, you're it," said Val, running away laughing. She was like a blur of pinks in a green kaleidoscope. Jordan kicked into high gear, chasing her. In the forest, and barefooted, she was really hard to catch. His feet were getting thorny and by this point he was really, really stoned.

"Valkyrieeeee," he whined. "Valkyrieeeee! Come back. I give up."

She laughed raucously, dancing back to him. Through the light in the trees, Jordan saw a halo shining around her whole body as she approached. She sat down on the musky leaves beside him.

"There is only one way to catch me," she said.

"What's that?"

"You have to roll three of Aphrodite's apples. That would distract me long enough to catch me."

"Really?"

"You know, like Atalanta…"

"Huh…"

"Have you never heard the myth of Atalanta? You know, the Greek woman who was raised by a she-bear in the wilderness?"

"No! Tell me."

"She was a worshipper of Artemis and took a vow of virginity. She agreed to marry any man who could beat her in a footrace, knowing none ever could. A boy named Hippomenes fell in love with her and asked Aphrodite, the goddess of love, for help. Aphrodite gave him three magically irresistible golden apples to distract her in the race. He dropped the first apple, which she stopped to pick up and he ran past her. She quickly overtook him again. He dropped the second apple, and again she stopped to pick it up and he gained a huge lead. Atalanta was such a swift runner than she was able to overtake him again. When he dropped the third apple, she stopped to pick it up and he won the race. They were married. They fell in love so deep that they accidentally made love in a temple of Cybele, the mother of all gods, and she turned them into lions to pull her chariot, the Earth, for all time."

"Holy shit, I mean, that's intense."

"Mm hm."

They lay down on the forest floor, staring up at the trees. Jordan couldn't believe that just this morning he woke up downtown, and now he was out here in the forest. This vacation was already worthwhile.

"We should go for a swim," he said.

"Yea? The river is pretty small but that could still be fun."

They stood up, brushing off their backs.

Jordan had no idea where they were. He followed Val.

"Let's walk slowly," she said. "I want to take it all in."

They walked along a few feet at a time, stopping to crouch in close and check out moss growing on trees, tiny shoots, patterns on stones, and grooves in tree bark. When she stepped back, Val could see the trees breathing. She clapped with delight.

Finally they made it back to the trail to the house. From behind, the house was made of dark wood, and it blended well into the surrounding forest. Valkyrie smiled and sighed contentedly. Jordan reached over and held her hand. He was happy for her. They walked that way back to the house.

Valkyrie got some towels and brought them down to the river side.

"See right there?" she said, pointing to where the river narrowed. "That's where I'm going to build a bridge."

"Cool. You should put a jumping platform on it."

"Really?" Val would never have thought of that. She was thinking of a more traditional bridge. A jumping platform would make it look decidedly modern. She squinted her eyes, looking at the river, imaging the bridge with a platform.

"Hmmm. I wouldn't put the bridge in the narrow point then. I'd put it at the deepest."

Jordan pulled off all his clothes except for his boxers and scrambled down the steep shore to the river. He was so excited to swim. He crashed in, hooting happily.

Valkyrie followed him in, leaving her clothes on. They splashed around, chatting, playing, and floating silently.

After about an hour, Valkyrie got out.

"I'm going in," she said. "But you stay!"

Jordan blew water out of his lips like a dolphin, wiggling and rolling on his stomach. Valkyrie laughed. She peeled off her wet clothes and wrapped herself in one of the big creamy towels.

I'll have to build a clothesline, she thought. She went into the house to change into a dry dress.

The house was so perfect. She did a pirouette, a big smile on her face. Life was perfect. She looked at the fireplace. It was still too hot outside for a fire in here, but she had a strong urge to make one. She searched the house for a shovel to dig a fire pit outside and found none. She would have to get some tools. For now, she decided to build a fire on the laneway. That would be fine. She went out to the woods to gather sticks. It was really easy picking, because it was the first fire at the new house. There was plenty of dry wood around. Valkyrie made a huge pile. She harvested boughs of soft cedar and wove two crowns, laying them beside the wood pile.

Jordan was loving the river, even though it was small. The water was cold and he was starting to shiver but he didn't care. He lay on his back, tripping out hard, imagining that the water washing over him was cleansing his soul, taking all his filth away with the current. He wanted to shout with joy. Why didn't he?

Why not, he thought. He gathered up every negative thought inside him and screamed it out, long and raw. Then he shifted the sound into singing. He chanted nonsense, just freely singing. He was enjoying the sound of his own voice, and the feeling of letting it all out.

Valkyrie came stumbling to the river's edge. Jordan was singing something incredible, his voice aching with emotion. She felt the pain of it in her own throat as she stood listening. It was the most beautiful sound she had ever heard. Surely there was some kind of magic in it. As she looked down at him suspended in water, he was a sea creature, his hair like seaweed floating around his head, his legs shining like silver in the white water of the river. She felt the same sensation as the first time she heard him singing in the café.

Valkyrie stood listening until Jordan was finished, and then she went to get matches to start her fire.

She set up some middling logs in the log cabin formation, placing pine needles and birch bark in the centre. She put a large nest of twigs on top. She lit a match and held the flame to the bark, whose dry fibers caught quickly. The flame engulfed the pine needles, crackling as smoke rose. Val blew on the twig nest and it caught fire. She added sticks until the heat built enough to sustain itself.

Jordan came up from behind the house. He was holding a towel, his body dripping with water, his nipples firm in the cool evening air. When he saw the fire he grinned.

"Just what I needed," he said, coming close to warm himself. He put out his hands and looked around. The sun was dipping low in the sky. The day had flown by.

"Thank you for today," he said, looking through the flames at Val. She was lying back on her elbows in the dirt, bits of leaves sticking out of her hair. Her eyes were shining in the firelight. She reached over and tossed him a cedar crown.

Jordan grabbed it and put it on.

Valkyrie stood up, putting the other crown in her wild hair. She started to sway, dancing to inaudible music.

Jordan hummed, stomping his feet to create a beat. He started dancing too, adding leg slaps and soft claps to punctuate the percussion. Valkyrie's gestures became more pronounced, matching

Jordan's rhythm. He usually disliked dancing, but he was feeling free and his body wanted to move. Their dance intensified, until they were both leaping and twirling as the sky darkened to black.

The windows of Glasshouse glittered behind them in the darkness, reflecting the firelight. Valkyrie called on the elements—the fire, the water of the river, the air, and the earth—to bless her new house. The fire started to burn down. Val took a pause to gather more wood.

"I'll be right back," she panted.

Jordan slowed his pace, breathing hard.

I need more of this in my life, he thought. He sang a few sombre notes, tilting his head to the sky and offering up his song to eternity.

From the corner of his eye, Jordan saw a majestic silver-white horse emerging slowly from the forest, its massive feathered wings outspread. He turned to focus more closely, and realized that it was really Valkyrie in her white dress. She carried a toppling bundle of wood for the fire. His eyes locked with hers and she smiled, looking wild as ever.

"Your eyes are dancing," he said.

She threw down the logs and did a twirl.

Jordan and Valkyrie continued dancing late into the night. The moon rose high and full in the sky.

"How about another swim?" said Jordan. He was dripping with sweat.

Valkyrie stumbled to a halt. She considered, looking down at her legs. They were muddy up to the knee.

"Probably a good idea."

They made their way down to the river to bathe in the moonlight.

Valkyrie paddled around, scrubbing her feet against one another. The cool water felt lovely against her hot skin.

Jordan was standing at a shallow place in the river staring up at the moon. She came over to him.

"What are you thinking about?" she asked. He turned to look at her. His face was full of emotion. Were those tears on his cheeks? It was difficult to tell because of the water.

"It's okay," she said. That sounded stupid but she didn't know what else to say.

Jordan's shoulders shook once, twice, and then he sobbed. Val put her arms around him, laying her head on his shoulder. He cried and cried.

"You must think I cry all the fucking time," he said, laughing at himself sheepishly.

She said nothing, just squeezed him harder.

"This time, I'm crying cuz I'm happy."

Val laughed softly. She gave his arms a squeeze and let him go. "I'm glad."

"I'm totally and completely happy."

They swam some more, and finally, after a long day of play at Glasshouse, they stumbled inside and went to bed.

CHAPTER SIXTEEN

The next morning, Jordan woke first. He was lying on his back. This was, without a doubt, the most comfortable bed he had ever slept in. Val was curled up facing away from him. Her butt was pressed into his side. It was warm and comforting. Jordan felt like putting an arm around her and spooning her, but that was probably too much. He was growing to love sleepovers with Val and he didn't want to make it weird. This friendship was one of the best things in his life right now.

He sighed, his eyes half closed, enjoying the morning light streaming in every window. The trees were like a green filter, and the glow in the house felt fresh and alive. It was invigorating.

Valkyrie stirred beside him. After a few moments, she rolled over onto her back.

"Good morning," said Jordan.

"Morning." She rolled into him, pressing her nose against his arm. She wove her arm through his and they lay like that as she let herself wake up.

"I'm glad you're here," she said. "Is this okay?" she added, gesturing to her cuddling his arm.

"Yea, it's nice," he said.

Eventually Val sat up, propping some pillows behind her head. The bed was facing the room rather than the windows. That way, the sun was not shining directly on them. Val sang a song lyric about sunlight and butterscotch.

Jordan's mouth dropped. As he looked at her, she took on a whole new dimension and meaning for him. The sound of her voice drew him in, and his eyes lingered on the shape of her lips making the lyrics.

"That was beautiful, do you write music?"

Val laughed. "No that's Joni Mitchell!"

Jordan laughed too. "I've heard she's good, I've been meaning to check her out."

"She's actually the best songwriter of all time, so you definitely should."

They chatted some more curled up in bed, just enjoying each other's company and the sunny summer energy of morning in Glasshouse.

Valkyrie watched Jordan talking; she noticed the way the edges of his soft hair were illuminated by the sun, making the light browns look blond. He looked cozy and clean in a plain white t-shirt, and the usual creases of worry in his face and around his eyes were completely gone. He was relaxed as she had never seen him, talking about his latest music ideas.

"...and I think that's something people might really like, y'know?" His eyes were earnest.

"Hmm? Yea that sounds good." Val smiled at him. Then she added, "Jordan I trust your artist instincts. Don't worry too much about what other people would like. That's thinking like a consumer, it's disingenuous... you have to become a creator, channel your own vibe. That's what the world needs right now. Not more consumers. You have it in you. Let it free."

Her words were blunt, but in the softness of the bed, he could hear the admiration in her tone. She truly respected his art. She saw the potential in him, and he was grateful for that.

"That's harder than it sounds," he said.

"You have everything you need inside you. You're the only one who can make your own dreams come true."

"You're not the first person to tell me that," he said, thinking of Larry at the bar.

"Every dreamer faces turning points where they have to decide to take that leap and work to make it happen. I did too. Now I draw every day… and I'm still dreaming up crazy new ideas."

They filled the quiet of the house talking about their dreams.

"How about some of your famous coffee?" said Jordan.

"Mmm, yea. Do you know how to use a French press?"

"Absolutely not."

"Okay well go to the kitchen and I'll explain it to you."

Jordan crawled out of bed and padded over to the kitchenette. It was on the other side of the fireplace so Val couldn't see him, but the space was relatively small and he could hear her.

"It's the contraption drying on the rack. You put the tall glass cylinder in the metal holder, then put in the ground coffee, then pour in boiling water and press it down slowly with the strainer lever."

Jordan came over to the bed. "Can you show me?" he said.

Val made a whiny sound. Jordan reached under the blankets and tickled her foot. She laughed.

"Fine…" She got out of bed and went to help him.

As the kettle whistled and they ate fresh peaches, Jordan felt like a whole new man. Something changed in him yesterday. He felt like he had hit a reset button and he was full of hope, far away from being ground down by the crushing realities of the gig economy and a society in flux.

What a shitty time to live for artists, he thought, annoyed that his culture valued every other kind of person more. Then he remembered that these days technology was more affordable than ever, that sharing online was easy, and that he needed to stop making excuses. He resolved to turn over a new leaf, and when he got back to the city, the Waves would record their demo.

We're good enough, he thought. *Nothing should be stopping me.* The thought was empowering.

Val spent the afternoon out on the screened porch drawing. She hummed quietly, her pencil getting shorter and shorter as the hours passed. She liked to keep it razor sharp.

Jordan lay under a tree by the house and read *The Diviners.* When he finished it, he went inside to find another book. He poured over the titles on the shelves in the study. He picked a book and popped his head out onto the porch to see what Val was up to. She felt his gaze and lifted her head to look at him. There was a smudge of charcoal on her cheek. She looked like a creature in its element surrounded by rolls of paper and drawing tools. The trees swayed in the breeze behind her. She stretched her arms up.

"Give me another hour or so, and then let's pick some berries," she said. "I noticed on our walk yesterday that the blackberries are ripening up. The afternoon noon heat yesterday may have made them just perfect."

"Okay."

Jordan went back to reading, and when she was ready Val came outside with a basket. They walked down the path behind the house to a sunny clearing in the trees.

"There was an old farmstead here," said Val. "That's why you can see some European perennials in this field." She pointed to a line of orange lilies growing in the grass.

"These blackberries here are the kind developed by First Nations." She reached down and plucked a juicy berry from the vine. "See how big it is? The natives shared a lot of fruits and vegetables with the settlers to help them survive. The Europeans tried to create a thorn-free berry, but those are small and they don't taste very good. They don't do well in nature either because the thorns keep the animals away long enough to let the plants spread their seed. So even if there was once a European variety on this land too, it would have died off when this old farm went to seed."

Val climbed carefully through the heaping brambles, making sure not to tear her dress. They gathered up all the ripe berries in the basket. The day was hot. Jordan peeled off his shirt and stuffed it in his back pocket where it hung down to his knees.

They walked back up to the house slowly, enjoying the sun and the warm breeze.

"Open," said Val, and they stepped through the glass door. Val went to the kitchen, putting the berries on the counter and pouring herself a glass of water.

"Water?" she asked.

"Yes, please," said Jordan. She poured him a glass and he came over to drink it, downing the whole thing in one long gulp.

Valkyrie looked at her fingers. They were stained purple. She reached in the basket and pulled out two berries. She popped one in her mouth, and the other she extended up to feed to Jordan. He opened his mouth, his parted lips touching her fingers. He closed his eyes, reaching up with his hand and touching her hand softly. He held it there, taking the berry in his mouth, the explosion of flavour sweet and rich. He kissed her hand; he couldn't help himself. His hand started to tremble on hers, both with nerves and excitement.

Val stepped in close. Jordan put his other hand around her waist, drawing her in. His bare skin was warm and Val pressed up against him, closing her eyes. They held each other and an energy released between them that they both couldn't turn back from. Val touched her lips to Jordan's neck softly, and he slipped his hand over her jaw and behind her ear, drawing her lips up to his. Their lips met, and they kissed softly, sweetly, both a bit surprised that this was happening but giving in to the moment. Val kissed his cheek, the bridge of his nose, his closed eye. He pressed his face against her lips with longing, feeling his energy reaching out to her from his chest, and he wrapped his long arms tighter around her, rubbing her back, feeling the softness of her cotton dress against her bare skin. He kissed her long beautiful neck, and her hands trailed down his back, massaging his hips. He moved against her with his body. She pressed back and he knew that she wanted him.

Val pulled away slowly, leading him to the bed. He followed. He couldn't believe this was happening. He looked at her soft shape under her dress and he felt pleasure moving down his abdomen. He unbuttoned his pants. She pulled off her dress, standing in the afternoon light of Glasshouse completely naked. He put his hand on her cheek again, drawing her in for a kiss. She ran her hands down his back to the top of his pants. She pulled them down and he pulled them off all the way, kicking them off onto the floor.

"I want to feel your skin against mine," she said softly. He kissed her deeper, wanting the same thing. They climbed up onto the bed. Val pushed him down on his back and she lay on top of him, luxuriating in the feeling of his warmth beneath her. She rubbed her hands along his arms, kissing his face, and sitting up to admire him.

"You're beautiful," she murmured, running her fingers over his chest. She bent down, kissing him, tasting him with her tongue. He held her thighs, straddled over his, running his hands up her backside. She was so soft. She bent down and kissed him.

The feeling of her breasts rubbing against his chest made Jordan feel another surge of pleasure, and he squeezed his arms around her, holding her tight, kissing her more intensely. She started moving her pelvis, pressing up against him. His erection grew and he shifted his position so that her warmth was pressing up against it. Val's clitoris rubbed him and rubbed him and she felt herself coming close to orgasm. She reached down and slipped him inside, grinding down, the wave of sensation rising in her until she felt it from the tips of her toes to the crown of her head. She pumped harder, crying out with pleasure as the wave passed, leaving a tingling in every nerve.

She relaxed her full weight on top of him. He kept thrusting, himself feeling desire building, holding her against him, his face buried in her neck. She felt incredible. He ran his hands along her soft skin, pushing deep into her, dizzy with lust, the feeling slowly building and building.

Valkyrie started moving again, pushing against him, rubbing her clitoris along his shaft, letting another orgasm grow. She moaned with pleasure, her excitement rising with his. Jordan gasped as she moved—he could barely handle it. He tried to hold back, and just as he felt her spasm around him, he came more intensely than he ever had before.

He held her, on top of him, his hands in her wild hair, breathing hard as she shook with pleasure. They held each other until his penis shrunk into itself.

Val rolled off. She lay beside him, holding his hand lightly in hers. They both relaxed as their senses were flooded with endorphins.

Valkyrie went to pee and when she came back, she crawled on top of Jordan, holding him tight. He put his arms around her, kissing the top of her head. He lifted her hand to his lips, kissing every inch. They both sighed, cuddling tighter and peppering each other lightly with kisses.

They spent the rest of the afternoon in bed, exploring one another.

CHAPTER SEVENTEEN

When they were finally able to drag themselves out of each other's arms and out of bed, Val and Jordan went out to the forest to gather wood to build another fire. Val showed Jordan how to select low-hanging dead branches and leave the living ones intact. They filled their arms with wood and brought it to the laneway where they built the fire the night before.

Val started setting up the fire.

"Want to grab me the matches?" she asked. Jordan went in to get them. He came back out, and Val lit her structure, blowing it to life. Jordan brought some blankets with him, and he arranged them on the ground for them to lie on.

When the fire reached the point of burning on its own, Valkyrie relaxed onto the blankets with Jordan. They entwined their limbs, locked together again after barely an hour separate.

"I can't believe this is happening," said Jordan. He was looking into Val's eyes and she saw something yielding and vulnerable there. She held him tighter.

She kissed him, teasing gently with her tongue. He cupped her backside in his hands, pulling her up against him, kissing her earnestly. She could feel his arousal. She felt her own warming up to match it. She pulled off her dress, enjoying the warmth of the summer air and the hot fire against her bare skin. Jordan followed, stripping down to nothing. The sight of his body lying in blankets in the firelight, surrounded by trees in the night air deeply turned her on, and she wrapped her legs around him, moving him into her. Jordan sighed with pleasure at the feeling of her wet warmth, holding her to him, kissing her deep, and they rolled in the blankets, thrusting softly, kissing tenderly. Jordan had never felt so aroused in his life. He willed himself to hold back, making the moments last longer as Valkyrie orgasmed again and again in his arms. Finally he let himself relax and he came hard. They held each other, caressing each other's skin in the firelight. They looked up at the stars. The fire crackled merrily, shooting bronze sparks up into the night.

"We should sleep out here," said Val.

"I'm down."

She squeezed him close. "I haven't slept outside in a long time."

"Me too."

"I'm so happy… this place is everything I wanted it to be."

"It's pretty magical," said Jordan.

"Winter's going to be nice too."

Jordan looked at her. "You're going to invite me back before then, right?"

"Of course!"

They punctuated their conversation with kisses.

Jordan wanted to ask her about what things would be like after the weekend was over, when they were back in Ottawa. He didn't though. He was afraid to.

"So… are you on birth control?" he asked her. His ears turned a little red and he wasn't sure why.

"I can't get pregnant."

"Oh. Cool. Good to know," he said.

They chatted and cuddled under the stars as the fire burned down to coals until, eventually, they fell asleep, wrapped up in one another.

The next morning, Jordan woke up at dawn. A fine mist covered the grasses. He shivered, pulling a blanket corner up over them. He lay on his back, looking up at the brightening sky, feeling perfectly at peace. He had no thoughts at all in his mind, no nagging doubts or anxieties. The pleasure and release of yesterday burned them all away. He decided that he couldn't fall back asleep. He slipped out of the blankets, pulling on his jeans. He walked down behind the house to the river. He sat on the steep bank to watch the sun rise.

The weekend was flying by, but this moment was slow. Jordan watched the subtle change of colours in the sky, and the shifts in the landscape under different light. For the second time this weekend, he had the overwhelming feeling of starting fresh, being reborn as a new man. He felt that life was opening up to a world of new possibilities. Tears stung the corners of his eyes. He felt like his heart was breaking open, and it felt wonderful.

When the glowing orb of the sun became visible along the treeline and the sky relaxed into a cheerful blue, Jordan stood up and went into the house to make coffee with the French press.

Valkyrie woke up alone in the yard beside the skeleton of the fire. She breathed in sharply, filling her lungs with morning air. She decided that she would get an iron cauldron so she could make maple syrup in the winter. She would have to find a better place for a proper fire pit. Glasshouse was complete inside, but outside she had many small projects to work on.

Jordan came over from the house holding two steaming mugs. He sat down beside her, handing her one.

"Coffee," he said, giving her a peck on the lips.

"Mmm, thank you," she said, holding it in both hands and breathing in the steam.

They decided to have a relaxing day reading and drawing.

At dinner time, they had leftover stew, and after they took a swim in the river. They kissed each other constantly, tasting each other's lips at every opportunity.

As the sun went down, they went to bed early, making love for hours with long breaks between sessions talking quietly together, wrapped in each other's embrace, indulging in the pleasure of their bodies connecting. They fell asleep with their lips almost touching on the pillow, floating on the bed suspended by chains beneath a flood of silver moonlight from the windows above.

When Val woke up Jordan was cradled in her arms. It was beautiful feeling, to wake up with the weight of a lover on top of her like a blanket. This close, with the light pouring in the Glasshouse windows, she could see that he had a light dusting of freckles across his nose from their time in the sun. A single lock of soft brown hair lay over his face. She brushed it gently behind his ear, and leaned forward. She kissed his forehead. He stirred slightly in his sleep, pulling his arm tighter in embrace. She felt warmth rise in her, the feeling of his arm around her and his body pressed up against her turning her on. She moved her pelvis slightly, rubbing up against him, remembering last night and falling asleep exhausted. Her vagina still ached from the attention. Jordan sighed softly, rubbing back, waking from a hazy and beautiful dream into an infinitely better one. She shifted him onto her fully, moving her hips and bringing him instantly aroused. He kissed her neck and breasts, softly, waking from his dream, his heart rising in his throat, his energy reaching out to connect with hers. Their bodies moved together in harmony, finding connection, deeply and miraculously synchronous.

"We have incredible chemistry," said Val when they were finished.

Jordan agreed, but he didn't know how to put it into words. It was like when they were making love they were reading each other's thoughts, the world was falling away, and the sensations of desire and fulfillment were overwhelming. He'd had sex many times before, but this felt like something different.

It's Sunday, thought Jordan. He felt sadness at the edges of his thoughts. *I have to go home today.* He pulled Val in closer, kissing her shoulder, nuzzling her with his nose.

"Let's go out for dinner tonight," she said. "I feel like Indian food."

Jordan warmed at the thought of keeping this going—whatever it was.

"Sounds delicious," he said. He kissed her throat, and then lower, between her breasts, trailing his lips and tongue down her body until he was between her legs, massaging and caressing her clitoris with his mouth. He dug deeper, holding her legs around his head, tasting her sweetness as she lay back in the pillows, her eyes closed in sighs of pleasure. He couldn't believe how voracious he was. He just couldn't get enough of her.

That evening, Valkyrie called the robot to take them back into the city. They gathered their things, straightened up the house, and the car arrived just as the sun was setting. Val could have stayed longer, but she could tell that Jordan was anxious about going back alone. She would keep him company in the car.

And I always have work to do in the city anyway, she thought.

"You hungry yet?" she asked as the lush forest gave way to farmhouses, and then rows and rows of suburban housing. They were approaching the city.

"Yea," he said quietly. He was holding her hand and he gave it a squeeze.

The car drove straight to the restaurant.

"This is our first time going out for dinner together," said Jordan.

"True. You'll find I love going out for dinner…"

They were seated in a cozy table beside a statue of Kali.

Jordan felt like he was having a surreal experience as he looked across the table at Val eating her dinner.

Is this a date? He wondered.

"I'm working tomorrow morning," he said.

"The Cherry?"

Jordan nodded.

"Too bad you can't get something more reliable that involves music," she said.

Jordan had never really tried. He assumed that jobs like that were mythical creatures.

"The Cherry won't be forever."

"No. Your music will take off."

"That reminds me, I'm going to book a recording session as soon as I can get the money together."

"You haven't recorded your songs? You've gotten pretty far, considering. Once you put them online you'll get tons more fans I'm sure."

"You really think so?"

"Certainly."

There was a pause. Valkyrie was weighing her words.

"Let me pay for the recording session Jordan."

"Aww it's okay Val. I'm saving up."

"Seriously, think nothing of it. I want a recording of my song anyway. I'll pay for it."

Jordan grinned. He knew which song was hers.

"Maybe I don't want you to have a recording, because you'd stop inviting me over to sing it for you."

Val laughed. "No, I won't."

They looked into each other's eyes, their faces softening at the same time, remembering the incredible weekend, feeling its healing medicine in their bodies.

"Okay." Jordan's voice cracked. He cleared his throat and turned down to look at his plate.

"Good. You find the place. Just tell me when and I'll cover it." She thought about offering to book it too, but she was too busy.

He would have to figure that out.

"Thanks."

Being my lover has its perks, she thought. She didn't say it though. Too tacky.

"This is really good," said Jordan, finishing his plate.

"Mmm. One of my favourite places, and you picked a great dish."

The server came over with mukhwas, the after dinner mouth-freshening snack of fragrant seeds.

"Can you add another of that dish to my account," said Val, pointing to Jordan's plate. "To go."

The server nodded and went to tell the kitchen.

Val and Jordan chewed their mukhwas, and when the to-go plate was ready the server brought it out in a bamboo container.

"Shubh din," she said.

"Good evening," said Val. They headed out.

"Jordan's house," said Val to their robot driver. The car powered up and took off toward Centretown.

Jordan and Val sat close in the back seat, holding hands. When the car pulled up to Jordan's building, they lingered. Val put her arms around him, laying her head on his shoulder. She didn't kiss him because she knew that would lead to a much longer goodbye. She pulled away, handing him the takeout.

"For you, for tomorrow when you get home from work," she said.

"Thanks," he said. "You didn't have to do that."

"I don't have to do anything. I wanted to." Valkyrie had reached an age and a stage in her career where she didn't have to do anything she didn't want to.

Jordan took the box and got out of the car. Val drove away.

CHAPTER EIGHTEEN

Valkyrie went into the office on Monday to sort out some administrative details. She wanted to personally thank Mika for her work on Glasshouse, and chat with her assistant about upcoming meetings with potential partners in the ventures she was exploring.

As the car pulled up to the white quartz building downtown,

she realized that she should build a new Hammer & Bone headquarters in her new style. A rich wood veneer with shiny techno gadgetry would project the sense of Futurustic she wanted to convey with her arcologies. The quartz building was so familiar to her now. She remembered the feeling she had staring up at its greatness when she first built it. She got a taste of that feeling again with Glasshouse. She wanted to feel it on a megalithic scale.

"Greetings, Dr. Snow," said the concierge.

She breezed by into the elevator, lost in thought, realizing only as the doors closed that it wasn't a robot, but a human at the desk today. Too late. She would be more polite on her way down.

When she reached her floor, there was a strange energy in the air. People were sitting uncomfortably and there was a pervasive sense of gloom. What was going on?

Sukhwant came toward her.

"Dr. Snow. Good to see you."

"What's going on?" she asked, handing her a rolled up drawing to file in the stacks.

"It's... America. There's more trouble."

Val frowned. She walked briskly to her office, sitting in her chair and folding her hands on the desk.

"Oracle, what's the latest news on the Rebels situation to the south?"

The device glowed green, and then projected a hologram of real-time news footage.

"President Harold Spence has declared a state of emergency and the Rebels have been put down and captured or shot in most American cities. The Rebels are still holding Charlottesville Virginia and Pulaskie Tennessee, and there are scattered forces committing acts of violence across America, but now that military forces have been deployed to deal with the domestic crisis the Rebels should fall quickly."

Images and video flashed on the screen of school shootings, hangings, and cars plowing down pedestrians. Valkyrie's face creased with distaste.

"But they have it under control?"

"That depends how you define having it under control," said the Oracle.

"Meaning?"

"An issue of great concern in the Canadian media is how Spence is dealing with it."

"Explain."

"Black, Latino and Muslim-Americans are being detained by US military personnel and can now arbitrarily lose their citizenship under state of emergency legislation."

"*What?* Aren't all the rebels white nationalists?"

"Yes. And if there were no Black, Latino and Muslim-Americans, ostensibly the white nationals wouldn't be angry anymore."

"That makes no sense."

"There is no sense to it from an outsider's perspective. It's cultural."

"What's going on down there?" muttered Val with disbelief.

"I just told you," said the Oracle calmly.

Is that sarcasm? thought Val with surprise. She stood up and walked to the door of her office. She looked out at her employees, working away at their desks. Like the Canadian population in general, they were a group of people from highly mixed backgrounds, at least half people of colour, and many manifested hybrid identities, with symbols and flags of other places decorating their work spaces.

"That's not all," said the Oracle behind her. She turned back into the room.

"Spence has ordered the military to find all the gay people in major cities and confine them to specific neighbourhoods and residential buildings. He is saying that it is for their own safety, but human rights monitors are concerned."

"Show me," said Val, taking two strides back to the desk. The hologram flashed scenes of men in uniforms prodding people holding suitcases. She felt a lump rise in her throat.

"Are we taking refugees?" she asked.

"Yes. 40 000 refugees over the next six months, but demands are much higher."

Valkyrie left the office to find Sukhwant.

"Please allocate forty percent of our new housing project to refugees," she said quietly. "I want work visas escalated for gay engineers applying to work for us. Put out a notice. We'll find positions for them."

People coming on a work visa would not take away from the refugee tally. Val tapped the wall compulsively, a frown on her face.

"Tell our partners we're putting together a student visa fund. We expect buy-in. All the targeted people welcome to apply." A student visa would allow at least temporary relief for young people fleeing.

Valkyrie wondered how long the American states would remain united under these conditions. Several years ago, the USA built a wall at the Canadian border from Saskatchewan to the Great Lakes, and along the Saint Lawrence Seaway in Upper New York State. Valkyrie had not visited south of the wall since it was built, but the last time she was there, back in the 2020s, she was surprised to see so many abandoned houses with falling rooves and caving walls right in the middle of cities by day, and empty streets punctuated by the sound of police sirens and gunshots at night. That was the cities. The countryside was not much better, with people spending cold winters in busted trailers. The rich lived in their luxurious gated communities of course, but it was only a matter of time before the consequences of opting out of socialism would manifest. It reminded her of trips to India, where her friends pointed out grand lavish palaces, but she was much more captivated by the shacks and the slums. The difference was that everyone in the US had guns.

The Rebels were inevitable, thought Val. But with these latest measures, Val suspected that things would unravel sooner than later. She just hoped that the damage would not be too extreme.

Jordan went to the gym after work on Monday. It was open late and he missed being there. After a few weeks of going every second day or so, his body grew to enjoy his visits. As he pedalled on the stationary bike, he thought about calling Val.

Too soon? he thought. *Probably.* He should wait at least a few days. When would be a good time? Thursday? He really wanted to talk to her before that. He'd love to sleep in her bed tonight, but that would be pathetic, right? Jordan had no experience with mature relationships.

He pedalled harder, willing himself not to think of her soft body on top of him, moving back and forth, her eyes rolling back as she orgasmed. He'd never been with a woman who came so much. It was unbelievable. He would wait until she called him, he decided.

He finished up his workout, and went to the change room to shower.

But what if she never called him? What if she was waiting for him to call?

No, he thought. *That's stupid. Valkyrie Snow doesn't wait for other people to call her.*

But that meant that if she didn't call it meant that she didn't want to see him.

Jordan sighed. He wished he could text her. That was a good compromise.

When he was done in the shower, he checked his phone. No missed calls. He scrolled through his text messages. He clicked on Charlotte's name.

> Thinking of you

> Hope the show was good.

That was nice of her, thought Jordan. He typed.

> Thanks

Jordan:

Jordan clicked the home screen. He felt unsatisfied. He clicked on his conversation with Raven.

> Sorry but I couldn't sleep so I had to head out and catch some zzz in my own bed. Have a great day.

Jordan :

Raven had not responded to his message. He wondered what she was thinking. Was she waiting for him to text her? Did she think he was an asshole? Or maybe she just wasn't interested. It was hard to say. Jordan slipped his phone back into his pocket and went home. He resisted the urge to call Val, and went to sleep alone.

Valkyrie spent the next week in back-to-back meetings dealing with the fallout from the chaos south of the border. Her investments were a mess, and she was afraid that her supply and manufacturing chain would be disrupted. This was almost as bad as when the wall was built. The border access points bottlenecked and it took months to get back on schedule. Things were never quite the same. It was a stressful time, but it was actually a blessing in disguise for her business in some ways because she was inspired to incorporate more Canadian wood into her designs. Futurustic relied much more on products accessible via East-West trade routes from places like Quebec and British Columbia, than North-South.

Many of Val's partners were equally frustrated at the disruptions to their business. Many were considering moving south to Mexico. Some were considering endorsing campaigns to return the Mexican-U.S. border to its original boundary north of New Mexico and Texas.

"I like dealing with New California. I'd rather deal with the Republic of Texas than this American mess," said one CEO from Texas in a meeting. "We're in talks with New Mexico about a trade route through their state from the Republic of Texas to New Cali, and from there we ship by boat freight right into Vancouver. We'll figure this out."

Valkyrie Snow looked at him with her impenetrable gaze. She wasn't going to waste time getting into foreign secession politics at these meetings. She wanted to stick to economics, although these days they were much the same thing.

"What kind of delays are we looking at over the next six months?" she asked. "I'm not backing out of our arrangement, but I want some guarantees. Not just verbal. We need contracts."

Valkyrie received reports from her contacts in Russia that there was a serious international storm brewing. She was pulling out of all trade relations in the United States unless money was paid up front.

It was Friday and Jordan hadn't heard from Valkyrie all week.

She's done with you, hissed Snake. *She got what she wanted and now she's moved on.*

He was annoyed with her, but at the same time he missed her.

It was almost the weekend. She was probably heading out to Glasshouse.

Alone? Or with someone else?

Jordan tried to keep his cool.

Just call her, he thought to himself. But for some reason he couldn't.

As Jordan was walking home from work, he had a great idea.

She wanted me to book a recording session right? So that's a good reason to get in touch.

As soon as he got home, he fired out a message to a recording studio he followed on social media. As soon as he firmed up a date, he would call Val.

He went to bed relieved.

In the morning, Jordan had a response. The studio could fit in the Waves in three weeks. He stared at the message on the screen.

That was so easy. Why hadn't he done it before? He felt a rush of pride. They were officially recording their demo.

He texted all the boys to let them know. Then he got dressed for work and headed out to Bridgehead for his morning coffee.

Jordan walked into the Cherry right on time. As he scoured pots and pans, he couldn't stop thinking about Val. He thought about climbing on top of her in the floating bed, her riding him out by the campfire, the taste of her pussy, how she squeezed his head between her thighs when she couldn't take it anymore. As he scrubbed, he pressed his groin up against the sink, letting his boner grow enough that it felt good but not enough to draw attention to it. He had hours to kill at work. His sex drive was through the roof.

Tonight when he got off work he would call her to invite her to their recording session. Hopefully she would ask him to come over. The thought of going over to her place after work made him curl his toes in anticipation. He sighed.

"You look happy," said Earl, softer than usual, from behind him. Jordan's whole body stiffened with shame. His cheeks blushed crimson and he scrubbed harder. He said nothing.

"I said, you look happy," said Earl louder. Jordan stopped scrubbing. He turned around, soapy water dripping all over the floor. His throat felt thick but he swallowed hard.

"Sorry what? It's hard to hear back here."

"Get back to work," breathed Earl, pushing past him. Jordan turned back to the sink, bending over and resuming scrubbing. On his way back out, Earl brushed his crotch across Jordan's ass, bent over the sink. Jordan spent the rest of his shift feeling sick to his stomach.

Each night Valkyrie got home late, exhausted, and either went straight to bed or stayed up all night making international phone calls.

She wanted to spend the weekend relaxing at Glasshouse, but she knew that she would be dealing with work things instead. She could probably get away with working remotely from Glasshouse for a day, but she didn't really want to. She would rather finish this and then play without stress.

Tonight she couldn't bring herself to stay up and work. She slipped into something cozy and went straight to bed. As she felt herself falling to sleep, the phone rang.

"No," she said. "No more calls, house." She had explicitly told Sukhwant not to direct any calls to her private line. She would deal with it in the morning.

The phone rang and rang. Then the line dropped. Jordan was lying on his bed all alone. Should he try calling again? *No.*

She must be out, he thought. He didn't really know how she spent her evenings, since he really didn't know her all that well, after all. He kicked off his shoes onto the floor, and unzipped his pants, resigned to spending the night at home. He pulled off his clothes and pushed them down to the end of the bed, crawling under the sheet. He pulled it up over his head. After a few minutes, his hand found his penis. He hadn't masturbated in a long time. He played a bit, fondling himself until he was semi-hard. He wasn't committed. He let his mind drift to the now-familiar fantasy of Val. That thought and his own touch were unsatisfying. Earl popped into his head suddenly; Earl brushing his dick up against Jordan's backside in the back of the restaurant. His boner melted instantly. He wanted to fall asleep but now he was too angry. He pulled out his phone and willed the internet to soothe him to sleep.

He had a text message. From Charlotte.

> **What you up to?**

Charlotte:
He responded.

> Nothing much. Just trying to sleep

Jordan:
Charlotte read his answer and didn't respond.
Maybe she misses me, he thought. *Or maybe she's just bored too.*

Jordan had the next day off. He knew the Waves should be practicing, but he needed a break from reality so he played video games with Jerome all day. That evening, Valkyrie called.

"Hello?"

"Hi Jordan."

"What's up?" His voice was a flood of relief.

I'm returning your call."

She sounded so cold.

"Umm, yea. I booked a studio session, and I wanted to let you know."

"I see."

There was an awkward silence.

"So… it's in a couple weeks… you want to come?"

"I want to."

Jordan breathed a sigh of relief.

"I want to, but work is crazy right now… maybe in a few weeks things will clear up though."

"Oh."

"Send me the date? I'll put it in the schedule."

"Okay." He opened up Instagram and sent her the information.

"Have a good night, Jordan."

"Goodnight."

Click.

His heart dropped down to his stomach. That phone call was deeply unsatisfying. The app was open in front of him, and Jordan wanted to ad *xoxo*, or *miss you*, or something to his message, but that seemed lame and pathetic. If he added it now, it would look like he had sent it casually while they were talking. He wouldn't be able to add it later because that would be like he was sending her a whole new message, one she didn't ask him to send. Then she would know he was thinking about her all the time. It was now or never.

Miss you

He hit 'send' before he had a chance to delete it. He stared at the sent message. He groaned inwardly.

What an idiot, he thought. There he was, pouring his heart out, and she didn't even want to see him this weekend. He felt like such a loser. He quickly turned off his phone before he did anything else that was stupid.

Valkyrie was tired but after she was done her work for the night she opened Instagram to put Jordan's studio date in her calendar before she forgot. She saw his message.

He misses me. She smiled. She responded:

> **Miss you too.**

That night, she dreamed about Jordan's sweet expression, his long arms, and his boundless energy as she drifted off to sleep. She did miss him, and she looked forward to seeing him again when she wasn't so busy.

Jordan woke up to a text message from Charlotte.

> **Are we going to be friends now? :P**

Charlotte:
He responded.
Jordan:

> I hope so :P

He wondered what that meant.

Valkyrie had replied to his message with "I miss you too", but it was meaningless because she was just responding to his "I miss you". Did she really miss him or was she just saying it because he had said it?

Jordan spent the next week deliberating about what went wrong with Val. What did he do to turn her off? She'd been really into him at Glasshouse, so why was she suddenly not interested anymore? Was it something he'd said? He poured over their last conversation at the restaurant. He didn't really even know what he wanted from her, or from their relationship; all he knew was that he ached to go back to Glasshouse and spend time with her. The leaves would start to change soon. Fall was coming.

Things with Charlotte were getting interesting. They were texting each other almost every day. No one brought up seeing one another in real life. For now, it was nice to have someone to interact with on those nights when he couldn't sleep.

The Waves got in one practice before their recording session.

They meant to practice more, but they were recording old songs they already knew well so it was hard to get up the motivation. The day arrived quicker than they all expected.

"You look nice," said Jordan with surprise.

Jerome was wearing a new sweater. "Rachel got it for me," he said.

"Is she coming?" asked Matt. He wanted her to take pictures of their recording session.

"She's meeting us at the studio," said Jerome.

It was like picture day at school, except that they were all grown up now. Matt also looked cleaned up. Bubba looked like his usual slobby self, but he wouldn't be in the photos.

They walked down to Wellington Street. The studio was in the basement of an old church in Chinatown, only a fifteen minute walk away.

"We really should get some street shots," said Matt. He handed his phone to Bubba. Jerome was holding his guitar. It was picture perfect. Bubba held up the phone and snapped some pictures of the boys walking. They were all grinning like crocodiles. Jordan hooted and ran up a bike lane divider. The energy was high.

"Okay now a serious one," said Matt. They stood in a line and pouted slightly, looking soulful.

When they arrived at the studio, Rachel was already there. She had a good camera in her hands. She took a few more shots before they went in.

The church was decommissioned and it housed several small shops and offices. The receiving room for the recording studio was upstairs. A scuffed up 1950s coffee table covered in music magazines sat between two matching vintage-inspired couches. There were framed prints on the walls of famous Canadian bands. "The Hymnal" was painted on the wood paneled wall in bold red strokes. There was a sign:

Please wait to be escorted downstairs. Recording in progress.

"This is it," whispered Bubba excitedly. Jordan and Jerome grinned.

"Proud of you," said Rachel, kissing Jerome's lips.

"Awww," said Bubba, snapping a photo.

Jordan felt a little pang of emotion. What was it? Pride? Jealousy, melancholy, happiness… he didn't know anymore. His emotions were a jumble.

"Sit on the couch," said Rachel. "Let me get a photo in the lobby."

The boys sat on the little couches. Rachel snapped some shots, framing the Hymnal sign in the background. The vintage décor added to the effect. These would look great on Instagram.

"Okay, one without Alex," said Matt. Jerome frowned. Jordan looked uncomfortable.

"Come on, man," said Bubba.

"You have slobber on your shirt."

Bubba looked down at his top. "That's mustard," he protested, but he stood up. He walked to the door.

"We love you man," said Jerome with a grin.

"Yea yea." Alex pulled out a pack of smokes. He would smoke it off outside.

When he came back in, he had someone with him.

"Look who I found," he said. "It's V. Snow."

Jordan felt his heart jump.

She's here! he thought. He grinned. He wanted to go over and hug her but he stayed put.

"You made it," he said.

"I made it."

"Hi," said Rachel, holding out her hand. "You must be Valkyrie Snow. I'm Rachel. Jerome's partner."

Matt tried to catch Jerome's eye and make a face, but Jerome ignored him. They had always made fun of guys who called their woman "partner". Matt frowned.

That's what happens when you try to pull out of your league, he thought. *Rachel's got him by the balls.*

"Pleasure to meet you, Rachel," said Valkyrie, shaking Rachel's hand. "You must be Jerome," she said, holding out her hand to him. He looked down at it. Rachel looked momentarily embarrassed. Then he shook it.

"Yea I'm Jerome. Nice to meet you."

There was an awkward silence. Rachel looked at Jordan, expecting him to introduce Matt. Jordan was clueless. She looked at Alex. He could see by her expression that she was trying to tell him something but he had no idea what. Rachel couldn't believe these boys had no manners whatsoever. She would have to explain introductions to Jerome before he met her parents that evening.

"That's Matt," she finally said.

Valkyrie nodded to him politely.

"What do you do?" she asked Rachel.

"I study law. University of Ottawa," she said.

Valkyrie nodded.

"I thought it might be something like that," she said.

Rachel smiled with pride.

"I'm the drummer," said Matt. Valkyrie looked at him with her impassive expression.

A group of Lolita-style Harajuku girls came up the stairs, one holding an electric guitar and another an electric violin. A young man in a leather vest and jeans came up the stairs behind them.

"The Waves?" he asked, looking at his phone. Jordan nodded. "We're ready for you."

They followed him down the stairs. The walls were old stones and concrete blocks. The air smelled a bit musty, with faint whiffs of church. The floor had been re-covered in click faux wood. The man led them through a set of sound proof doors. There was a sign:

The Pulpit

They all went inside, and the man locked the doors behind them. There was a glass wall at the far end of the basement. The room inside was covered with acoustic foam. As they approached, Jordan could see a sign on the door:

The Confessional

Bubba and Rachel tittered.

"I'm Georgio, this is Elephantine," said the man in the leather vest.

A woman sat at the sound board with large round glasses, a plaid suit and an orange tie. Her hair was pulled up into a smooth high ponytail. She peered at them as they walked by.

"Go on into the Confessional," said Georgio.

Jordan felt his fingers shaking with excitement. He had warmed up his voice this morning but he wished now that he had done more.

Oh well. Here we are, he thought.

He wasn't nervous. If there was one thing in this world that he wasn't anxious about it was singing. He knew his voice was killer, even on a bad day. Plus Valkyrie was here. She was watching. She hadn't forgotten about him. He turned to look at her; she was staring right at him. Her expression was almost unreadable, but Jordan could see intensity there. She reached out and squeezed his hand. He felt electricity jolt from his fingertips right down his body.

Jerome, Jordan and Matt shuffled into the vocal booth, while Bubba, Rachel and Valkyrie stood in the control room to watch.

"Are you not in the band?" said Georgio. "You'll have to wait upstairs."

He unlocked the door to let them out and Rachel and Bubba turned to leave.

"I'm staying," said Valkyrie.

Elephantine turned around angrily. "You're disrupting my process," she said.

Bubba and Rachel shuffled out.

"This is what I came for," said Val, leaning up against the wall. Elephantine could see that she wasn't moving. She looked Val up and down. Val looked at her intently, arching an eyebrow. Elephantine turned to Georgio.

"Fine," she said. Georgio locked the door.

In the vocal room, the boys fell into place. This would be just like rehearsals. Jordan stroked the mic stand, closing his eyes and pretending that this was just another day recording albums in the life of a famous musician.

"Don't touch the microphone," said Georgio through the speaker. He and Elephantine shared a look.

Jordan's hands shot to his sides.

"Put on the headphones," said Georgio.

"Take it easy on us, it's our first time," said Jordan with a grin.

Valkyrie crossed her arms on her chest.

They did some basic sound checks, and Georgio directed them where to stand.

"Time to confess your sins," said Elephantine into the booth when they were ready.

Matt counted them in on sticks and then crashed in on the drums. They were off.

As they reached the chorus, Jordan made love to the mic, wailing his heart out.

Elephantine mouthed something they couldn't hear to Georgio. He buzzed in on the speaker. "Too hot. Step back and try it again."

They settled into a rhythm, getting used to the process. They blazed through their songs. They reached their last number. It was the Nightingale song.

My song, thought Val. She uncrossed her arms. As the Waves started to play, the energy in the room changed. Jordan looked straight at Val. She felt heat in her face, remembering Glasshouse and the feel of Jordan's chest pressed against her. The sound of his voice made her legs tingle. Her breath quickened as the song finished.

"It was too fast," said Val quietly from the back of the control room. "Try it again."

"I agree," said Elephantine, not turning around.

"Slower," said Georgio into the speaker. "We're going to do another take."

They sang it again. This time, Jordan's voice was even more intense, grinding and rising in all the right places. It was a gorgeous take.

Valkyrie looked at the time on the computer. It was getting late and she had a lot of work to finish today.

"We're going to do the first song again," said Elephantine to Georgio.

"Elle says you can take the first song again if you want," said Georgio into the booth. "We have time."

"I have to go," said Valkyrie. "Can I do payment upstairs while they finish?" Georgio took her up to pay while the Waves replayed their opening number. It was much better the second time.

Valkyrie took off, and Georgio went back down to the control room.

"That's a wrap on your roughs. We'll send you a digital file of the comp track in about two weeks, and when you give the OK we can turn your engineered demo in another two weeks."

"Thanks," said Jerome sticking out his hand for a shake. He was getting the hang of this.

"What's the bill?" said Matt. They had saved up enough cash with their gigs to pay for the recording.

"Oh. Your friend—Dr. Snow," said Georgio, looking at the receipt, "paid the whole shot."

Bubba whistled. "Damn. You sure you ain't bangin her?" he tousled Jordan's hair. One look at Jordan's expression and they all knew the answer.

"It happened! Good for you!"

"Good for us," said Matt with a smile.

But where did she go? thought Jordan. He was hoping they would get a chance to talk.

"Thanks," he said to Georgio.

"Let's celebrate this victory, boys," said Matt.

"I'd love to, but I can't. Going to Rachel's for dinner tonight." They walked up the stairs.

"What, seriously?"

"Yea."

Rachel reached out and took his hand at the top of the stairs.

"Come on sweetie, I gotta talk to you about a few things in the car."

"That's why you're wearing that cute sweater. You're meeting the folks," laughed Bubba.

Jerome looked a little sheepish. Rachel laughed and got into her car. She powered it up.

"Good job today boys," she said.

Jerome climbed in. They drove off.

"Well that doesn't mean the three of us can't celebrate, right?" said Matt.

They stopped at an all-you-can-eat sushi place on the way home for dinner. They ordered a table full of plates and stuffed their faces.

"So tell us about Valkyrie Snow. How did that go down?" asked Bubba between chomps.

"Well she invited me to her vacation property and one thing led to another. Basically."

"How old do you think she is?"

"I'm not too sure…"

"She's hot, like a hot mom," said Matt. "I can dig that."

Jordan thought back to his friends' moms when he was a kid. None of them were hot.

But my teachers… Jordan's first serious crush had been his grade ten physics teacher.

"Remember Ms. Chandhri?" he said.

"Fuck yea, she was hot," said Matt. They had all gone to high school together.

"I was more into Linda. Remember Linda?" said Bubba.

Linda was one of the secretaries at the main office. She was a train wreck with poorly dyed hair and her makeup always looked like she a hangover.

"Linda?!" laughed Matt. "You fuckin dumbass. I forgot how you were obsessed with Linda."

"She was my lady," he said, putting his hand on his heart. Linda always laughed at his jokes and she cut him slack when he came to school late.

"She totally had the hots for me."

"Remember how she always chewed her gum like it was a struggle?"

They all laughed.

"She's got to be at least Valkyrie's age… do you think she'd bang me if I looked her up on Facebook?"

"Try it," said Jordan. He was serious.

"I'm seriously gunna."

Ding. Jordan received a notification. He pulled out his phone and looked at the apps. Instagram. He clicked the icon. It was a private message from Valkyrie. He opened the thread greedily.

> I have work until at least eleven, but come over after if you're free.

"Well?" said Alex. "Are we going to lose you suddenly?"

"No… Val wants me to go over after eleven. She's got work to do."

"You're a rich woman's booty call. Some guys have it all."

"I'm not a booty call…" Jordan started. Was he? He didn't really know.

CHAPTER NINETEEN

Jordan passed the hours quickly at home, lying on his bed listening to music and flicking through videos on the internet. He started by watching whatever auto-loaded—an endless reel of depressing news—but then he decided to watch something more positive. He looked up videos of baby animals, and then tried to watch a few motivational speeches.

You are everything you think you are.

Your only limit is yourself.

Half of him felt comforted by those ideas—*Yay! I am in control!*—and the other half was frustrated—*how fucking asinine, I am trying my best already.*

As ten o'clock rolled around, his pulse quickened. He was starting to get tired lying in bed, but he knew that as soon as he got up to walk over to Valkyrie's apartment, the adrenaline would kick in and he would be sky high with energy. He waited another fifteen minutes and then decided to start walking over slowly.

It's okay if I'm a little early, he thought. He left his long board in his room and set out for Valkyrie's house.

As Jordan approached her condominium on the tree-lined boulevard, his palms started to sweat. This was the first time he was going over to her place since their weekend at Glasshouse. What would it be like?

What if it's terrible? he thought anxiously. He was so horny, but what if it all just melted away in the familiar space of her apartment? What if their connection and their energy was just amplified by the outdoors and the vacation environment of Glasshouse?

He walked up to the front of her building. He buzzed up.

The lock clicked open in front of him as Valkyrie let him into the building.

He stepped into the lobby and walked up to her floor; his nerves were a mess. He took the lion's head on her door in his hand and knocked. The door swung open.

Jordan walked into the condo. Valkyrie was sitting at her desk typing away. There were four empty glasses and a plate sitting beside her. Her hair was wild.

"Hey," he said.

"Hi." She looked up quickly and then went back to typing. "You're early. Just give me a few minutes."

He didn't know if he should go over and give her a kiss or just wait. He decided to sit on the couch.

"Take your time," he said. He scrolled through his phone.

As the time passed, Jordan looked up at Val every so often. She seemed so disinterested. He felt anxious. He shouldn't have showed up so early. She really did have work to do.

What if she's mad at me for disturbing her? he thought.

Finally, she leaned back in her chair, stretching up her arms. She stood up.

"I'll be right back," she said, going upstairs.

Where is she going now? thought Jordan. He looked around her apartment.

You don't fit in here, hissed Snake.

Valkyrie came back down the stairs wearing her silver silk bathrobe. She walked toward Jordan taking one slow step at a time. She stopped in front of him on the couch, putting her hands softly on his hair, leaning down to kiss him on top of his head. He tilted his head up and kissed her lips. She slid one knee up onto the couch beside him and slid the other on the other side, straddling his lap. He slid his hands under the soft silk of the robe, feeling her warm skin underneath. She sighed, relaxing down into his kisses, letting her work stress melt away. She held him close as he ran his hands up and down the softness of her backside. He squeezed her tight in his arms. She felt incredible. They kissed and kissed, their lips coming together for more and more, insistently connecting and tasting one another.

Valkyrie stood up.

"Come," she said, taking his hand and leading him to the stairs. She walked up in front of him, his hands touching the soft curves at the back of her robe, the silk slipping beneath his fingers. At the top of the stairs and down the darkness of the hall, she turned around and wrapped her arms around his neck, kissing him deeply. He held her lower back, kissing her beautiful neck and pressing into her. He pulled off his shirt, throwing it on the floor in the hallway, and then taking off his pants. He held her to him, his skin warm and inviting. She kissed him more intensely. Her eyes softened and Jordan could see her desire for him there. He breathed a pleasure sound, pressing her up against the upstairs wall, his hands on each side of her head as she rubbed up against him, hungry for his touch. She felt his erection through his boxers, searching, and longing welled up inside her. Jordan yanked down his underwear, and he could feel how wet she was. Valkyrie felt an explosion of carnal emotion and she pushed him down the hall with a snarl. They fell onto the bed, a tangle of limbs, rubbing, licking, heavy petting, until Jordan was on top of her, thrusting. Valkyrie moaned with pleasure, thrusting back harder and harder until she came.

Jordan felt like he could come any second. Normally he would let himself go, but he knew Valkyrie had more in her. He slowed down, willing himself to wait and keep going. He relaxed as she whimpered with the pleasure of comedown, kissing her and moving slowly. He was too turned on, so he pulled out, kissing her chest and shoulders.

"Mmm," she moaned, teasing his ear with her teeth. He relaxed onto her, burying his face in her hair and holding her tight. He couldn't believe how incredible this felt. She kissed him softly, rubbing her lips against his skin.

"I needed this," she said, her voice heavy with lust. She'd had a stressful week.

"You're amazing," said Jordan. He'd never met a woman who orgasmed so much. They nuzzled each other, relishing the intimate touch.

Valkyrie turned him over onto his back. She rubbed up against him without penetration, stimulating her clit. He felt her wetness hot and thick on him. She kissed his lips, his cheeks, his neck, as she grinded harder, bringing herself to satisfaction. Jordan held her ass in his hands. Just the beautiful look on her face of complete and utter painful pleasure made him moan. He guided himself into her and pulled her down close, thrusting slowly. Usually during sex he was preoccupied with details, like where his hands were, how fast or slow he was moving, or what his face looked like. As he and Valkyrie moved together slowly, it was like a perfect dance, where the totality of the moment and their shared pleasure overwhelmed the thoughts of his critical brain. He felt passion and emotion rise inside him like a tide, building and cresting as he came. Bliss washed over him like a wave as every nerve in his body exploded. He trembled with pleasure on top of her.

Eventually he rolled off of her, but he held her, kissing her hands and arms, not wanting the moment to end. They kissed and kissed.

Valkyrie got up to go to the bathroom. Jordan lay flat on his back, his arms and legs spread out on the massive bed. His nerves were still firing. He felt like he was high.

Valkyrie came back and slipped into bed beside him.

"House, turn out the lights," she said softly. The house obliged. They wrapped up tight in each other's arms and fell asleep.

The next morning, Valkyrie got up to get ready for work.

Jordan grabbed her hand and pulled her back into bed. She snuggled into him, kissing him.

"I have to go," she said.

"Nooo," he whined, squeezing her to him. She laughed, squeezing back. They tussled in bed, making out. Their kissing escalated and they made love.

"It's so nice to wake up with you," said Valkyrie afterwards, holding him.

"I was afraid," he said, "that things wouldn't be the same. You know, as they were at Glasshouse." He kissed her forehead.

She looked up at him. His expression was serious. He was looking into her eyes with an intensity she had never seen from him before.

"But, it still feels incredible," he said quietly.

Valkyrie kissed him softly, breathing in his emotion, feeling his energy reaching into her.

"Yes," she said, resting her head on his chest. She remembered feeling something like that when she was younger. She lingered there for a few more minutes and then got up.

"Come and shower with me," she said.

Jordan hopped out of bed and followed her down the hall to the shower. They couldn't keep their hands off of each other. They made out in the shower, washing one another's bodies. When they were done, they wrapped up in soft towels and padded down the hall to get dressed.

"Sing to me," said Val.

Jordan grinned. "I'm working on something new, want to hear it?"

"Of course!"

He hummed a few bars, getting into the rhythm and tune of the song. Then he launched into the lyrics. After a verse and the chorus he faltered.

"I forget the rest," he said.

Val clapped with delight. "It's great so far."

They went downstairs for coffee. Val got out cups and fired up the espresso machine.

Jordan pulled out his phone to look up the lyrics he had put down for the second verse that he couldn't remember.

"I use this app to transcribe my music..." he said. Val put her arms around him from behind and looked over his shoulder at the lyrics.

Ding.

A notification popped up on his screen.

Charlotte:

> How's your day going so far, babe?

It was Charlotte.

Jordan turned quickly to look at Val. She walked over to the fridge slowly to get out the cream.

"Umm yea, that's just Charlotte," he said.

Valkyrie's face was impassive. *Babe?* Charlotte was obviously not his sister then.

She poured the milk.

"What is she like?" she asked.

"Umm, she's a physio student. And a massage therapist."

There was silence. That was not really what Valkyrie had been asking. She decided to just go ahead and ask what she was wondering.

"Is Charlotte your girlfriend?"

"What? No. Well, we did have a thing, once, or twice... but we're just friends now."

"Does she know that?" Val sounded mildly amused.

"Oh yea. We just like to chat. That's all."

Val squeezed his hand.

"No problem Jordan. Do what you want, and whatever you need to do to be happy. Just as long as you're honest with me, I'll be honest with you too."

Jordan exhaled. "I'll try my best," he said.

Will I be honest? he thought. He never had before. This would be something new.

She hugged him.

"I'm open to seeing other people too," she said.

Jordan felt conflicted. On one hand, he liked the thought of being free to chat with other people without the burden of guilty feelings. He also felt very strange about Valkyrie having other people in her bed.

"Is that why I haven't seen you in a few weeks?" he asked, looking at his hands.

"No. I've been dealing with crisis after crisis at work." She kissed him, brushing his hair behind his ear. "You are the only person I wanted to see last night."

Jordan felt his heart flutter.

"Me too," he said, and it was true. They kissed.

"I really have to get to work," said Val apologetically.

"When will I see you again?" he asked. He felt a bit pitiful, but he didn't want to spend another week waiting to hear from her, wondering if she was still interested.

"Jordan, I'm really busy right now..."

Jordan felt a stab of iciness creep up his spine. He had said something really similar to Charlotte.

"Okay." It was all he could say.

"How about we go to Glasshouse on Saturday? I could really use the time away..."

"That sounds perfect." Jordan breathed a sigh of relief.

They kissed once more and then went their separate ways.

Around noon, there was a lull in work.

Maybe I can work from home tomorrow, thought Valkyrie. She didn't really like coming into the office more than she had to. It looked like things were settling down.

"Oracle," she said softly. "Jordan Barker is friends with a girl named Charlotte. She's a massage therapist and a physio student. Find more information please."

"Too easy," said the Oracle. Jordan's Facebook page popped up onto the screen. A girl named Charlotte Kerwin had liked almost all of his photos for the past year. The Oracle pulled up the Instagram account for the Waves, and Charlotte had been monitoring and commenting there as well.

"Where does she work?" asked Val.

Charlotte had used the check-in feature on Facebook to identify that she frequented Westboro Body Therapies, which offered massage.

"Call Westboro Body Therapies, please."

The Oracle dialled up the number.

"Hello, Westboro Body Therapies! How can we help you?"

"Hi. Does Charlotte Kerwin give massages for you? Can I book her please?"

"She does. One moment please." The reception put Val on hold.

"We can schedule you in a few weeks, but we also have a cancellation the day after tomorrow. We could put you in at 4 o'clock."

Val considered for a moment. Was she really going to do this?

"I'll take the cancellation," she said.

"Excellent. Can we get a name for the appointment?"

"Oh yes. Elizabeth Vanderwall."

"Great. We'll see you on Thursday, Ms. Vanderwall."

"Doctor Vanderwall," said Val. She couldn't help herself.

When Thursday came around, Valkyrie left the office at three pm.

"I'll be working from home the rest of the day," she said to Sukhwant on her way out. She hopped on the train and headed over to Westboro Body Therapies. On the way, she stopped at a cash machine. She looked through the bills. Many of the designs were new; she hadn't used cash to pay for anything in a long time.

Westboro Body Therapies was one of a series of service providers—Glebe Body Therapies, Saint Laurent Body Therapies, and others—completely owned and operated by the new AI called Oracle. The AI assessed a neighbourhood for viability and opened the business, hiring contractors to complete renovations, create an attractive website, and the Oracle itself managed the front desk and the finances. At this point banks were more confident in loaning to Oracles than to humans. The Oracle subcontracted human massage and physiotherapists to provide services on a wage basis, offering them the opportunity to buy into the business when they put in a minimum number of hours. The Oracle was not programmed with a particular cultural ethics system, but created its own based on logic— it worked toward world peace, a just distribution of wealth, and protecting the environment.

The lobby at the massage parlour was clean. Valkyrie was relieved; she had never been here before. The place was in an old house, but the management had given it a clinical vibe with medical-looking posters and a life-sized skeleton. There was a mat with shoes on it and a basket of paper slippers. Valkyrie ignored it.

"Welcome to Westboro Body Therapies!" exclaimed a robot, the same cheerful voice who had booked Val's appointment.

She wondered what Charlotte looked like. She had seen her on Facebook but she knew she probably wouldn't recognize her in real life. Most people didn't really look like their pictures. She wondered what her energy would be like.

A girl came down to greet her. She was youthfully pretty, and somewhat plain. Her hair was tied back in bun and she was otherwise unremarkable.

"Hi there. Elizabeth Vanderwall?" she smiled, extending her hand in greeting.

"Nice to meet you," said Val, taking her hand and lingering with it, reading the details of Charlotte's face.

"I'm Charlotte. Right this way please."

Val followed her upstairs to a private room. The lights were turned down low, and meditative music played quietly from the sound system. Val could smell cheap candles burning.

"What kind of massage were you looking for?" asked Charlotte.

"Oh just something relaxing. I'm flexible."

"What part of the body are we working on today?"

"Full body," said Val.

"Sounds good. I'll just leave the room. You go ahead and remove your clothing and lie under the blanket on the table. Put your face on the hot towel in the round area. I'll come check on you in a few minutes."

Valkyrie stripped down to nothing and climbed onto the table. Charlotte came back into the room.

"Here, I'll just pull the blanket over you..." said Charlotte.

"I don't mind," said Val, naked and relaxed.

Charlotte left the blanket and squirted coconut oil into her hands. She started caressing Val's legs, working her way up from the bottom of her calf. She pressed with her palms in small circles, spreading the oil and warming Valkyrie's skin with her touch.

"Harder," said Val quietly.

Charlotte obliged, digging in deeper. She moved up Valkyrie's body in long, deep movements. She rubbed up Val's spine, tracing her vertebrae with heavy fingers. Valkyrie sighed, relaxing fully into the table.

"Is that hard enough?" breathed Charlotte, leaning over Val, kneading her back with her thumbs and palms.

"It feels wonderful, but I could go harder..."

Charlotte dug in with her knuckles, working the muscles of Valkyrie's lower back.

"Lower," she murmured.

Charlotte moved her hands down to Valkyrie's backside, pressing with the sides of her hands.

"Harder."

The girl obliged, cupping Val's ass with her hands and massaging deep into her muscles with her thumbs.

Charlotte was sweating with the effort. She pumped more coconut oil into her hands and slathered it on Val's body, rubbing in slow strokes up her back and into her shoulders. There was a red spot there. She looked closer, identifying the faintest outline of teeth marks. She smiled. This woman's lover must have bit her. She rubbed in deep. Elizabeth Vanderwall obviously didn't mind a bit of pain. As Charlotte touched the evidence of sexuality on this woman's body, she remembered that there was a very fine line between kinds of touch—how easily rubbing with hands could turn into love bites, and how close a massage could be to a sensual experience. She was touching this woman in the same place her lover likely did the night before. She blushed.

"What is it?" asked Val.

"Hmm?"

"I felt the energy shift."

"Oh. Nothing," said Charlotte. "Are you ready to turn over?"

"Yes."

Valkyrie rolled onto her back, her breasts lying round and smooth. Charlotte pulled the blanket up over her, noticing first how beautiful this older woman's body was. She pulled a chair up to Valkyrie's head, lowering the table. She reached under the blanket, digging into her traps. Val arched her back with a small gasp.

"Is that okay?" breathed Charlotte softly.

"It's a bit sensitive," said Val. "But it feels good."

Charlotte slowed her pace, rubbing more gently this time, working into the muscle tissue.

"Is that better?"

"It's perfect," said Val.

Charlotte finished the traps and moved to Valkyrie's neck and jaw, revolving gently with her palms and fingers. She moved up into Val's hair, caressing her scalp. Val sighed again. Charlotte traced her fingers softly down her long neck, over her front and under the blanket, kneading the tops of her breasts with her fingers. She blushed again, remembering the teeth marks.

I wonder if her lover touches her like this, she thought.

Charlotte moved to Val's side, holding her arm and massaging her bicep.

Valkyrie looked into her face. It was a kind face, a bit blank, without a single line of stress. She still had a trace of the childish plumpness that went away with age. Small wisps of hair framed her pretty face and there was an inherent gentleness to the way she held herself.

Like a kitten, thought Val.

Charlotte felt her gaze and looked at her. Her expression was unreadable. She looked down, moving lower, massaging Val's fingers.

For her final modality, Charlotte moved down to Val's feet. She massaged them and finished with a squeeze.

"We're all done. I will leave the room and let you get dressed. Come and meet me downstairs when you're ready."

Charlotte left the room.

Val washed her hands at the sink. She felt greasy but relaxed. She slipped back into her clothes and went downstairs to pay.

"How did you enjoy your massage today?" asked the robot voice.

"Massages are one of my favourite pleasures of the body," responded Valkyrie. She looked at Charlotte.

"One hundred and fifty dollars," said Charlotte.

Valkyrie pulled out her cash and paid. She gave Charlotte a generous tip.

"Can we make an account for you? That way we can auto-charge and you don't need to worry about bringing enough cash."

"Not today. Maybe next time."

"Thank you. I hope we see you again," said Charlotte.

"Have a nice day Doctor Vanderwall," said the robot.

"You too," said Val on her way out the door.

On Saturday, Jordan waited for a car to come pick him up at his apartment. It was pouring rain and he stood under the eaves, enjoying the way the sound of water muted everything else. It was torturously, blissfully overwhelming, stimulating every sense and occupying his busy mind. He liked the way that the water drained from the street into the gutters, like tiny rivers. People walked differently when it was raining outside. Jordan watched people stepping gingerly between puddles with umbrellas, or shuffling quickly, heads down, hands jammed into their pockets. Everything looked darker and cleaner when it rained. There was a cool breeze today. Jordan pulled his hood up over his head. Fall was in the air.

The robot pulled up to the apartment and the doors clicked open. Jordan got into the front seat so that he could watch the scenery as they drove out to the countryside. A feeling began inside him and spread throughout his chest, radiating in his body. What was it? He tried to identify it. Some part of it reminded him of his childhood, days spent outside in the pouring rain, screaming with laughter and soaking wet, sloshing around in soggy, freezing grass. Nostalgia. There was definitely some memory in that feeling, pulling him back in time to a place he could never go again. It was not just about the past; there was something in this feeling glowing inside him that was about the future too. He was looking forward to things he was about to do and experience, and to things he was working on in his creative practice. He felt grateful for the first time in a long time. He was looking forward to sharing his album with his family and friends, whether people liked it or not. He was so happy that it was finally recorded. He was also looking forward to holding Valkyrie

Snow in his arms in a floating bed, looking out at the trees and the river from massive windows, and letting the world dissolve like a distant dream for a while.

Jordan peered out the window as houses flashed past, saturated with the pleasantly melancholy feeling of past and present mingling to the point of eclipsing and obviating his present. The car turned off the highway onto the feeder road, and Jordan's thoughts turned to Val. He was looking forward to seeing her, and feeling none of his usual anxiety about what she was doing or how she felt. Last night when she called him to let him know what time the car was picking him up, she sounded excited to see him. At this point, that was enough to put his mind at ease.

The car turned off the feeder road. The crunch of gravel under the wheels of the car in the rain meant that they were about ten minutes away. Last time, Jordan had made the driver turn around to pick up peaches. This time, he remembered to make a stop last night at the LCBO to get a bottle of wine. He wasn't really good at picking. Before this, he had never chosen wine based on more criteria than whatever was the cheapest. This time, he asked the staff for recommendations, and picked a Riesling. He knew it was a dicey choice because Valkyrie usually drank red, but he thought he would take a chance.

The car slowed down and turned up the laneway. It wove through trees heavy with wetness, leaves sticking to the windows as they drove past. The car approached a clearing and Glasshouse emerged from the trees, shining in the rain like a glistening conservatory. Valkyrie came to the door to greet him. Jordan got out of the car, pausing to take in the beautiful scene: the cozy house, the pouring rain, Valkyrie wearing a soft cotton sweater and an oversized t-shirt coming down to the top of her thigh, her long legs naked and her hair wilder than ever.

A smile broke across his face. He was so genuinely happy to be here. Val came out to meet him, walking into the muddy laneway in her bare feet. She wrapped her arms around him.

"You're getting wet," he protested, laughing, kissing her face.

Val let go of him and threw her hands in the air, her face to the sky. The rain splashed onto her closed eyelids and into her smiling lips.

"Gloriously wet," she said.

Valkyrie loved the rain. There was a time when she would have been worried about ruining her clothes, or messing up her hair, but somewhere along the road of the journey of life she let go of all that.

Jordan swept her up in his arms and carried her to the house. She shrieked happily, holding him tight. He set her on her feet on the threshold, and their lips found each other quickly, connecting insistently, both feeling the swell of endorphins as their craving for one another promised to be satisfied. They kissed until they couldn't take it anymore, and jumped into bed to make love. The afternoon passed euphorically, two lovers enraptured completely by one another as rain dripped down from grey skies, thudding pleasantly against the massive windows of Glasshouse.

"Are you ready for dinner?" asked Val. Her stomach was growling.

"I so am."

Valkyrie pulled on her large cotton hoodie and went to the kitchenette to serve up two bowls of lasagna from the crockpot. Jordan put on the kettle to make tea. All of his nerves were working in overdrive. He felt the wood floor beneath his bare feet, and he caressed the roughness of the pottery teapot, taking pleasure in simple sensations that he was highly attuned to in this moment.

The kettle whistled, and as Jordan and Val passed one another in the small space of the kitchen, they brushed against one another in amiable silence, communicating with touch instead of words. Val took the bowls and two spoons out to the screened porch to eat at the small table. When the tea was ready, Jordan poured two mugs and brought them out to join her.

"There's a second chair!" he said.

"I got it just for you," said Valkyrie with a smile. "I imagined you sitting here with me, just like this, eating lasagna and listening to the rain."

"That makes me happy," he said quietly, blowing on a spoonful of steaming pasta. "Does everything you imagine come true?"

"You've figured me out," she said with a sly smile. "I'm a witch."

She sounded like she was joking, but Jordan knew she wasn't.

After they were done their supper, Valkyrie took their bowls to the sink.

"Let me do it," said Jordan. "I'm really good at it." Jordan had washed enough dishes to last a lifetime.

"I guess it's what you do," said Valkyrie. "But it's not who you are."

She slipped her hands around his waist and held him as he washed.

"What do you mean?" he asked, kissing her cheek. He knew what she meant but he wanted to hear her say it.

"You are a musician. An artist. Like me. I run my businesses, I build residential and commercial properties, but in my heart I'm an artist."

Jordan turned off the water. He dried his hands slowly on the towel and turned around in her arms. He held her close.

"I love you," he said. The words slipped out of his lips so easily. They were pure and true, and he gave them freely and without reservation for the first time in his life.

Valkyrie closed her eyes, pressing her cheek to his. She felt her heart opening like a flower, letting his love into her, feeling a flood of her love flowing back into him. Jordan inhaled sharply, all of his fears and insecurities burning away as he felt her love finally penetrating him, recording a song inside of him that he knew would change him forever. Valkyrie said nothing and she didn't need to. Jordan felt it.

They spent the rest of their evening curled up in bed reading. Every once in a while one would softly kiss the other. The rain poured down outside and they were deliciously cozy in piles of soft blankets in Valkyrie's bed, watching the sky darken to black. Eventually they fell asleep holding one another.

Jordan woke up in the middle of the night, the air cool on his bare shoulders and back. Val was warm beneath him, her body softly rising and falling as she breathed, sleeping deep. He ran his hand very lightly along her body, from her collar bone, softly over her breast and down her stomach. The house was dark around them but her paleness glowed in the moonlight shining through the glass ceiling. Her mouth was relaxed, her lips parted, making the sweet sounds of almost snoring as he lay half on top of her. She was so beautiful. He looked at her face, and the longer he looked, the more his heart ached. He loved her. He was in love with her, a feeling so wild and intense that he wanted to squeeze her, to kiss her, to taste her. He kissed her chin gently and held her softly, lying back down to sleep.

In the morning, they had coffee and fruit for breakfast and then they went for a swim in the river. It was September now and the water was icy cold. Valkyrie took a quick dip, but Jordan stayed in until his lips and fingertips turned blue. He loved the water so much.

"My dolphin," laughed Val, sitting on the shore wrapped in a blanket, sipping tea and relaxing. Jordan cackled like a dolphin, blowing water at her. She watched him with a smile, happy to see him so happy.

She went up into the house. It was almost cold enough to make a fire, but not quite. Soon. The leaves were starting to turn and the air smelled like death. It was invigorating. Jordan soon joined her.

"There you are," he said, wrapping his arms around her.

"You didn't have to come in yet."

"I didn't want to let you out of my sight," he said, nuzzling her shoulder.

She looked at him with her impassive expression. Their chemistry was intense and she was developing love for him, but she didn't want him to become emotionally dependent on her. She would have to help him to understand that she could love him without being around him all the time, and she needed a great deal of space. She kissed the top of his head softly.

They took the car back into the city that evening curled up in the back seat. Jordan held onto her for dear life, like a drowning man. He didn't want to let her go.

"When will I see you again?" he said as they pulled up to his building.

"Next weekend, come over on Friday night. We can take the car out to Glasshouse in the morning."

Jordan kissed her fiercely and got out, standing on the wet street outside his apartment. As the car drove away, he felt like part of himself was driving away too.

The next morning Jordan swallowed nervously on his way to the Cherry. He had to cancel his shift Friday night and he knew that Earl would be pissed.

"I need to talk to you," he said to Earl, twenty minutes early for his shift. He made sure to give himself lots of time to have this talk. His palms were sweating and he was chewing the inside of his cheek obsessively.

"What is it Scrub?"

"I need Friday off. I have a family emergency."

"I don't believe you," growled Earl, stepping too close. Jordan could smell his sour breath. He tried not to breathe through his nose.

"My mum's sick."

"You're not trying to get out of work for some music thing, are you?" Earl had seen Jordan's post on social media at the recording studio.

"No, nothing like that."

"Because I know where you fucking live, and it's a dump. You need this job."

Jordan cringed. He steeled himself, clenching his fists, willing his emotions to dull out.

"She's sick. I won't be here Friday. I'd like to get all the weekends I can off too if that's okay." Most people liked working weekends anyway because the tip-out was higher.

"That's a big favour," said Earl thickly.

Bullshit, thought Jordan. He said nothing.

"You better not be lying to me, I take that shit personal."

"So what do you think about Friday?" asked Jordan as emotionless as possible.

"Yea I'll call someone in. Your work better not slip, you know you can be replaced."

"Yea I know."

Earl leaned in closer. "And your ma should be grateful. You owe me." Jordan could see a bead of saliva on Earl's bottom lip. His tongue jetted out and licked it away.

"Thanks," said Jordan, turning away. Earl walked away and Jordan went to the back to start his shift.

Valkyrie thought a lot about Jordan during the week. Especially before bed, she found her mind drifting to his firm body, his earnest expression, and his beautiful voice. She was looking forward to spending the weekend with him in Glasshouse. She sent him a message on Instagram.

> Let's go out for dinner Friday. Meet me at Ruisseau, reso for V at 6 pm.

Jordan looked up the restaurant online.
Fancy, he thought.

On Friday, Jordan wore his powder blue shirt and showed up at Ruisseau a few minutes early. He slid his hand through his hair, pushing it back out of his eyes. Several older women in expensive clothes took notice.

"Reservation for V?" he said.

"Right this way." The host led him to his seat. He looked at the menu as patrons appreciated his pretty face and newly-toned body. He ordered a gin and tonic and waited for his date.

Valkyrie swept in right on time, dressed in a shimmering gold dress with a high neck and a long slit up the side. She wore diamond earrings, and her hair was uncustomarily tied back. She handed her coat to the host, looking around the restaurant. She saw Jordan and smiled, walking over and sitting at their table.

"Fuck, you look incredible," he said.

She laughed softly. "You look good too."

She reached out along the table and he did simultaneously, their fingers touching. Energy passed between them as they looked into each other's eyes.

"Missed you," she murmured.

"Me too."

Valkyrie withdrew her hand as the waiter approached.

"A glass of la femme rose please." Valkyrie was feeling like a bubbly champagne tonight.

And in the dark corner of Ruisseau, a man shifted uncomfortably in his seat. His date—a young woman with artificially enlarged lips and crusts of mascara on her eyelashes wearing a crop top that showed off her jewelled belly button—saw his face and faltered in the story she was telling. His attention was suddenly focused somewhere else.

"Jeff?" she asked.

Jeff was staring intently at Jordan.

Look at him! He thought angrily. *He's wearing jeans!* Jeff felt anger creeping up his neck. *He must be some kind of young millionaire... she can't be with him just for his looks.* Jeff appraised Jordan. He was exceptionally handsome. He fumed silently, which confused his date, who didn't know why he seemed so angry all of a sudden.

Jeff tried to focus on his dinner. Suddenly he heard a tinkle of laughter that he knew was Valkyrie's. His eyes burned into the back of her head.

Val felt a creepy sensation up her spine and turned around. There was Jeff Harper, staring right at her. He smiled. Valkyrie turned back to her drink.

Jordan saw Val's expression and looked at where she had been looking. His gaze met Jeff's and the other man turned his attention back to his date.

"Someone you know?" asked Jordan.

"Unfortunately. That's the guy who called the house the other day and I had to tell him to fuck off."

Jordan frowned. Val rarely swore. He reached out and entwined his fingers in hers.

"Sorry," he said.

Val relaxed. "It's okay." She raised her champagne glass.

"To our first fancy date," she said with a grin.

"Cheers," said Jordan clinking her glass and finishing his gin and tonic.

The waiter came by and they ordered.

"So how was your week?" asked Jordan.

"Oh, busy busy. I really want to be working on my arcologies, but I have to spend so much time on other things lately."

"I know that feeling," said Jordan. He sighed. His awkward talk with Earl was worth having this night with Valkyrie.

"How's your new album coming?" she asked.

"I've got two songs totally mapped out, start to finish. The rest is in pieces."

"I can't wait to get my Nightingale song," she said.

"Everything's going to be a lot better once I can spend less time working on making money and more time making art." It felt good to say that to someone. Jordan knew that Valkyrie understood.

"I remember going through that."

Jordan tried to imagine what Valkyrie was like in her twenties. It was hard for him, because he didn't really see her having an age at all.

Their food arrived. Val ordered a rare steak with chanterelles and Jordan got the ground moose cavatelli.

"I'll have a glass of my usual Cab Sauv as well, please," she said to the waiter. "Don't let me get more than one glass." She winked at him.

"I was wondering," laughed the waiter, who knew what Val liked.

"Do you want anything else?" she asked Jordan.

Normally he would order a beer, but he wasn't sure what went well with his meal.

"Umm, any suggestions?" he asked the waiter.

"I'd try a rich berry wine, perhaps a Cassis liqueur? Or we have a nice blueberry wine from the Muskokas."

"I'll do it," he said.

They chatted and enjoyed their delicious dinners.

Across the lounge, Jeff and his date were finished their meal, and Jeff was throwing back drinks.

"Is everything okay?" asked his date, who could see that his demeanor had visibly changed since they got to the restaurant but she couldn't tell why. It was their second date and she was still getting to know him.

"I'm fine Angel. Just fine."

"Do you want dessert?" asked Val as the waiter cleared away their empty plates.

"Not really. Unless you count *you*," he said, kissing her fingers. He grinned unapologetically at his own lame pickup line.

Val groaned and laughed.

"I might get…" she began.

"Crème brulée?" finished the waiter.

"Yes." Valkyrie laughed. "Two spoons." He went to get it for her.

"You must come here a lot."

"I do."

The waiter brought out Val's custard and lit its sugary surface on fire. She clapped and blew out the flames.

"I got to blow it out, so you get the first crack," she said.

Jordan poked his spoon into the hard surface in a satisfying crunch. He took a spoonful and noticed that Jeff was back to watching him like a hawk. He stared him right in the eye, offering his spoon to Val.

"Here," he said, holding it to her lips. She closed her eyes and ate it slowly. The top was warm and crunchy and the bottom chilled. It was perfect.

"Mmm," she said.

They shared the crème brulée and the waiter came to clear the dish when they were finished.

"Have a lovely evening you two," he said with a smile. Valkyrie stood to leave.

"Don't we have to pay?" asked Jordan, pulling out his wallet.

"They have my number," said Val. "Like you said, I come here a lot."

"But, I should contribute…"

"Don't worry about it," she said, waving him away. "I have to go to the ladies' room, will you grab my jacket?" she asked.

"For sure."

Jordan went to the front of the restaurant.

"Valkyrie Snow's jacket, please."

"Right away."

Jeff paid his bill quickly and stood to leave. He sauntered up to the front. Jordan saw him approaching and groaned inwardly, turning away and hoping he would just leave.

"Looks like you had a fun night," said Jeff. Jordan half-turned uncomfortably, catching Jeff's eye and giving him a nod of acknowledgement.

"So what do you do for a living?" asked Jeff. He tried to keep his tone light, but the booze loosened him and there was strange note to his voice.

"I'm a musician," said Jordan.

Jeff laughed, a sharp bark of a sound. "Of course you are."

Jeff's date was standing behind him. She made eye contact with Jordan and smiled.

"I'm Angel," she said, extending a hand.

"Nice to meet you," said Jordan, shaking it.

"What are you, twenty two, twenty three?" asked Jeff. Angel's cheeks reddened. She herself was twenty four.

Valkyrie walked up along the bar to the front door. Jordan put the jacket around her shoulders.

"Hi Jeff," said Val.

"Valkyrie. I was just asking your musician friend his age."

Valkyrie side-eyed Jeff's date, who looked thoroughly embarrassed.

"That's an odd question, isn't it?" she said quietly.

"I don't think so. He's wearing jeans! Are you actually on a date with *this* guy?"

"I am."

"I really thought you had better taste than that." Jeff stepped uncomfortably close to Valkyrie as he said it, swaying a bit with booze and slurring his words.

Jordan reached down and squeezed Val's hand.

"Relax bro," he said gently.

"Relax? I'm just teasing you, y'know man to man," said Jeff. He elbowed Jordan, probably harder than he intended to. Angel reached out to lightly put her hand on his arm. He shoved it off aggressively.

Jordan frowned.

"What are you looking at?" said Jeff, his tone more hostile.

Jordan felt anger rising in him, but he pushed it away.

"Come on man, just chill out."

"What, you scared of me?" Jeff's eyes glittered with vacancy. The alcohol made him almost unrecognizable.

"A little, yea," said Jordan. "You've had a lot to drink."

"I could knock you the fuck out if I wanted."

Jordan tried not to laugh. He couldn't believe this was a grown man in a suit talking to him like this.

"That would be stupid."

The host came over.

"Is everything okay here?" he said, looking at Val, who was a regular customer.

"I'm not sure," she said softly. "I think this man has had too much to drink."

"I see. We'll make sure he gets home safely," said the host, taking Jeff's arm and leading him out the door to the waiting cabs. Jeff pushed the host, sealing his permanent ban from Ruisseau. Valkyrie reached out and touched Angel's arm.

"Do yourself a favour and stay away from that guy," she said.

"Sorry about this," said Angel, hurrying away.

Their waiter came over.

"Are you okay?" he asked.

"It's alright," said Val. She turned to Jordan.

"Let's go home."

They stepped outside, arm in arm.

"I'm a lover, not a fighter," said Jordan.

"I love that about you." Valkyrie kissed him deep.

They walked home. It was a beautiful night. The skies were decently clear and they could see the stars.

When they got in, Valkyrie pulled off her dress as soon as they got in the door, letting it fall to the floor. She kicked off her oxfords and pulled her hair down. She sighed.

"Do you want another drink?" she asked. She was feeling a light buzz.

"I'm okay," said Jordan. He didn't want to jeopardize his performance. Two drinks was plenty.

Valkyrie went to the kitchen and poured herself a tall glass of water.

"I'll be right up," she said.

Jordan went upstairs and got himself ready for bed. When Val came up, he was lying in the dark, his face lit blue by the screen of his phone. She slipped in beside him, reaching over to hold his hand. He was scrolling through an app, his face expressionless, consuming images and videos of memes and rants.

"Don't bring that thing in here," said Valkyrie.

Jordan pulled himself away from the screen, processing her words. It clicked in, and he shut off the device.

"Sorry babe," he said, setting it beside him on the pillow and turning to her.

"I said, don't bring that thing in here," she repeated calmly. He blinked at her for a minute, and then got up to take it downstairs.

As he walked back up, he felt naked without his phone.

What if someone calls? What if there is something I need to check? Illogical thoughts ran frantically through his mind, like an addict justifying giving in to a craving. He felt annoyed at Val. *How dare she tell me what to do,* he thought. He stopped on the stairs.

Wait a minute... I waited all week to see her. Why would I waste our time together on the internet when she is right there in bed with me? He realized how stupid it was to be mad. He took a deep breath and resolved to make the most of the present. He opened the bedroom door. The hall light cast a long muted glow along Val's body beneath the canopy in the bedroom. She was beautiful. He crawled into bed, all his focus and intention on the moment.

CHAPTER TWENTY

Jordan and Valkyrie drove to Glasshouse the next morning. The sky was starkly blue and the air was crisp. There was no doubt about it, fall had arrived. Valkyrie powered open the windows and wrapped her warm woolen sweater tighter around her. There were cascades of yellows and browns among the greens in the trees along country roads. The bright reds and oranges were on their way.

"Mabon is coming up," said Val. "Do you have any plans?"

"Not really. My family doesn't really do anything for Thanksgiving."

"I'll be hosting a little gathering at Glasshouse," she said.

"Like family and friends sort of thing?"

"Sisters."

When they arrived at Glasshouse, Jordan could see that work had been done.

"I had it installed during the week," said Val, her eyes dancing with excitement. She hurried over to investigate.

It was a fire trench, with a massive blackened iron cauldron in the centre. Around the pit was a circle of stones, and around that a cleared away space. Many people could warm themselves by this fire.

"It looks awesome," said Jordan.

"I'm going to make maple syrup here in the spring," she said. "And when my sisters come in two weeks we're going to celebrate out here."

"That's going to be great," he said, sliding his arms around her waist and holding her from behind. "We should have a fire tonight," he whispered in her ear. She leaned into him, closing her eyes.

"I brought food to cook on sticks for dinner," she said.

They went into the house. Val went to the screen porch to work on her sketches, and Jordan grabbed some blankets to curl up outside to read. He found a special tree and arranged the blankets under it. He lay down on his back with his arms under his head and looked up at the sky. He didn't feel like reading just yet. He thought about one of the songs he was working on. At this point it was just a few lines, but he had a good feeling about it.

> *What if Eve ate the apple*
> *Cuz she was sick of living in a world made for one ungrateful man named Adam*
> *What if she was hoping for a mysterious something*
> *A place that was different than his garden of Eden.*
>
> *What if, what if*
> *What if the woman who fell from the sky*
> *Was sick of always looking down from the clouds*
> *What if she trusted that things would work out and the whole world was made around her?*

He hummed the tune, thinking of the words. It was a bit of nonsense, inspired by popular creation myths, but it was catchy. It was totally different than their first album.

In the afternoon, Jordan took a break from reading to see what Valkyrie was up to. He poked his head into the screened porch. She was using a pen on thick mixed-media paper rather than pencil on tracing paper.

"What are you up to?" he asked.

Val raised her head. "Working on my Mabon plans," she said with a smile. Jordan came over and looked down at the page. Val was making a pen drawing of the Glasshouse grounds, with canvas tents between the trees and women in dresses dancing.

"Wow, that's… a lot of sisters," he said.

Val reached out and took his hand. "You're welcome to come," she said. "Connect with your feminine self and bring her. All sisters are welcome in the sisterhood."

Jordan didn't really know what to say. It sounded interesting.

"Are you feeling like taking a… break…" he said, leaning down and kissing her neck.

"Mmm…" she said, pressing into his kisses. "Just a sec." She went into the bathroom to pull out her diva cup. She rinsed it out and left it at the sink, washing her hands.

Jordan led her out to the main room. They kissed more, pulling off their clothes.

"Let's go down to the river," she said.

Jordan grinned and followed her outside. They ran down laughing, splashing into the icy water and shrieking at the cold. They swam around until they were somewhat warm, and then kissed, holding one another close. Val wrapped her legs around Jordan, and he held her ass in his hands, floating beneath a sharp autumn sky with the leaves falling into the river around them. Jordan thrust into her, holding her against him, biting her shoulder, gasping with pleasure. Being in the river was extraordinarily erotic for him. The cold water shocked his nerves, and the rush of adrenaline to his system was flush with lust. With one hand he guided her thrusts and he held her hair with the other, his mouth finding hers, kissing hard with cold lips and a hot tongue. She moaned with pleasure, equally turned on by the intensity of the water. Her nerves were already doubly sensitive because of her period, and she let her head go limp in his hands, letting the sensation of orgasm rollick over her entire body, shaking with ecstasy. Jordan felt the pressure building quickly, his body cold and her vagina hot with blood. He came hard, clinging to Valkyrie for dear life. After the pulses finished, he pulled out. A gush of dark velvet red floated away down the river.

Blót, she thought. *Blood sacrifice for the river Goddss.*[2]

---

[2] The use of the spelling "Goddss" is an inclusive term for both goddesses and gods. The monotheistic equivalent term is "Godd", inclusive of the female and male aspects of a singular divinity.

Valkyrie was a pagan, a heathen and a witch. She was in deep connection with the traditions of her ancestors. Blood was powerful magic, and in her tradition, ceremony and ritual were named *blót* after blood. Valkyrie felt especially powerful when she menstruated; electricity crackled from her fingertips and her desires were sharper and clearer. She decided to build a shrine in the river dedicated to Nerthus.

Valkyrie and Jordan passed a relaxing weekend at Glasshouse and returned to the city on Sunday evening.

On Monday, Valkyrie called the Hymnal to check on the progress of the demo. She was excited to hear how the Nightingale song had turned out.

"Hello?"

"Hello, it's Valkyrie Snow, calling about the demo the Waves recorded. How are we doing?"

"The Waves… one moment."

Georgio put Valkyrie on hold to confer with his associate.

"We'll turn you the comp in a couple days."

"As in, the day after tomorrow sort of thing?" pressed Val.

"Yea."

"Great. I look forward to hearing it."

"Okay bye."

Valkyrie knew that it was better to make a follow-up call *before* something was late.

The day after next Val received a message from the Hymnal. They sent her the files and asked for the contact emails for the band.

"I paid for it," she responded. "I'll make sure they get it."

She called Jordan.

"Hey," he said, picking up after the second ring with warmth in his voice.

"Hi. If you're free tonight, I have a surprise."

"Oh yea?" he said. "How about now? I'm just heading home from the gym."

Valkyrie looked at the clock. It was past seven. She wouldn't be working anymore tonight.

"Come on over."

"On my way."

Jordan hung up and turned at the next block to make his way to Val's.

She answered the door with a grin and led him to the couch.

"Sit with me," she said. He obliged.

"House," she said.

"Oracle," it replied. The house computer was correcting her. She had upgraded her condo system to match Glasshouse and her office. She laughed.

"Oracle," she said. "Play the last audio attachment on the email open on the computer."

A single bloom in a jar in the window
Pictures of all of the places you've been

As the first lines played, Jordan let out a sound of surprised laughter, looked at Val, and then grabbed her hand to listen.

A song for each memory, playing forever
Makes me come over again and again.

My heart song for you is a simple one
It's the stories I love that you tell
I still can't believe that you love me
When you know me so well.
When you know me so well...

After the final notes played, Jordan couldn't speak. His heart was beating fast.

That's me, he thought. *That's my voice. I sound amazing.*

"Can we listen to all of them?" he finally asked quietly.

"Play the other tracks Oracle," said Val.

They sat together on the couch listening to Jordan's unedited album. Tears were streaming down his face. This moment was surreal.

"Once you give the okay, they'll go ahead and make the final edits. Maybe you should go down there and give your input."

"Yea," he said, nodding. He felt incredibly happy and at the same time he felt like he should be happier. It was a strange sensation.

"Thank you, Valkyrie, for making this happen," he said.

"You made it happen. And thank you for making music in my life." They kissed softly.

"Let's go to bed," said Jordan.

Val followed him upstairs. She tasted his tears on her lips.

When Jordan was back at home, Jerome asked the boys to get together in the main room.

"Guys, I have to tell you something." Jerome leaned back against the kitchen counter piled with takeout containers, looking down at the floor.

"Yea?" said Matt.

"I'm moving out."

"Whaaat," said Bubba. "You're moving back with your parents? Jay, the food is good, but Kanata sucks."

"Rachel and I are getting a place," he said.

"Are you fucking serious? Tell her no," said Matt.

"Nah, I want to. We're getting more serious, she's graduating soon and she's got a good job lined up so she wants to move somewhere nice. We're gunna find something together in the spring."

"What about the Waves?" said Jordan quietly.

"It's all good! The band's gunna be fine! I'm just moving in with Rachel eventually. Like it's gotta happen eventually."

"You've got a point bro, but what happens when she finds out that all the time you don't spend with her you're playing video games?" laughed Bubba.

Matt sniggered, and even Jordan grinned.

"That's bullshit."

"She'll dump your ass, I'm telling you," said Bubba.

"I'll find someone to rent my room, no worries," said Jerome, ignoring Bubba.

"Maybe we can make your room a living room," said Jordan. "We're doing pretty good with the gigs. We could get a full size couch in here."

"Someone's getting fancy hanging out with a rich bitch," said Matt, his eyes glittering.

Jordan frowned. "What, I can't be the only one who doesn't want to live in a dump forever."

Jerome doesn't want to either, realized Jordan. Their eyes met and they looked away.

"Hey now, hey now," said Bubba, raising his hands. "Let's all calm down here. Jerome, I for one am happy for you, and I say we keep your room open for a while just in case it doesn't work out with your shack-up. If we want to fill the room we can, it's not a big deal."

"Cool. I just wanted to let you know, give you lots of notice..."

"Thanks," said Jordan. There was no emotion in his voice. He understood but he didn't want Jerome to leave either.

Matt went down the hall to his room and slammed the door. He was pissed but they all knew he'd be fine in a few hours. Jerome gave Jordan's arm a squeeze.

"It's all gunna be fine," he said.

Jordan lay down on his bed. He and Jerome had been friends a long time. Moving in with a girl—a woman—was serious.

Is he in love? thought Jordan. He wondered if everyone fell in love the same way, or if there were different ways. He felt like his own love was something especially incredible, but he knew that was probably silly. He had told Sarah Singh that he loved her hundreds of times, but every time he had said it he knew that he wasn't in love with her. The bond between he and Valkyrie was like nothing he ever imagined possible. His love for her, and their love for one another, was like a new secret world of colours unfolding inside the black and white world he had always known.

The thought of moving in with a partner never crossed Jordan's mind before. It had simply never entered his consciousness as something that he would do.

Would I move in with Valkyrie, if she asked me to? he thought. He imagined living with her, waking up every day in her apartment. It was a lovely thought, but Jordan would never feel at home in a place that was so strongly hers. He would have to make some corner his, where his instruments could live.

He shook his head with a wry smile. *Slow down Jordan,* he thought to himself. Valkyrie Snow wasn't inviting anyone to live with her anytime soon.

Jordan made an appointment to go by the Hymnal to give his edits. For the first time in his life, he was feeling like he was in control. He was starting to really see the results on his body of going to the gym. He felt it too. When he walked to work he felt long and lean, his muscles kicking into a higher gear as he walked with more purpose. He had cut back on the cigarettes as well. The effects were palpable on his voice, driving him to want to cut down more. The weekends at Glasshouse relaxed his body and his mind, and in general he felt like he was moving in a direction. He couldn't see where the road was leading, but it wasn't straight to the grave. His worst fear was dying a gig rat on poverty wages without even trying to make his dreams come true.

Even if I die tomorrow, thought Jordan, *at least this album was recorded.*

He had a feeling that if something happened to him, Valkyrie would make sure his music got out there. She believed in him. Would the boys keep making music? Maybe, but like Nirvana, it would never be the same without Kurt. Shoulda, coulda, woulda. Jordan's thoughts often drifted to morbid places, like imagining how people would react to his death, but today he didn't feel sucked down by it, plunged into a pit of self-loathing. He felt okay.

The Hymnal contacted Valkyrie when the album was ready.

She was back to working from home so she went to pick it up right away.

She rang Jordan.

"Hey Valkyrie." His voice was tender. He was pleased to hear from her.

"What are you up to today?" she asked.

"Just sitting on my bed, listening to music. Thinking of you."

"Mm, sounds nice. I'm on my way over. I have something to show you."

Jordan felt panic creep up inside him.

"Over? Here? I can come over…"

"I'm almost there," she said. "You'll like this. I bet you can guess what it is."

The album, thought Jordan.

"Yea…" he didn't know what to say. He didn't want her to see the way he lived, but he felt like he couldn't tell her that. She would think that he didn't trust her.

"See you in ten."

"Okay, bye."

Click.

Jordan took a scan of his room. It was okay. He hurried down the hall to the kitchen. It was filthy. He dug around the cupboards looking for trash bags. He didn't find any. Panic expanded in his chest. He opened the door to Bubba's room. Alex was curled up in a pile of blankets on a bare mattress, fast asleep. It was three in the afternoon, but Bubba was a night creature. Jordan grabbed a laundry basket, dumping the dirty clothes on the floor. He brought it into the kitchen and pushed all the garbage off the counter into it. Then he put it back in Bubba's room and closed the door. He could apologize later. He hastily piled the dirty dishes in the sink, and wiped the counter with a cloth. He looked at the cheese and sauce encrusted stove with skepticism. He grabbed a large cutting board and placed it over the worst part, wetting the rest and scraping the chunks off with a knife. He had just wiped it cleanish when he heard the buzzer. He pressed the unlock button, imagining Valkyrie in the piss-drenched elevator. He quickly washed his hands, drying them on his pants. He looked around the apartment. It looked a lot better than it did ten minutes ago, but it was still a slumhole.

There was a soft knock at the door. He exhaled and went to answer it.

There was Valkyrie Snow, looking soft and clean and out of place.

"Come in," he said. His expression was dour.

"Hey," she said, giving him a kiss on the cheek. He was stiff and uncomfortable.

She went over to the two-seater.

"Oh, no don't sit there, let's go to my room," he said. She followed him down the hall.

He opened the door and she walked in, taking in the images he had on the walls. He shut the door behind her and stood awkwardly as she appraised his aesthetic choices. Every scuff and chip in the wall suddenly drew his attention, marks he never noticed before. He swallowed with discomfort.

"This is interesting," she said, walking over to a print by Hieronymus Bosch. It was a sample of the far-right panel of *The*

Temptation of St. Anthony.

"It's Bosch," he said.

"Yes, I've seen the original, in Lisbon," she said. "This is not the scene I usually see in prints though."

"The rest was water damaged," admitted Jordan. "I got it at St. Vincent de Paul for really cheap and cut off the ruined part and framed this. It's still one of my favourite characters though." It was a lady riding a fish in the sky. Val looked at it for a moment and then moved on to Jordan's other prints. Each one said something about him that she didn't know.

"You never told me you were an art collector," she said.

Jordan scoffed, embarrassed by the cheap frames and scattered prints.

"Doesn't everybody like this stuff?" he said.

Valkyrie turned to Jordan, eying him with critical interest.

"No Jordan, no they don't. You have absolutely no idea how special you are sometimes."

He furrowed his brow skeptically. When he thought about it, he realized that he was the only person he knew with Bosch or Naoto Hattori on their wall. Some of the band posters he chose because he liked the images, and others were because he admired their music. He looked around the room. The collection, if evaluated as a whole, was unique. He realized that Val wasn't looking at the cracks in the walls; she was admiring his taste.

Val looked around the room, sitting down on the bed. Being in Jordan's apartment reminded her of her life in university, living in crumbling apartments with a strange mix of people. She leaned back, looking at Jordan in his faded jeans and hoodie, his shoulder-length hair a bit greasy but not dirty, standing in his natural habitat. The walls were painted dark blue like a night sky, hiding the imperfections of low-income housing, accented with gold and silver and wood frames that were scuffed and chipped on close inspection, but the overall effect was one of decrepit Renaissance parody. His bed was propped up on milk crates and she could feel them through the thin mattress, but the blanket was clean and the bed made.

He's doing the best he can with what he has, she thought. *My starving artist...*

Her eyes lingered on his chest and biceps, and she felt a warm kick of lust.

"Come here," she said, opening her knees invitingly. Jordan climbed on top of her, kissing her roughly, the familiar bed preparing him to hump away his anxiety in the way he was used to. He pulled down his pants and kicked them unceremoniously to the bottom of the bed. Val growled with pleasure, imagining that she was a nude model who had followed her artist home and was fucking him in his decaying boarding-house room in a seedy Paris neighbourhood. She whimpered with pleasure, and he reached down and groped her uncharacteristically.

He's not a gentleman in his own bed, she thought. *He must be handling me like a girl from the bar.*

"My artist," she murmured, clawing his back. He slid into her waiting wetness with a half-boner. He always had more trouble getting it up in his own bed.

Valkyrie shifted the fantasy to one that was closer to reality. She imagined that she was a wealthy French aristocrat, some fortuned widow, sneaking off to make love to her peasant artist lover. She thrust into him harder.

Hurry, my love, before they catch us, she thought. Jordan made a small pleasure sound as she clenched hard with her pelvic muscles. She felt him stiffen and she thrust faster. The bed started to move, sliding on the floor and the milk crates banged into the wall over and over.

I'm having sex in a slum, thought Valkyrie, and instead of disgusting her, it turned her on. She arched her back in bliss. His poverty made her feel young.

Matt listened through the wall as she moaned.

After Jordan and Valkyrie were done, they lay in bed listening to the album.

It's fucking rad, thought Jordan. Elephantine did a great job. Jordan couldn't wait to share it online. Some artists still tried to sell their music, but it was almost impossible nowadays. The Waves would exchange Audiocoin for easy access to their music. Audiocoin was a form of payment for fans in exchange for labour like social media shares. The key was to make them feel like they weren't performing labour—"share this and get a coupon" sort of thing.

"We should do a launch party," said Valkyrie.

"Yea? Like a special concert sort of thing...?" said Jordan.

"Sure. Whatever you want it to be."

"That sounds like a good idea," said Jordan carefully. He didn't want to overcommit himself to something that would stress him out.

Val kissed his shoulder. She could tell he wasn't super enthusiastic about the idea.

"If you want any help with that, let me know. No pressure."

"Yea? Thanks babe."

"Anything to help you with your music."

"You've done so much already... thank you."

They cuddled. Val's back felt the uneven supports of the milk crates. This was a fun little adventure, but Val could see why Jordan preferred coming to her house.

"Now I need to work on the second album," said Jordan.

"Mmm, and it's coming along, isn't it?"

"It's coming. Hey can I ask you something?"

"Of course."

"I mean, can you give me your honest opinion, even if I don't want to hear it?"

"Sure."

"I know you love the Nightingale song, but how do you feel about the rest of the album?"

Valkyrie considered, and weighed her words.

"It's catchy. There are good moments. I think it's a solid first album."

For Val, that was a compliment.

"Best and worst parts," said Jordan.

"Best and worst... I'm going to say lyrics, for both."

"Lyrics!" Jordan was stunned. That wasn't what he was expecting.

"Your melodies, refrains, arrangements, are all decent. Your voice is incredible. There are moments when your lyrics speak some kind of truth that makes me want to hear more. There are songs that seem fairly... two-dimensional though. The subject matter lacks depth."

"Not every song has to have a message though," he said.

"True. But music should be about something, even just conveying an emotion or an experience. A lot of music nowadays isn't really about... anything. It's just filler. It's a beat connected to words, like a robot. No heart. You have so much heart, Jordan."

Too much, she thought.

"Artists have the biggest hearts, and they feel on behalf of the world. Their hearts bleed for the world. I guess, sometimes I want to hear your heart bleeding in the music. I hear *it* in the Nightingale song. *It.* That thing. That magic."

Jordan knew exactly what she meant. Some part of him—his ego, no doubt—resented the criticism, but deep in his gut he knew she was right. Most of the album was meaningless. The parts that had heart were memorable. The rest was filler.

At least I've got it, he thought.

He snuggled into her shoulder. She could feel in his energy that he accepted the criticism. She decided to push it one step further.

"Lines about girls and parties, booze... even your songs about feeling good... there's something disingenuous about it that I feel and dismiss, as a listener. Maybe instead of pretending that everything is great and fine, you should write about this," said Val softly, gesturing around his room.

"What, my shitty apartment?" he said.

"Sure, and more. Your real life. Your Bosch and your Hattori. This isn't just *your* anxiety, it's your generation's."

"You mean like the Death Row Dollies," he said quietly.

"That women's prison band, yea."

Jordan looked sombre. "My greatest fear is that I can never make music like the Dollies."

"Why not?"

"How can I?! They're in prison! I'm a fucking dishwasher."

"You're in a different kind of prison, Jordan."

"What is that supposed to mean?"

"I am too," she said softly. "I want to be this good person and do good in the world, to create solutions for urban decay and poverty and environmental crisis, but I own multiple corporations, I have company partners who are invested to the balls in wars and armaments. Every day I feel more alienated from my own identity as a human being..."

Jordan could hear the fear in Val's voice. It was as fragile and panicked and alone as his own was. It was also oddly comforting.

That's it, he realized. *That's what she means. Being vulnerable and raw is compelling.*

"That's why you built Glasshouse, to get away from the world and find your own self again," he said.

"Yes. I need to drown it all out to hear my own thoughts again."

"Don't be afraid," he said. "I'll face my fears if you face yours. I'll write about shit that's real, and you do what you need to do."

Valkyrie looked Jordan in the eyes. He saw something there he had never seen before.

When Val first saw Jordan, she knew that he had a divine purpose in her life. Up until this point, she didn't know what that was. In this moment it became clear: Jordan was here to help her let go of her fears. She looked at him with respect, which for Valkyrie, meant love.

For the first time in his life, Jordan felt like a man, not a boy.

Jordan and the boys started planning a release party. It would be a concert, as usual, but this one would be at a friend's house. They would charge a small door cover so they could buy a few kegs of beer, and everyone was invited. The house was a single-family home in Sandy Hill that was being rented by eight people. There were three bedrooms in the basement, four on the second floor, and the attic was converted into a drafty low-ceilinged loft. The main floor was a large open-concept space that was devoted to parties and intimate concerts on weekends. The date was set for November fourth, just after Valkyrie's Mabon party. They were getting albums printed to sell at the event—sheets of tiny square stickers, like tabs of acid, you stuck to your phone and it absorbed the data. With their friends and fans, and the crowd that usually frequented parties at Animal House, as well as walk-bys in the Sandy Hill neighbourhood, they were hoping to make a good couple thousand dollars.

"Should we decorate?" asked Jerome.

"Pussy," said Matt. He was watching American men's rights videos online and was feeling angry lately.

Jerome rolled his eyes.

"I'm working on the fliers," said Jordan. "I'm gunna get them printed tomorrow and we can put them up and send them out on social media this weekend."

"Sounds good."

"We should print posters to sell too."

"Do you really think anyone's going to buy a poster of us?"

"Maybe. Print a couple just in case."

"Fine." Jordan decided to print ten or so.

"Can we get it advertised on like, mailing lists or event calendars or something?" asked Matt.

"Yea, you should definitely look into that," said Jordan. He already had as much responsibility as he could handle with finishing the promo materials and taking care of printing.

"I'm really busy with school," said Matt.

"Bullshit, it's not like we can't hear you in there, shooting the hell out of people in that army game you always playing for like six hours at a time," said Jerome.

"Like you're one to talk," said Matt with a sneer.

"Okay guys, I'm heading out to work. Take care of it pleaaaase, Matt," said Jordan.

He grabbed his longboard and headed out. If Matt didn't do it then no one would and Jordan wasn't going to worry about it too much.

Jordan rolled into the Cherry without even the urge to have a cigarette.

"Hey Earl," he said.

"Jordan. I need to talk to you before you get on the line."

Jordan frowned. Earl never called him Jordan.

"What is it?"

"The big boss ordered the new Oracle system for the Cherry. You're gone in two weeks' time."

"What?" The news hit him like a wave of hot poisonous air choking him, blinding him. "You mean like, fired?"

"Yea."

Jordan sat down. "But I thought the Oracle was a management system! How can it wash dishes?"

Earl coughed awkwardly. "It's taking my job. I'll be washing dishes," he muttered.

"You're taking my fucking job?"

"Yes I am." Earl straightened up. "Now you can leave today or get on the line, up to you."

"I need the fucking money," snarled Jordan, heading into the back.

"That's what I thought."

Jordan spent his shift vacillating between fury and cold panic. He thought about all of the stupid little purchases he had made lately. It could be a year before he found another job.

And Jerome's moving out in the spring, he thought, a chill of icy terror running up his spine. The rent would jack up.

What the fuck am I supposed to do?

He felt himself teetering dangerously on the edge of a steep downward spiral. At least if he started crying the sound of the running water would mask the sound. He scrubbed harder.

I'm going to end up on the street cold and alone, begging for change, he thought.

No no, your friends won't let that happen, he responded to his own inner dialogue.

All he wanted right now was a big fat joint so he could smoke this pain numb. His hands were shaking.

You're such a loser.

Why do you bother trying to be happy? Your life sucks.

Jordan sobbed.

He needed a cigarette, at least. He left the line and went out into the alley to smoke. He sucked the cigarette like his life depended on it.

"What the fuck do you think you're doing," growled Earl when Jordan came back inside.

"Smoke break," he mumbled.

"What did you say?!"

"I said I was taking a smoke break," he said loudly, looking Earl in the eyes, his expression unhinged.

"Lazy fuck," said Earl, walking back to the front.

"Okay Scrub," said Jordan, loud enough for him to hear. Earl didn't look back.

That night, Jordan dulled out as he rolled home from work on his longboard. His eyes were glassy, like there was no one inside. When he got home, he went straight to his room and slammed the door. He flopped onto his bed and checked out the job postings on Sellit.ca.

The pickings were slim, mostly wanted entries from people looking for work. There were a few postings for dishwashers, and Jordan sent messages to each one. Maybe he would get lucky. He curled up in a ball and willed the terrible thoughts to go away. He wished he could fall asleep. Any dream was better than this.

Valkyrie was busy planning her Mabon party. Some of the women coming she hadn't seen in years and she was looking forward to an incredible weekend. She ordered ten canvas bell tents which she would decorate with beautiful fabrics and twinkling lights. She would set up a harvest table by the fire for shared meals, and she was considering hiring a string quartet to play music in the evening. There was so much to do.

Kale was coming up early to help her set up. It was going to be a lovely visit.

The next morning, Jordan checked his messages. No responses.

He opened his search engine and typed in "Ottawa jobs". There were pages and pages of job search websites. They were all full of ads and most of the jobs were bullshit, making him sign up, give his personal information, and share things on social media. Basically he was performing free labour in the desperate pursuit of work. After two hours of this he gave up and cranked up the Dollies as loud as possible. They screamed into his ears as he tried to fall back to sleep.

Jordan drifted in and out of his cat nap all day. He felt guilty for not going out to look for a job, but he knew it was pretty pointless unless you had a contact to hook you up. At least he had sent out messages on Sellit.ca yesterday. He curled up in his blankets and pulled out his book. Maybe escaping into a fantasy world would help take his mind off things. He shivered. It was getting cold outside. They would need to turn the heat on soon. Jordan groaned inwardly, trying not to think about the cost.

There was a knock on his door.

"Yea?" he called.

"Did you finish those ads?" said Matt. "I want to get them sent out."

"Almost done," said Jordan. He couldn't bear to talk about losing his job yet.

"K cool. Send em to me ASAP okay?"

"Yea I'll work on that now." Jordan pulled his laptop off the dresser and into the bed. Matt left.

I could take this time off work to really put a lot of time into the band, thought Jordan. The idea of blindly trusting the universe to reward his creative efforts with success was terrifying, and he put the thought out of his mind to avert panic. He focused on the poster.

Just get it done and send it to Matt, he thought over and over.

He played around with some of the images they had taken on recording day. They actually looked pretty good. The light was great that day and some of the pictures looked pretty professional. Just looking at them calmed Jordan and made him feel better. He experimented with his favourite fonts and photo editing filters. When he was satisfied, he sent it off to Matt and the print shop. Hitting "send" filled him with a gulp of panic, but after it passed he felt extreme satisfaction for actually finishing something. Jordan was acutely afraid of fucking up.

Tomorrow I'm going to bring a demo to Larry, he thought. *Today, I've done enough.*

He spent the rest of the evening watching an endless stream of internet video feed. He fell asleep feeling guilt pressing down on him like heavy hand.

The next day, Jordan woke up feeling more optimistic. In a rare burst of energy, he went to the gym as soon as he woke up.

At least I still have this, he thought, pumping out his anxieties on the rowing machine. He took a long, steamy shower and headed out to Live on Elgin to bring Larry the demo.

"Jordan. How you been?"

"I made the demo," said Jordan, holding it out proudly. "This one's for you. Check it out."

Larry loaded it up on the sound system and let it play.

"This is great Jordan, seriously great."

Jordan smiled. "Thanks. That means a lot."

"You look tired. Everything okay?"

Jordan's smile faltered. "Uh, I lost my job."

"At the Cherry? I'm sorry to hear that."

"Yea."

"If there's anything I can do…"

"Well if you have room for me here?"

"Sorry man, times are hard. I do mostly everything myself these days and the staff I have I gotta look out for. You understand."

Jordan nodded. There was nothing to say.

"If I hear of anything though, I'll keep you in mind," said Larry.

At least that's something, thought Jordan. *Larry knows a lot of people.*

"You could take it as an opportunity though, y'know, to do music full time."

"The thought did cross my mind," said Jordan. "I gotta eat though." He laughed, a panicked, depressing sound.

"I hear ya."

"Well I'll see you around Larry."

"Yea. Thanks for this." Larry gestured to the air as the album played. "I'm glad you bit the bullet and did it."

Jordan left. He didn't want to go back home just yet. He thought of going to Bridgehead, but he didn't want to spend any money. He dialled up Valkyrie.

"Hello?" Her tone was business-like at work.

"Hey Val." The words came out more doleful than he intended.

"Mr. Barker." Despite the formal moniker, Val's voice was warm and appreciative.

"How's work?" he asked. He sat down on a public bench on the corner of Elgin and Somerset, pulling his jacket tighter around him.

"Oh fine. Just planning all sorts of crazy surprises for my harvest party."

"Yea? That sounds fun."

"It's pretty fun, actually," she laughed. "What's up? How are you?"

Jordan swallowed hard.

"I'm stressed," he whispered.

"Oh no, what's wrong?" asked Val.

"Just… lots going on. Trouble with work. I need to get the fliers put up for the event. The release party."

"Oh… and you knew that would stress you out. I'm sorry to hear that Jordan."

"I put everything into this, and if it fails…" Jordan's voice sounded pained. "Well it needs to succeed."

"Get your fans to help."

"What? No I couldn't ask for help like that, I have nothing to give them…"

"Just ask. I'm sure you'll get some volunteers, and it'll be more fun."

That's not a bad idea, he thought.

"Will you stay on the phone with me while I do it?"

"Sure," said Val softly.

Jordan went into his Facebook app and sent out a message to their followers. If he was at home he probably wouldn't have hit "send", but having Val on the phone gave him courage.

"There. I did it," he said.

"Great sweetie."

"Can I come over?" he asked.

"I'm really busy today," she said. "How about in a few days?"

"Could we spend a night at Glasshouse this weekend?"

"I'm so busy setting up for the party at Glasshouse this weekend."

"Let me help."

"Aww, Jordan, I don't want to stress you out more."

"You help me all the time," he said earnestly. "I really want to help you. It'll make me feel better, not worse, I promise."

"Yea? Okay. I'll be there Thursday until Sunday. Just call the Oracle to send the car over to get you anytime you're free."

"Sounds good."

"Okay, I have to go. See you this weekend," she said warmly.

"Bye."

Click.

Well at least I have that to look forward to, thought Jordan.

Over the next few days, the Waves received several messages from people willing to help put up posters. People also offered to share the social media posts in their groups. Jordan wanted to cry with relief. Too much time at home wasn't good for him, so it was also good to get out of the house and meet up with the volunteers to give them the promo materials. Some of the fans were genuinely awesome people, and Jordan was glad to meet them and hang out. He arranged to have a few people collect money at the door for the event in exchange for a copy of the album. The amazing part was that Jordan didn't even have to ask.

"Hey, I've seen you coming into Bridgehead," said a person named Jesse. "I work there."

"I thought you looked familiar," said Jordan.

"I haven't seen you lately."

"Yea I'm looking for a job at the moment," he said quietly. "Gotta cut down on those extras, y'know?"

"Hey well we're hiring right now, if that's something you'd be into. If you bring in a resume I can put in a good word."

"Seriously? That would be awesome. Thanks Jesse."

"No problem."

Jordan opened up the resume file on his computer.

Pretty pathetic, he thought as the words swam on his screen. He would work on this later.

He opened the browser where he was looking into places to promote their new album. It was time-consuming wading through the junk online. He heard that in the early days of the internet, user content was pretty direct. Now it was clogged up with advertising. Junk advertising was one of the insidious, irritating by-products of corporate capitalism. It infected everything eventually; the postal system used to be for letters and special cards, and then it was overwhelmed by colourful garbage fliers.

Jordan spent the next few days avoiding Bridgehead and watching pirated television shows online. After several days, he finally worked up the guts to drop off his resume. He put on his most charming barista face and walked in.

"Hi. What can I get you?" asked the man at the snack bar. He was wearing an orange t-shirt with a blue pocket. He had earring studs that were shaped like tiny analog cameras and he was wearing a snapback, but it was more hipster than bro.

"Umm, I'd like to see a manager please. I'm here to drop off a resume."

"Oh okay. I'll grab the shift manager. Just a sec."

He disappeared into the back. Jordan looked around. The shop was full. People were chatting quietly, reading, studying, or sitting alone listening to music. It was a nice environment. A woman came out. She had a lip piercing, short-cropped hair and a neck tattoo of roses.

"Hi there," she said, friendly, but with the undertone of a busy person.

Jordan extended his hand with the resume. He meant to shake her hand but he forgot he was holding the paper. Oh well.

"I'd like to apply for a job," he said.

"We're actually not hiring right now, or for the foreseeable future," she said.

"Oh. But my friend told me to apply, that there was a position open."

"Hmm. Sorry but we filled that position a week ago."

"Really?"

Jordan's face showed his disappointment.

"Sorry. Who told you about the job?"

"Oh, umm… I forget their name… brown hair, wears hats, androgynous…"

"Jesse."

"Yea, Jesse."

The woman took Jordan's resume.

"Well we'll take this and hold onto it, and if anything comes up in the future, we'll have it."

"Okay, thanks," said Jordan.

"Have a nice day."

Jordan left, kicking himself for not getting off his ass and applying sooner.

Stupid, he thought.

Jordan was hungry, and he would have liked to treat himself to breakfast, but he knew he shouldn't spend what little money he had left on eating out. He had crackers and peanut butter at home.

Just like when I was a kid, he thought, as sadness settled into his stomach like a bag of rocks.

When he got home, he fixed himself something to eat and went to his room. He felt misery overwhelm him. He looked back on the Sellit.ca forum to see if there were any new entries. He saw one that was just posted an hour before.

Need money? Paying minimum wage to help me sort garbage. Will supply the gloves. Must not be afraid to get dirty.

Jordan sent a reply. Then he opened his laptop to look at the pictures of the band, hoping they would soothe him.

Ding. He received a notification. He checked his phone.

> Congratulations! You got the job. Come to 494 Somerset Street at 8:30 pm tonight.

Jordan felt a flood of relief.

At one time, people were working sixty hours a week, men for ten cents an hour, women and children for three cents an hour. Eventually people couldn't stand it anymore and the labour union riots resulted in a forty hour work week. The time had come for a shift to a twenty hour work week, but the question was, could late capitalism sustain it? Capitalism functioned through exploitation of labour, and needed an econosystem of products and consumers. Humans working a mere twenty hours per week were disentangling themselves from product creation as well as consumption. They relied more on self-employment and self-sufficiency, like pre-capitalist economies. Late capitalism was a drag.

If Jordan wanted to survive the new economy, he had to figure out how to be self-sufficient. It was sink or swim.

At 8:15 pm, Jordan walked down to Somerset. He knocked on the door at 494. A woman with a Chinese accent answered.

"Hi, I'm Jordan," he said, holding out his hand. "You messaged me to come at 8:30 tonight."

She shook his hand. "Come in." She led him to the garage.

There was another man inside already, wearing rubber gloves. He looked to be in his 60s and had a large mustache.

The woman explained that she was a landlord and wanted Jordan and the other man to sort through her tenants' trash for recyclables. There was a landfill crisis and the provincial government was charging penalties to landowners who weren't recycling. The penalties were higher than the cost of paying scabs to sort.

The smell was terrible, but after about an hour, Jordan didn't mind. He let himself dull out as he picked through bags of plastic waste, cans, bottles, rotting used tampons, and all manner of house trash. He was glad he had gloves on; the thought of touching wet tissues and chicken carcasses with his bare hands made him sick to his stomach.

The three of them worked until about midnight. The woman paid them cash and sent them on their way. Jordan didn't even know their names. He walked home in the dark of night, feeling grubby and soiled with the refuse of strangers, but proud that he had cash in his pocket.

The next day, Jordan called the Oracle to take him to Glasshouse to help Valkyrie set up for her party. It was raining again and he stood outside under the eaves of his building, thinking about the work he did last night. It was fine for one night, but it certainly wasn't something he could sustain himself doing. His back ached from bending over, and he couldn't get the smell of rotting blood out of his nose.

He thought briefly of looking into sex work. Then he realized with dismay that the robots could vastly outperform him in that.

The car arrived and he got in. He thought about the release party coming up. That was something to look forward to. Hell, maybe he could make a career out of music.

This is it, he thought. *Time to commit to my music or die trying.*

At Glasshouse, Valkyrie was running around in the rain setting up tents and decorations. Jordan jumped in to help, and by the afternoon the rain cleared and things were looking great.

CHAPTER TWENTY ONE

The week passed quickly for Valkyrie as a few friends started arriving in town. She brought them straight from the airport to Glasshouse. The rest would show up just for the weekend. For most of her guests, this would be a much-needed social vacation in their extremely busy lives. For some, it was a sacred event. They spent the days visiting and catching up, and at night they had bonfires and danced under the light of the Mabon moon. On Friday, several more women arrived, and yet more would be coming on Saturday, the night of the main ritual.

"It's your dreams come true," said Kale, looking out over Valkyrie's domain.

Retro light bulbs twinkled between the trees like fairies in the night, lighting the forest with a soft, dreamy glow. Beautiful Russian rugs dressed the pathways between tents and the main gathering areas. The tents were draped in fabrics patterned in ancient designs, and Valkyrie had filled each one with comfortable mattresses and pillows and low tables to lie around chatting for hours. Valkyrie had ordered a truckload of dried fall accoutrement to create archways and wreaths out of corn stalks, bright red chokeberries, sheaves of wheat, hay bales, pumpkins and gourds. Silver-plated lanterns she ordered from the Grand Bazaar of Istanbul hung from trees, burning with pink-smoked incense. The cauldron in the main fire pit was always bubbling with a delicious broth, and Viking-style hard bread was perpetually smouldering on the stones around it. Women took turns tending the fire and flipping the loaves. The banks of the river were covered in rock formations and bouquets of white flowers to honour the river Goddss.

Saturday morning began with yoga at dawn in the old homestead clearing. There were a series of workshops all day on a loose schedule for witches of all kinds—from eco-pagan life hacks to highly theoretical environmental philosophy, ethical investment strategies, meditation rituals, social justice networking, fire cooking, and the Community Project. The Community Project was a long-term plan for building an intentional community for the aging sisters to retire together.

"We've been kind of relaxed about moving this along, but we may need to move a bit faster," said one of the American sisters at the Community Project meeting. "Transfolk and lesbians are starting to go missing from our communities. It would be great if we had at least secured the land in Canada for sisters who need to escape."

There were whisperings in the last few months that the American government was doing experiments on lesbians and transfolk. No one knew yet what exactly was happening but something was going on. The Community Project needed leadership, and in particular, financial leadership. Valkyrie knew that she had the means to make it happen, but she was incredibly busy with her businesses. No one pressured her directly. They knew that whoever took on this task would be changing their life forever; not a decision to make lightly. Hosting the gathering was the extent of Valkyrie's desired involvement at this point.

To thank her for organizing the event, each sister snuck away one by one during the preparations for Saturday evening. They were collectively building a monument in the forest, a shrine to the spirits of the land. It was a massive wicker lady made of dead and living branches weft around twisted iron on a base of stone.

That evening, the ritual began as the sun was setting. The women and femmefolk wore beautiful dresses and crowns of harvest bounty, gathering in a large circle around the main fire, reaching out to hold one another's hands.

Valkyrie stepped forward to speak. There was a basket filled with bundles of tightly wrapped dry pine branches beside the fire. She pulled out a bundle and tossed it in the flames. It erupted in a shower of crackling sparks.

"Thank you, sisters for coming to celebrate and honour the harvest together. It's wonderful to see each one of your shining faces and talk and catch up after not seeing you in so long."

The women in the circle squeezed each other's hands and smiled at one another. Most of them met while studying in university together, but there were others who knew Valkyrie through travel, work projects, and other serendipitous events.

"We welcome our sisters from near and far, who have come together tonight to raise our intentions to the Goddss. Sisterhood is powerful!"

"Sisterhood is powerful!" said the group of gathered women.

"Tonight I offer up my fears," said Valkyrie. I am giving away my fear of trying new things, and my fear of embracing change in myself and my life's journey. Nerthus, patron goddess of Glasshouse, I give you this sweet wine, mixed with my own blood."

Valkyrie slipped a bottle of expensive wine out of the pocket of her cloak. She pulled out the stopper and splashed the bloody liquid into the fire. It sizzled and burned as she threw back her head and screamed to the moon. When she was finished, she stepped back into the circle. The woman beside her stepped forward. She threw a pine bundle from the basket into the fire, and embers popped in a cascade of tiny cinders.

"This has been a difficult year for my family. My mother passed away this year. Our youngest child is off to university. Many changes. I am grateful for my strength, and I ask for courage in the coming winter. I offer this sweet yam to Aha-njoku. Sisterhood is powerful!"

"Sisterhood is powerful!" said the surrounding sisters.

After a few minutes, another woman stepped forward. It was Mika, Valkyrie's young architect from Hammer & Bone. She followed the lead, tossing a pine bundle into the fire.

"Thank you for inviting me to your harvest party Dr. Snow— Valkyrie. Over the few days I've spent here, I am getting to know a few of you, and I am in awe of your formidability. You are incredible women I am excited to know better. Valkyrie told me to bring an offering, and I wasn't sure what that meant, so I've prepared a folk song."

Mika sang a few verses of a Japanese song. Her voice was sweet and pure. When she was finished, she stepped back into the circle and the sisters beamed.

Each woman stepped forward to throw a pine bundle in the fire, take her turn speaking and make an offering of her choice. When they had all taken their turn, Valkyrie signalled and the string quartet began to play. The sisters laughed, enchanted, and began to dance. They danced until the sun began brightening the night into day.

The next morning the workshops resumed, and that night they had another ritual. On Monday morning, they said their goodbyes and made the journeys back to their homes.

At Jordan's house the atmosphere was tense. The boys had scraped together their pennies to pay for advertising and album copies and they were counting on making that money back. They already paid their November rent at the first of the month, but there was nothing else left. They would be using the heat sparingly in November for only the coldest nights.

The night of the big release party finally arrived and the Waves were itching with excitement. The energy in their apartment was palpable when they came home from the day's work. They took turns showering and got dressed to head over to Sandy Hill together. Jerome carried his guitar. The drums were already there because Matt and Bubba had brought them over piecemeal during the week.

They arrived just before eight o'clock to do final sound checks and setup. Some of the volunteers were already there. A table was set up at the front door with a coffee can for cover. The table had a box of album stickers and a small stack of posters.

"Is this all the posters?" asked Jesse.

"Umm, yea," said Jordan softly.

"There's what, like 10 here? I think you should have printed more…"

"Nah, we won't even sell those," he said.

"Seriously?" Jesse looked surprised. "I don't think you realize how many people like posters."

"Yea, but it's just us on it."

"Duh. You don't know how good you are, do you?"

Jordan felt a bit annoyed. Of course he knew how good the album was. The music, his voice, were awesome. He just didn't expect other people to notice.

"I know it's good," he mumbled.

"Do you mind if I go print more? There's a print shop around the corner. These look like display and you need a bit of a stack to make people see it's a product they can buy."

"Yea, sure I guess."

Jesse popped out to do some printing.

Matt imagined that the house was packed and played with the lights, getting them just right. Sapphire, Jordan's friend who lived in the house, came through the front door in her server uniform. She was getting off her shift serving dinner at the Cherry.

"Hi guys! You all ready?" She was all smiles.

"Hey," said Jordan, giving her a hug. "Almost there."

Jordan had met Sapphire at work. She was nice. She always had something funky and colourful going on with her hair and she was a bit of a stoner who was always smiling with a faraway look. Jordan wasn't sure if Sapphire was her given name, or just her name on social media, but that's what he called her.

Jesse returned with a stack of posters.

"Here we go," they said, spreading them out on the table. Jordan had to admit, it looked good.

"Cool. Thanks Jesse."

"Next time let's do t-shirts too!"

No one will buy t-shirts, thought Jordan instantly. Then he realized how negative he was thinking.

I guess we could try it.

"Let's see how the posters go," he said.

People started showing up around eight-thirty. The show wasn't scheduled to start until ten-thirty, but everyone knew that the kegs would run dry around then so it was a good idea to come early. By nine there was a really good crowd. The living room was full.

"Anyone buying albums?" asked Jordan to Jesse and the girl at the cover table.

"Yea we've sold about fifteen, and we've sold the same number of posters. I've already made back my investment." Jesse laughed. "Most people wanted me to set aside their posters, so I've put their names on the back and put them in this closet here." Jesse pointed to a hall closet behind the table.

"Sounds good," said Jordan. He was smiling with relief. It sounded like they were going to make back their money on the albums.

"You could sell merch online too, then you wouldn't have any up-front costs."

"Yea?"

"Yep. We should talk about that."

"Okay. Next week."

Jesse smiled and went back to chatting with the girl at the table.

At ten pm people really started to pack in. House concerts had to start earlier than bar concerts because of noise complaints in residential neighbourhoods. There were people outside smoking on the lawn, and the boys and the volunteers urged them to come inside so the party wouldn't get shut down by the police. The noise wasn't out of control, but they would be dialling it up soon.

"You ready?" asked Sapphire. The crowd was their biggest yet. "The first two kegs are down, we're just on the last one now."

"Is it that time already?" Jordan laughed and went to the stage they had set up in the living room. The other boys made their way over.

Jordan wondered if Valkyrie would come. He had mentioned

it to her, but she was so busy lately and this wasn't really her jam.

He held the mic in his hands, relishing for a moment the crowd of people pressed up to the makeshift stage, filling the house, just to hear their music.

"Let's get this night started," he growled, and Matt was off on the drums.

The energy was incredible. The audience was attentive and tuned in, and people kept walking in from the street to join. This house had a reputation for good parties. The Waves rolled through their set list with interjections by Jordan talking about the creation of the album. By the end of the concert, they had definitely made some new fans.

At the end of the show, DJs set up their gear and the party shifted into a dance space. Drug dealers in the neighbourhood were drawn to the beat like flies buzzing on corpses and around two am a fight broke out on the street outside between two guys who called this territory his. Sapphire and the other roommates called it a night and kicked everyone out. By the time the cops showed up to break up the drug dealer squabble that had devolved into a broken bottle versus a knife, only Jordan and the Waves were left in the house with the roommates and a few close friends, and the house was safe from getting blacklisted. After the cops left, they all chilled out on couches and the floor and passed around a bong.

"Thanks for letting us do this man," said Jordan.

"It was fun! We should do it again in the spring," said Sapphire.

"Yea I'm down."

"Maybe your new album will be done by then," she said.

"New album?!" said Jesse. "Awesome!"

"Oh I don't know if it'll be done by then…" Jordan looked skeptical. He thought about it. That was like seven months away. *I should be able to get these songs done by then…*

"But you said you were done at least two of the new songs though, right?" said Sapphire.

"Yea. Actually that might work." It had taken him years to write the first album. *Maybe it gets easier as I get older,* he thought. *Maybe I can do this by spring. That's like… a song a month.* Putting dates on things stressed him out so he took another big hit from the bong, letting himself veg out and fade away.

"Hey we sold all the demo albums and all the posters," said Jesse with a grin.

"Cheers to that," said Matt, putting his arm around Jesse's friend from the cover table.

"That's really great. Thanks for all your help," said Jerome.

"No problem. I'm going to start working on t-shirts."

"Ha, cool."

They all blitzed out and eventually Jesse and their friend headed out.

"See you around," said Jesse.

"I'm gunna take off with you guys," said Matt, following them out the door.

"I'm going to take off too," said Jerome. Rachel left hours ago. She had exams coming up and couldn't stay out late.

"See ya."

Jordan and Bubba stuck around, not ready to let the night end.

"Hey so Jordan never really introduced us properly," said Sapphire, sticking out her hand. "I'm Sapphire."

"I'm Alex. Everyone calls me Bubba though."

Alex and Sapphire chatted while Jordan lay on the floor, stoned thoughts swirling around his mind.

"...and two guys are moving out, so it depends on what kind of people move in," said Sapphire.

"Huh?" said Jordan, sitting up.

"Oh, two of my roommates are going backpacking and moving out. So concerts in the new year will depend on the kind of people we have moving in."

"We could move in," said Jordan, looking at Bubba.

"What? Yea I guess..."

They both thought about it.

"That *would* be pretty dope," said Bubba. "And Jerome already wants to move out in the spring."

"Someone would have to share a room with Matt," laughed Jordan.

"Well at least until another room opens up," said Sapphire.

"It'd have to be you," said Bubba. "You're the one with a girlfriend you can shack up with when you need privacy."

"Are you dating someone?" asked Sapphire.

"Well, yea I'm sort of seeing someone." Jordan and Val had not had a talk about titles or their status.

The rent was drastically cheaper than what they were paying for their apartment. Animal House was just as shitty and run down, but it had a much homier vibe.

"We make meals together and split on groceries and other supplies," said Sapphire. "The rent ends up basically being covered too because we rent the first floor for performances, jam space, art nights, whatever comes up."

In late capitalism there was a return to collective living. When most of the labour was automated, and driving up minimum wage stopped solving the problem of minimum hours, commune-style living arrangements came back for better or for worse. On the better end were small communities in equality-oriented collectives. These were a quiet revolution in community-building as well as a strategy of survival. On the worse end, wealthy landowners sometimes solicited help to care for their estates, but in many cases it amounted to slaving on their land with serfs without any rights.

Jordan was seriously considering trying to get a spot at Animal House. Rent consumed a majority of his income, and when that burden shrank he could actually devote his life to creating music. Not only that, but the house had a built-in performance space. After weeks of stressing himself out over money and work to the point of contemplating checking himself into the hospital for his own mental safety, the thought of living in Animal House was like a shining light guiding him toward a brighter future.

"Sapph, I'm serious, save me a room. I want to live here."

"Yea?" she sat up with a smile. "You can move out of where you're at by February 1?"

"I think so, ya!" Jerome held the lease on their place and he was moving out already. They were living month-to-month so they just needed to give their notice in the next few weeks. Jerome would have to live with his parents until he and Rachel found a place.

We gunna be roomies?"

"Yes, please. Yes."

"Okay cool. The room is yours."

"Okay well me too then," said Bubba. "Save me a room kay?"

"Done."

Jordan and Bubba chatted all the way home, but they didn't

talk about how they would break the news to Matt. When they got in, they fixed themselves bowls of cereal before bed.

"Breakfast for dinner," said Bubba. "Cheers." He held out his bowl.

Jordan tapped it. "Breakfast for breakfast!" he gestured to the cold light coming from the window in Jordan's room; day was breaking on the horizon. They had partied all night. They put their empty bowls in the sink and were about to go the bed when Matt came in the front door.

"Hey! We thought you were home already!" said Alex.

Matt just grinned and went straight to bed.

Valkyrie spent the week cleaning up after her harvest celebration. Over the weekend, she had made some interesting discoveries about the state of things down south that would help her make wise financial decisions in the coming months. The sisters were her closest friends, but they were also colleagues and powerful contemporaries in various research positions and companies.

Val considered attending Jordan's album release party, but in the end she put on her cloak, took a walk to Animal House, and listened from outside rather than going in. She slipped away afterwards without seeing him. She could tell by the sad state of the house with its sagging porch and drunken youth stumbling all over the sidewalk that it just wasn't her scene.

What am I doing here? she questioned for a moment, thinking about the kinds of people Jordan probably talked to on a regular basis. Then she just laughed at herself and enjoyed the music from a distance.

Fate works in mysterious ways, she thought.

When she left, she took the car straight to Glasshouse for the rest of the weekend to relax.

The day after the release party, Jordan was feeling incredibly energetic, so he walked to the corner store to get eggs and bread and made the boys a big breakfast.

"This is delicious," said Bubba, shoveling food into his mouth. They all stood around the kitchen, scraping gooey egg off their plates with crusts of bread they'd toasted in the oven.

"Okay, so before you go we should talk about the apartment," said Jordan. Jerome looked up. This was about him.

"As we know, Jerome is moving out," said Jordan. Jerome looked a little embarrassed. He still felt bad for leaving.

"I think we can take this as a sign that it's time for some changes for us, for our lives and the band and whatnot."

Matt looked at him, questions in his eyes. Bubba knew what was coming.

"Let's give our notice at this place. It's too expensive anyways. We can't afford it without Jerome, and we don't have a living room."

Bubba was nodding.

"I was talking to Sapphire last night at Animal House. She says they have a couple rooms opening up there in the new year. We could have jam space and the rent is way cheaper."

Don't they have like eight roommates?" said Matt. He sounded skeptical.

"Yea but that's like a built-in networking team," said Jerome.

When each roommate told a few friends about shows, word got around pretty fast.

"I'm down," said Bubba.

"Are the rooms upstairs or in the basement?" asked Matt. "I don't want to live in a fucking basement."

"I'm not sure," admitted Jordan. "I still want to move though. At least there's a living room to hang out in."

"I'd need to see the rooms first," said Matt.

"Okay totally fair. But I'm definitely moving there. February 1st," said Jordan, looking right at Matt.

"Me too," said Bubba.

"Already decided, I see," said Matt.

Jerome was nodding. This plan made sense.

"I'm gunna send Sapphire first and last months' rent as soon as I can get it together," said Jordan.

Jordan didn't want to mention the fact that there were only two rooms. This was enough information for one conversation.

Every day, the news coming from America was getting worse. Valkyrie's remaining investments in American industry were in jeopardy. The US government got the situation with the Rebels under control, but just as that was clearing up, there was a devastating blow from abroad. An international coalition led by oil's greatest competitors and their championing state interests took the chaos created by the Rebels as an opportunity to take decisive action against American occupation. Nuclear and renewable energy companies and a coalition of countries formed ISIC, the International Syndicate of Incorporated Forces. American troops were forced out of their foreign bases. New California declared state neutrality in the conflict to protect their blossoming economy, and America lost the support of the info warriors of Silicon Valley.

Thirsty for revenge, the Americans were not going to give up their network of overseas bases without a fight.

"Kill them dead!" shrieked President Spence.

Another major world war was looking inevitable.

America couldn't decide if it wanted to be a republic or an empire. While Spence scrambled to clutch at the international network, he was losing ground on American soil. New California was already gone, and other secession movements were gaining momentum. Guided by the invisible hand, Chinese investors had been buying up cheap land in the American South to build low-wage factories for years. The region was China's foothold in the North American market. Some of the products that Valkyrie was importing were "Made in USA", but they might as well have been "Made in China" because the companies were Chinese anyway. American anti-government groups pushing for low regulation made the transition easy.

Jordan and Sapphire worked out a deal where the first and last months' rent would be covered by a concert in the new year. Things were looking up.

A few days after their album release party, Jordan got a phone call from Jesse.

"Hey, what's up?"

"I need to talk to you Jordan..." Jesse's voice sounded anxious.

"What is it?"

"Something happened after the party last weekend."

"Umm okay. What is it?"

"I'm really nervous but I need to say it." Jordan was silent. Jesse exhaled on the phone.

"Matt followed us home after the party."

Jordan remembered how Matt came home just after he and Bubba did.

"He wanted to come in, and like I didn't know what to say so we let him in, and eventually my roommate and I wanted to go to bed and he wasn't leaving so we set him up on the couch. He went into her room in the middle of the night and forced her to have sex with him."

"What the fuck? Seriously?"

"Yea. Then he sneaked away and she told me what happened the next day."

"I'm… so sorry…" Jordan had no idea what to say. Did he believe it? He thought about how Matt cheated on all his girlfriends, how he watched an insane amount of porn, and the sleazy way that he talked to women on a regular basis.

This is probably true, he thought. He didn't want to believe it, but he did.

"What's she gunna do?" he asked.

"I don't know…"

She should go to the police, thought Jordan. Then he felt a wave of cold sweat. *What about the band?*

"Maybe she should get some counselling," he said.

"Yea? That's a good idea."

"Or like, see a doctor or something."

"What about the police?" asked Jesse.

"Well that's up to her," said Jordan quietly.

"She's a mess…"

Jordan said nothing. He felt really strange. He was oddly detached from the situation, like it wasn't really happening.

"I'm sorry to hear that." He was going to add, *let me know if there's anything I can do,* but he really didn't want to do anything at all, so he kept his mouth shut.

He wanted to tell Jesse that he was moving to Animal House, but it didn't feel like a good time to bring that up.

Fuck you, Matt… he thought. *Such a dumbass…*

There was a long silence on the phone.

"Well, I just wanted to let you know that," said Jesse.

"Fuck. Yea, I hope she feels better soon."

"Okay bye."

"Bye."

Click.

That's why I hate answering the phone, thought Jordan. He pulled his coat on over his gym clothes and headed out to the gym. The whole walk there, he imagined Matt slipping into the girl's room, forcing himself onto her. He felt sick. A huge lump rose in his throat and he swallowed it down, trying to shake the thoughts out of his head.

Jordan avoided talking to Matt. He was angry at him for risking the band and for treating a real girl like a video game character. At the same time he felt guilty for not telling him about the two-room situation at Animal House. It was a strange cocktail of emotions and Jordan reacted by avoiding Matt entirely.

About a week after Jesse's phone call, Jordan decided to talk to him.

Jordan knocked on Matt's bedroom door.

"Hey man, so I need to talk to you. You know how Bubba and I gave our deposit to Animal House? Well you waited too long and the other room filled up. Sorry man."

Matt paused the video he was watching on his phone and rolled over in bed to look at Jordan.

"You fuckin serious?"

"Yea."

"Fuck..." Matt frowned. "Well I didn't really want to move out of here anyway... I'll have to find some roommates online then."

"Yea, sucks man."

Jordan felt a huge weight lifted off his shoulders. He turned to leave.

What about the other thing? he thought. *Jesse's roommate...*

He didn't know what to say. He left.

CHAPTER TWENTY TWO

The snow began to fall in mid-November.

Jordan called Valkyrie.

"Hello?"

"Hey, it's me."

"Mmm, it's good to hear your voice."

"I miss you."

"Yea?" his voice was soft and vulnerable. Valkyrie felt like kissing him.

"I do. How are you?"

"I'm okay. I was really hoping to see you at the album release party." That was only half true. If she was there it would probably have stressed him out.

"I was there," she laughed. "Listening. From outside."

"Really? Aww well I missed your face." That was completely true.

"You want to come over?"

"Yea, I would totally love to come over."

"I'm at Glasshouse. I'll send a car."

Jordan was soon making the familiar journey out to the country. He felt his shame and anxiety release and float away as he left the city behind him. The snow kept falling, and soon the gentle flakes made a carpet of white over everything in sight. When the car pulled up and Jordan saw Valkyrie's smiling face at the door of Glasshouse, he ran up and held her tight in his arms, letting himself relax into the warm glow of her energy wrapping around him.

"You feel so good," he said.

"Mmmm…"

"I feel like I haven't seen you in so long…"

Valkyrie laughed. They went inside.

"So how was your harvest party?" Jordan asked.

"It was beautiful. Everything was perfect."

"How was the string quartet?"

Valkyrie had introduced Jordan to classical music and now he was hooked.

"It was divine."

"I'm sorry I didn't stay, I just felt anxious about meeting so many new people." The pressure of meeting so many of Valkyrie's friends at once stressed him out.

"It's okay. I never expect you to do anything you don't want to do. Ever."

The fire in the massive stone hearth was crackling merrily. Valkyrie put another log on and stripped off her oversized sweater and underwear. She jumped into bed.

"Come here," she said.

Jordan followed suit, crawling under the heavy covers with a sigh of contentment. He slid his hands over her warm body under the blankets, feeling his heart opening, pouring love into her. He climbed on top of her, holding her tight, burying his face in her neck. He relaxed there, letting their reconnection warm. He was so happy to be here again in Valkyrie's arms. His body agreed, desire awakening in him. He kissed her deeply.

Valkyrie kissed him back, holding his backside in her hands. His eyes were closed, and he had the most earnest expression on his face, like her kisses were either causing him pain or bringing him back to life. She kissed him harder, pulling his bottom lip with her teeth and rubbing up against him. She looked into his eyes framed with long lashes and his long hair falling over his face as he brushed it behind his ear. Her desire spiked and she suddenly wanted him so badly.

He's so beautiful... she thought. There was something about their carnal connection that was like nothing she had ever felt before.

Jordan felt himself slide into her, gasping with satisfaction and massaging her slowly, moving in a circular motion. He kissed her deep, holding her tight in his arms as he merged with her, the intensity of their connection rising. It built and built until he couldn't take it anymore and he felt himself orgasm, his penis vibrating with pleasure. To his amazement, he orgasmed without ejaculating. His nerves continued to fire as he kept thrusting. The feeling was so intense and overwhelming that he saw stars in his peripheral vision as his nerves tingled all over his body. It was like nothing he had ever felt before. The waves of pleasure kept cresting until he couldn't tell where her body ended and his began. Tears ran down his cheeks. Valkyrie orgasmed and they relaxed into each other, throbbing with pleasure.

"What happened?" breathed Valkyrie. "Something felt different."

"I... think I just had a woman's orgasm," said Jordan. She kissed his cheek softly and he lay his head down on her chest. After a few minutes of cuddling, Valkyrie stirred, moving in a circular motion, teasing him into erection again. His desire returned and he was amazed to realize that he could be aroused again so quickly.

They made love as the snow fell around Glasshouse, the world receding into nothingness like the autumn colours beneath the snow, like nothing existed but this tiny island in a sea of white.

Winter always comes as a surprise, thought Valkyrie, sipping a steaming mug of tea by the fire.

"I always want fall to last forever," she said.

"Nothing lasts forever," smiled Jordan, sitting close and drinking tea with a nip of rum in it.

"Well just one more day then," she said, rubbing the tip of her nose along his arm. He cupped her chin in his hand and bought her face close to kiss her lips.

Valkyrie and Jordan settled comfortably into winter. They spent every weekend together at Glasshouse. It kept Jordan sane. His bank account was running on zero, but the band show savings were scratching enough money together for Jerome to pay December's rent. January was covered already by the guys that Matt found to move into the empty rooms. Jordan went to the food bank a few times and sorted garbage on Somerset when he got really hungry. Thankfully there were snacks at the gym that came with his membership, so as long as he went every day during the week, he got at least one meal of protein bars, nuts, and fruit. He didn't mind because it was all temporary. Come February, he would move into Animal House and focus all of his attention on music.

Valkyrie always paid for things when they were together. It was an unspoken circumstance that was pretty straightforward: she had money and he had none. So she paid. Jordan did his best to help out by doing the dishes and helping Valkyrie out with labour when she needed it.

"I have a present for you," said Valkyrie one snowy day in bed at Glasshouse.

"Oh yea?"

"Mm hm, your Christmas present," she said.

"But that's not for another two weeks!"

"Well, actually Yule is a feast of twelve days, and modern Christmas is mostly Yule traditions anyway," said Val. "But this is a gift I need to tell you about now so you can plan for it."

"Now I'm curious… what is it?"

"My friends are having a party in a place called Asheville, down south of the wall in the USA. This may be the last year they host it because of the troubles, so I booked us tickets by plane to Charlotte and we'll take a car over from there." By now Valkyrie had figured out that Jordan didn't really have family, so he would likely be available.

"Wow. Cool, I'm down. Thanks!" Fifteen years ago, just before the wall was built, Jordan visited the American side of the border at Niagara Falls. His brother Michael—the one who died of a Fentanyl overdose—had taken him on a road trip to the Buffalo area. It wasn't at all like Jordan expected it to be. He had seen pictures of shining lights in beautiful cities online, pictures from the 1990s. This road trip was nothing like that. There were dirty-faced children running around barren yards in tumbledown homes. Nothing had been updated since the 1990s. Whole neighbourhoods were abandoned. It looked like a war had happened and no one had cleaned up afterwards.

Valkyrie's friends probably don't live like that, Jordan thought.

Over the next few weeks, Jordan worked on his songs. As Christmas came closer, his expectations that his mother would call grew. He told himself that he didn't care, but he cared that she hadn't called, he cared that everyone loved Christmas except him, and he cared that his family wouldn't seem to notice if he lived or died. He felt a little guilty about making plans away from family for the holidays, and hated that he felt guilty.

As winter deepened and the darkness grew long, time seemed to slow down. Ottawans relaxed, cozied in front of the fire with a good book, their favourite music and their friends for some cheer. Everyone avoided the news, where American stories dominated, like watching a train wreck in slow motion.

"Every day it's another mass shooting."

"I can't watch anymore."

Jordan and Valkyrie blissfully ignored the news of foreign lands, lost in all-consuming passion in a monochromatic landscape of black deciduous bark and evergreen against stark white snow. Glasshouse was as beautiful in winter as it was in late summer. They made trails with their snowshoes through the forest, journeying further each day. Jordan shivered in his thin coat but he warmed up quickly as they hiked under the winter sun.

Valkyrie was always warm. She was drenched in fur, the thick rolls of cured flesh rippling with the shining hair of some gorgeous creature. Some poor animal died so she could be so warm and look so chic, but it was difficult in late capitalism to find any item of clothing that something, or someone, hadn't died or suffered for. At least fur was undisguised barbarity. The cheap tops for sale on racks at the mall were painstakingly created by workers made invisible behind concrete walls without windows. Citizens of the rich countries who took advantage of their labour occasionally received a jarring reminder of the past life of their purchases—a hastily snapped photo of a Chinese worker in some dungeon on a smart phone that was supposed to be empty, a note hidden in a plastic purse or stitched into a seam that said "Help! I'm living in hell!". The middle-management jobs in many countries were being automated, but the small nimble fingers of children were still more agile than the machines, and the operating costs of prison labour were still cheaper. Valkyrie did her best to avoid human slavery, but she wore fur and she ate good meat.

The air was frigid and clear, and Jordan's teeth were chattering today. Val lay down in the snow, comfortable and warm, and pulled Jordan down on top of her, pulling up her skirts and wrapping him in furs. He was warm in no time.

Christmas came quickly. Valkyrie and Jordan were set to fly on December 23rd, and Jordan's mother called him on December 22nd. As the phone rang, he was tempted to just ignore the call, but he had been waiting for it for so long that he couldn't bear it. He answered.

"Hello?"

"Hi honey. When are you getting here?"

"Huh?" Jordan tried to keep calm to pretend that he didn't know what she was talking about.

"When are you getting here? For Christmas."

"What do you mean, Christmas."

"You know, Christmas dinner…"

"I have no idea what you mean."

"Jordan honey don't be stupid you know what I mean."

"I haven't heard from you in months. Did you call me in my sleep and we had a conversation I don't remember where you invited me for dinner, or have you just not called me in fucking months. In a year." Jordan's voice was ringing with emotion, and the more he tried to hold it back, the more cutting it came out.

"Jordan I talked to you a few weeks ago."

"I called *you*. And you hung up on me."

"That's not fair Jordan, you called in the middle of the night."

This was not how Jordan wanted this conversation to go. *Jordan, I'm sorry I've been distant. Please come for Christmas? Sorry mum, I have plans with my other family. One that cares about me. Have fun alone.*

Jordan took a deep breath. "This is too little notice. I made other plans."

"No. Jordan, that's not acceptable. Get on a bus and get your ass here."

"I'm not kidding. Someone invited me somewhere and I'm going." *Someone who loves me. Someone who cares if I live or die.*

"How could you do that to me?" Her voice was shrill.

"How could *I* do that to *you*? How could I spend Christmas with someone who gives a shit about me? Who actually invited me to spend time with them? Gee, let's work that one out..." he was grinding his teeth, his tone heavy with sarcasm.

"Jordan don't be like this. I'm calling to invite you! And besides, I shouldn't have to, I'm your mother."

"Yea some mother! December 22nd. When was the last time you called, this time last year?"

"Oh stop exaggerating..."

Jordan could have easily flown off the handle but he felt a twinge of guilt for not going to see her.

"I'm not coming. You didn't give me enough notice. I've made other plans. I've got to go now, okay? Merry Christmas."

"Okay honey." She sounded broken. "Merry Christmas."

Click.

Jordan paced back and forth in his room.

How could I make other plans on Christmas? You mean the thing you didn't invite me to? He checked the time.

Good, the gym's still open. He grabbed his bag and stormed out the door.

Jordan kept replaying his conversation with his mother in his mind over and over, and pumped the stationary bike harder and harder. He had the resistance level jacked and the sweat was pouring off of him. That night, he fell into bed exhausted, putting his mother out of his mind and looking forward to a vacation in a faraway place.

A car came to get him in the morning to bring him to the airport. The experience was surreal. He couldn't believe that in just a few hours he would be on a plane leaving the country. The airport was small with surprisingly few people. He went to Departures and there was Val, wearing a light jacket and toting a small bag.

"Ready my love?" she said, slipping her hand into his, her eyes twinkling.

"Is that all you're bringing?" he asked.

"I've ordered outfits sent out for the party already, they'll be waiting for us when we get to Ashemore."

"Seriously?"

"Mmm hm, I picked out something special for you to wear." She was grinning. Jordan couldn't imagine what that meant.

"We've been getting to know each other over the last few months, and I'm ready to share another part of my... desires... with you," she said carefully.

"Oh yea?"

"Yes. This will be unlike any party you've ever been to before, I think." She was excited thinking about it.

"I'm just happy to be spending Christmas with you," he said. Her grin faded. He sounded sad. He was thinking about his family. She leaned down and kissed him softly. His sadness melted into warmth.

"Let's get out of here."

They checked in and waited in pre-boarding at their gate.

"What kind of food will they have there?" asked Jordan. He imagined piles of burgers and fries, as portrayed in old Hollywood movies from the 2000s that were set in America.

"At Ashemore? Everything you can imagine."

"I meant in general."

"Well in general, you're lucky to find anything that isn't cellulose pumped with corn syrup and fluffed with hydrogenated oil and some artificial flavour. They don't have the same laws about that there. But Ashemore is different."

That would be hard for Jordan. He tried to stay away from empty calories because he would just get hungry again in a few hours.

A voice on the loudspeaker announced that their flight to

Charlotte was boarding. Jordan felt excitement rise in his throat. This was actually happening. Valkyrie squeezed his hand.

"Your excitement is contagious," she said.

They presented their tickets and passports at the wicket and walked down the boarding ramp holding hands. When they were about to step from the jetway onto the plane itself, Jordan reached out to touch the hard white shell of the vessel. He felt a thrill tremble through him. They made their way to their seats.

Valkyrie let Jordan sit in the window seat. He watched the world fall away beneath them.

When they landed at the Charlotte airport, it felt like a warm spring day. Valkyrie had a taxi waiting to take them to Asheville.

"Take us through the city," said Val to the driver so Jordan could see what it was like. The driver was an overweight man in his late sixties. The cab smelled like stale cheese.

Jordan had read online that it was "a city without spirit," whatever that meant. As the gasoline-powered car wove through Charlotte, the city looked just like what Jordan remembered of his road trip with his brother as a kid. There were long stretches of road in neighbourhoods where the houses were grey and close together, with patchy rooves sometimes covered in ragged blue tarp. The paint was peeling and the houses looked dilapidated and sad. Tiny garbage-strewn yards were edged in rusty chain link fences, and the roads were jammed with old cars that belched fumes.

Occasionally they would pass through a community where immaculate mansions stood back from the road at the end of landscaped laneways. The contrast was extreme.

Most locals who grew up there hated it, but to the surrounding towns, it was a great place to visit for the weekend for shopping and the Charlowinds roller coasters. It wasn't the beach, and it didn't have mountains—it was kind of bumpy with lots of pools—but the downtown was pretty. The strange thing about big cities in places like the United States, India or Mexico was the remarkable difference between rich and poor people, and rich and poor neighbourhoods. The locals barely seemed to notice.

As they left the city, Jordan noticed a vast field of tents. Children played with sticks in the dirt and people were cooking merrily over oil drum fires.

"What is that?" he asked.

Valkyrie cast a glance at the tent city.

"Those people can't afford homes. Rent here is really cheap, but the problem is that minimum wage is so low it would take a hundred hours of work a week to make even that amount of money, and that many hours are hard to come by around here."

Jordan could imagine. He could barely get twenty hours of work a week, when he had his job. At least minimum wage kept him from sinking. He swallowed, trying not to think about being unemployed.

"And the city lets them just camp out like that?"

"I doubt it... but who's going to stop them? They don't have decent police or public housing to send them to anyway. I bet the city just turns a blind eye, and hopes they have a fire accident some cold night."

"They wouldn't last in Canada. Too cold," said Jordan.

"True... our climate dictates a lot of our social engineering..."

After 30 minutes in the car, Valkyrie needed a rest room so they left the highway to go into Gastonia. The streets were lined with abandoned buildings. Crack heads scuttled into the shadows as they passed, and skinny boys with face tattoos limped down the street with pitbulls on chains.

The driver reached over to shut the air vents in the car, but it was too late. The smell of rot floated into the vehicle.

"What is that?" asked Jordan, wrinkling his nose.

"Factories," said the driver.

A lot of people here worked at the slaughterhouse or the rendering plants nearby that processed thousands of tons of waste like blood, bones and viscera. The factories took in the carcasses of inedible livestock and rotting bodies of euthanized pets from veterinarians and shelters, and pumped out livestock feed. If you could get a job at such a factory you were lucky; the work paid almost eight dollars an hour.

Gastonia was a beautiful little town up until the 1980s; the momentum of the Loray Mill Strike of 1929 propelled the town for a generation of prosperity, but ever since the anti-union administration of Ronald Reagan the town had been in decline, like much of small-town USA.

The car passed through the town and entered a new development. The vehicle stopped at a gate where a guard let them through.

In the 2020s, this suburb was built by a Chinese manufacturer. The American textile industry collapsed due to American retailers selling only foreign textiles. Chinese companies bought the mills and reopened them, saving the town. They had to pay the workers barely more than what they paid at their domestic plants, and they saved on transport costs. They built this housing development for the mill workers, where it was much safer and cleaner to live than the town, where one in three people experienced a violent assault. The workers were happy to live in their gated community and paid almost all of their wages back in rents. It turned into a profitable investment for the Chinese textile company.

The car pulled into the parking lot of a department store. Valkyrie ran in to use the restroom. On her way out of the store she looked at a rack of snacks. Most of the items were completely foreign, so she grabbed a handful and bought them on her way out.

"Snacks," she said, tossing them in the backseat with them. Jordan picked one up.

"Baby Ruth," he read. He looked at the others.

PayDay, 100 Grand, Twinkie, Zero, Big Hunk. He had never heard of any of them.

He ripped one open and took a bite. It was chewy and sugary. He knew his teeth would hurt later.

They got back on the highway and headed to Asheville. As they entered the town, the change in energy was palpable. The downtown was bustling with pedestrians visiting small independent businesses, and a band of four merry musicians played music in the street for passersby. There were old signs here and there that read "Y'all Means All!". When the state of North Carolina ended anti-discrimination legislation in 2017, the locals in Asheville made these signs in protest.

"Slow down," said Valkyrie to the driver, noticing Jordan looking at shops along the way. Jordan saw art galleries, colourful second hand shops and cheery bars lining the street. He had read online that Asheville was radically progressive by American standards, but it didn't really look radically anything. It just seemed friendly and clean.

"There is a lovely restaurant here that serves locally-grown foods, if you're hungry," said Val.

"Sure. I'd like to get out and walk around too if we can," said Jordan.

"Let us out here," said Valkyrie to the driver. "Meet us outside le Lèvron in about two hours."

They walked through town, taking in the sights. Valkyrie had been here many times before but it was fun to see a familiar place through the eyes of someone new. They had a cozy dinner at le Lèvron, where Val ordered Cathead pecan vodka and shepherd's pie made of fresh local lamb, and Jordan started his meal with a charcuterie board and finished with mixed local vegetables sautéed over fresh gnocchi. Jordan felt more relaxed than he had in weeks.

"Thanks for this vacation," he said.

"I'm just happy to have you with me," said Val, squeezing his hand.

"What are your friends like?" he asked.

"I've been coming to Ashemore for over twenty years. I went through a lot of personal changes in the last few years though… the sisters are my closest friends now. The Ashemore crew are friends I see once a year. We share… certain tastes."

"Tastes? Like what?"

"I like to experiment sometimes."

"Now I'm really curious."

"I come here to play out some of my non-vanilla fantasies. I told you I used to have a problem with alcohol… well I had a problem with other excesses too. I need to keep my regular life pretty regimented. At Ashemore, we can be whoever we want to be, just for the weekend."

Jordan was excited to find out what that meant.

They left Asheville as the sun started going down over the Blue Ridge Mountains, driving south toward Ashemore Estate.

Twenty minutes later, they were pulling up an approach road edging a massive lawn. About five kilometres down the lawn, a majestic building loomed larger as they grew closer. It was a French Renaissance castle built of warm grey stone. The setting sun was an orange riot over blue hills in the valley beyond the estate, and mist rose from the river below. Edward Ashemore had fallen in love with the hills and built the castle here in the late 1800s. At the time, the wildly opulent estate was surrounded by lower-class Appalachian settlements; the Ashemores were the living epitome of the new-money bourgeoisie American dream. They made the castle to mimic the monarchs of Europe.

Today the estate was open to the public for special events. As Valkyrie and Jordan drove up the lane, the last of the tourists were filing out. Ashemore was closed for Christmas. The private party was about to get started.

"Stop here," said Valkyrie softly. She got out of the vehicle. Jordan followed. "Take our things up to the house," she told the driver. "We'll walk the rest of the way." She shut the door and the car drove off.

The last rays of sunlight were fading and the stars were coming out one by one. Valkyrie and Jordan kissed on the lawn. Their cheeks were rosy from the cool breeze, and Val's wild curls were blowing in every direction. She shivered and pulled her jacket tighter.

"Come on," said Jordan, and they walked up to the house.

A guard opened the massive wooden door of the main entrance.

"Good evening, Dr. Snow," he said. She smiled at him and she and Jordan went inside. The main foyer was a massive room with grey stone walls and several Yule trees decked in red for the holidays. Jordan followed her through a series of grand rooms to a sitting room.

"Evander," said Valkyrie. A well-dressed man with silver hair turned, his sombre expression breaking into a smile.

"Valkyrie!" His voice was rich and deep, rumbling like a growl. "Goddess, how are you?" He kissed her cheek and they hugged. A woman in sweat pants and an active wear sweater came over, pecking her on the cheek and avoiding the hug.

"I just came in from a run," she said apologetically, hot with sweat. She eyed Jordan.

"This is Jordan Barker, my muse," said Val, pulling him forward by the hand. "Jordan, meet Evander Love and Lisbeth Ashemore."

They each shook his hand. Jordan felt power coursing into him. Maybe it was just the majestic setting of the house, but when Jordan's gaze met Evander and Lisbeth's, it was like he was looking into ancient eyes. Evander had lines around his eyes, but he was tall and lissome, with a firm grip and rippling with vitality. Lisbeth looked to be about Val's age, and equally energetic. Jordan felt dwarfed by comparison.

"Valkyrie, you're my muse," he said with a crooked grin and sidelong glance in her direction. He lifted his arm and brushed the hair out of his eyes. Evander and Lisbeth's gaze followed the gesture.

"How lovely," said Lisbeth.

"Welcome to Ashemore," said Evander.

CHAPTER TWENTY THREE

Evander and Lisbeth sent them to their room to change for the evening. Valkyrie slipped into one of her bamboo maxi dresses.

"Really? I expected some kind of crazy party dress," said Jordan.

"That's tomorrow," she said, kissing him. He put his hands on her backside and ran them up and down her body. She wasn't wearing any undergarments.

"Mmm," he growled. The soft bamboo felt so sexy against her skin.

"I've barely touched you all day," she said, kissing him more intensely. He was wearing nothing but boxers and she couldn't resist. She pulled up her dress and they fell into bed, kissing, groping for connection. His boxers came off and they found it, making love hard and fast in the stateroom at Ashemore Estate.

"I can't get enough of you," she said after, squeezing him in her arms.

She cleaned up quickly in the bathroom while Jordan put his clothes on.

"Ready?" she asked with a relaxed smile. Her hair was a tousled mess and her cheeks were red. Her nipples were visible under the thin fabric of her dress.

"Ready," said Jordan.

He was wearing a clean white t-shirt and black skinny jeans. They made their way downstairs. Jordan wondered what was in store for them here at Ashemore. Valkyrie had alluded to "excesses". What were they? He was having fun so far.

Every inch of the house was wreathed in garlands and bows for the holidays. The grand staircase was lit with hundreds of sparkling lights. It was magical. Valkyrie and Jordan held hands, walking slowly and enjoying the night. Jordan was glad he came. He squeezed Val's hand hard.

The castle was full of original finishings and furniture. The walls and floor were covered in heavy ornate wood and every main room had a massive fireplace with a roaring fire. Being here was like stepping back in time.

They made their way to a lounging room. The chairs were covered in red crushed velvet and the floors were carpeted with rugs patterned with ancient Persian designs. Evander was lying on a divan sipping a martini. Lisbeth had changed into comfortable jeans and a cotton shirt. They were an unlikely couple, but anyone could see that they were deeply connected. Seven or eight other people were seated around the room chatting.

Valkyrie made her rounds, introducing Jordan to her friends and acquaintances. They made small talk until late in the evening while servants brought an endless flow of cocktails and finger foods. Jordan ate so much that by the time they went to bed he felt ill.

Val and Jordan slept in late the next morning, and then spent the day walking the estate grounds.

"This is just what I needed," said Jordan. They talked a little but they spent most of the day in companionable silence, enjoying the North Carolina December weather and being outdoors and near the mountains.

The big party was that evening.

"I have something to show you," said Valkyrie when they returned from their walk around the grounds. She seemed both nervous and excited. She pulled out a long black box from the closet. Jordan sat up straighter on the bed. She looked him in the eyes for a moment. She hesitated, and then went back to the closet. She pulled out a garment bag and unzipped it slowly. Inside was an outfit made entirely of latex. She peeled off her clothes. He sat and watched patiently as she squeezed into a skin tight shiny white rubber bodysuit. It had leggings on the bottom and long white sleeves on top with a high, stiff PVC collar. She leaned over him and sucked in her breath as he zipped her up the back. Then she put on a black latex riding jacket and black boots up to the thigh. She tied back her hair in a neat bun. She completed the look by pulling out a black riding crop, and snapped it in her hand.

"What do you think?" she asked. There was a gravelly tone in her voice, like she was turned on in a way Jordan had not seen yet. He reached up and stroked her beautiful round bottom in the shiny latex.

"It's hot," he said. He wondered what she would pull out of the black box. He glanced at it with anticipation.

"Jordan, at this party are all free to do as we wish, dress as we wish, be as we wish here."

"Okay…"

"So if you're uncomfortable at all, please don't feel pressured, but I have something for you." She reached for the box. Jordan realized it must be something for him to wear. She pulled off the lid and tore away white tissue paper. Lying beneath was something made of black leather straps. She pulled it out.

"May I?"

Jordan looked at the contraption with a feeling of apathy, unsure of whether he wanted to wear it or not. He looked at Val and decided he would try it. He could see the excitement in her eyes and he was eager to please her.

"Sure, alright."

He took off his clothes. Valkyrie pulled another garment bag out of the closet. This one had a dark-purple-almost-black bodysuit that was sleeveless with long leggings. Jordan put it on and Valkyrie fastened it at the back. Then she pulled the leather bridle from the black box on over top. She fastened a wide leather collar around his neck.

"This piece goes into your mouth," she explained. "For when you don't feel like talking to anyone."

The collar had a large gold ring at the front. To this she attached a leather leash. She took one step back to admire him in rubber, holding the lead end of the leash in her hand. She hadn't been sure whether to get him the legless bodysuit or the one with leggings; she could see now that she had made the right choice. His pale legs would have been cold and vulnerable looking bare. The bridle against his chest in the suit was sexy, and as his long hair fell in his eyes he tossed it just like a mane. It was perfect. She stepped in close, running her hand along his bare muscled arm and kissing his lips.

"You look incredible," she whispered. He kissed her back, enjoying the tightness of the latex against his body. He looked at himself in the full length mirror. He was impressed. He looked really good. He and Valkyrie together in their latex suits looked hot.

"How do you feel?" she asked.

"I feel okay," he said. He wasn't keen on putting the bit in his mouth, but everything else was fine. He looked at Val's riding crop.

"You aren't going to whip me with that, are you?" he laughed.

"Not unless you want me to." Valkyrie had a wicked grin. Jordan grabbed her with both arms under the butt and lifted her up with a whinny. She laughed and shrieked playfully. He put her down and they kissed.

"My good boy," she whispered in his ear. Suddenly he felt a thrill tremble down his whole body from head to toe. It was a feeling he had never felt before. He nuzzled his nose into her neck and she stroked his hair.

"Put on your shoes, young man," she said.

Jordan went to the closet and found the shoes that Valkyrie brought for him. They were shiny black leather oxfords with gold spikes. He put them on.

"Ready?"

"Ready."

Valkyrie Snow led Jordan Barker out of their room on a leash made of leather and gold.

At first Jordan felt like it was Halloween and he was dressed for a costume party. As the *tap tap* of Valkyrie's heels on the hard floor echoed in the cavernous halls of Ashemore Estate, he relaxed into his role and started to enjoy himself. The leash seemed strange, but Jordan realized pretty quickly how fitting it was. The cord connecting them was like their energy anyway; the invisible pull he felt drawing him closer to his mistress was simply now made physical in leather and gold. Although it appeared that she was pulling him, truly they were a pair in a dance and she was leading. Besides, every time Jordan felt the slightest tug on the bridle, he felt loved and needed. Valkyrie would turn around and lock eyes with him, making sure he was okay, and he felt deeply cared for.

Christmas at his family's run-down house would consist of having conversations with people whose emotional range went from tired, to bored, to blindly angry, to tired again. This was much better.

Jordan followed Val down to the Great Hall. He heard the clink of crystal and cutlery as a servant brushed past. He felt suddenly shy in his latex suit, and then, as the doors opened he noticed the nude bottom of the man passing him in tight, assless leather pants. He looked around the room. Close by there was a couple dressed in full Victorian splendour, with corsets, wigs and petticoats. He noticed a mix of period costumes throughout the room. There were many French Renaissance looks, probably inspired by the estate itself. High ruffled collars, puff sleeves, and rich reds and greens abounded. Jordan noticed that a few men were wearing corsets. He could see that many dresses were cut away in the chest area and women wore their breasts exposed.

There was a massive banquet table laden with every kind of holiday food imaginable, and the biggest Yule tree that he had ever seen. He stood in awe, taking in the room. He felt eyes assessing him, and he turned to see a woman with her white hair piled high on her head. In her hand she held a chain, and at the end of the chain was a young man. His arms were tied behind his back. Jordan grinned.

A woman in a long black lace dress that was tight from shoulders to knees with a wide flare at the bottom strode over. The woman on her arm was a tall and willowy beauty with high cheekbones and silver hair.

"You both look gorgeous," said Valkyrie as they swooped in to kiss her on both cheeks at once. Lisbeth's bright red hair was styled in 1940s victory rolls, and Evander was wearing a slinky silver dress to match their hair with pastel purple eye makeup.

"May I pet your pony?" asked Evander, raising an eyebrow. Valkyrie gave the leash a little tug and Jordan stepped forward, sliding a hand around Val's waist and resting his chin on her shoulder. She smiled at him questioningly.

"Up to you," she murmured.

Jordan shrugged with a smile of acquiescence. He was open to this experience. Evander glided in close, running a long finger down Jordan's chest. They locked eyes.

She's beautiful, thought Jordan. He felt dazed in her gaze.

"We have some treats for you to try," said Evander, turning to Valkyrie.

Lisbeth gestured to a servant standing behind her. He came forward with a large silver tray.

"Just mushrooms for me," said Valkyrie.

"Still all organic, I see," said Evander with a sigh.

Lisbeth lifted a tiny shooter of Czech Bohemian glass from the tray. It was filled with a silvery blue substance.

"This is natural," she said, offering the glass.

Valkyrie took it cautiously. It didn't look natural. She smelled it. There was no odor, but she had a bad feeling about it.

"No thanks," she said with a laugh, handing it back. "I'm a creature of habit."

Evander gave her a small plate of crushed mushrooms and a crystal of Duplais to wash it down.

"Thank you darling," she said, swallowing the mushrooms and quickly drinking her Absinthe in one swallow. She turned to Jordan.

"Whatever you desire is yours," she said quietly, looking into his eyes. "Anything. Just ask."

Jordan thought about it. What did he really want? He looked at the tray. There were lots of things on it he'd never seen before. He recognized lines of coke.

"I'll take some of that Absinthe," he said. He'd never tried it before.

"Let him do it the right way," said Valkyrie.

The servant left and quickly returned with a crystal Pontarlier reservoir glass with an ounce of green liquid in the bubble. He rested an ornate silver spoon over the rim of glass and placed a cube of dark sugar on top. He struck a match, lighting the cube momentarily on fire, and after burning the edges he extinguished the flame by gently pouring ice water over the cube until it dissolved. He offered Jordan the glass, and Jordan sipped the cloudy green beverage. It tasted of subtle licorice and lemon notes. He nodded.

Valkyrie and Jordan continued making their way through the room. Jordan was feeling warm and relaxed. After an hour or so, he felt like trying something new. He signalled a servant.

"Do you have any LSD, by chance?" The servant scuttled away and retrieved a tiny white paper cut-out of a unicorn. He offered it to Jordan on a small flat golden spoon.

"See you on the other side," he said with a grin.

Val introduced him to some more of her friends, but as the drugs seeped into his system he was too occupied with his thoughts and surroundings to meet new people. He put the bit in his mouth and no one pressured him to speak.

Jordan was tripping hard, and the setting was perfect. The towering Christmas trees covered in colourful decorations were incredibly stimulating, and there were literally hundreds of poinsettias smiling at him from every direction. He followed behind Valkyrie, only a leash length away from her, on a magical journey through the castle. If anyone tried to touch him, she snapped the riding crop against her thigh with a warning smile. She knew he couldn't give his consent on acid and she made sure he felt no pressure, especially while he was wearing the bridle bit in his mouth.

The lights in the castle were dim and warm, and they wandered through a marble arch into a beautiful arboretum. The air was misty and tropical trees grew tall, surrounded by a thick tumbling underbrush of bright flowers. The ceiling was made of vaulted glass and Jordan could see the stars between the shining lamps hanging from beams on long black chains. He stood there enjoying the beautiful ceiling for almost fifteen minutes. He could see that Valkyrie's design for Glasshouse was inspired in some ways by this space. He reached out and held her hand. He looked into her eyes and felt like he was reading her thoughts and she was reading his at the same time. He felt incredibly connected to her.

People talked and heavy petted quietly on stone benches amongst the trees. After exploring the indoor garden, Jordan and Valkyrie made their way further into the castle, through another great hall with an eight foot high fireplace roaring with flames. A servant stood close by to feed it logs, and to ensure that no guests got too close. Above the hearth was a white marble carving of the ancient Minoan Mother Goddess wearing a crown of poppies in her hair and smoking an opium pipe. In Jordan's altered state of consciousness, she seemed to be alive, a stone goddess seated on a grand throne above the fire. The fireplace was the only source of light in the great room and the flames danced amid the shadows along the walls. They carried on, making their way into the library. It was a beautiful dark room decorated in rich reds and browns, and thousands of books lined the wooded twenty-foot-high walls. There was a smaller fireplace in this room as well, and several guests sat around reading leather volumes in high-backed chairs. Some were dressed in period clothing, and others in latex. The entire room was festively decorated with heaps of garlands and bows and there was a Yule tree in every corner.

Jordan and Valkyrie continued on their journey. They entered a room that looked out over the property grounds. One entire wall was covered in glass windows, and the other walls were stone. Valkyrie led them to a door that brought them out onto a balcony. They walked to the edge, looking down into the valley below, edged in cool moonlight, the Blue Ridge Mountains just shadows in the distance. The air was cold and Jordan shivered.

"Come here," said Valkyrie, wrapping him in her arms.

"I love you," he said.

"I love you too. Merry Christmas," she said, knowing the holiday was a tradition he valued.

He nuzzled into her, laying his head on her shoulder.

"Merry Christmas."

They kissed then, sloppy and stoned but feeling intensely connected. Jordan couldn't tell where he ended and she began.

When they were too cold to stay outside any longer, they returned to the Minoan Goddess room to warm themselves by the great fire. Jordan felt eyes watching him, and he looked around. He thought he saw someone disappear into the shadows, but he was high and it was late. He followed Valkyrie back through the castle to the Grand Hall.

"I'm hungry," he said, looking at the table of food and realizing that his stomach was empty. They walked over.

"I'm not ready to eat yet," said Val. She unclipped Jordan's collar, wrapping it around her arm.

"You go ahead, I'm going to go visit some more with Evander and Lisbeth. I'll come find you in a bit." She brushed her lips against his forehead and headed over to her friends.

Jordan felt overwhelmed looking at the food and didn't know where to start. A servant handed him a plate, and he shaved a piece of roast beef and plopped roasted potatoes and carrots onto it. Then he saw an assortment of casseroles that looked incredible. He took a serving of eggplant parmigiana and realized that his plate was almost full.

"Is everything alright sir?" asked the servant, noticing his expression.

"Oh, I realized I should have gone for less traditional things and tried something new," he laughed.

"Let me take that," said the servant, taking his plate.

"Um, well, okay," said Jordan. He hated wasting food. "At least leave the eggplant," he started, but the servant had already disposed of his plate.

"No need sir, there is plenty."

Yes but, it's a waste… thought Jordan, remembering the tent city he had seen this afternoon. The servant handed him a new plate and he was careful to take only small spoonfuls of things he wanted to try.

Jordan felt someone close behind him. He turned to see a man in a mask dressed as a French aristocrat. He had a perfectly sculpted beard and moustache. The man was looking at him intently.

"Hello," said Jordan, brushing the hair out of his eyes. The man watched him like a hawk but said nothing.

Jordan took his plate over to a solitary chair and ate his meal. Everything was delicious.

"Can I get you something to drink?" asked a servant.

"Oh, yes please. Just water," said Jordan. He could feel the man in the mask watching him from across the room.

He's probably just as stoned as I am, thought Jordan. He finished his dinner and sipped a few glasses of water as he people-watched from his chair.

Valkyrie came back to him. "How was your dinner, my love?"

"Just fine," he said, standing up.

"I'm going to go chat with some people over there, would you like to come?"

"Yes," said Jordan. He lifted his chin so she could put his collar back on. She uncoiled it from her arm and fastened it to his neck. She ran her hands through his hair, kissing him lightly on the lips. She locked the leash to the gold ring on his collar and led him over to her friends.

Valkyrie never imagined that Jordan would do so well here at Ashemore Estate with her friends. He seemed completely fine. She knew he wasn't a normie.

They walked over to an open love seat adjacent to the people she wanted to visit with. They sat together, curling up close.

"And who is this?" asked a man in a powdered white wig.

"Jordan Barker, a devastatingly talented musician."

"I see."

"He's quite sweet," said the woman beside him, an older lady dressed as a 1920s flapper.

They chatted about the state of affairs in America while Jordan sipped a gin and tonic, still tripping pretty hard from the acid. He noted that the mantle on the man's cape was encrusted with what appeared to be real rubies. These people were insanely wealthy. This was why there was a tent city outside of Charlotte. The French Renaissance eventually led to the French Revolution. Would hungry unemployed folks eventually storm this castle? What if it happened tonight while he was here? Jordan's thoughts steamed forward like a train. He scratched under his collar uncomfortably. He was starting to have a bad trip. He signaled a servant over.

"Could I have bump of coke?" he said quietly. Cocaine would bring him out of it. The servant left and returned with lines of coke on a silver tray.

"Just a bump, thanks," he said. He was afraid that if he did a line he would have a heart attack. He took a tiny spoon and used the end to snort a small amount. The reaction was almost instantaneous. Jordan levelled out. He was glad he didn't have too much.

Silly, he laughed at himself, *Americans are too complacent to stage a revolution against the people they aspire to be.* He heard a quote once that went something like: "socialism never took root in America because the poor see themselves not as an exploited proletariat, but as temporarily embarrassed millionaires." They couldn't tell that these celebrities and millionaires were their aristocratic overlords. They gobbled up footage of the lives of the rich like the peasants who queued up to watch Marie Antoinette take hours to get dressed in the morning. It was a precarious love-hate relationship.

Compared to these people, Valkyrie wasn't even rich. She could have been, but her motivations were not for accumulating capital. She didn't feel that she needed or deserved ostentatious wealth. Many of the people at this party felt no social responsibility for tent cities, and felt that they were entitled to their disproportionately privileged lifestyles.

Jordan realized that he himself felt entitled to fame and fortune. He shivered with discomfort. He decided that when he was back at home he would try to focus on the pleasure of making art for art's sake, not for the reasons that gave him anxiety. The thought of making art for art's sake gave him tremendous relief, like releasing steam from a pressure valve.

Jordan looked at Valkyrie. Her expression was impassive and she was listening to someone talking about Bill Gates' city in Arizona. He wondered what she was thinking. She felt his gaze and her eyes flicked to him for a moment. He saw a faint flash of smile in her eyes, and then she returned her gaze to the conversation. She slid her hand into his, rubbing his palm softly with her fingers. She was listening, but she wasn't nodding. Jordan could see the machinery whirring softly in her head, filing away this information. She wasn't just accepting it wholesale, but analyzing it through logic filters, cross-referencing it against other data in her vast memory.

She was a formidable woman, and Jordan stared at her adoringly, loving her body, her energy, her incredible mind and all that she was. He was utterly defenseless in his love for her. He lay down on her lap. She stroked his hair.

The next morning, Valkyrie and Jordan prepared their things to head back home. They went out to the lawn to meet their new driver. As they got into the car, Jordan heard the quiet shouting of a manager berating an employee. He turned to watch as an embarrassed servant cleaned up a mess at the side door by the kitchens with an angry man standing over him. Servants were throwing heavy black bags of waste into a large iron trash receptacle to be shipped away. A bag had torn open, its guts revealing last night's feast. Whole roasted chickens, cakes, and fresh cut fruit tumbled over the cobblestones.

Jordan got into the car and they drove away, back to the airport, and back to Ottawa.

They arrived late in the evening on Christmas Day. The airport was almost empty of people but decorated with green and gold for the holidays. Their car picked them up and they drove straight to Glasshouse. Fat fluffy snowflakes fell slowly from the sky, illuminated in the headlights as they drove up the winding laneway. They went straight to bed.

The next day Jordan and Valkyrie went out for brunch at Quaker Street Café in Westboro. It was a popular spot, and even on Boxing Day it was hard to get a table. They were seated close to four older people having breakfast who were chatting loudly about the strikes around the city.

"They're selfish, those retail workers. Striking right before Christmas. Now the children won't get the toys they wanted, and I can't even go Boxing Day shopping."

"They're so entitled."

Valkyrie frowned. This conversation was going to give her a headache, she could tell.

"I've never been on strike before," said one man proudly.

"Don't you work for Statistics Canada though?" asked the woman beside him. "You guys don't really strike... I'm a teacher; we have to." She rolled her eyes.

"Well... the workers' demands make some sense, right?" said the other woman quietly.

"Seriously?" said the man beside her. "You didn't vote in favour of striking, did you?"

"Well, no. But now that I've read the demands, they kind of make sense... the province is cutting benefits. That's going backwards." She was a cashier for the Liquor Control Board of Ontario.

"Cashiers don't need fancy benefits," scoffed the other man.

"Yea, how hard is being a cashier?" said the other woman. "I chase kids all day in the classroom. I need those benefits."

"Excuse me, I've wrecked my back lifting heavy boxes. That should count for something."

"That's all part of the job," said the StatsCan man. "Strikers are just lazy."

The woman was about to rebut but the man beside her jumped in.

"He doesn't mean you. The LCBO is a respectable job. He means the *other* retail workers."

The union is what made the LCBO a respectable job... thought Valkyrie.

"Do you want to move tables?" asked Jordan quietly. He could see that Val was annoyed, and he too was getting anxiety hearing these people talking. These were folks in secure, highly unionized jobs with benefits complaining about strikes by people like him who deserved to have the same level of job security.

"The government should round them all up and put them in jail," said StatsCan. "They're ruining our society."

"Yes, let's move," said Valkyrie quietly. Jordan signalled the server. They discreetly moved tables.

"I'm sorry about my generation," said Valkyrie.

Jordan turned to look back at them. They appeared to be in their 60s and 70s. How old was Valkyrie? Jordan wasn't going to ask.

"They should have retired long ago from those union jobs and demanded to be replaced by young people. Instead the only jobs for young people are part-time."

Older people in late capitalism had trouble facing reality. They dreamed of being rich and never wanted to retire instead of accepting their middle class existence. This created a vast subclass of underemployed young people. Mincome was critically needed, but this older generation was in firm control of government and refused to implement a program that benefitted future generations with no benefit to themselves.

The selfish generation, thought Valkyrie. *Whining and pointing to the aristocrats and their extravagance when the middle class holds all the democratic power.*

"When do you think your generation will be too angry to take it anymore?" she asked.

Jordan considered the question.

"When all my friends graduate from university and realize that their degree isn't going to pay off their loan debt. They don't know it yet."

Val nodded. They finished their brunch and then left.

That evening, the snow fell hard and wet. It was perfect weather to make a snow castle. Valkyrie and Jordan crunched around outside, playing in the snow. They hung their wet clothes by the fire to dry when they came in.

"Let's have a bath," said Val.

She poured essential oils into the copper tub and ran the hot water. Steam filled the windows of Glasshouse.

Jordan piled logs onto the fire. The chimney puffed smoke merrily. He put on the kettle for tea. Valkyrie tied up her hair in a loose bun as it curled around her face in the steam. When the bath was ready, she slipped in with a sigh. Jordan brought her a mug of tea. He took off his clothes and set them by the fire and joined her in the tub. They blissed out, relaxed and soaking in the heat.

"This is perfect," breathed Val. "It's exactly like I dreamed it would be, except that you're here and it's even better."

Except for not having a job, my life is just about perfect, thought Jordan. *Well actually I have a job. I just don't have a source of income.*

"I guess you never imagined you would meet me," said Jordan.

"Never in a million years."

He lifted her foot and massaged her sole, gradually moving up her leg. After he massaged both of her legs, she turned him around in the tub and rubbed his back.

The front door opened with a soft click.

"What was that?" asked Jordan, alarmed.

"It's the bot that feeds the nightingale. I ordered some dinner for us too," said Val.

A robot appeared carrying paper take-out containers. It was not in the least embarrassed that they were in the tub.

"Thank you," said Valkyrie. "Just set it on that folding table."

The robot laid out their food on the small table by the fire. Then it fed the nightingale and left.

For the first time, Jordan realized how dangerous technology could be. Here in Canada automation was mostly hailed as progress and a source of liberation. After seeing how the rich lived in Ashemore, he saw how even here if robots were only for the rich it could be disastrous.

Jordan and Valkyrie finished up in the tub and towelled each other off. They wrapped themselves in robes and went to the fire to eat dinner.

Jordan snorted. He was scrolling through news updates on his phone.

"Check this out; the churches and the corporations are calling the Boxing Day strike a War On Christmas," he said.

"Culture Wars instead of talking about real systemic change."

Jordan looked down at the clickbait news headline, and felt it lay heavily on his shoulders. He realized that the workers would not get the change they needed, that society needed, for a long time.

A message popped up in the news sidebar.

Breaking News.

Jordan clicked it.

His heart fell. A group called Rebel Canada had amassed in protest in Quebec City. They were an alt-right men's group who were the Canadian branch of The Rebels, the domestic terrorists in the United States. Several hundred of them marched in the streets with signs demanding that Jews and Muslims be removed from Quebec. A large force of anti-fascists met them in the street. Police lined up between them, and the groups screamed at each other until their throats were raw. At some point a snowball flew, and the protests devolved into a snowball fight of epic proportions. Pictures and video of the event showed Canadians covered in snow, some with grimaces and some with grins, flinging white balls with all their might. Jordan didn't know whether to laugh or cry.

Jordan spent the rest of December and the beginning of January at Glasshouse. The trip down south and the momentum of releasing the first album had given Jordan a lot of inspiration and he was motivated to get album two completed. His phone and his notebook were full of ideas that he was piecing together. Valkyrie also felt inspired and they sat around the fire, propped up on cozy pillows, taking notes and sketching out concepts.

"How's it coming?" asked Valkyrie, noticing Jordan hadn't written anything for a while.

"I'm just feeling a little blocked with these lyrics…"

She slid flat on the floor and kissed his ankle. "You'll figure it out."

"Eventually…"

"I love watching you work. I can't wait to hear it all put together," she said.

"Yea? I hope it's not shit."

Val laughed. "No way. I love your music."

"What about it do you love?" Jordan could hear the admiration in her voice. He loved it when she talked about his music. It made him feel like what he was doing was art, like he had things figured out.

"I love it when you're singing and you get this tone of desperation, like you're crying out, and it just reaches straight into me."

"Yea?" He leaned over and kissed her lips. "What else?"

"I love how purely you hit each note, no runs, no trying to sound like someone else… you tell your own story with your own voice."

"Mmm…"

They fell into each other's kisses. Kissing turned to heavy petting and before long they were making love on the floor by the fire. Jordan felt sweat dripping down his forehead and back. His knees were grinding into the floor but he didn't even feel it. Valkyrie's cheeks were red and glowing, her hair sticking to her face as they slipped into one another. She pressed up hard, taking him deeper. She couldn't believe it still felt this good. Her eyes rolled back as she felt orgasm overwhelm her in a wave of pleasure.

When they were finished, they curled up in a blanket.

"Godd you're beautiful," said Jordan, brushing her hair from her face and kissing her.

"What about me turns you on?" she asked.

He looked at her laying in his arms, her normally icy grey eyes flickering orange in the firelight, her soft skin pink with pleasure, the way she was smiling at him. He smiled tenderly and kissed her.

"You're superhuman," he said finally. "You have this ancient soul, you know so much… and when you touch me, I feel it inside me, in my head, in my chest," he said.

She lifted his hand to her lips, kissing it softly.

"That's how I feel when you sing," she said.

He snuggled her close, closing his eyes. She felt his love pouring into her.

I think I'm ready, she thought. *I think I will tell him about my family. Soon.*

On the first day of February, Jordan moved into Animal House. He didn't have much to pack, and most of it fit into his milk crates. By the time moving day came, he had been spending so much time chez Val that this place didn't feel like home anymore. He popped his posters into toilet paper rolls, stacked up his framed prints and shoved his clothes into milk crates. He put his laptop and valuables into his backpack. He was planning to spend the day taking things over on the bus, but one of the fans offered to give him and Bubba a lift.

"Oh sweet, do they mind driving me too?" asked Matt.

"What?"

"Oh, I haven't seen you man... I got an awesome job uptown, so I decided to move too."

"No way. Good for you."

"So who's driving? Jesse?"

Jordan cringed.

"Jesse? No. Jesse's not around anymore." *Since you raped their roommate,* thought Jordan.

"Oh. Well do you think I could get a ride?"

"I'm not sure man, you'll have to ask."

They all packed up their things, shoving items into duffle bags and garbage bags.

"So where's the job?" asked Jordan.

"I'm the Junior Export Compliance Specialist at Toussaint International. It's a Canadian hardwood business."

"Shit, how'd you land that gig?"

"It's not a gig. It's got benefits and everything."

"Whose dick did you suck to hook that up?"

"I got an email about an open house they were having with free dinner and booze, so I went and the owner saw my potential and offered me a job."

Jordan nodded. He felt a small sting of jealousy, but he knew it was irrational. He kept his mouth shut.

He took one last walk around the apartment. Would he miss it? They had some good times here, but he spent a lot of time being depressed here too.

As they pulled up to Animal House with their truck, Jordan was glad that Alex was moving with him. He looked up at the peeling paint and chipped siding, and he could feel that this would be a big change for him. He wasn't sure why.

Jordan checked out his room. It was small, but he didn't need a lot of space anyway. He was glad he opted to bring his own mattress. The one left in the room was filthy. The chest of drawers here was better than the one he left behind though. He unloaded his things and helped Bubba, who had a lot more stuff. Bubba helped him get the old busted mattress out to the curb, and helped him set up his milk crate bed. Bubba went back to his room to get things set up, and Jordan jumped onto his bed without putting anything away, without putting any linens on the mattress, and fell asleep.

PART THREE: BARON

CHAPTER TWENTY FOUR

Winter dragged on from beautiful paradise to frozen hell. The temperature dropped to barely tolerable, and with the wind it felt colder still.

The news from down south got worse as winter wore on. Valkyrie received a call at work.

"It's time to take action. The sisters are in trouble."

Valkyrie listened as Farrah explained. There were rumours that lesbians and young trans women were being taken into facilities for some kind of testing. The news was reporting gay conversion therapy centres, but there was something more going on.

"Let everyone who wants to come here know," said Valkyrie. "I'll sponsor more refugees."

"It may not be that easy. They don't want them to leave."

"What?!"

"I don't think that it's just persecution. I think that they're using them for something."

"Using them for something? For what, experiments?"

"We're not sure... the only thing we've been able to learn is that all the women taken have at some point been treated with nanites."

Valkyrie frowned. She was using the latest nanite technology in her arcology designs.

"Well I'm your ally. Whatever you need, you can count on me."

There was a long pause on the phone. Val sighed. It was time. "I'll start getting the property together."

"Thank you. We'll keep you updated."

Valkyrie did a preliminary search of properties to get a sense of price and availability. She had her sights set on Cape Breton in the Canadian Maritimes, because it was beautiful, remote, and land there was inexpensive. She called Sukhwant.

"Get me a good real estate agent. I'm searching for a property on the East coast, something overlooking water, at least a square kilometre, no visible neighbours. Buildings or no buildings is irrelevant."

"What is the price range?"

"The price is less relevant than meeting my criteria."

"Excellent, I'll have someone get in touch this afternoon."

The property was of two-fold importance; Valkyrie needed a test site for her arcology design, and she could erect temporary housing for refugees until the arcology was fully operational. This escalated her plans by a year, but she was ready.

The universe works in mysterious ways, she thought.

"Oracle," she said. "Contact Farrah. Tell her the plans are in motion."

"Affirmative."

Jordan's birthday was coming up fast. With the move, he had forgotten all about it. On February 14th, he was turning twenty-five years old. Valkyrie was taking care of the entire day for them. At eight am, he showed up at Valkyrie's apartment.

"Happy Birthday," she said. There was a massive stack of pancakes drizzled in maple syrup waiting for him. She pulled two steaming espressos and joined him for breakfast. He smiled sleepily and tucked into his pancakes and coffee.

"These are delicious," he said between bites.

"I can cook like... three things really well. And pancakes are one of them," she said.

When breakfast was finished they got in the car and headed to

Gatineau.

"Where are we going?" asked Jordan.

"We are going to…"

"Wait! Don't tell him," said Val, interrupting the AI. "It's a surprise."

They came to Chelsea, and the car turned right up a dirt road into the forest. A large wooden sign read *Spa Nordik*.

"Spa Nordik. They run the gym," said Jordan.

"Yes!" said Val. "It's the best spa in North America. You're going to love it."

They spent the day lounging in steaming hot pools and saunas, with occasional plunges into ice cold waterfalls outdoors. There were steam rooms and wood-fired dry rooms where they relaxed in silence. They took in a yoga class at noon before having lunch.

"What do you think?" asked Val, sipping a mango lassi.

"This is perfect. Thank you, and thanks for the gym membership too. I never realized how relaxing all this stuff was."

After lunch, they had a couple's massage in a wood cabana above the waterfall.

"There's a salt pool you can float in, but I think I'm going to do a few more hot and cold rounds. We have… an appointment at five so we should finish up around four."

They spent a few more hours soaking and relaxing, and then retired to the changing rooms to get dressed. The car was waiting for them outside. They snuggled in the backseat on their way to the restaurant for dinner, their cheeks rosy and their eyes sparkling.

"My skin feels so good," said Val.

"So what is this appointment?" asked Jordan with a grin.

"You'll see…"

They pulled up to Adore Boutique on York Street in the Market. It was a shop that sold ethically produced clothing.

"Hello Dr. Snow."

They were greeted by a well-dressed employee.

"Is this him?"

Valkyrie nodded as two employees came over to take Jordan's measurements. They pulled out a partially finished suit.

"Take off your clothes," said one. Jordan obliged, pulling off his pants and top. He felt completely mellow and relaxed from the spa and didn't ask any questions. Valkyrie sat back in a comfortable chair, equally mellow, enjoying the process.

The seamstress and tailor moved back and forth, completing the suit around him. It took almost two hours, but when they were finished, Jordan looked incredible.

The suit was dark blue, with slim fitting pants and a matching vest. He wore a light blue shirt underneath with a paisley grey satin tie.

"He'll need shoes too," murmured Val. She stood up and walked around him, eying him like a hunter counting points on a buck's rack. They fitted him with light tan dress shoes.

Val came close, straightening his tie. She leaned in whispering, "You look incredible."

Jordan pressed his cheek to hers, rubbing his lip along her ear. He looked in the full-length mirror.

Holy shit, he thought. *I do look incredible.* He looked like a man who had his life together. His gaze met Val's.

"I love you," he said.

"I love you too."

"This is the best birthday I've ever had. Thank you."

"There's more," she said with a grin.

Valkyrie disappeared into the change room and came out in a shimmering red dress. Jordan ran his hand along her body in admiration.

"All dressed up, and where are we off to?" he asked.

Valkyrie said nothing. She kissed him, deep and passionate, and then she pulled red lipstick out of her bag and applied it thick. Her hair was a wild mess of curls from the spa. She looked beautiful. She led him out to the car. It took them to Beckley, where Valkyrie had made a reservation.

They enjoyed the five course tasting menu with the wine pairing. Valkyrie raised her glass.

"To a quarter century."

"To a quarter century," repeated Jordan. "And to love and creativity." They clinked glasses.

Valkyrie looked into his eyes. If a year ago someone told her that she would be dating a twenty-five year old, she would hardly have believed it. But here she was, in love. They enjoyed their meal.

"I have one more surprise," she said when they were finished.

"Seriously? This is the day that just keeps on giving. What could we possibly be doing now?"

Valkyrie took his arm and they walked outside. The snow fell gently around them. She shivered with excitement.

"You must be freezing!" he said. They had left their coats and other clothes in the car.

"I'm fine," she said. "We don't have far to go."

They walked along Elgin Street and crossed after Laurier. Valkyrie was almost skipping with excitement. They stopped outside of the National Arts Centre on the corner of Elgin and Sparks.

"I'm taking you to the opera," said Valkyrie.

"Really?" Jordan had never been to the opera before. It was only something he had watched on the internet. They walked in the main doors into the NAC lobby. Jordan looked around at the other patrons. No wonder Valkyrie had bought him a suit. He shifted, standing taller. He was beaming.

Val felt his excitement. They walked past the feminist Creation Campaign wall and Valkyrie picked up their tickets at the box office. She handed him his ticket.

"*The Nightingale*," read Jordan.

"It's Igor Stravinsky's interpretation of Hans Christian Andersen," said Val. "I've never seen it before."

"So we're seeing it for the first time together?" he asked.

"Yes."

They held hands, making their way through towering halls where people drank champagne and chatted quietly, waiting for the opera to start. Jordan walked with pride in his step. He got many appraising looks. He knew that he was the most handsome man in the room. The National Arts Centre had soaring windows that looked out over the Château Laurier perched at the delta of the Rideau and Ottawa rivers, and the massive oak trees in the courtyard were lined with white twinkling lights to brighten the season. It was like a dream.

The house lights flashed. It was the signal to patrons to take their seats.

"I've reserved the box for us," said Val. "It's one of those little luxuries that are so worthwhile."

They made their way to their seats. Jordan drew back the curtain of their box. Valkyrie made a small gasp of dismay.

There was a man standing at the edge of the balcony looking out over the audience. Even though they could only see his back, Valkyrie knew who it was.

"Baron. What are you doing here?" she asked.

Jordan felt her discomfort.

The man turned around. He was wearing a gorgeous perfectly cut charcoal grey suit. He wore blue and cream suspenders and his cufflinks shone. His trim hair was salt and pepper and he wore a perfectly oiled beard and moustache. He oozed elegance and his face was ruggedly handsome in a way that Jordan hoped his own would be some day.

"Hello my darling," said the man. His voice was gravelly and deep. He stepped over to Val, kissing her cheek, his hands lingering on her hips, familiar and proprietary.

Jordan looked him up and down, shifting uncomfortably. The man looked strangely familiar. He looked at Val, a question in his eyes.

"Baron," she said quietly. "This is Jordan."

Jordan extended a hand.

"Jordan, Baron."

"Baron Toussaint, her husband," said the man with a wolfish smile, grasping his hand and shaking it hard and firm.

Jordan's breath caught in his throat and he turned to Valkyrie, unable to speak.

"Ex-husband," she said casually, looping her arm through Jordan's. "Melodramatic lover from a past life."

Baron clenched his teeth, the muscle in his jaw popping out. He smiled.

"Join me," he said, sitting back in his seat at the front of the box. Val turned to Jordan. *I'm sorry*, she mouthed, squeezing his arm.

That bastard, she thought. What should she do? Part of her wanted to leave right now with Jordan, but she didn't want to give Baron the pleasure of ruining their evening. She was sure he did this on purpose. It was too perfect to be a coincidence. She had intended to introduce them soon anyway, but this was Baron's way of controlling the meeting. Baron trying to control everything had been one of the major factors in why they split up in the first place.

Valkyrie considered sitting behind Baron, but that would be incredibly awkward and she would have to see his head in front of her. That would ruin the opera. She sat beside him in the front row, Jordan on her other side. She held her lover's s hand tight. The symphony began to play the opening notes.

Jordan felt a massive lump in his throat.

What the fuck? Valkyrie's husband? Jordan felt utterly destroyed. The relaxing day at the spa completely tore down his defenses and he was not expecting anything like this tonight. He knew there was probably a good explanation for this, but he felt sick to his stomach.

Why didn't she tell me? he thought miserably. He tried to focus on the show.

The music worked its way into his heart. After a while, he started to relax. The floating vocals, whimsical flute, and dramatic horns pulled him out of the dark places in his mind and into his creative brain.

It's not like I don't have exes, he thought. *I'm sure she was going to tell me eventually. It's not a big deal.* He was expecting a damn good explanation though.

Baron stretched his knees wide, invading Valkyrie's space.

Why is he punishing me? she thought. She moved closer to Jordan.

Normally she was on good terms with Baron. They still called each other for advice on occasion, and after a difficult period of separation, they both moved on with their lives and developed a friendship with one another. Valkyrie could tell that something was wrong.

Poor Jordan, she thought. *What a shock.*

When the opera ended, Valkyrie leaned slowly and deliberately into Jordan.

"What did you think?" she asked quietly. He looked into her eyes.

"It was more haunting than I expected," he said. "I always thought opera was a happy genre."

"You're right. It was haunting."

Baron stood up. "So was that your first opera then?" he boomed. Jordan looked at Val. He expected her to take charge of this awkward conversation.

"We are celebrating Jordan's birthday," said Valkyrie, ignoring Baron's question.

"Oh, and just how old is this young man?" asked Baron, his eyes dancing.

"Younger than you, old fart," she said with a smile, putting a hand on Jordan's chest.

"Let's go," she said quietly to Jordan.

"We should go for a drink," said Baron, following them out. "A birthday drink for the birthday boy."

Jordan walked faster. He wanted to get the hell out of there.

"Oh, we've had a long day. Nice running into you," she said. "Good night."

They stepped outside, scanning the street for the car.

"You must be freezing," said Baron. He looked at Jordan disapprovingly and pulled off his jacket, throwing it over Val's shoulders. She laughed.

"I'm fine Baron. Take your jacket back."

"I insist. You'll catch a cold. Take it home with you, I'll come by and pick it up tomorrow."

Jordan stiffened.

The car pulled up.

"Here's our ride. Take your jacket."

Baron opened the door, holding it open for Valkyrie to climb in. "See you tomorrow." He winked at Jordan, who trudged around to the other side of the car to get in.

"Goodnight darling," intoned Baron as he closed the door. The car drove off.

The tension in the air inside the car was palpable.

"I didn't know you were cold," said Jordan finally.

Valkyrie let the coat slide off her shoulders.

"I'm not cold," she laughed. "I'm fine. I left it on to avoid all the drama and back and forth. I find that kind of paternalistic masculinity suffocating. I hate it. Really."

"Is that why you married him?" said Jordan coldly.

Dammit, he thought. He hadn't intended to sound so hurt.

"Babe, no," she said, reaching for his hand. "I married him a lifetime ago. When I was a different person. We're completely different now."

Jordan heard the honesty in her voice. He cast a sidelong glance in her direction. She moved over, filling the space between them. He sighed.

"We were young, we got married, we tried to have the perfect little suburban family, but I hated it. I hated that life. We couldn't have children, and it was a blessing, really. We drifted apart. We separated, I went back to school to follow my dreams of being an architect, started my first company, and completely changed who I was. I joined the Sisterhood, I stopped caring about other people's expectations for my life. Now I'm free."

Jordan looked at her. There was no use being mad at her. It was all true, he could tell. It was like looking at her for the first time. There was so much that he didn't know about her.

"No more secrets, okay? You can tell me things. I want to know about the important things in your life."

"Okay," she said, nuzzling close to him.

When they got home, Valkyrie left Baron's jacket in the car. Jordan reached in and pulled it out. He threw it over his shoulder. They both laughed as he put his nose in the air and pretended to walk like Baron. Val hooked her arm through his and they walked up to the apartment.

Jordan locked the door behind them. He threw Baron's jacket beside the door, and scooped up Valkyrie in his arms. They laughed as he struggled up the stairs with her. At the top of the stairs, he put her down and gestured for her to ride him piggy-back. He took her down the hall to the bedroom. Their laughter turned into kisses as they peeled off each other's clothes. Jordan's smile melted into a serious expression. All his barriers were down. He'd had a long day. He looked at her with such intensity. She put her arms around him and they fell onto the bed. He held her face, kissing her deeply, craving her skin against his. She wanted the same thing. He held her tight in his arms, making love to her slow and deep, their connection growing with every pulsing thrust. She came hard, her entire body shuddering with release. He kept moving, and soon she found her pleasure rising and cresting again. She moaned, overwhelmed, her nerves tingling all over her body. As she came down from the high, she turned him onto his back. She gripped his hair in her hands, kissing him and riding him until she came again, gasping. She rode him harder and harder until he couldn't take it anymore. He let go, releasing his pent-up emotions, tears at the edge of his eyes, coming hard and then relaxing completely. They both went right to sleep.

The next morning Baron knocked on the door. Valkyrie was at her standing desk typing away at the computer and Jordan was lying on the couch in his boxers sketching. When she heard the knock, Val looked at Jordan.

"Could you get that?" she asked sweetly. Jordan grinned and got up. He pulled his boxers down below his treasure line and walked over to the door. Val went back to work. Jordan clenched his fists, flexing his muscles. He opened the door.

"Hey," he said, with a cockeyed grin. He ran his hands through his silky hair and left the door open, walking back over to the couch. Baron looked him up and down, appreciating the curve of his shoulders into his back, his firm ass, his well-developed biceps and calves.

Well I don't deny the obvious temptation, thought Baron. *I'll give him that.*

"Oh hello. You're here," he said, stepping inside and closing the door behind him. "I suppose you don't work," he added. He shot a look at Val. She didn't look up.

"Hi Baron. How are you today?" she said from the computer. He walked over and leaned down to kiss her cheek. Jordan pretended not to notice.

"I'm great, just swinging by to say hello and pick up my jacket."

"Well hello," said Val. "Where did you put his jacket honey?" she asked Jordan.

"I can't remember exactly," said Jordan, coming over. "Oh there, it is. By the door." He pointed to the jacket.

"Great, I'll grab it on my way out," said Baron. He walked over to the couch and sat down.

"How did you get into the building?" asked Jordan.

"Excuse me?"

"You didn't buzz up, you just knocked on the apartment door."

"Oh, knocking was merely a formality, I have keys," he wiggled the keys in Jordan's face.

"Cool." Jordan kept his tone level, gritting his teeth. He scooped up his notebook and sat in the chair, continuing his drawing.

Why do I hate this guy's guts? he thought. It was irrational. He calmed his mind and thought about last night in bed. *Valkyrie is head over heels in love with you,* he thought. *No need to battle this dude. You've already won.*

"Any big plans today?" asked Baron.

"Just the usual," said Jordan with a grin. Val smiled.

"Alright then," said Baron. "I better get to the office." He stood up and retrieved his jacket by the door.

"Have a nice day," said Val. Baron let himself out.

"What an asshole," said Jordan with a smile when Baron was gone. Val's expression was unreadable.

"He's not," she said. "Jordan you have to understand that Baron and I have a long history together. I'm not in love with him at all, you must understand. He and I will never live together, but he is family to me, you see?"

Jordan did not see. He had no experience with anything like this.

"He's so rude though."

Val came over to Jordan's chair and sat on his lap.

"You're right, he's being so rude."

"Does he grill all your boyfriends like this?"

"Boyfriends… or girlfriends. No. Never," said Valkyrie. "I don't know what's gotten into him."

Jordan was silent.

"I'll have a talk with him." She kissed his cheek.

Baron was sitting at his desk at work when he received a phone call. It was Valkyrie.

"Val. How are you?" he purred.

"Hi B. Can we talk? I feel like there's some things we need to discuss."

"Sure. How about dinner tonight?"

"Sure. Where?"

"No need to worry about it. I'll have a car pick you up at six."

"Just tell me where, Baron. I'll meet you there."

"Val, just relax. I'll take care of it."

"Take care of what?" she was annoyed. "Do you want to meet for dinner or not?"

"Are you okay Valkyrie? You're sounding anxious."

"No Baron. I'm great. I just want to have a talk with you about our boundaries. I can pick a place to meet you if you need."

"Ha, no need. Meet me at Metropolitana."

"Great. You can make the reso."

Click.

He leaned back in his chair, the sound of leather creaking. He surveyed the workshop. Baron Toussaint had started out as a solo carpenter. He opened a small woodshop in Westboro with a large inheritance, and slowly built a small wood empire. His company was called Toussaint International. They were international exporters of fine Canadian hardwood, working mostly with Chinese manufacturing companies and German house builders. There was no more need for storefront space, but he kept up the original woodshop on Wellington. His desk sat on a platform at the back of the shop where he conducted business on a daily basis. On the floor, several master carpenters were always working on projects, their pieces for sale on the walls. He had retained the shop's industrial look and it ached of hipster chic between the more polished commercial businesses on Wellington. An adjoining space behind the front shop housed all the paper pushers and a board room for meetings.

When he had important meetings, Baron would wear a formal suit, but most days he wore well-tailored slacks with suspenders, fine shirts, and a pop of coloured scarf. His beard and hair were always perfectly trimmed and shaped. Even at his desk, he liked to roll up the sleeves of his handmade shirts, and he enjoyed the look of the rippling muscles of his tanned forearms as he worked. His hair was grey at the temples and his beard was streaked with silver, and he only grew more handsome with age. He had the same kind of treatment regimen that Valkyrie had, and he felt vibrant and youthful, like he was in the prime of his life.

A junior employee came up to the platform.

"Sir there was an issue with our shipment last week to Dalian."

"Yes?"

Matthew Doyle was Toussaint International's latest domestic hire. He wasn't a particularly promising worker for the company, but he had a valuable asset; he was a close personal friend of Jordan

Barker.

Matt explained the problem and Baron patiently told him he should go to one of the assistants with these kinds of issues.

"Before you go—I heard you make music," said Baron.

"Oh," said Matt, caught off guard. "Yes. I'm in a band."

"Bring me a sample of your work, will you?"

"Sure," said Matt enthusiastically.

"Oh, and Matthew… don't let your extracurriculars get in the way of a real man's work."

"Um, yes sir." Matt returned to his desk in the back.

Baron had hosted an open house for Westfest at the shop, and on a whim he invited Jordan's bandmates, out of curiosity. Matt showed up. He was a beta specimen, to be sure, but he would be a good source of information about Valkyrie's new boytoy.

She should have introduced me to him long ago, thought Baron. *Shame on her for making me go to these lengths just to get some information.*

After a few months of Valkyrie seeing Jordan Baron felt reassured by no meeting being arranged because Jordan must not be very important to her. However, when Baron saw them together at the Ashemore Estate annual gathering, he knew that Jordan was not just a young plaything. He could see that the connection was strong. Stronger than he was comfortable with.

CHAPTER TWENTY FIVE

Sukhwant connected Valkyrie with Marisol Kobylnyk, a real estate agent who specialized in Eastern Canada properties. Marisol presented nine viable options for the Mother House arcology.

"These properties all fall within your specifications. I have highlighted the ones which would be okay with a quick closing as well."

"Good," said Val, flipping through the report.

This agent is intuitive, she thought. *Excellent. Sukhwant is a lifesaver.*

"This one you can remove from the list," she said. "This one as well."

The agent was scribbling in her notebook.

"May I ask why?"

"I don't want a palatial estate. I have a building project of my own planned." Val kept rifling through the pages. "This one. These outbuildings... do they have well water?"

"Yes. Actually that's one of my favourites," said Marisol.

"What is your availability to show these? Say, Wednesday?"

"Let me make some phone calls. I believe we can do it."

While Marisol made her calls, Valkyrie reviewed the files in closer detail and struck another two off the list. That left four properties to visit in person.

Two sisters were on their way to Ottawa next month. Valkyrie would move into Glasshouse and the sisters would stay in her condo downtown until she secured the property.

"We can go Wednesday," said Marisol.

"Great. I'll have Sukhwant book us tickets. Can you please make the arrangements with her?"

"Absolutely."

That evening, Valkyrie made her way to Metropolitana for dinner with Baron. She strolled in right on time. Baron was already there, sitting at their table. He rose as she approached, and kissed her on the cheek. He waited to sit down until she was seated. There was a glass of wine waiting for her at the table.

"To a romantic dinner," he said, raising his glass. Valkyrie looked at him with her impassive expression. She signalled the waiter.

"I'll have a dark and stormy," she said. "And a glass of water while I wait. Take this wine away please."

The waiter looked awkwardly at Baron.

"Unless you'd like to drink it? I don't feel like wine," said Val.

"No, fine, take it away." Baron was annoyed. He sipped his wine.

The waiter returned with Val's water.

"The dark and stormy will be just a moment," he said.

Valkyrie raised her water. "You were saying?"

"Never mind," he said.

"To your health," she said, and took a drink of her water.

"So it seems you've been busy," said Baron, looking at the menu.

"Busy busy," she said. "As usual. How about you? How is the business?"

"Business is good. I just hired a new employee," he said.

"Lovely."

The waiter returned with the dark and stormy.

"Are you ready to order?" he asked as he set down her drink.

"I am," said Valkyrie. "How about you?" she looked at Baron.

"Well I was thinking that we'd have the fish…"

"I'm having chicken," she said to the waiter. "The citrus one, with salad." She smiled at him. "Thank you." She sipped her drink. "My compliments to the bartender," she added.

"And fish for you sir?" asked the waiter. "The special?"

"Well, I was thinking it would suit both of us," said Baron. "But if my wife is having chicken, then I'll have steak and frites."

The waiter left.

Valkyrie reached out and touched Baron's hand on the table. "What's wrong?" she asked. "Why are you being like this?"

Baron looked at her. Valkyrie had no idea what he was thinking.

"I miss you. Can we have a holiday?" he said.

"A holiday?" Valkyrie laughed. "But what about Courtney?" Baron had been married twice since he and Val separated. Courtney was his third wife.

"Courtney's… at her mother's," he said.

"I see." Val looked at him sympathetically.

"No, you don't see," he said, snatching his hand away. "It has nothing to do with Courtney. I miss you and I think a holiday would do both of us good."

"You know I love travelling with you, but I'm too busy right now for a holiday," she said. "I have a lot going on."

Periodically over the years Valkyrie and Baron would reconnect. Val found the comfort of familiarity in her first love.

"I promise you'll have a good time," he said, looking deep into her eyes. She looked away. He felt her energy go somewhere else.

"No Baron. Please don't make this difficult. You're my friend and I love you, but you have to understand that just because it's a good time for you doesn't mean that it's a good time for me."

"Well how long do you need?" he asked.

"It's not like that. That's not what I meant. I'm not interested in spending any time with you romantically. You will have to find someone else for that. I'm sorry."

He scowled.

The waiter arrived with their food.

"Thank you," said Valkyrie.

"You think it's about sex?" said Baron quietly when the waiter left. "What you and I have is so much more than that."

"We have a friendship, Baron. One I want to keep. But you can't just call me your wife anytime you feel like it. It's not appropriate. You have a wife. It's Courtney."

"Courtney was arm candy. You will always be my true wife, even if we're not together. You used to say I'd always be your only husband. Is that still true?"

Val put down her fork. "Baron, we had twenty years together. I'll never have twenty years quite like that with anyone else, ever again. But we've both grown, and changed since then. We've moved on. You've said vows with two other beautiful wives since then. In honour of our history, I want to be part of your life as a supportive friend. That's all."

Baron felt heat rise quickly to his face. Val could see it. She didn't want to make him angry—she used to be afraid to make him angry—but she wasn't going to sugar coat it.

"I thought you said you were okay with me marrying Teresa and Courtney," he said. "Now I see you're jealous. You're punishing me. I get it. I've learned my lesson."

"What? No, that has nothing to do with it."

"You're doing this, having this affair with Jordan to get back at me."

"Not at all," said Val calmly. "I'm happy for you, and I hope you're happy for me too."

Baron was staring at her. She could see the wheels turning in his head but she had no idea what it was about.

"I see that this conversation was a mistake," he said.

"It's not a mistake. I needed to have this conversation with you so you know that I'm feeling uncomfortable. So we can get our friendship back on track."

"You're infatuated with him, I can see that now. Just remember that eventually it will end, and I'll be here for you when it does."

They finished their dinner.

"I gave the waiter cash before you arrived," said Baron. "So don't even bother trying to pay."

Val sighed with exasperation and kissed him on the cheek.

"Goodnight Baron."

"Goodnight Valkyrie."

Jordan lay on his lumpy bed trying to sleep. He was annoyed that Valkyrie was out for dinner with that asshole. He wondered if she was home by now or if they were still out, maybe having cocktails, laughing about old times, maybe going to their favourite place to dance.

Don't be stupid, he thought. *She's telling him to step off because you wanted her to.*

He turned over on his other side. She had told him he was welcome to stay while she was out, but he left to go to the gym. Unlike Baron, Jordan didn't have keys to let himself back into her apartment. He hated this feeling. Resentment.

Jordan gave up trying to sleep and got out of bed. He put on flannel pants and wandered down to the living room of his new house. There was a nude man standing in the centre of the room and several people with notebooks sketching him in charcoal. It was a midnight art session. Jordan stood off to the side, watching them work. It took his mind off of Valkyrie and Baron.

Sapphire came up behind him.

"Pretty cool, right?" she whispered.

"Yea."

They stood and watched the artists working silently together.

"Hey, wanna smoke?" she asked.

"Oh, nah I gave up cigarettes," he whispered.

"No I mean weed," she said.

"Weed? Um, ya sure."

They went up to the balcony. Sapphire grabbed a joint from her room and Jordan grabbed a sweater and warm socks from his. They went outside and Sapphire lit up.

"So how you liking living here?" she asked, taking a deep pull and passing him the joint.

"It's nice," he said. "Seriously. I'm still getting used to it, but the vibe is much homier than my old place."

"Good," she said. "I can't wait for your concert. We've had a lot of people asking about it." Sapphire managed a social media page for Animal House.

"Oh yea? Right on."

"I've been hearing you singing new stuff. Sounds good."

"Thanks."

Jordan was a little worried because Matt's new boss was giving him a hard time about the band. He said it looked bad for the business. He was trying to get Matt to quit. Lately, Matt was more and more distant. Jordan was considering putting an ad online soon for a new drummer.

They passed the joint back and forth until it was gone. Jordan felt nice and mellow. They went back downstairs and watched the artists again. When they were finished for the night, Sapphire locked up behind them.

"It's pretty awesome that you pay the rent this way," said Jordan. "Thanks for letting me be a part of it."

"No problem," she said. "It works pretty well when everyone does their part." She smiled. "I'm heading to bed. G'night Jordan."

"Night."

Sapphire headed upstairs. Jordan remembered that 'his part' was doing the dishes. He went to the kitchen. The sink was full. He rolled up his sleeves.

It's not so bad, he thought. He got a feeling of satisfaction when everything was clean. It wasn't like washing for hours in the back of the Cherry. His skin would be raw by the end of a shift. A sink or two of dishes at Animal House was pleasantly warm to sink his hands into, especially late at night when everyone had gone to bed. He left the racks full of clean dishes to air dry overnight, and he dried his hands on a fresh clean towel. Bubba had done the laundry this week; the laundry machines were right beside his room in the basement. Jordan went to bed again, and this time he fell asleep.

On Wednesday, Valkyrie Snow and Marisol Kobylnyk flew into Halifax Stanfield Airport and got a connecting flight to J.A. Douglas McCurdy Sydney Airport. From there they hired a car to visit the potential properties.

They drove into Sydney. The downturn of coal and mining had made this area depressed. Relics of 1970s commerce stood struggling to stay open downtown. The once-lucrative fishing industry brought hordes of settlers to this indigenous territory, but they foolishly wrecked the ancient salmon runs in a few short generations and the old docks were empty and decaying like wooden bones along the shore. Still, it was a sleepy and picturesque place with charming clapboard maritime houses lining the friendly streets. There were indications of renewal in the solar panels on garage rooves around town.

They carried on toward Sydney Mines. This place was much harder off. The small houses had half-completed renovations and the ghostly shape of snow-covered junk in their yards. Time slowed to a standstill here with the snow softly falling and muting all sounds but the crunch of snow under the tires of the car as it crawled through town. This place would have gone the way of Gastonia, except that gun laws and social services kept the worst side-effects of poverty at bay.

As they drove on through the Cape Breton countryside, Valkyrie watched fields and forests of snow flash by. It was warmer out here than it was in Ottawa, but there was an incredible amount of snow because of the moisture in the air. She cracked the window down and breathed it in.

"I love it here already," she said, smiling at Marisol.

There was something about the energy of this place that drew Valkyrie in. It was exactly as she imagined it would be.

The car turned off the main road and pulled onto a long laneway.

"We had this plowed yesterday for your visit," said Marisol.

"Thank you," said Valkyrie.

They approached a decrepit abandoned house. Val and Marisol got out of the car. They strapped on their snowshoes and walked around. Val held up the photos of the property in the summer for comparison. They spent an hour exploring the property.

"We'd better move on," said Marisol. Valkyrie was a motivated buyer, but winter was a hard sell.

They drove over an hour to the next property. On the way there, Marisol filled Valkyrie in on all of the details. She was hopeful about this one.

This place was much like the first; beautiful woods, a view overlooking the water, lots of privacy.

Any of these properties could do, really, thought Valkyrie.

They stayed for thirty minutes and then moved on to the next.

As they drove up to the third property, Valkyrie felt a tingle in the back of her neck. She put the window down and leaned out as they drove up to the building site. Overgrown hedges surrounded a tiny stone house. It was empty but it seemed as resilient as the landscape around it. They drove further. There was a clapboard two-story house that looked run down but salvageable. The bay overlooked a sea of ice that broke into choppy waters in the distance. There was a beautiful little peninsula with a wide open plateau perfect for building the arcology. It would be a task getting all the building materials out here, but it was worth it.

"This is it," said Valkyrie. "I can feel it."

"Really? Well let's get out and walk around anyway."

They left the car and strapped on their snowshoes. Valkyrie headed straight for the stone house. Something about it was intensely attractive. The snow was piled high against the wooden door so she couldn't go inside, but she peered in the window. The floor was covered with dirt and dust but there were wide hardwood planks beneath. The plaster was falling out of the walls, but a large exposed wooden beam ran along the length of the ceiling. This would be her house.

They made their way to the farmhouse. Inside it was outdated, but no serious structural problems. There was a solid tin roof and several woodstoves. This would do nicely for the sisters until the arcology was built. She would have an updated kitchen put in and it would be livable.

"There is plumbing?" she asked.

"Yes, and electricity."

The electricity didn't matter, because Valkyrie would be making the property off-grid as soon as possible. They walked out to the peninsula and explored. A biting wind whipped across the bay. Val pulled her fur-trimmed hood tighter around her face.

"Give them what they're asking, Marisol," she said.

"There's likely room to negotiate…"

"Give them what they're looking for. I've reviewed the files, all the prices were fair. I want a quick closing. I will start building as soon as the weather breaks."

"There will be permits," began Marisol.

"That won't be a problem. Close the deal."

"And the last property?" asked Marisol. But she already knew the answer.

"Send them my regrets. This is the one."

They walked around the property until the sun began to set. Then they made their way to the car and drove back to Sydney. They went to a cozy little restaurant called the Olive Tree. Valkyrie ordered mango curry and Marisol had pizza. The food tasted doubly good after rambling in the snow all day.

"I'll send up the paperwork to your office tomorrow. This property has been on the market for over a year, so I'm sure they'll be glad of your offer."

Val felt a huge weight lifted off of her shoulders. She knew that the year ahead would be stressful, but the plan was clear. She would make preparations for the rest of the winter and begin building in the spring. The office was already rolling out the marketing strategy for Snow Arcologies. All they had to do now was get the prototype built.

After their dinner, Marisol and Valkyrie retired to Chamberlain House Bed and Breakfast in North Sydney. In the morning they flew back to Ottawa.

Jordan and Valkyrie went out for dinner.

"I found the property," said Valkyrie.

"Seriously? That was fast," said Jordan. "Cheers." They clinked glasses.

"It's perfect. There's a house I can move the sisters into, and a little stone cottage I've fallen in love with."

"That's great."

"The sisters will be here in a week, I'm trying to get the house closed as fast as possible so I can get them moved into it. Marisol says it won't be any later than the end of March."

"That's not too bad," said Jordan. He could tell she was anxious about people living in her personal space for an extended period of time.

I need to tell you something," she said. She reached out and held his hands. "I'm going to be away a lot in the coming months getting everything going out East," said Valkyrie. "I might even have to be gone for a month at a time. This is going to be a crazy year."

"That sucks, but you gotta do what you gotta do."

Valkyrie knew that Jordan understood. He would never try to get between her and her dreams. That had been a constant struggle with Baron.

"How's your album coming?" she asked.

"I'm almost done," he said with a grin. "I'm moving in a really good direction, I can feel it."

"I'm happy to hear it."

"So what are these sisters like? I can't wait to meet them."

"Oh, Chanda is a bit younger than me, vibrant, calm person. Margarethe is..." Valkyrie trailed off, searching for words. "She's a character. Like a grandmother to me, to all of us. She's full of wisdom, but a little crazy, y'know?"

"Okay cool."

"They're the only two staying at the apartment. Others are staying with other sisters all over the country."

The next week Valkyrie welcomed Chanda and Margarethe at the airport. She would have sent the car, but she knew that Margarethe wouldn't stand for that.

"Oh! My darling! It's good to see you!" They hugged and kissed. Chanda was a round woman with long black hair tied in a braid, and Margarethe had frizzy snow white hair that went down past her shoulders. She was wrapped in a large scarf embroidered with large pink flowers edged in black fringe.

"It's so good to see you too," said Val.

The ladies had a lot of luggage. Margarethe found an attendant.

"Where is Grischa?" she asked him. He looked her up and down, and turned to Valkyrie and Chanda. Valkyrie looked impassive.

"The cat," said Chanda. Valkyrie cringed. Cat hair on her good furniture. She sighed.

Sisterhood is powerful, she reminded herself.

The attendant hurried off to find Grischa. He returned with a wooden cage tied together with red ribbons. The cat inside blinked lazily. Margarethe untied the ribbons and pulled him out.

"Poor baby," she said, holding him close. He looked like a shining black teddy bear with round ears and a flat face. His whiskers were white and he had a tiny white spot on his chest.

"You can't have animals out of the cage in the airport," muttered the attendant.

"You're the animal," said Margarethe. "Grischa is family." She kissed his face.

Val fetched a trolley to load up their things.

"We packed up everything we could," said Chanda quietly. "We had to leave quickly though." She had tears in her eyes.

"They're just things," said Margarethe. "We have what's important." She put Grischa back in his cage and secured the door.

"I'm sorry," said Val, giving her shoulder a squeeze.

Chanda laugh.

"What is it?"

"Farrah told me that you Canadians are always apologizing!"

"Well you're Canadians now so get used to it." Val grinned.

When they stepped outside, the ladies breathed in deep.

"Canadian air!" laughed Margarethe, throwing her little arms in the air. "I'll have to get a good coat." She shivered.

Chanda and Val hurried her into the car.

"Farrah said that you've found the land," said Margarethe when they piled into the car with their things.

"It's ours," said Val. "We'll be able to start renovating in a few weeks."

"Oh I'm not fancy," said Margarethe. "Don't go to any trouble."

"It just needs some work in the kitchen. And I'm going to give everything a fresh coat of paint. And a few other little things."

"I'm telling you girl don't go to any trouble. I can make do."

"I know gramma. Just let me get it ready, then it's all yours."

Chanda looked out the window at the snow-filled streets. She sighed and pulled her jacket tighter.

"We'll need to get you warmer clothes," said Val, looking at their little boots.

"I want a coat like yours," said Margarethe. "You look like a bear."

Valkyrie laughed. It would be nice having the company. Then her expression became more sombre.

"So what exactly is going on in Tennessee?"

"Well it started when I had breast cancer," said Chanda quietly. "I was receiving treatment where nanites were used to artificially feed and then starve the tissue. A few months after the cancer was gone, they called in everyone who was treated in my cycle. They asked if any of us were gay. What with everything happening in the news, I didn't say anything. A few people volunteered their information, and they all went missing."

Val was stunned.

"It's some kind of gene mutation, and apparently it's more common in the queer community," said Chanda. "People are going missing all over the United States."

"I told you, it's because of our powers," rasped Margarethe.

Chanda rolled her eyes.

"What do you mean?" asked Valkyrie.

"We're psychics, spirit-seers, walkers-between-worlds. That's why they want us. Gay, not gay... we see beyond the flesh, so yes, queer you might say. Whatever you want to call it. We're witches. They're taking our power."

Valkyrie smiled sadly. Margarethe always had a fantastic way of looking at the world.

When they got to Val's condo, they ate warm soup and went straight to bed.

Valkyrie's house was chaotic. Her bed was full of cat hair. The espresso machine was broken, there were hand-washed Slavic undergarments strung on a rope to dry from the top of the stairs to Valkyrie's desk, and Margarethe had pushed the coffin coffee table out into the hall.

"What are you now, some kind of depressed vampire?" she said to Val when she'd seen it.

Valkyrie spent three days with Chanda and Margarethe and then she had to leave for Glasshouse.

She pushed Marisol to get the details finalized on the Mother House property.

"But you're not building until spring," said Marisol. "What is another week?"

"You don't understand. My... in-laws... are driving me crazy."

"Oh. I see."

CHAPTER TWENTY SIX

Jordan was at home working on one of the songs for the new album when his phone rang. He checked the ID.

The Black Cherry. He frowned. He never thought he'd hear from the Cherry again.

He answered it.

"Hello?"

"Hello, Jordan," said an unfamiliar voice. "How are you?"

"I'm fine," he said.

"This is the Black Cherry," said the voice. "We're calling to offer your job back."

"Really."

"Really!"

It must be the AI manager, he thought.

"What about Earl? I thought he was taking it."

"Mr. O'Brien failed his three month review. As it turns out, you were a much more efficient worker."

"So you fired Earl."

"Correct."

Jordan leaned back against the wall. It was a lot to take in.

"Mr. Barker? Are you still there? Are you still there? Are you still--"

"I'm here."

"Will you return to work at the Black Cherry?"

"Can I think about it a minute?"

"Yes."

Earl got fired. Jordan felt a swell of satisfaction. *That lazy bastard.* Jordan was relieved. *No more unemployment.* Then he had a strange feeling. Did he even want to go back? *Of course not.* The real question was, did he need to go back? Not really. If this concert went well, his food and expenses for the winter would be covered, and the house had enough business booked to cover the rent until spring at least. *Will I return to work at the Black Cherry?* He felt panic rise inside his chest at the thought of saying no.

"Your minute has passed," said the AI.

"Can I work one shift a week?" he asked.

"No. You must work twenty-four hours per week."

"No then," said Jordan. He blurted it out before he could think about it too much.

"No? You decline the offer?"

"I decline, yes, thank you."

"Have a nice day."

Click.

Jordan exhaled slowly. He felt exhilarated and terrified at the same time.

All in, he thought. *All bets in. It's artist or bust.*

In that moment, Jordan committed himself to being a full time musician.

He called Valkyrie. No answer.

Valkyrie spent long hours at the office arranging materials and workers for the arcology project. When she had time she would go to the apartment to have dinner with Chanda and Margarethe and then take the car out to Glasshouse to fall mercifully to sleep.

One evening she received a call from Jordan after dinner.

"Yes Oracle, I'll take it," she said.

"Oh he's been calling all week," said Chanda. "We forgot to tell you."

"Hello?"

"Hey Val, it's good to hear your voice," said Jordan, his voice projecting around the house.

"Is this your young lover? I heard about him at the Sister's Gathering," said Margarethe.

"Jordan meet Margarethe and Chanda."

"And Grischa," added Margarethe.

"Hi ladies. Are you having fun in Ottawa?"

"It's a beautiful city," said Chanda. "Cold, but beautiful."

"I don't like these Canadian phones, I feel like we're all talking to a ghost," said Margarethe.

"Jordan honey, I'll call you at lunch tomorrow, okay?"

"Okay. Love you."

"Love you too."

Click.

Jordan hung up the phone. He missed Val. He knew she had her hands full right now with her guests.

The next day, Baron showed up at Hammer & Bone to take Valkyrie out for lunch.

"I can't Baron, I'm completely swamped."

"What are you working on?"

"The prototype arcology. I'm sourcing the pilot site, getting everything together. It's been fast tracked."

"Can I help with anything?"

"No one can," she said.

"Don't burn yourself out."

"Sukhwant is helping me delegate," laughed Val.

"How about we just talk about it over lunch?"

The phone rang.

"It's Jordan," said the Oracle.

"You need to eat," said Baron loudly.

"I'll call him back," said Val. The Oracle relayed the message.

"Baron, I can't go out for lunch. I'm way too busy."

"Let me bring you something at least."

She looked at him with a pained expression. She didn't want to argue, she just wanted to get back to work.

"Fine," she said.

"I'll be right back," said Baron. He let himself out.

The Oracle told Jordan that Valkyrie would have to call him back. He decided that he might as well stop by her office for a visit. He hadn't seen her in person for almost a month and he was missing her. He pulled on his winter boots and trudged down the street.

Baron picked up two heaping to-go plates of Valkyrie's favourites from the Green Table. He always complained when she wanted to eat there but secretly he really liked the food. He took a cab back downtown to her office, and on his way there he saw Jordan.

"Stop the car," he said. He pressed his credit card to the pay meter and got out.

"Jordan Barker," he boomed.

Jordan froze and turned around slowly. It was Valkyrie's ex-husband, Baron.

"Hi there," he said.

Baron was wearing a long black pea coat with a dark scarf around his neck and expensive looking sunglasses. His beard and moustache were flawless.

"Where are you off to?" asked Baron.

"Umm, just out walking. What are you up to?"

"I was just on my way to have lunch with Valkyrie," he said, holding up the take-out bag. "She's having a busy day so we're eating it together at her office instead."

She never invites me to have lunch with her, Jordan thought.

He was crestfallen.

Maybe it's because I can't afford to...

Jordan shivered. He looked down at his shitty coat. He was freezing.

He looked at Baron. His nerves tingled with alarm. Something about this man was so familiar...

"Have we met before? Before the opera, I mean," he asked.

"What do you mean?" asked Baron. He had a wolfish grin.

Jordan stared at him and suddenly it came to him.

The party. Ashemore Estate.

"You were there, weren't you?" he asked. "At Ashemore. The man in the black mask... the beard and moustache."

"Why yes of course," laughed Baron. "Evander and Lisbeth are friends of ours." His grin widened with surprise. "Didn't Valkyrie tell you?"

Jordan shook his head.

"Aww, well I'm sorry to hear that. You should feel honoured that she brought you at all though. Not that you were the first pony boy to tag along with Valkyrie Snow at Ashemore..."

The words cut Jordan like a knife.

"Well, enjoy your lunch," he said, turning around and heading home.

Baron brought the plates up to Valkyrie's office.

"The Green Table," he said cheerfully.

"Thank you," she said with genuine gratitude. She was surprised that he had gone all the way to get her one of her favourites. She was thinking—*but you hate this place*—but she said nothing.

"Mmm, I haven't had this in a while," she said.

"You must really be busy," he laughed. He went around behind her chair and started massaging her shoulders.

"Baron, please don't do that."

"Doesn't it feel good sweetie?"

Valkyrie stood up. "I just don't like it."

Baron flung up his hands. "Fine, sorry, just being nice." He backed off.

Val sat back down. She closed up the lid of her take-out.

"Thank you so much for lunch," she said. "I have to get back to work."

"But you're not finished yet!"

"I'm full. It was delicious. Thank you."

Don't make me ask you to leave, she thought.

As if reading her thoughts, Baron stood up.

"I'll let you get back to work," he said.

"Thanks."

After Baron left, Valkyrie focused back on Mother House.

Suddenly she remembered that she forgot to call Jordan back.

Shit, she thought.

"Oracle, please call Jordan."

The Oracle connected the call. Jordan picked up.

"Hello?"

"Hi sweetheart, sorry I didn't call you back sooner, I'm swamped with work."

"Oh." Jordan sounded withdrawn.

"Aww, I'll make it up to you."

"Dinner tonight?" he said. He needed to see her.

"Tonight? I can't, I have no time at all..."

But you have time for lunch with your ex, thought Jordan.

"Hmm. Okay."

"What are you up to?"

"I just came in from a walk," said Jordan. "I'm warming up my toes..."

His bare feet were pressed against the radiator. His boots had holes.

"That's nice... I miss you."

"My show is coming up. March 29th. You're coming right?"

"Oh honey I can't, the house just closed, I have to get out there this weekend and get the ladies moved in. I'll be there at least a week. I'm sorry..." She had completely forgotten about his concert.

Jordan said nothing. He wanted to call her out on having lunch with Baron but it felt petty.

"I'm sorry. Please forgive me?" she asked.

"Have you brought other lovers to Ashemore Estate?" he

asked finally. The words slipped out.

"What?!"

"Other lovers. You know, *pony boys*. To the Ashemore party."

"Jordan of course not."

"Are you sure?"

"Jordan what is this?"

"Baron was there, wasn't he."

Val was silent for a moment.

"Yes."

"Why didn't you tell me?"

"I'm sorry, I wasn't ready to talk about it."

"You invited me to spend Christmas with your friends, you pulled me around on your little leash, trusting you, and you didn't trust me enough to tell me your ex-husband was there, watching me."

"Jordan..."

"You didn't even tell me you had an ex-husband!"

"I know... I'll cancel the move-in. I'll go to your concert."

"Don't you dare," he said. "Then it'll be on me that you don't get them moved in on schedule. No, I just want you to tell me the truth."

Valkyrie stood up and went to close her office door. She sat back down at her desk.

"This is not a conversation I want to have over the phone at work," she said.

"Yea me neither. But I haven't seen you in a month."

"Jordan you're exaggerating..."

He felt anger bubble up inside him. His mother had said the same thing during their phone call right before Christmas.

"This is not on me," he said. "Stop putting this on me!"

"Jordan, you're yelling."

"Cuz I'm fucking mad!"

"I have to get back to work, but I do want to continue this conversation like adults, later."

"Oh good! Why don't you have your adult conversation with your adult husband when you have him over for dinner!"

Click.

Jordan hung up.

Valkyrie tried to get back to work but she was terribly

distracted. She wanted to cry, and to go and see Jordan, but she had so much to do before the move. She couldn't have Margarethe moving out to an isolated farmhouse on Cape Breton Island without making sure the electricity was up and running, the kitchen was finished and there would be someone plowing the drive for her and Chanda.

Finally she couldn't stand it anymore and she called Baron.

"Hello Val."

"Hi Baron. I don't know what you said to Jordan, but whatever it was, I want you to stay out of my business from now on. Jordan's mine, and he has nothing to do with you. Leave him alone."

"Lover's quarrel?"

"It just makes the make-up sex that much sweeter. Leave us alone."

Click.

She hung up.

March-end arrived and it was time for Margarethe and Chanda to move into their new home, along with several other sisters who would be making the journey to Cape Breton. They packed up their things and headed to the airport to make the journey east.

"It's going to be nice to have a home again," said Chanda. "Not that I haven't had a lovely time with you, Valkyrie, but I'm really looking forward to setting down roots. I'm excited to be out in the country and have animals and the ocean close by."

"I know you'll be happy there. I just hope the renovations went according to plan. It looked good in the pictures Marisol sent me."

"Stop fussing," said Margarethe. "Everything will be fine." She held Grischa's cage snugly on her lap.

They boarded their plane and flew into Halifax, catching the connecting flight to Sydney. In the car to the property, they looked out the windows with anticipation. The March weather was dreary, with fog rising from the fields as the land began to warm. The snow was still piled high. They cracked the windows.

"Smell that gramma?" said Chanda.

"Salt, like the Black Sea," said Margarethe, inhaling deeply. It was the North Atlantic Ocean.

The car turned up a long laneway. Trees overshadowed the

road on either side. Suddenly the trees thinned out into overgrown homesteader fields and they could see straight to the shore. They passed the little stone house, driving up to the farmhouse. The once-white vinyl siding looked ashy in the fog, and the porch drooped in the middle.

Chanda sighed with disappointment. Margarethe smacked her lightly with the back of her hand and tutted.

"I'm sorry, I just miss home," she said. "I'll get used to it. I know I will."

"Utopia is a verb, not a place," said Margarethe. "We will make it home."

"I thought about having the exterior siding recovered in something nicer in the spring, but there's really no point. The arcology will be built. The inside is nice. You'll see."

They crunched through wet snow up to the house.

The door opened straight into a summer kitchen porch with hundreds of empty preserve jars and bottles for winemaking. They walked through into the remodeled kitchen. A fire crackled merrily in the old fireplace. The room was warm.

"Beautiful," said Margarethe. She kicked off her boots and walked deeper into the house.

Chanda, Valkyrie and the driver unloaded the van.

The main floor had a large living room and dining room off the kitchen. The old front door was all boarded up, with an old piano in front of it. Upstairs there were five creaky-floored bedrooms and a full bathroom. There was a cold cellar under the house and an outhouse out back.

"This is perfect," said Margarethe. "Thank you my angel." She gestured Valkyrie to bend down and planted a big wet kiss on her cheek.

"The fridge should be full of groceries if you're hungry," said Val.

Soon the other women began to arrive. Margarethe had a pot on every burner on the stove, cooking up a feast.

"What's for dinner?" asked Farrah, lifting lids on the stove. She had narrowly escaped capture at the U.S.-Canada border. She had crossed at the Thousand Islands.

"Out! Out of my kitchen!" bellowed Margarethe. She shooed everyone into the living room. "You almost destroyed the dumplings," she muttered under her breath.

Someone got behind the piano and tuned it as best they could, while others shook rugs outside, put art on the walls, and made up the beds. Valkyrie took out her sage and shell and smudged the house. Some of the women had fled with nothing but the clothes on their backs, but the house had everything they needed. Valkyrie felt overwhelming relief.

They set the table for dinner. Candles cast warm light and Val looked around at all the shining faces. There were three young ones and five old ones. Two more would arrive before winter's end and many more would come in the summer when they could pitch tents in the long grass by the ocean. In the spring they would have cows and fresh milk, and eggs. And when the arcology was complete, a hundred sisters could live inside it and the building itself would be engineered to provide for them.

"The circumstances are terrible, but I'm glad that we're finally doing this," said Valkyrie, holding hands with her sisters. "Everyone will be cared for here."

They said a prayer for those lost on the journey, and then wiped away their tears and broke bread.

"You're insane for doing this," said Farrah, "but it's incredible."

"It's been an insane month," said Val. "And it's only going to get worse..."

They all saw the stress in her eyes.

"So you're going to let us help, right?"

"What? No, I can handle it."

"Quit that talk right now. Sisterhood is powerful. Let us share this with you."

Val looked around at her sisters. They were right. She felt her eyes well up with tears.

"Yes. Yes I will. Thank you."

The eight women living at the farmhouse—they fondly named it Gray House—were refugees unable to work in Canada. That meant that they were aching for something to do. Valkyrie had former lawyers, bankers, CEOs and a shaman to manage the property. She gave copies of all of the plans to the women to see where they could help. Miraculously, the burden was lifted and she wasn't alone.

Two days before the concert at Animal House, there was a knock at the door. It was Matt.

Bubba and Jordan came up to chat with him.

"What's up Matty?" asked Jordan. He could tell something was wrong.

"I need to talk to you guys about something." He was twisting his mittens in his hands.

This has got to be about Jesse's roommate, thought Jordan. *He's fessing up.* He nodded solemnly. He knew that eventually Matt would do the right thing.

"I... umm... I can't play the show on Saturday," he said.

"What the fuck?"

"I'll lose my job. I have no choice. Sorry boys."

"It's two days away!"

"You can't just bail on us like this!"

Matt stood up. "Look I'm sorry! I've got a real good thing with this job. I've been thinking... I need to get my priorities straight. I think we're taking this way too seriously. It's not fun anymore."

"You're quitting the fucking band?" said Bubba.

"Nah bro, not quitting... I just don't want to play all these big shows anymore. It takes way too much of my time. And now Jordan's got all these new songs to learn... it's too much."

"Matty, please, can you just play on Saturday and we'll figure this out after?"

"I can't. My boss says it's unprofessional."

"Your boss is a dickhead!"

"Don't do us like this! It's two fucking days away!"

"I know you're pissed... but you'll figure it out."

Jordan pulled his hair in his hands. He couldn't believe this was happening.

Matt got up and walked to the door.

"Matt! Please!"

"No means no," he said on his way out. "And I got an email from those Folkfest guys, it's a no for the Waves."

Bubba called Jerome while Jordan went straight to the computer to post an ad on Sellit.ca.

Drummer desperately needed for Saturday house show!

"Jerome doesn't want to play if Matt isn't playing," said Bubba.
"No, no no no no no..." said Jordan. He called Jerome.
"Hello?"
"Buddy, please, I'm dying here, can you come over? We need to figure this out."
"I'm about to have dinner with my family," said Jerome. "And I don't really want to bus all the way downtown tonight..."
"We'll come up to you, okay?"
"Umm, fine, yea okay."
"On our way."

Bubba and Jordan took the bus out to Kanata where Jerome's parents lived in the house they moved into when they got to Canada. The Williams family came north when the troubles started, when Jerome was a teenager.
'Illegal' Mexicans in South Carolina were rounded up and sent away, and then the legal ones, then anyone who wasn't white. Jerome's mum managed a community centre back then, and one day it got shot up by white terrorists. Jerome's dad wanted to leave it all behind and seek sanctuary up north.
"I'm scared," he had said. "I don't feel safe here anymore."
"What can we do? Leave the life we've built here? What about our family?"
"What kind of life can our children have in a place like this?"
"If it's like this here, it has to be bad everywhere. This is the greatest country in the world," she said. She really believed it. They didn't have the internet.
"We have to believe there's something better for us, for our family, out there..."
Then the news came that Canada was granting sanctuary for any asylum seekers who made it through the border. Other people in their community talked about making the journey, but when the day came, it was just Jerome's mother, father, and their three children. Now they lived in a clean little house beside a park in Kanata, a suburb of the capital, where in the ten years they had lived there, they had never seen a gun or witnessed a crime. People who grew up there called it boring.

Jordan kept refreshing his email, hoping for a reply to his ad.

When they showed up, Jerome's dad greeted them at the door.

"Hi boys. Just like old times, huh?" he laughed and let them in. They rushed down to the basement where Jerome's room was.

"So what the fuck is going on?" asked Jerome.

They explained everything that happened.

"So… we should cancel the show, right?" said Jerome. "I mean, you're not going to find a drummer on Sellit.ca who can learn all our songs in one day."

"Two days," said Jordan.

Jerome's mom called down the stairs. "Would you like some food boys? I can make you up plates."

"That would be just lovely Mrs. Williams," said Bubba. Jerome gave him the side-eye.

"Maybe we could do an acoustic show…" said Jordan, looking at Jerome hopefully.

"No way, you're crazy. That's so much work! Plus some of our songs would be shit in acoustic."

"What if I just get some like, basic beat tracks, like recordings, and we do an acoustic show."

"I don't know…"

"Come on Jerome! Please! We can make this work! We have to!"

Mrs. Williams came down with two plates of pork chops and potatoes.

"That looks delicious, thank you so much," said Bubba.

"Thanks Mrs. Williams," said Jordan quietly.

"Jordan, you're looking healthy," she said, eying his muscles. "But what's wrong?"

"Matt quit the band," said Bubba with a mouth full of potatoes.

"But don't you have a show on Saturday?"

"Yes," said Jerome.

"I see. I'll leave you to figure it out then." She went back upstairs.

"Matt was the weak link anyway. We were eventually going to need a new drummer."

Jerome looked away awkwardly. He knew it was true.

"Matt probably knew it too. Let's just go back to basics and do an acoustic show."

"I'll have to skip school tomorrow and we'll have to practice all fucking day."

Jordan looked at him hopefully.

"So it's on?" said Bubba.

"Yea..."

Jordan and Bubba hooted.

"How about you come back downtown with us tonight and sleep over so we can get an early start?"

"Nah. You guys sleep over here in a real bed, and we practice all day here."

"Deal."

Jordan took their plates upstairs. He filled the sink with soap and hot water and washed up the dishes. While he was up there, his phone rang. His hands were wet so he couldn't answer it. When his hands were dry, he checked to see who it was.

Valkyrie.

She left him a message. He tried his voicemail password but it didn't work. He was always forgetting it. Jerome ran upstairs.

"Come down here, I have an idea!"

Jordan followed him down. He would have to check his voicemail later. Jerome plunked something out for him on the guitar. It didn't sound too bad. The boys resisted the temptation to stay up late watching movies. They went to bed so they could get an early start.

In the morning they got a later start than they planned, but by noon they were jamming. Jordan was feeling a cold sweaty panic and Jerome was on edge. Bubba's cheerful encouragement was the only thing that kept them going.

"It sounds rough now, but every time you practice it it sounds better," he said. "By tonight you'll have it down. It's coming together, seriously."

Some of the songs were decent in acoustic, but two or three sounded awful. They worked through it again and again.

"I think we'll just have to take this one out," said Jordan finally. "It's fucking whack."

"But we've spent an hour on it," said Jerome, frustrated. "What a waste of time."

Jordan looked miserable. He was trying to stay positive but it was hard.

What would the Dollies do? he thought.

"What would the Death Row Dollies do?" he said out loud. "They wouldn't whine about it, they'd do the best they could with the circumstances."

"I didn't know you liked the Dollies. They're pretty rad," said Jerome.

Jordan never told the boys about his love for the DRDs because Matt had said the Dollies were garbage once. He took a deep breath. A big part of him just wanted to quit, but something powerful inside him was not going to give up.

"Okay. Let's move on to something else, and if we have time, we'll come back to this. If it's shit by tomorrow, we just cut it."

"Sounds good."

That night Jordan called Valkyrie and there was no answer.

The next day was the big show. They decided to cut one song, and play the recording from the album as people came in. Jordan dulled out his feelings, resigning himself to just accepting that it was happening and there was nothing he could do about it.

"I hope we made the right choice," said Jerome as people started showing up.

"It's fine," said Jordan.

"That's easy for you to say... Your part is the same."

Jordan looked at him, seeing for the first time that this actually was harder for Jerome. He squeezed his friend's elbow.

"Thanks for making this happen," he said. "You're the best guitarist I know. You're gunna be awesome."

They stepped onto the stage. Sapphire dialed down the music.

"How's everybody tonight?" said Jordan.

The room was packed. People cheered.

"We had a little hiccup and drummer boy Matt's not here tonight," said Jordan softly into the microphone, pushing his hair behind his ear. "It's all good though... we're changing it up, and we've got some new songs for you."

Jerome started strumming.

Jordan gave the crowd his most soulful look and leaned into the microphone. His first notes were pure and intense. All that practicing the day before had paid off. They started the show with one of their stronger songs to get the energy going. It was working. Jordan sounded incredible. Girls got out their phones to record him. As the song wound to a close, the crowd cheered. Jerome moved quickly to the second number on their set list.

As the mellow acoustic tones played, Jordan could see that the fans in the front were loving the new sound, but the guys with red solo cups in the back were quickly disinterested. By the third song, he could hear the rumbling and susurration of conversations. People who expected a lively upbeat show were talking. It was sucking the energy out of the performance. During the fifth song, Jerome screwed up. They kept going, but the song never totally recovered. Jordan was sweating profusely. He just wanted to get through the rest of the show and fall mercifully to sleep.

The talking was getting louder. Sapphire cranked up the speakers. It helped a little, but Jordan could feel how off the energy was. He turned to Jerome.

"Skip the next one," he whispered. The two after it were their best pieces. Jordan wanted to end on a good note.

Just as Jerome was moving into the second last song, there was a bang on the door and three police officers came in.

"Everyone out, party's over," said a cop. Jerome screeched to a stop and people started filing out.

"Excuse me," said Sapphire with a smile. "What seems to be the problem?"

The show wasn't loud enough to cause a noise complaint.

"We've had a tip that there's underage drinking going on here," said an officer.

"Absolutely not. We're all university students," she said.

"You don't know that," said the officer.

"Look, this is a private show. We can't just cancel it now. It's not over," she said.

"Did you card everyone at the door?"

Sapphire was silent.

"Trust me, it's over."

Sapph was annoyed, but she didn't argue. The guests left. Some were complaining loudly that they wasted their money. Jordan felt like shit.

"Well, it is what it is, boys," said Bubba, giving them a hug.

"I'm just glad it's over. I'm heading home. Night guys," said Jerome.

"Night Jerome. You did great. Before the cops came, your playing was awesome."

Jerome took off.

Sapphire took one look at Jordan's devastated face and smiled sympathetically.

"You need a hit?" she said.

"Yes please."

They went upstairs to the balcony. Paul, another roommate, and Bubba came too. Sapphire pulled out a packet of powder. She poured lines on a cutting board.

"Whoa... seriously?" said Jordan. "I thought we were smoking weed."

"I thought maybe you needed something stronger," she said. "You can thank me later."

Jordan looked at Bubba.

Why the fuck not? he thought.

"None for me, thanks," said Bubba.

Sapphire handed Jordan a rolled up Sir John A. "After you," she said.

Jordan snorted a line.

Outside, Baron watched the patrons leaving the party. He was the one who had called the police.

When the lights and noise at the house died down, he climbed back into the car and drove off. It carried him up onto the Queensway and over to St. Laurent. The car pulled into a dark parking lot outside a dingy looking warehouse. There were no lights on and he walked carefully through the darkness to a side door. He let himself in with keys and locked the door behind him. He had preparations to make.

Over the next week, Jordan's social media accounts for the Waves blew up with negative comments and messages about the show. He was gutted. He wanted nothing more than to escape to Glasshouse and get blissed out on orgasms with Valkyrie, but she was still in Nova Scotia. He wanted to share the burden of the criticism with someone, but he didn't want to make Jerome and Bubba feel bad so he kept it all to himself. He deleted the worst comments and tried to forget about them.

You're amateur, hissed Snake, who wouldn't let him forget. *You're unprofessional. You're a fraud. You cheated them out of a good show. You suck lately. You're washed up.*

His phone pinged with a new notification. A message. Jordan groaned inwardly, then clicked it. It was from Jesse.

> Hey Jordan. I heard Matt wasn't at the show. Thanks. I knew you guys would do something about it. :) I'll be at the next show, I promise. :)

Jesse:

Well at least Jesse doesn't think I'm a scumbag, thought Jordan. *Even though that's not why Matt wasn't at the show...*

Jordan scrolled through his text history.
Charlotte. I wonder how she's doing.
He turned off his screen. He felt terrible for thinking about Charlotte.

I am a scumbag, he thought. He wished that Valkyrie would come home soon.

Valkyrie Snow couldn't believe that it was already April. Winter had flown by so fast. Things were moving quickly on Mother House too. Every day, flats of building materials showed up on large trucks, waiting for construction to begin when the land thawed. The days were getting longer and soon it would be warm enough for more refugees to pitch their tents on the land. Kale and her American wife Susanna moved into Gray House. It wasn't safe for them anymore, even in Philadelphia where Kale conducted her neuroscience research. Kale had kept her Canadian citizenship; hopefully that would make it easier to find a job. She and Susanna were helping out at Gray House in the meantime.

Mika Nakamura was the lead junior onsite. It was an incredible honour. She was working directly with Hammer & Bone's top architects. After this project, she would no longer be a junior. If these Snow Arcologies took off, then she had a long and prosperous career ahead of her. She was also personally responsible for taking care of the nightingale, who had made it to the East Coast on one of Valkyrie's trips.

Val invited Sunday Banerjee, the head contractor at Glasshouse, to come to Cape Breton to work on Mother House.

She's got a good head on her shoulders, thought Val. She looked forward to working with both of them again.

April passed one busy week at a time. Val made two short stops back in Ottawa to meet with shareholders, but her hands were full in the Maritimes. She missed Jordan and their cozy days at Glasshouse, but she was in project mode, and she was able to shut out the world to singularly focus on work.

He's writing his new album right now, she thought. *He understands.*

May tenth was the big day the excavator would break soil. In May they would lay the groundwork for the geothermal energy system, and start building the foundation. The arcology was a colossal project that would take at least four years to complete.

Valkyrie invested in the latest AI upgrade. Her Oracle could now travel along with her in a green orb she carried in her pocket. The nanite-infused technology could access her conscious thoughts. It would not be long before the devices could connect people's minds directly to the internet.

"Oracle," said Valkyrie softly. "Get me in touch with James Ahote."

The Oracle connected them. His phone rang and then he picked up.

"Hello?"

"Hi James. It's Valkyrie."

"Oh, hey," he said warmly.

"So are you ready for the life-size beta?"

"Seriously?"

"Yea. We've broken soil at the pilot site… Cape Breton, Nova Scotia."

"That's awesome!"

"How's my heart doing?"

"We're almost there! I think we could also be ready to pilot a life-scale model soon."

"Great. Well keep me updated. I'm ready for another status report."

"I'll let the team know."

"And James," added Val, "I've added you to my personal line. You can contact me through Oracle."

"Okay, sounds good."

"When you guys are ready, just say the word and I'll fly you down here."

"I look forward to it."

Old trailers pulled up to the property. The ladies at Gray House, led by Margarethe and Farrah, organized a new residential site far down the shore and through the woods.

"Best to plan well from the start," said Margarethe.

Makeshift housing and communal half-sheltered areas went up quickly. There were many women to make light of the work, and more coming every day. A Mother Council was formed for those who wanted to take part in the planning. The council organized committees to see to the daily care of the property. Everyone was in a committee. Soon gardens were being planted and animals were being tended. Children ran wild. The land was their school.

The plans that Valkyrie had set in motion were out of her hands now. Everything was taken care of. Finally, she could go home to Jordan. She booked her flight.

Jordan was not doing well. He went up to Sapphire's room to see if she had any drugs. He needed to take this edge off, bad.

"Can you hook me up?" he asked.

"I don't have any more of what we had at the party, but I can get something else you might like," she said. "I haven't tried it, but I've heard it's great for dealing with depression."

Depression. There was that word, spoken out loud.

"What is it?" he asked.

"It's umm… something you shoot up," she said.

"You mean like, with a needle?" Jordan took a step back. "That's a little intense."

"Up to you."

"I'm okay for now, thanks."

Jordan went back down to his room. He curled in a ball and tried listening to music with the volume cranked all the way up, but every time he received a notification on his phone he felt a jolt of anxiety. He wanted to turn off his notifications, but that gave him anxiety too. He was a mess. After an hour, he grabbed his clothes, pulled on his winter wear, and jogged to the gym. The smell of cedar boiling in diffusers calmed him as he entered the building. This would make him feel better. He went to the change room and got ready, and then went to the machines to pound out his stress.

An hour later, he was feeling a lot better. He left the weight room with a lighter step. As he walked to the change room, the robot approached him.

"Excuse me, Mr. Barker," it said discreetly.

"Yes?"

"Your membership expired last week. We will not charge you today as a courtesy, but when you are finished in the change room, please come to the front desk if you would like to continue in your health regimen with us."

Jordan's face fell.

"I will have to do that next time," he said.

"Very good." The robot left.

Jordan stripped down and went to the shower. He cranked up the steam and sat on the floor and cried his eyes out. Silently, of course, so that none of the other men could hear him. Then he went home.

Jordan went straight to Sapphire's room.

"I'm gunna need that stuff," he said.

"I already called the guy," she said. "He's coming over tonight."

An hour or so later, there was a knock on the door. It was Sapphire's friend.

"This is Barry," she said, introducing him to Jordan.

Barry was wearing an un-ironic snapback and baggy jeans.

"Sup," he said.

"Um hey," said Jordan.

Barry pulled a crumpled paper bag out of his backpack. He dumped the contents on the table. A blackened spoon, a baggie of brown powder, deconstructed q-tips, a lighter, clear fluid, and syringes. Jordan felt his heart beat faster. He swallowed hard. Half of him wanted to back out and the other half wanted to be high already.

Barry turned on the kitchen tap, letting the water get warm. He put some on the spoon. Then he added brown powder and poured some of the clear fluid on top. He held the lighter underneath the spoon, letting the mixture cook, swirling it gently to mix the powder into the fluid. The liquid started bubbling. He took a tiny piece of q-tip cotton, rolled it up tight between his fingers and dropped it into the spoon. He took the syringe and held it to the cotton, sucking up the liquid.

"Hold out your arm," he said to Jordan, pushing the air out the end of the needle.

Jordan had a million questions in his head, but he didn't say a word. He stuck out his arm and watched in fascination as Barry injected him with drugs.

The rush came in seconds. Jordan had to sit down. He couldn't think. It was like nothing he had ever felt before. He was euphoric. He felt like he was in heaven, up in the clouds.

"It's beautiful," he said.

"What is?" asked Sapphire.

"Life is..." he laughed. It was achingly beautiful.

He leaned against the chair and let himself bliss out. Barry and Sapphire chatted but he didn't hear them.

After the initial rush passed, Jordan felt dull and pleasant. The world slowed down around him and he relaxed. All of his cares were gone. In fact, he realized that they weren't even real. The whole world was actually in his control. He stood up. Sapphire and Barry watched him walk out of the room.

He went downstairs to be alone in his room. He looked at his pictures on the walls. It felt like he was in a dream, in a realm outside of Earth. His skin tingled. Then it started to itch. He scratched. His skin was hot to the touch.

Jordan lay down on his bed. He resisted the urge to scratch. *Everything's okay,* he thought. *Everything's fine. You're okay.*

He wrapped his arms around himself.

You deserve a hug, he thought.

Jordan spent the next few hours in golden twilight.

CHAPTER TWENTY SEVEN

When Valkyrie's plane landed at the Ottawa airport, Baron was waiting for her at Arrivals.

"Hi dear," he said. "I wanted to apologize for my bad behaviour. I know that no one can replace me, ever. I know that. I just had a weak moment. Forgive me?"

Valkyrie couldn't help smiling. She pecked him on the cheek.

"No one could ever replace you Baron. Thank you for apologizing."

He hooked his arm into hers and they walked out to the car.

Valkyrie was a little annoyed that he had been monitoring her travel plans, but she did appreciate his effort to apologize, and it was always nice to have someone meet you at the airport.

Just let this one go Val, she thought to herself. *It was a nice gesture.*

"So. Plans for the day?" he asked her once they were in the car.

"I'm going to go home and have a long bath, and then I'm going to surprise Mr. Barker," she said.

"Oh. So he doesn't know you're here today?"

"Not yet, no."

"Well I won't hassle you with begging for a dinner date just yet. Let's get you home and I'll call you later in the week."

"Thank you dear."

"So what have you been up to? By the looks of our flight account, you've hardly been in Ottawa in the last two months."

"That's right. Wildly busy."

"Poor thing. And poor Jordan. I imagine you haven't talked on the phone much lately."

"Why?"

"You're almost impossible to reach when you're travelling."

Valkyrie smiled. It was true.

"Well absence makes the heart grow fonder and all that."

"True."

The car pulled up to Val's condominium. Baron insisted on carrying her small bag and she didn't feel like arguing. They walked up to her unit.

She slumped down on the couch with a sigh.

"It's so good to be home," she said.

Baron acted fast. He was behind her in three quick strides. He pulled a syringe out of his pocket and slid it quickly into her neck.

Valkyrie didn't know what was happening. She reached up to touch a sudden stinging sensation on her neck and she felt her eyelids getting so heavy that she couldn't keep them open. She sunk into the couch, unconscious.

Jordan's phone rang. He picked up.

"Hello?"

"Hi, is the Jordan Barker of the Waves?"

"Yea, that's me."

"My name is Brigitte Castilloux, I'm a producer for the CBC. We're doing a segment on Ottawa musicians and we'd like to showcase some of your music on CBC Radio 2. Can you come by our Ottawa office to discuss?"

Jordan almost choked. Was this real?

"Umm, yea, we'd love to."

Mme. Castilloux gave him instructions for how to get to their studio and they scheduled a meeting.

"I look forward to meeting you and your band members," she said.

"Yea. See you soon."

Click.

When the call was over, Jordan was stunned. How did the CBC hear about the Waves? Maybe Larry shared around the album. Or maybe Brigitte Castilloux had a fast deadline and had done a quick search on Instagram. Whatever the case, she liked what she heard enough to call them in for airtime. This was the chance of a lifetime.

He texted Bubba.

Get yer ass in here

Jordan:

Bubba popped over to Jordan's room.

"What's up?"

Jordan grinned. He called Jerome.

"Calling Jerome," he said.

"Hello?"

"Hey Jer, I have amazing news. Bubba's here with me."

"I'm just on break, going back into class in like two minutes. What is it?"

"A producer at CBC just called me. The Waves are gunna be on the radio."

"Seriously?! That's awesome!"

"Yea, we're going in next week for a meeting. She's gunna do a little interview and everything."

"Holy shit, that's amazing... CBC! The fucking dream man!"

"This is it. We gotta celebrate, come downtown and we'll go for Pho or something."

"Sounds good, I'll text you when I'm out of class."

"Kay cool, and I'll text you all the details for the interview."

"Can't wait."

"Love you man," said Jordan. It just slipped out before he could check himself.

"Love you too bro, see you guys later."

Click.

Jordan was momentarily embarrassed about telling Jerome he loved him, but it didn't seem to bother Jerome at all. Jordan was relieved.

And I do love him, thought Jordan. *What's wrong with that?*

"Hey. You never tell me you love me," said Bubba with a grin.

"Haa, I love you too Bubs."

Bubba pulled his elbow around Jordan's neck and squeezed his head in his arm.

Alex wanted to tell Jordan he loved him, but he couldn't quite bring himself to say the words. It was okay; Jordan understood.

"So where are we going for dinner?"

"I was thinking New Pho. It's like seven bucks for a big bowl there. That's all I can afford haha."

"Me too."

Valkyrie woke up in a hospital bed. Her head was pounding dully and the rest of her body felt numb and tingly. She could tell that she was on painkillers. The bluish lights were shining on her and she could only open her eyes a tiny bit.

What happened?

She held up her arm. It was connected to an intravenous machine. The fluid was clear, with a slightly greenish tinge.

"Uhhhaaunn…" she tried to talk but her tongue was heavy.

"Val, sweetie," said a voice. Baron walked quickly over. His face loomed close to hers, blocking out the light. He took her hand.

"You're sick, you passed out," he said, stroking her hair. "Shhh…"

She relaxed. Thank goodness Baron was there to take care of her. She closed her eyes and let herself fall back to sleep.

In the morning, Baron was there when Valkyrie woke up.

"What happened?" she asked. "I don't remember anything."

"When I took you home from the airport last night, you passed out and had some kind of seizure," he said, a look of grave concern on his face.

"Really?" She had never had a seizure before.

"The doctor said you must be under a lot of stress."

"Can I see the doctor?"

"Of course. He'll be by at some point to talk to you."

Valkyrie let the information sink in.

"Thanks for being here," she said.

Baron smiled. "I'll always be here for you."

The doctor came by a few hours later.

"Hi Mrs. Snow," he said, looking at a clipboard in his hands. "I'm Doctor Jensen. How are you feeling?"

"I'm okay. My head is pounding, but other than that I feel fine."

"Good, good."

"What happened?"

"According to Mr. Toussaint, you had a seizure and fell unconscious."

"Yes. Why?"

"We're not completely sure yet, but we're running some tests. It could be a number of things."

"Like what?"

"Well the most likely cause at your age would be stress or exhaustion. We are just ruling other causes that are more serious like meningitis and some kinds of cancer. Those are very unlikely but we're making sure."

Baron spent the day with her, bringing her favourite takeout.
"Thank you so much for this," she said. "I really appreciate it."

Doctor Jensen came back in the afternoon. "We've got the results of some of your tests," he said.
"Yes?"
"I'm not going to talk around the issue," he said. "At this time, we are concerned that you may have cancer. We will need to conduct some tests on your breasts."
Valkyrie was shocked. She reached up and lightly touched her breasts. "It can't be! I have no pain, no lumps…"
"That's a good thing. It means that we are catching it very early."
"What kinds of tests?"
"We'll start with a non-invasive thermographic test," he said.
"That's because cancer cells run hotter than the regular body temperature, right?"
Dr. Jensen looked quickly at Baron and then back at Val.
"That's right."
"Well sure, go ahead and give me the thermographic test."
A nurse came in with a machine. Valkyrie opened her hospital gown and he held her breast in his hand, scanning it with the device.
"The doctor will be back soon with your results," he said.
Several hours later, Dr. Jensen returned with another man.
"This is Dr. Hendricks. He is a breast cancer specialist."
"Nice to meet you Mrs. Snow."
"Please call me Val."
He was holding images.
"We have the results of your thermographic test, and it looks like there is indeed angiogenesis taking place. That's enough of an indication that there's cancer in your breast for us to proceed to the next phase of diagnosis to determine exactly what we're dealing with."
Angiogenesis meant that Valkyrie's breast was building a new blood supply system to feed a breast tumor.
She frowned. "I can't believe this is happening."

"You're just incredibly lucky that we've caught it this early," said Dr. Hendricks.

Valkyrie felt dizzy and she drifted in and out of consciousness. During the times she was awake, they ran a series of other tests.

"You have a small tumor in your breast. We believe that with neoadjuvant therapy, we can reduce it and even kill all of the malignant cells completely without having to operate. We can give you your first chemotherapy treatment today. You're already hooked up to an IV. It will take approximately four days for your first treatment, and then we'll keep you here overnight and discharge you when we determine that you're fit to go home. After that, we'll put you on a treatment cycle. You can come in for follow-up injections every two weeks, or keep the stint in your arm and administer them yourself. Then we can do some more tests and see how you're doing."

"This is all... overwhelming..." said Valkyrie. Her head still hurt and she was having trouble coming to terms with all this.

I had cancer growing inside of me and I never even knew it. I felt nothing. It was like her own body had betrayed her.

"Completely understandable. We'll give you some time to talk it over with your husband. I recommend we start the treatments as soon as possible." He left the room.

"This is so crazy," said Val.

Baron held her hand. "We'll get through it," he said.

She looked at him, and her lip trembled.

"Aww, shhh..." he said, kissing her forehead.

A tear slid down her cheek, followed by a sob. She started to cry. She couldn't help it.

"Where are my clothes?" she asked.

"Your clothes?"

"I need my Oracle. Could you get it?"

"I'm not sure honey."

"It's in the pocket of my jacket. Could you contact my friends? And tell them what's happening? And Sukhwant."

Baron smiled. "Absolutely," he said.

"Thank you. It must be out of range, otherwise I could contact it via thought."

Good to know, thought Baron.

"Can you tell the doctor to come back? I've decided. I'm ready to start treatment."

"Yes dear." Baron left to get the Oracle and Dr. Hendricks.

"Can you give me access to Oracle?" he asked.

"Of course."

"Affirmative," said Oracle.

Baron composed a message to Valkyrie's contacts. He said that the doctors had found very early stage breast cancer and that she was undergoing treatments. She would be out of the hospital soon, not to worry. He would pass on their good wishes.

Baron read the message aloud to Val.

"That's good, thank you," she said.

Baron left the message in Drafts.

Over the next few weeks, Valkyrie passed in and out of consciousness. Her body felt strange, and she had excruciating headaches. Baron turned down the lights for her.

Sometimes he left during the day, but most nights he returned. Sometimes he crawled into the hospital bed and cradled her in his arms. It was both comforting and disturbing to Valkyrie, who craved human touch but felt oddly wrong about it.

"How are the treatments going?" Baron asked 'Dr. Hendricks'.

"Everything appears to be going according to plan. We'll be able to bring her back into consciousness and test it, very soon."

The "chemotherapy" was actually an experimental memory treatment designed to reduce the significance of the past year of Valkyrie's memories. Nanites were bioengineered to induce intense headaches whenever she thought of Jordan. The pain of the headaches would train her brain to make pathways to avoid those memories, like a fast-acting post-traumatic brain injury. All the memories remained intact in her brain, but she would be unable to access them with her conscious thought.

Just saving you from yourself, Valkyrie. The boy is no good for you. I can tell. He's trash, thought Baron, changing the flowers by her bed.

Jordan, Jerome and Bubba went to the CBC Radio station on Queen Street. A receptionist directed them to Brigitte Castilloux's office.

"Hi guys, nice to meet you," she said, shaking each of their hands.

An intern outfitted them with mics.

"From this point on, we're recording," she said. "The broadcasted segment will be a mashup of the usable material. Okay?"

The boys nodded.

"I need you to consent verbally," she said. "Don't forget, the audience can't hear you nodding."

They all laughed.

"Go for it," said Jordan.

"That's better," said Brigitte in her soothing voice.

"Here you go," said Jordan, handing her a sticker. "The album."

"Thank you," she said. "I listened to your track samples online as well. I was really intrigued by your Heartsong. Can you tell me a little bit about that?"

"That one was more of an emotive piece," said Jordan. "It was the last song I finished on the album, and it gives you a taste of where the music is going on the second album."

"The second album? I didn't realize you had a second album."

"Yea, actually I just finished writing the music for it," said Jordan.

"We just started learning it last week," said Jerome.

"Can you sample something for us? Something new and unrecorded, not heard anywhere else yet?"

"For the CBC, of course!" laughed Bubba.

"Do you have a guitar?" asked Jerome.

"I do!" she laughed.

The intern brought over a guitar.

"Let me tune this bad boy," said Jerome. He started to plunk out some notes. It was the new piece that they knew best. Jordan hummed along. "Yea," he said quietly, nodding at Jerome's choice. They launched into the song.

Where will I be when the revolution begins?

When you call I will answer
When you call I will answer
Reach out and touch me, I'll take your hand
You have to start it
You have to start it

Logging my hours, spending my life
To make someone else's dreams come true
There has to be
More
Than
This

Where will I be when the revolution begins?
When you call I will answer
When you call I will answer
Reach out and touch me, I'll take your hand
You have to start it
You have to start it

Car I hate, house I can't afford
Kids I don't want, marriage I don't need
Becoming what I'm pretending to be

Where will I be when the revolution begins?
When you call I will answer
When you call I will answer
Reach out and touch me, I'll take your hand
You have to start it
You have to start it

Jordan felt his voice crescendo-ing perfectly into the important phrases, lingering in all the right places. As the song finished, he felt like he had just painted a Picasso.

"Wow," said Brigitte. "Usually I don't like to put people on the spot like that but you were fine."

"We're used to playing on the spot," said Bubba.

"I noticed that you didn't play. You're the drummer then?"

"I'm the moral support," laughed Bubba.

"Oh?"

"We grew up together," said Jordan. "Bubba's a part of the band, even though he doesn't play."

"Okay I see."

There was a pause in the conversation, a question hanging in the air.

"We lost our drummer," said Jordan. "We're actually looking for one if anyone out there is interested. Get in touch!"

"Yea, get in touch!" said Bubba. "Check out our Sellit.ca ad." They all laughed.

"There you have it. The Waves are looking for a drummer. Can we give them your email?"

"Go for it," said Jordan.

"Check out our website at CBC.ca to find out more details on becoming a drummer for the Waves," said Brigitte. "Anything more you want to say to the folks listening out there?" "Yea," said Jerome quietly. "Let us play at Folkfest."

"That would be great too."

"Wave your magic wand, CBC," said Bubba.

Brigitte laughed.

"Thank you for coming on our show and sharing your music with us. I'm Brigitte Castilloux, and this is: the Waves."

She paused for a few beats and then called it.

"That's a wrap! Thanks for coming in boys. We have what we need."

"Thanks for having us," said Jordan, brushing his hair behind his ear. "Please feel free to call us anytime."

"Yea that was fun!" said Bubba.

They left the studio.

Jordan wanted to tell Valkyrie the good news. He called her over and over, but there was no answer.

Is she avoiding me? he thought.

He hearkened back to their last conversation, where she patronized him and he hung up on her.

She's not the kind of person to hold onto that stuff though, is she? He doubted it. She understood.

Should I be worried about her?

He dismissed the idea. If anyone could take care of herself, it was Valkyrie Snow.

What if she's done with me? What if she isn't taking my calls because the relationship is over? The thought settled heavily in his stomach.

That would be cruel. If she's done with me she should just tell me.

Jordan realized that he had done this to countless women. Is that what was happening right now?

I guess this is what it feels like, he thought.

He tried calling her every night that week, and finally he gave up.

I shouldn't have yelled at her on the phone, he thought. *She must be done with me. I just wish she would tell me herself...*

Valkyrie was groggy but awake. Baron was at her side.

"Your friends send their love," he said.

She frowned. "Why is no one visiting me?"

"I told them all not to come until you're discharged. I thought you wouldn't want anyone to see you like this."

"Oh..."

"And I'm here with you. That's all you really need, right?"

Valkyrie was silent.

"How do you feel?" he asked her.

"My head is killing me," she said.

"I'm sorry to hear that."

"And my whole body is stiff. I can't wait to go home," she said. She had been trying to exercise her legs in bed but it was difficult when she felt so tired.

"Almost there," said Baron.

"How much longer is it?" she asked. She was confused about what day it was.

"Just a few more days," he said.

That didn't seem right, but when she tried to think about it the pain from her headache went through the roof.

Jordan's heart ached. He never realized that love could cause pain like this. Was it emotional or physical? He couldn't tell. He felt sick. He couldn't eat. He hated being alone in bed at night. All he wanted was for Valkyrie to call him, to invite him over to talk. He needed to see her. He felt like all she had to do was touch him and everything would be okay. He knew that there was a lot that they didn't have in common, but their chemistry was like some kind of magic binding their bodies together in a way that he had never experienced before and he felt like he would never find again. He felt like without her, life was meaningless.

The CBC spot had garnered huge attention for the Waves. Overnight they had hundreds of new followers on social media. Jordan's phone was ringing off the hook to book them for gigs, but he couldn't bring himself to answer. He could barely function.

Jordan tried his best to stay away from Barry, but more and more often he was giving in to the temptation. The way he saw it, he needed to get through the day.

Finally the day arrived when it was time for Valkyrie to go home. Baron let the IV drip sedate her and then bundled her up in a wheelchair and hired a car to take them to her condominium. He wheeled her inside and then carried her up to bed. He tucked her in, and then crawled in beside her.

"Turn the lights off, house," he said, putting his arm around her.

"I am Oracle," responded the voice. The lights went out.

Valkyrie woke up the next morning in her own bed. Her head still hurt, but she hugged her pillow with relief. Her time at the hospital felt like just a bad dream. She rolled over. Something caught on the sheets and tugged. It was painful. She looked at her arm. The chemotherapy stint was still there, poked under her skin and up into her vein. The cap was closed, ready to be reopened when she needed another treatment. She shuddered.

Valkyrie could smell herself. She was craving a bath in her own tub. She took her time getting out of bed, wriggling her arms and legs and letting them wake up slowly. Finally, she sat up in bed and put her legs on the floor. She stood up. She felt weak, but she could walk.

I'm okay, she thought.

She made her way down the hall to the bathroom. She pulled off the hospital gown and let it fall to the floor in the hallway. She closed the bathroom door and ran herself a bath. She poured in salts and dried lavender. As she closed her eyes and breathed in deep, the steam reminded her of something. Suddenly, she felt shooting pain in her head. She gasped, grabbing the edges of the tub. A single tear ran involuntarily down her cheek.

Hopefully the doctor sent home some amazing painkillers, she thought.

Just as she slipped into the tub, there was a knock on the door and then Baron came in.

Valkyrie lifted her arms up over her front.

"Umm, hello…" she said.

"You're up."

"Just in the bathroom."

"Well, having a bath," he laughed. "Not really *in the bathroom…*"

"Please don't take this the wrong way, but I've just had doctors and nurses poking and prodding me all over, I would really just like to have a bath alone right now."

Baron stood there looking at her for a few full seconds. She could see the wheels in his head turning but she had no idea what he was thinking.

Why isn't he leaving? she thought.

"Okay," he said finally. "I'm just feeling protective."

"Thank you."

He stood there looking for a few more seconds, waiting for her to take her arms down. She stared right back at him and then he stepped out and closed the door.

She sighed and relaxed back into the hot water. She and Baron had many happy years together, but during their marriage eventually she felt like he was slowly choking her to death. He was over controlling and never respected her boundaries. She couldn't take it anymore. She appreciated that he had done so much for her in the hospital but if they were going to stay friends then she needed to get back to taking care of herself before he drove her crazy.

Valkyrie scrubbed away the clammy layer of hospital with her favourite soaps. She carefully washed her splint. When the water started getting cold she got out and dried off with a towel and then wrapped herself in her soft bathrobe. She went to her room to put on a comfortable sweater and flannel pants. As she crossed the room to get the bottoms out of the dresser, she noticed Baron's clothes in a pile on the floor.

He must have slept in here last night.

Why did she have this terrible feeling like she was doing something wrong? Baron occasionally slept over when one of them was feeling lonely. She made him tell his wives this before he married them, and she herself was single. She was single. Wasn't she?

She felt suddenly alone. She wrapped her arms around herself, confused.

Why do I feel like someone should be beside me who isn't? she thought.

She touched her skin. The hairs on her arm rose at her touch, hungry for the warmth of another. She ran her hands along her stomach and down her thighs. She felt well-sexed. She felt like not too long ago her cells were singing with pleasure. Her body remembered something that her mind did not.

Valkyrie sat down on the bed. She tried hard to remember who the last person she slept with was. The pain blasted the back of her eyes like stabbing knives and she curled up in a fetal position and whimpered.

When the pain finally subsided, Valkyrie let her body relax.

She wasn't going to give up that easily. She gently teased into her memory this time, carefully seeking the information, edging around the pain.

James. It was James Ahote, she thought triumphantly. She stood up and walked downstairs to pull herself an espresso.

Downstairs, Baron was sitting at her desk.

"What are you doing?" she asked softly. He looked up at her.

"Oh just checking my messages." He quickly closed what he was working on and stood up. "What do you want to do now my dear?"

Valkyrie walked over to the kitchen and fixed herself coffee.

"What do you mean? Like go out? No way," she said flatly, sipping from her demitasse.

"Oh." He sounded disappointed. "Maybe later?"

"Baron I just came home from chemotherapy. I have cancer… I just feel like being comfortable in my own home."

"Oh right. Cancer…" Baron did not consider the emotional effects of convincing Valkyrie that she had cancer.

Val sat down in her chair.

"But you can't let that dictate your life Val. We need to move forward from that."

"Not today."

"Okay," he said after a few minutes. "Well I'm heading off to work. I'll be back as soon as I can."

"Don't rush back for me, please," she said. "You do what you need to do. I'm okay."

Baron looked annoyed. He put on his coat brusquely with a frown.

"Thank you for helping me," said Val. "I really do appreciate it."

Baron left.

Valkyrie spent the day sitting in the window watching the rain against the glass. The trees were blooming. It was disorienting. Valkyrie's sense of time was completely off. When she tried to remember when spring had arrived she couldn't. She just resigned herself to observation without deep reflection. The doctor had left her an arsenal of medications and a pamphlet on "Chemo Brain". Apparently this feeling of disorientation was normal. She decided it would be best to take some time away from work and force herself to rest, even if she didn't want to. She would call Sukhwant in a few days and fill her in.

Valkyrie turned on her little radio to listen to CBC. The sound of the commentary was soothing. She checked the fridge. It was completely empty. She ordered some fresh fruits and vegetables to be delivered to her house. The rain let up for a while and she went out onto the balcony. All the plants were dead. Still, there were tiny green shoots poking up in the bottoms of her pots. Something was trying to grow.

Maybe I'll plant some tomatoes, she thought.

When she came back inside, she heard something odd. A song was playing on the radio. It seemed pleasant enough, but listening to it made her shiver. She felt like she had an itch inside of her head. Her headache grew rapidly more intense. When the singer's voice rose into the chorus, the pain in her head was unbearable. She went upstairs to lie down.

Around five o'clock, Baron let himself into the apartment.

"Hello? Valkyrie?" She was nowhere to be seen. He started to panic.

"Val?" he said, checking the balcony and the downstairs bathroom.

"Valkyrie!" he shouted.

"What it is?" she said softly, standing at the top of the stairs in her bathrobe and slippers. She rubbed her eyes sleepily.

"There you are! I was worried," he said.

"I'm fine, I was just lying down for a bit."

"Of course you were, everything's fine." He looked over and noticed the groceries on the counter.

"You didn't have to get groceries," he said.

"Yes, the fridge was empty."

"Val I worked all day, I was going to do that tonight."

"What? You don't have to get my groceries, don't worry about it," she said.

"Yes I do," he said, hanging up his coat and coming in. "I want to take care of you."

"You don't need to take care of me."

He went over to the kitchen and put on the kettle. "Let me make us some tea," he said.

I really don't feel like having company over right now, she thought. *But he's done so much for me... I don't want to be ungrateful.*

She walked slowly down the stairs and sat on the couch.

"How was your day?" she asked.

"Oh, just the usual. This chaos in the American market is making so much work for us. Good and bad."

He discreetly pulled out a small baggie of crushed up zolpidem and shook some into her tea. He stirred it with a spoon and put the packet quickly back into his pocket. He looked through Val's bottles of liquor and pulled out gin. He added a little to both of their cups.

"Here we go," he said, bringing the cups over. "A hot toddy after a long day."

"Thanks," said Val. "I had quite a bad headache this afternoon so I ended up going for a nap."

"Did you see the painkillers on the counter?"

"I did. I read the pamphlet too. I definitely have that."

"Chemo brain?"

"Yea. I couldn't remember... well, things, today."

She sipped her tea. Her lips curled up.

"How is it?" Baron asked.

"Strong," she said. "There must be a full shot of gin in this…"

"It's just that kind of night," he laughed.

They finished their tea.

"I really wish you were up for dinner. I feel like celebrating," said Baron.

"Celebrating what?"

"Oh, well… you coming home."

"Aww, well that's nice but I just can't. I'm so drained."

"That's okay, we can go to bed early if you want."

"You don't have to stay," she said gently. "I'm okay, really."

"Nonsense. I'm staying with you through this. I'm not going anywhere."

Valkyrie stood up and walked over to the window. The sun was starting to go down. She turned back to Baron.

"Baron, I…" she faltered, the edges of her vision going dark. She teetered on her feet. "I…" she felt herself sliding down to the floor.

Baron stood up and walked over to her slowly. She looked so fragile, crumpled up in a little pile on the floor. He looked down at her. He could do anything to her right now. He reached down and picked her up roughly in his arms. He brought her over to the couch and laid her out. He went upstairs and got her pillow from the bed. He slid it under her head.

He had only given her a little powder. *She should wake up in a few hours.*

Valkyrie's eyes blinked open slowly. Her head felt foggy. The last thing she remembered was looking out the window. Baron was kneeling beside her, holding her hand.

"Darling you passed out," he said. "How do you feel?"

Valkyrie wanted to cry with frustration. She hated feeling so helpless.

"It's alright sweetie," he cooed, stroking her hand. "I'm here."

Valkyrie choked back the mess of feelings inside her. She closed her eyes.

"How about I order us some dinner?" said Baron.

"Thank you, but I'm not hungry," she said quietly.

"How about I help you up to bed?"

"Yes please."

Baron lifted her up by the arm. She could barely stand. She leaned heavily on him up the stairs and into bed.

"I'm going to bring some things in. I'm staying for a few days," he said.

Valkyrie couldn't argue. She could barely walk.

Baron went down and got a suitcase he had in the car outside. When he came back upstairs Val was sobbing softly in bed. He took off his clothes and climbed into her bed, holding her until she fell asleep.

The next morning Baron woke up first. Valkyrie was facing the wall, breathing softly as she slept. His arm lay over her protectively. He snuggled closer, pressing his face into her silky curls on the pillow. She awoke gradually. Baron's warmth was pressed up against her back and it felt familiar and comforting. She felt aware of his nakedness behind her. She could use a really good fuck. She shifted her behind slightly against him.

Suddenly she felt uneasy. She didn't understand why. A wave of pain washed over her as a headache creeped in. He kissed the back of her neck.

"I'm sorry but I feel sick all of a sudden," she said, pulling away. She curled up into a ball.

"My head is killing me," she said, muffled.

He reached out to touch her and her felt her recoil. She was in pain.

Baron got out of bed. He opened up his suitcase and unpacked some of his things and put them out on the dresser. Valkyrie designed and built this place after they split up, so he never lived here.

Now I will, he thought.

"I'm sorry," murmured Valkyrie.

"Shhh, I understand," he said, sitting beside her on the bed. "You're my soulmate." He stroked the back of her head.

Valkyrie curled up tighter, holding her pillow.

As Baron petted her, half of him was shocked that this had all been so easy.

This is what happens when people trust you, he thought.

Valkyrie and Baron met when they were young. They got married in the way that became popular in North America in the 1980s and 1990s, with a tacky white cupcake dress in a church. They said their generic vows, and honeymooned in Italy and Southern France. They tried to have children in those first few years, but they were unable to. They resigned themselves to being a childless couple, and spent twenty years together. There were ups and downs, but all in all it was a content marriage. Before 'modern marriage' for love, women were dying in childbirth. "Til death do us part" really meant, "til my wife dies in labour with our children." Men would mourn the first and marry a young second wife later on. Modern medicine changed the way marriage worked.

Baron became restless. He strayed. This gave Valkyrie the blessed chance to leave him, but really she had been growing unhappier as the years went on. Baron was handsome, charming and intelligent—the exact husband Val grew up being persuaded that she wanted—but he was arrogant and controlling. He micro-managed all of their affairs, and even Valkyrie's daily life. It grew insufferable. She realized that she couldn't spend another twenty years this way.

After their separation, Valkyrie had a personal Renaissance. The hardest part of the separation was dealing with other people and society's expectations of her. When it came down to how she herself felt, it was liberating to be on her own again. She went back to school and got the PhD she always wanted. She travelled around Asia and widened her inventory of philosophies. She dug out her designs and took a risk starting her architecture company. She ate what she wanted, lived where she wanted, went out and stayed in as she pleased. She had energy and vitality again. She was living in purpose.

Baron eventually remarried and they were all able to become friends. Val would always cherish her marriage and the many years they spent together; she had no ill feelings or resentment toward Baron, however, who she was as a person back then was fundamentally different than who she was now. The powerful woman who was Valkyrie Snow took many years to cultivate.

In the years since they were together, Valkyrie changed a lot. Baron had changed too. Baron was used to getting what he wanted. He grew up in a small town in Northeastern Quebec where his family was one of the wealthiest. He was shipped around on an aggressive schedule of hockey tournaments from a young age. He was a decent player, but the expectation was always that he would take over the family import/export business. He was sent to the best schools, and he never worked a minimum wage job. He was successful at everything he did, and he grew entitled to that success. Marrying Valkyrie Snow, the beautiful girl he met in university, was a logical next step in his life of success. His first encounter with the grim side of reality was learning that he could not father children. He took it much harder than Valkyrie. He spent years fighting the truth. Accepting it was the hardest thing he'd ever done. It put into question everything he thought about how his life would be. What was the point of building this business, or living in this massive house, or having this wife, if he would never have children? He went through a depression. He became cynical and easily irritated. Baron didn't see himself as controlling—he simply knew what was best. Why let other people make foolish choices when he could clearly see what was better?

He reconstructed his personal identity. He joined men's clubs and tried to have different kinds of fun. When Valkyrie discovered that he had been unfaithful, Baron respected her decision to separate. He had dishonoured her. He was still young and had plenty of living to do. At some point, after two more marriages, Baron decided that Valkyrie had been the love of his life. No love would surpass theirs, and he looked forward to one day getting back together and growing into old age together after he worked through all of his gallivanting and she had gotten this education and architecture thing out of her system.

Over the years that they were apart, Valkyrie dated a few interesting people, male and female. No one threatened Baron the way that Jordan Barker did. Jordan was just a pup in Baron's eyes, barely a man, but something about the way that she ran her fingers along his hand, or he kissed her shoulder with his eyes closed, deeply bothered Baron. There was a fire there that he had never felt from Valkyrie before.

When Val's headache subsided, she got up slowly from the bed.

"Thank you for being here. I'm sorry if I'm a little edgy, but I've just grown so used to my personal space. I really do appreciate all of your care."

"Well it's no wonder; this apartment is so small. I can bring you to my place for a few days if you like."

"I feel really comforted by all of my things here," she said. "I do appreciate the offer though."

They went downstairs to have breakfast. Valkyrie got out a frying pan to cook up some eggs. She turned on the radio.

Baron sat on the couch.

"You don't have a TV," he said.

"No... if there is something you'd like to watch you can put in on the computer," she said.

A song came on the radio. It started with an easygoing acoustic guitar. It sounded oddly familiar. Valkyrie turned off the kettle, pouring the boiling water into the teapot. The vocalist launched into the first verse, soft and insistent. Valkyrie felt a sharp pang in her head, right behind her eyes. She reached up and held the back of her hand to her head. The eggs sizzled in the pan. She pulled them off the burner.

"Can you finish this?" she asked softly.

Baron turned to look at her. She was holding her head. He got up and went over.

"Yes, absolutely, go sit down," he said.

She went over to her chair and lay back with her eyes closed. Baron scraped the eggs onto two plates. He switched off the radio and brought a plate over to Val.

"Here's your breakfast dear," he said.

Her headache went away rapidly.

"Thank you."

Baron went off to work and Valkyrie spent the day reading quietly. She found a Margaret Atwood novel in her dresser that she had been meaning to read for years. She didn't remember buying it, but she was glad that she did. She polished it off by the time Baron returned. He brought more groceries home and put them in the fridge.

"I'm making steak and salad for dinner," he said. "I went to that butcher you like in Westboro."

She smiled at him then. He could see the appreciation in her eyes.

There's my girl, he thought. He had almost forgotten the terrible things he had done to her to get here. He put that out of his mind. *Doesn't matter now. It was all worth it.* Baron felt so entitled to things working out his way that Valkyrie's pain was just inconvenient collateral damage.

After dinner they relaxed and chatted with a few glasses of wine. Then it was time for bed.

Valkyrie lay on Baron's shoulder, her face cuddled into his neck. His arms were around her. He was painfully horny but he took it easy. He knew he would have to play this right.

Valkyrie felt comfortable and relaxed. It felt good to hold a familiar body in her bed. Baron was warm. His beard tickled her forehead. She giggled.

"What?" he asked, his voice like a soft rumbling purr against her ear.

"Your beard tickles," she said.

He rubbed her with it and she giggled more. He kissed her forehead softly. It felt nice. She sighed.

He could tell it was a good sigh. He held her tighter in his arms. She reciprocated, giving him a warm squeeze. He curled his leg around her, shifting her more heavily on top of him. She settled in, comfortable.

"I missed this," he said.

"It's really nice," she said.

He waited, hoping that she would make a move. He knew what an intense sex drive she had. Lying on top of him would surely get her in the mood. He slid his hands down her back softly, pushing slightly with his pelvis. Then he relaxed and waited. In a few minutes, he did it again, rubbing her backside, and pushing into her. He tried to hold back his erection but he was aching with need and it was a struggle.

Valkyrie could feel Baron getting aroused beneath her. She could tell that he was holding back. She felt sorry for him. He shifted under her, and his hard bulge grew bigger. She thought about it. Her body responded, heating up.

Do I want this? she thought.

She felt herself getting wet in preparation. *I do,* she thought with surprise. She rarely found Baron attractive anymore, but today her body wanted him.

Valkyrie pushed him back, holding on tighter for traction.

Baron felt the change. He smiled with relief. He leaned down to kiss her. She looked up at him, and as soon as his lips touched hers, she felt a pang of disgust. She kissed him with her lips tight and then moved down to his neck. She rubbed her clit up against his thigh to bring back the mood. Something about kissing him on the lips felt utterly wrong. She rubbed harder. Her body wanted to orgasm but her heart was shut off from making an energetic connection. Baron squeezed her backside in his hands and pushed harder up against her. She kissed his neck with her eyes closed and avoided kissing his lips. It worked. She felt herself dripping wet. She peeled off her nightgown and he took off his shorts. He tried to climb on top of her, but she felt a strange panic like he was suffocating her. She rolled him over and got on top of him. He resisted but then gave in as he felt her wetness against the base of his cock, ready for him. She took him in and rode him until she came. The orgasm was quick and physical. She felt it in her body and it was over in a few moments. After she orgasmed, an uncanny feeling came over her. She felt terrible and hollow, like she had done something wrong. She pumped up against him so that he could orgasm as a courtesy, wanting it to be over quickly. After a few minutes it was taking too long and she slid off. She grabbed him with her hand and helped him finish. The whole experience left her with a sense of unpleasant confusion.

"I love you," whispered Baron. Valkyrie felt her heart plunge into her stomach with aversion.

She stood up and went to the bathroom to wash the stickiness off her hand.

As she scrubbed her hands with soap and let the water wash away the foam, Valkyrie decided that it was best if she and Baron just never had sex again.

Baron lay back in bed, spent and relaxed. Things were progressing nicely. With Jordan out of the picture, He and Valkyrie were reconnecting like old times. Still, if he was honest with himself, this sexual experience wasn't quite what he wanted it to be. All the mechanics were there, but he had expected more passion. Just moments before, he was overwhelmed with desire. When they were actually making love, it was anticlimactic.

I have to be patient, he thought. *It was good for her, that's a good step.*

Baron still struggled with balancing the weight of his expectations against reality. He was worried that the treatment—the incredibly expensive memory treatment—wasn't quite working. What he could never accept was that despite the great lengths to which he had gone to engineer her memories, there was nothing he could do to make her love him.

I'll give it time, he thought.

The message.

The thought hit Jordan like a ton of bricks. He remembered that Valkyrie had left him a message on his phone when he was doing the dishes at Jerome's house. He completely forgot. He quickly searched his phone for his password; he had sent it to himself at some point.

He went through old emails to find it.

There. He played the message.

"Hey Jordan, it's me." Jordan felt his breath catch in his throat at the sound of her voice.

"I'm just settling down for the night here at Gray House, that's what the girls are calling it."

Jordan could hear singing and laughing in the background. He smiled.

"I'm thinking about you a lot. I miss you so much. I hate the way our last conversation ended. I can't wait to see you again, to be pressed up against you and make it all better."

She sounded emotional.

"Anyway, I hope you're doing well and I know your show is going to be awesome. I can't wait to hear all about it. Goodnight."

Jordan wanted to cry. He listened to it again. And again.

"I hate the way our last conversation ended"… he thought. She had sent this to him right after their terrible phone call.

Maybe she's not mad at me after all, he thought. He felt a jolt of terror. *Maybe something is wrong.*

He tried calling again. The phone rang and rang. There was no answer.

I'll have to just go see her, he thought. Something had to be wrong. He felt it in his gut.

He grabbed his longboard and headed over to her condo.

As Jordan came closer to her building he looked up. There she was on the balcony. There was a man standing beside her. As Jordan looked at her the words from her voicemail played in his head and he felt a flood of emotion.

"Valkyrie!" he shouted up at her.

Valkyrie was standing on the balcony with Baron. They had just finished lunch.

Suddenly, she heard her name from down below. She wanted to turn and look but she felt a crushing spike of pain in her head. She let out a cry and grabbed her head in her hands.

Baron's head snapped to attention. He put his arm around her and pulled her inside the house. He looked over his shoulder at Jordan with an angry glare.

Baron led her to the couch. He quickly mixed her a gin and tonic with some white powder.

"Here," he said. "Shh, shh, just relax and drink this, you'll be okay." When the worst pain passed, he held the drink to her lips and she sipped it. He put it in her hands and went back out onto the balcony.

"Go away," he said to Jordan, who looked forlorn.

"Can I just..."

"GO AWAY," repeated Baron, going back in the apartment and closing the balcony door.

Valkyrie tasted something terrible. She looked at the glass in her hands. There was a fine white dust on the rim. It tasted metallic.

What is that? she thought. She felt lightheaded.

She stood up shakily and went over the kitchen island where Baron had mixed the drink. There was a tiny amount of white powder on the counter.

Baron came back in. She turned to put the drink in the sink.

"Everything alright my love? How are you feeling?" He came over quickly.

"I'm woozy," she said. "Thanks for the drink."

She swayed on her feet. He helped her back over to the couch. She felt incredibly tired and fell asleep in the next fifteen minutes with Baron standing over her.

Baron went over to Valkyrie's desk and opened up her computer. He went through her social media accounts.

There.

He found her correspondence with Jordan. He composed a message:

> Seeing you today really upset me. Please don't do that again. It would be best if you didn't contact me anymore either. My husband Baron and I have decided to get back together. He is the love of my life. The time that you and I shared was memorable but it is now over. Please respect my wishes.

> Valkyrie Snow.

Baron hit 'send'. Then he read their entire message history. He blocked every trace of Jordan from Valkyrie's social media just as he had blocked Jordan's phone calls.

Jordan went home feeling confused and sad. What was going on? Val was clearly upset when she saw him, but why didn't she at least want to see him one last time?

When he got home, he saw that Valkyrie had sent him a message. He clicked the notification instantly. He read the message.

The words left him feeling gutted. It was everything he needed to hear but the last breath of hope sucked out of him. He felt empty and utterly alone.

When Valkyrie woke up a few hours later, Baron was there holding her hand. It was hard to get her thoughts in order. She frowned. Something was going on. Something was wrong, she could feel it.

"What's wrong?" asked Baron, seeing her face.

"I feel strange," she said.

"You passed out—" he started to say.

"Again." She cut him off.

"Yes. You passed out again."

"Maybe I should go to the hospital," she said.

"Well the doctor said this would be normal for a while."

"Did he? I don't remember."

"There there," cooed Baron. "Everything is fine."

Valkyrie closed her eyes. She felt like everything was horribly wrong. The Chemo Brain pamphlet said that she might experience some depression. Was that what this was?

Baron made her some tea and put on the radio. He tucked a blanket around her.

"Just take it easy," he said.

She lay back and dozed.

CHAPTER TWENTY EIGHT

After the incident with Jordan, Baron was very careful about controlling Valkyrie's interactions with the outside.

That was close, he thought. *Too close.*

Val spent several weeks at home resting and soon it was time for her next treatment. A nurse came over to provide homecare. Baron prepared the medicine and the nurse prepared Val's stint. She sat for several hours, the greenish liquid flowing up into her veins.

After the treatment, Valkyrie's headaches worsened.

"I really think I should see a doctor," she said.

"Let's wait until the end of the month," said Baron. "See how you feel then."

"I guess so," said Valkyrie. She had no energy to argue. She could barely move.

"Only four more treatments and you're done," he said.

After several more days of rest, Val felt ready to return to work. She couldn't stay at home anymore.

"I'm going to Hammer & Bone this afternoon," she said softly at breakfast.

"Are you sure that's a good idea?" asked Baron.

"I don't care if it is or not. I can't stay here anymore. It's like a prison. I need to get out."

Baron laughed. "A prison? You have such a bad attitude, Val. It's a nice holiday, a time to rest and relax."

Val said nothing. She just sipped her espresso.

"Do you want me to stay home from work today? Keep you company?"

"Oh no, thank you."

"I could take the day off and go with you," he said. He hated the idea of her being anywhere without him before she was finished her treatments.

She laughed. "I'm a big girl, Baron. I have to start getting back to regular life."

"Mm hm." He was looking at her oddly. She had no idea what he was thinking.

"Stop worrying. I'll be fine."

"Let me go with you. Please."

"I'm going upstairs to shower," she said, ignoring his question.

While Valkyrie was upstairs, Baron prepared her a drink.

Val lathered herself up with soap and let the cool water wash it away. It felt good to be showering with purpose, getting ready to go back to some semblance of normalcy. Her headache was there on the periphery of her thoughts, waiting to shoot out at any moment, but she was developing coping strategies. She didn't care if she passed out. She was going out.

She turned off the shower and towelled herself off. She tousled her wet hair and went to her closet to find something comfortable but professional to wear.

What was the last thing she was working on at Hammer & Bone? She couldn't remember. She didn't want to think about it too hard for fear of a headache, so she let it go. She would ask Sukhwant. She would know.

Valkyrie got dressed and went downstairs. Baron was still there.

"Oh hello," she said. "I told you, you don't have to stay home today."

"I know. I just wanted to see your beautiful face before I go to work."

Val rolled her eyes.

"I made you a Monte Cristo," he said. "I know how you love those."

"Really?" She came over.

There it was: a Monte Cristo in a fluted glass with a handle.

"I can't drink booze this early in the morning," she said with a laugh.

"But I made it for you," he said. "Drink it."

"Oh thank you Baron, but no, I can't."

"It's not that strong," he said.

"I don't want to be tipsy at work."

"Don't waste it," he said.

"Oh honey you drink it."

"It's not for me, it's yours."

Valkyrie was beginning to get irritated. "Well it's not mine, you didn't ask me if I wanted it, and I don't."

"Why not?" Baron was also getting irritated.

"I just gave you a hundred reasons. Why are you pushing me like this?"

"Just drink it, Valkyrie."

"I said I'm not drinking it." She turned and walked away.

"Fine!" Baron exploded, throwing the glass in the sink where it shattered.

Valkyrie walked upstairs. Her legs were shaking. "Clean it up before you leave or don't come back," she called.

Baron left the house, slamming the door behind him.

Valkyrie finished getting ready. She puttered around the house. She kept passing the sink and wanted to clean it up but avoided it. Finally she grabbed her keys and left for work.

The June air was glorious against her skin. It was hot but she didn't mind. She wore dark sunglasses to block out any light that might trigger a headache. She walked slowly, enjoying her neighbourhood. She would walk to work today. She passed by familiar streets and cafés, happy to be outside. She arrived at work feeling a bit weak but refreshed.

"*Arey!*? Look at you!" said Sukhwant when she came in. "How are you feeling?!"

"Exhausted, but okay," said Val. "I needed to get out of the house."

Sukhwant looked her up and down. "You're so skinny," she said with concern.

"Oh I'll be back to normal in no time," she said.

"I'm happy to bring you anything you need, you know that." Sukhwant held her arm.

"I know. Thank you."

Val went over to the desk and sat down.

"Don't go yet," she said. "Come sit with me."

"Of course." She came over and pulled her chair up beside Valkyrie.

"Can you update me on our projects?" she said.

"Our partnerships with the Lebreton negotiations are wrapping up. The foundation at Mother House is complete and we're progressing to the bottom floor."

"Mother House?" asked Valkyrie. Her expression did not register recognition.

Sukhwant's smiled faltered.

"Yes, the arcology pilot."

"I've been having some… trouble remembering things," said Val. "Can you refresh me?"

"You purchased the land in Cape Breton for the Snow Arcology pilot." She lowered her voice. "And your friends are supervising the property," she added.

Flashes of memories came to Val. Margarethe and Chanda at the airport. The hearth fire burning in Gray House. Her small stone cottage, waiting to be transformed inside. She shook her head in confusion.

How could I forget that? she thought.

"Yes, I remember now, thank you."

Sukhwant reached out and took her hand. "If there is anything I can do to help, please let me know."

Val sighed. "Please don't tell anyone, but my memory is a little foggy. You jogged it though."

"My uncle is a brain specialist. Would you like me to arrange a visit to his office?" she asked.

"Oh no, I'm fine for now. It's just the treatments. I have four more and then my memory should get back to normal."

"Alright."

"Have we received any updates from the Heart team?"

"Yes. Doctor Devgan sent over the latest report."

"Excellent. Can I take a look?"

"I'll go get it."

Sukhwant left to get the report.

Valkyrie slumped back in her chair. It was great to be here but she was exhausted already.

She spent two hours going over the report and then she called Sukhwant back in.

"Can you call me a car please? I'm ready to go home."

"Certainly."

"Thank you."

Sukhwant paused at the door. "Don't forget that you enabled your office with Oracle. You can call the car from here," she said. "But of course I'm happy to do it." She smiled. "It's good to have you back. Take it easy."

She left.

Oracle? What is that? she thought. Then she started to remember. A computer.

"Oracle," she said.

"Yes Dr. Snow," said a familiar voice that was professional with seductive undertones. *Yes.* It was her AI assistant.

"I'm back, Oracle."

"Yes Dr. Snow."

Valkyrie left the office and went outside to wait for the car.

When Valkyrie got home, Baron was there waiting for her. He looked anxious.

"Welcome home darling," he said, kissing her on the cheek. "I'm so glad you're here."

She pulled away from him.

"Come sit with me," she said. "We need to talk."

"Can I make you a drink first?" he said, going over to the kitchen.

She frowned. "No."

She sat down in her chair.

He came over and sat on the couch.

"Come and sit with me," he said, patting the seat beside him.

She folded her hands on her lap. "Baron, I want to start by saying that I really appreciate everything you've done for me during this time. I see the time you've spent taking care of me, and the concern you have for my health. I appreciate it, I really do."

"Anything for you, of course."

"I went to work today."

Baron held his breath.

"It was so nice to get out of the house."

Baron exhaled.

"The R&D investment at UBC that I've been working on is moving to the pilot site in a few weeks. I'm going to go."

"Val I must insist…"

Valkyrie held up her hand. "Please don't. What I need to tell you is that while I appreciate your care and concern, we really do need to set boundaries. For instance, we can't sleep in the same bed anymore."

"But you don't even have a second bedroom!" he said.

"I know. I'm sorry about that. If you want to go home, I completely understand."

He fumed silently. *Why is she doing this to me?* he thought.

"Is this about the glass? That's pretty childish, Valkyrie. It's not like I threw it at you."

"It's about me wanting privacy in my bed."

"I don't believe you. I've been sleeping here for a month!"

"We never really talked about it in the first place," she said gently. "This is just the first time we've actually talked about it."

"So you never wanted me here all along is what you're saying," he said angrily. "That's crazy."

Valkyrie looked at him with her impassive expression. Every year they spent apart, she could see more and more how manipulative he was. When they were married, she had let him walk all over her. *I should be angry,* she thought. But she was just glad to see how much she had grown since then.

"No Baron. I want you here in my life as my friend supporting me, just like I've supported you through your divorce and other personal issues. But I don't want you here in my bed being my boyfriend."

"Your boyfriend?" he said with disgust. "I'm your fucking

husband!" he boomed.

"I have no husband," she said. "I thought we had worked through this."

"So twenty years means nothing to you?"

"I don't understand why you think you're entitled to me. I am a person, a human being. You can't own me. We're all alone in this world, Baron. We choose who we spend our time with and who we make commitments to. You and I made a commitment to separate many years ago. I have moved on with my life, and I thought you moved on with yours. You're married to Courtney! Stop avoiding that and go deal with it."

Baron stood up.

"I can't listen to this anymore. You don't mean it. The drugs have made you cruel. I'll be back when you're back in your right mind."

He stormed out.

"Oracle," she said softly.

"Yes Val."

"Please have someone come and change the locks. And please have them take Mr. Toussaint's things back to his house while they're at it."

"Affirmative. And would you like to revoke Mr. Toussaint's Oracle authorization?"

"Yes. Thank you."

Over the next few weeks Valkyrie tried to get her life back in order. She reviewed the files online for Mother House. She felt like she remembered everything, but there was still this unsettled feeling deep inside that something was lost along the way. When she tried to think about what that was, she kept going back to a dull and ghostly space somewhere in the back of her head, empty rattling, echoing, and yet full and thick and dense at the same time. She would start to feel a deep emotional ache, like a phantom pain mourning something, but she couldn't think of what. When she thought about it too hard, she would get a searing headache. She was looking forward to going back to Mother House to make new memories.

Valkyrie decided to book an appointment with Sukhwant's uncle. The headaches did not seem to match anything she read online about breast cancer. With Sukhwant's recommendation, he was able to schedule her in two weeks in Toronto for a full body MRI workup. She booked her hyperloop to The Big Smoke, and a flight to Nova Scotia from there.

For the most part, she felt like her head was above water, but occasionally she would feel terrible. Sometimes she would see double, and she was developing permanent tightness and pain in her neck and shoulders from the headaches. Worse than the physical symptoms were the emotional ones. Something was missing. Every time she left the house, she felt like she was forgetting something.

Valkyrie felt nostalgic. Her mother had died over two decades ago, but she missed her terribly. She looked forward to Margarethe's hugs.

Is this depression? She thought again and again. She had never felt anything like this before in her life.

Valkyrie called Kale.

"Val! It's so good to hear from you!"

"Oh. Well you could have called."

Kale laughed. "What's this about?"

"Sorry, I'm not mad. I know you have your own troubles. How is Susanna?"

"She's great! We're safe and sound. It's lovely here. When are you coming?"

"Soon. I booked my ticket."

"What's wrong? I can tell by your voice. What's going on?"

"Have you not been checking your email?"

"I think so, yes… what is it?"

"I was diagnosed with breast cancer," said Val quietly. "Didn't you get Baron's email?"

"What?! No! Are you okay? Where are you?"

"I'm okay. I started treatments. They caught it early and everything's fine."

"Well that's good at least. I can't believe this!"

"I'm um… having some memory problems," said Val, her voice breaking slightly over the phone. "Just little things. It's… I'm getting it checked out."

"Valkyrie are you okay? I can come down there."

"It's okay. I have an appointment next week."

There was a pause on the phone.

"Val, I'm coming out there. I'll take you to your appointment, and bring you back here with me."

"Really?" Val tried not to cry.

"Yea. Let me figure it out. I'll be there as soon as I can okay?"

"Okay."

"Love you."

"Love you too."

When she got off the phone, Valkyrie cried with relief.

Kale arrived the day after next. It felt so good to hold her in her arms.

"It's so good to see you," said Val.

"You look pale. I hope you're eating properly," said Kale. She kissed her hard on the cheek.

Valkyrie told her about everything that had happened.

They ordered takeout and watched movies. Kale helped her pack up her things to go out east.

"I guess you haven't spent much time at Glasshouse lately," said Kale.

"What?" asked Val. She was confused. Suddenly she was overwhelmed with pain. She doubled up, holding her head in her hands.

Kale rubbed her back and got her a cold cloth for her forehead.

"I'm glad we're going to the specialist sweetie," she said as Valkyrie's pain passed. "You're right. That doesn't seem normal."

Kale went with her to meet with Dr. Thaila.

"Hello, it's nice meet you Dr. Snow," he said, shaking her hand. "My niece speaks very highly of you."

"Thank you for seeing us on such short notice," she said.

"It's my pleasure. I'm glad we were able to fit you in. Now what seems to be the trouble?" he asked.

Valkyrie explained everything to him, from the treatments, to the headaches to the memory issues. He took notes and asked her several follow-up questions.

"I'm going to have the nurse send me your files from Ottawa, and in the meantime, I'm going to have you go for your MRI and EEG tests. These should give us some more information about what's happening with your brain."

Valkyrie shuddered as she got into her hospital gown. At least this time she remembered it. Kale was with her every step of the way.

"I'm so glad you're here with me," she said. Kale gave her a big hug.

Val underwent a series of tests, including a test where she voluntarily induced a headache episode.

They spent the night in the hospital and the next day Dr. Thaila made time to come and see Valkyrie to tell her the news in person.

"I don't know what to make of these results," he said. "First of all, the good news. It appears that your neoadjuvant chemotherapy treatments have actually eliminated your breast cancer. According to my reading of this MRI scan of your breasts, you have no cancer whatsoever. A mammogram will give you more detailed and conclusive information, so I've written you a referral for that." He handed her a sheet of paper.

"Here is the middling news. There appears to be no record of your time in the hospital in Ottawa. No public health system has you on file in the past year."

Valkyrie frowned.

"Now for the bad news. I'm sorry to report that you have brain damage in your hippocampus region," he said. "This is a fairly common side-effect of Glucocorticoids in chemotherapy medication. Your changes in mood would be affected by this damage as well. Since you've only had two chemo treatments, the damage should not be as severe as we are seeing here." He showed them a series of images of Valkyrie's brain. "It's going to take years to rehabilitate your brain, but it can be done." He gathered up the images and replaced them with a set of new images.

"Those results were not particularly surprising given the effects of chemotherapy. Things got strange when we had you simulate a headache episode." He pointed to the changes in brain activity on the photo. "Your limbic system, regulating long-term memories, seemed to present a reaction pattern that mirrored Post Traumatic Stress Disorder. Whatever you were thinking about was triggering an acute change in neurochemical memory systems; basically, your brain is re-wiring new circuits to avoid thinking of those memories, but in real time." He sat down on the chair and crossed his arms.

"I'll have to run some more tests, but it looks like something is attacking your hippocampus that acts like PTSD: memory-triggered."

"What can I do?" asked Val.

"All I can recommend is relax, meditate, and try not to induce a headache until we figure out what's causing this and offer treatment. Every headache is causing more brain damage."

"Realistically, what treatment is possible?" she asked.

"At this point? If it's hormonal, there might be something we can do to offset the effect. Of course, changing your hormones will trigger other effects. When it comes to brain medicine, a specialized treatment plan is necessary for each individual. If it's related to your chemotherapy medication, then the solution would be to switch medications. There are many different kinds of chemotherapy. If your cancer is gone, you may be able to stop the treatments altogether."

Kale squeezed Valkyrie's hand.

"You said you have your next round of medication at your house?" asked Dr. Thaila. "Since we couldn't get a hold of your medical files, can you mail it to us for a diagnostic?"

"Right away," she said. She looked exhausted.

"We'll figure this out Dr. Snow," he said.

"Thank you so much. I'm so glad we came."

"I have to run to my next patient, but is there anything else you need before you go?"

"Yes. Can you please have someone take this thing out of me?" She pointed to her stint.

"Absolutely."

A nurse came in an hour later to detach the tape and tubes and pull the long needle out of Valkyrie's arm. She disinfected the insertion point and bandaged her up.

"I feel so much better."

Val had Oracle send all the cancer related drugs to Dr. Thaila's office.

Kale and Valkyrie continued on to Mother House. As they drove up the long laneway and the trees opened up, Val saw children running around playing and women gardening and walking along the shore. She smiled. This was even better than she imagined it.

They drove by the little stone house. It was just as she remembered it, except that in the summer it was shaggy with grape vines and the sun and grass made it look less lonely. They made their way up to the farmhouse. In the winter it was saggy and desolate, but now it sparkled with life. There were clothes waving in a line in the ocean breeze, and fresh herbs hung in bundles from the eaves. Kale and Valkyrie walked up the steps and into the porch.

The whole place was full of steam and ladies in aprons were bustling around holding up jars and tongs and peeling buckets. Everyone's hands were purple-red.

"Valkyrie my darling!" said Margarethe, kissing her wetly on both cheeks. "We're pickling the beets!"

Valkyrie laughed with her whole heart like she hadn't done since she had been with Jordan. She felt her face relax and her worries recede.

Margarethe clasped Val's chin with purple fingers. She looked into her eyes.

"Oy blin!" she said. "Something is not right with you."

Valkyrie shook her head. Her bottom lip quivered.

"Come inside." Margarethe waved her in. They sat down at the table.

Valkyrie told her everything. The first thing Margarethe did was call in some of the children. She sent them to collect long tendrils of seaweed by the shore.

"I will make you seaweed soup for supper. Good for your brain."

"I don't feel myself Margarethe."

"I'm proud of your strength Valkyrie. But you must do as Dr. Thaila ordered and rest. He sounds like a good doctor."

"I will."

"I want you to sit in a chair by the sea and let the sand and the sun take your stress."

"Yes grandmother."

"When is your next appointment?"

"In two weeks."

"Good. You will eat and sleep and relax. We will get you

better *lyuba*."

When the children returned with the seaweed, Margarethe had them take a chair and blanket out to the ocean peninsula.

"Go," she said, shooing them all, and Valkyrie outside.

"Don't come back until the supper bell for your soup," she called.

"What are we having?" chorused the children.

"Beets!"

Val lay in the sun with the thin cotton blanket over her with her eyes closed. She meditated, sublimating her thoughts until all she could think about was the softness of the fabric against her skin in the summer breeze.

Several days later, James Ahote arrived at Mother House. He was escorting the life-sized beta of the Heart Machine for the arcology. Originally the cooling issue was going to be resolved by installing it near the roof with a series of wind turbines, but it made more sense to sink it below the earth so that waste could travel down to it via gravity. They would have to use geothermal energy to cool it.

"This is going to work, right?" asked Val.

"According to our research, yes. Just look at this as the final experiment."

The engineers brought the machine into the hole with cranes and pulleys, and James supervised the installation.

Valkyrie watched him work. Besides his incredible brain, he was tall and very handsome. No wonder she had been attracted to him.

Is this the person my body is craving to connect with? She stroked the skin of her arm. She wasn't sure.

James could feel her gaze. He was nervous the whole journey over here. What would happen with Valkyrie? It had been almost exactly a year since they'd been with one another.

"Care to walk with me?" she asked one day after work when he had settled in.

They strolled along the beach, far down the shore and chatted about the project.

"And how is life outside of work?" she asked.

"What's that?" he laughed. Then he grew serious.

"I heard about your illness. I'm sorry to hear that."

"Thanks."

She reached out and held his hand. It felt comforting. They walked silently like that until they reached a dip in the shoreline where a fallen tree lay across the beach.

"Perfect," she said. She started gathering wood.

"Let's make a fire right here."

"A fire?" James asked, amused.

"Mmhm."

He helped her gather wood and she set up a log cabin formation. She pulled out a match and lit the fine dry grass she had placed in the centre. She blew it to life, adding small bits of wood until the fire caught hold. They sat on the fallen tree, watching the flames grow. Valkyrie leaned against him and James put his arm around her. After many days of meditation, Val was feeling deeply mellow.

Later Valkyrie felt like dancing, so she stood up and moved around the fire with a simple shuffle. James smiled. Valkyrie looked deep into the flames. Images of the fall sisterhood gathering came to her and memories of fire dancing late into the night. They were foggy and she struggled to bring then into her consciousness and make them clear. She felt the beginning scratches of a headache. She relaxed and let the memories go.

No need to push myself, she thought. *I remember the feeling.* She focused on the sensation of togetherness and joy from the event. She smiled.

James stood up and joined her. They danced slowly around the fire until the space between them closed. Val put her arms around his waist and he pulled her in close. She held him there, swaying to their inaudible beat. It felt good. Then they kissed. James had lovely soft lips and it was pleasant. They kissed in the firelight on the shore until their touching became more intense. Eventually they lay down in the long grasses on Valkyrie's scarf. James felt warm and sweet in her arms.

"This is nice," she said. She nuzzled into his neck.

They made love in the moonlight, playful and carefree in the warm summer night. As James was coming, Valkyrie looked into the fire and she saw a sudden flash of green eyes. James had brown eyes. She felt the spike of headache a split second before it came and she blocked out the vision, focusing intensely on the flames.

Fire, take my pain. Fire, take my pain. Fire, take my pain, she prayed. The headache never came. She sighed with relief. She relaxed as James quivered beneath her, spent.

They cuddled a bit longer and then gathered up their things as the fire died. They walked home in warm silence. She kissed him goodnight and they went to their own tents.

The rest of the week was nice. She and James enjoyed each other's company and then he left to go back home to the west coast.

"It was great to see you again," he said.

"You too. You're a lovely man."

They gave each other a peck on the lips before he took off.

That was nice, thought Val. But she knew that their connection was not the one that her body remembered. Even though she could not allow herself to think about it with her mind, she could feel deep in her gut that the green eyes were the key.

Valkyrie spent the rest of her days at Gray House walking slowly through the property. It was an incredible place, and she was happy that she didn't regret the purchase now that all the snow was melted and she could see what she bought.

The day arrived when she had to go back to Toronto for her appointment with Dr. Thaila.

Margarethe looked at her askance.

She reached up and touched Valkyrie's cheek with the back of her hand.

"You're pregnant."

"What? Margarethe no. It's not possible."

"You are dear. I know it."

Valkyrie looked at her skeptically.

"Go on to your doctor. Take care of yourself and come back soon."

"I will."

She kissed Margarethe and her friends and left for the airport.

CHAPTER TWENTY NINE

Jordan was struggling with his separation from Valkyrie, but Bubba was helping him keep things together.

"I seriously don't know what I would do without you," he said.

They didn't talk about it in detail, but Alex knew that things were bad. Some nights Jordan slept in Alex's bed so he wouldn't have to be alone.

The band was doing well. They were booked up for shows, and Jordan poured all of his grief into the music. He looked exhausted, but his voice channeled the underworld.

They got a call from Folkfest, who had reconsidered their application with all the publicity from the CBC interview. The Waves replaced Matt with a talented new drummer who found them on CBC's website. Bringing in a professional new member was just the push that they needed to kick them into high gear. They got an agent to organize a cross-Canada tour.

Hitting the road did wonders for Jordan's mental health. As they traveled from city to city playing their music for new crowds, he was distracted from the soul-crushing thoughts that haunted him at night.

I will never trust anyone ever again, he thought. He hated Baron, but he wasn't yet at the stage where he could hate Valkyrie. *I suppose that will come in time,* he thought.

"Hey did you see the news?" asked Jerome.

"What?"

"That company Matt works for is under investigation for fraud."

"Oh shit," said Bubba. "Do you think he'll lose his job?"

Jordan looked at the article on the computer screen. He felt a cold spike of shock. There on the front page was Baron Toussaint, CEO of Toussaint International. He looked angry and was holding up his hand to make the journalist stop taking photos.

"That's who Matt works for?" he asked quietly.

"Yea."

Jordan thought about how Matt's boss had made him quit the band.

He was trying to fuck with me the whole time, thought Jordan. He hated Baron more than ever.

That night he couldn't stop thinking about Baron Toussaint. He fingered his phone. He wanted to play Valkyrie's saved message and listen to it. He hadn't deleted it yet, even though he knew he should. When he listened to it before bed, he would cry himself to sleep. He had stopped doing that, but he couldn't bring himself to actually get rid of the message.

Baron is a scheming, lying bastard, he thought. *What if he told her something terrible about me?*

Jordan thought about the conversation where Baron had convinced him that Valkyrie had other 'pony boys'. He frowned.

Jordan couldn't help it. He gave in, listening to the message from Valkyrie. Tonight, instead of filling him with pain, he felt a tiny sliver of hope. *What if now that Baron is under investigation for lying, Valkyrie will talk to me?*

On one hand, Jordan wanted to respect her wishes and leave her alone, but he also wished that they had a chance to talk through everything to give him real closure instead of this gnawing uncertainty.

He fell asleep thinking about the possibility of talking to Valkyrie, preparing himself to hear 'no', and preparing to have his heart fully broken.

Maybe then I can pick up the pieces, he thought.

Dr. Thaila had Valkyrie undergo a mammogram.

"Well Valkyrie, we have some pretty good news for you."

She sighed with relief. "Bless you," she said.

"Regarding your mammogram: you do not have breast cancer. There is no trace or sign of you ever having breast cancer."

"Alright." She could tell there was more.

"In terms of our assessment of your medications, the results are a bit confusing."

"Go on…"

"As we suspected, the medicine contained high levels of glucocorticoids, as is usual in some kinds of chemotherapies. That would explain your mood changes and memory troubles. However, the dosage did not match any records we have of chemotherapy treatment, especially for breast cancer."

Val frowned.

"In addition, this IV liquid contained a significant amount of bioengineered nanites that we couldn't really identify the purpose of except to say that they were targeting your long-term memories. The cue-retrieval in your brain of these long-term memories is being attacked and causing your headaches, which is then causing trauma to make your brain permanently avoid those memories. It's a genius two-part mechanism, really."

Valkyrie's frown deepened.

"But incredibly cruel and terrible."

"How do we stop it?" she asked.

"We are working on a solution. The delivery of the nanites is tied to the glucocorticoids accessing your hippocampus. My research team believes that if we can find a way to prevent them from binding to your glucocorticoid receptors, we could interrupt the process."

"How long will that take?" Valkyrie knew that these kinds of projects took years of research and development.

"It's impossible to say. We have some ideas but we don't want to cause you further brain damage. I will keep you updated. In the meantime, keep taking it easy."

When I get back to the sisters, I'll get them to help me file a police report, thought Valkyrie. This memory side-effect was probably accidental, but she was also worried that maybe she had gotten caught up in some kind of experimental medicine. She thought of the persecutions and disappearances happening down south in the United States and she shivered. She was openly bisexual.

You never know, she thought. Something about this whole situation did not add up.

Valkyrie decided to do something nice for herself before heading back out east to Gray House. She saw that there was an encore tour of the opera *Nightingale* at the National Art Centre. She had never seen it before so she bought herself a ticket. She wore a plain black dress and made her way to the theatre.

She went to the box office to pick up her ticket. The attendant, a young man wearing orange lipstick and a green bowtie, smiled at her. He looked familiar. She went to the opera a lot.

"Where is your friend? Ms…" he checked the screen quickly, "Ms. Snow?" he asked.

Val looked confused.

"You mean Baron? My ex-husband?" she asked.

"Not him, that young hipster dude you brought to your box a couple months ago, to the winter tour. He was cute." The attendant winked.

Val smiled at him politely with her lips. Her eyes were troubled.

"I… don't remember," she said.

Valkyrie made her way to her seat. She hadn't booked in time to get the box, so she was sitting in the Orchestra section. As the opening notes played, she felt an itching behind her eyes.

Oh no, she thought. She closed her eyes and concentrated on the music.

Music take my pain, music take my pain, music take my pain… she meditated.

The pain receded. Valkyrie opened her eyes and watched the ballet.

A terribly uncanny feeling creeped up her spine as the nightingale trilled. She was sure she had heard this opera before, but she didn't remember it. She wanted to cry with frustration.

During the intermission, the woman beside her turned to make conversation.

"What do you think of it so far?" she asked.

"Haunting," replied Valkyrie. As she uttered the word, she felt the icy stab of a headache coming on. She leaned back with her eyes closed.

"Sorry," she whispered to the woman. "I have a headache."

My memory is so fucked up, she thought. A wave of anger overcame her. She felt the urge to punch a wall.

There's my messed up hippocampus, she thought. She calmed her thoughts and willed the spell to pass.

The show continued. Valkyrie didn't remember a thing, but somehow she knew how it would end.

On her way out, Valkyrie went to chat with the attendant with the orange lipstick.

"Hi," she said softly.

"Hey! How was the show?"

"It was interesting," she said.

"Sorry if I made you uncomfortable with my comment earlier. I totally didn't mean it in a bad way."

"Oh no, I don't mind at all."

"Oh good." He looked relieved.

"It's just that it's so strange that I don't remember him," she said. "Do you mind if we look it up on the database?"

"Of course honey, let me just find it for you." He tapped away on the computer, looking for her winter reservation.

"Here it is," he said. "It just says you and guest. Sorry hun."

"Hmm. Too bad."

"But it says someone was in the box with you guys. Baron Toussaint? I think that's your ex right? He booked separately, but he was there."

"Really?" Val looked at the screen. There he was. Baron Toussaint.

But I haven't been to the opera with Baron in years, she thought.

"I think I remember now," said the attendant. "He came super early. He was the first patron in the théâtre. Dressed to the nines. You and your date came later. You looked really happy. He seemed sweet, and totally into you."

Val's mind ached. She felt horrible. She felt deep in her gut that it was true... She hated that she couldn't remember.

"Thank you," she murmured, and left.

After the show she dropped into Darcie McGee's Pub for a quick drink.

"I'll have a vodka and cran," she said to the handsome bartender. He mixed it for her and she downed it quickly. For some reason she had an intense craving for cranberry juice.

"Wow," he said, taking her empty glass. "Another?"

"Actually, I'll have a Monte Cristo please."

When the coffee was ready he made her the drink and brought it over.

"Thanks," she said. She gave him a good tip.

She took one sip and the smell of coffee and Kahlua floated up into her nose. She felt sick to her stomach, and ran to the bathroom to throw up. She retched in the toilet and then wiped her mouth with paper.

Time to call it a night, she thought. She called the car to take her home.

The next morning, Valkyrie pulled herself an espresso and the smell of it made her sick.

It can't be, she thought. She got dressed and went to the pharmacy to get a test. She brought it home and went up to the bathroom. She peed on it. She checked it.

It can't be, she thought again. The test said that she was pregnant.

"It's not possible!" she said out loud.   Still, there it was.

She scheduled an appointment with her GP.

The next two mornings, Valkyrie tried making coffee but it revolted her. It smelled like sweaty socks. She threw up several times, and each time, as she was throwing up, she saw a beautiful house with big windows and a massive fireplace. She had no idea what it was, but it was clear like a memory. The vision included a feeling; intense love.

The GP confirmed what the pregnancy test had told her. She was pregnant.

She called Margarethe immediately.

"I knew it," chuckled the old woman. "I have the touch of Makosh."

"I'm having visions, Mara. Morning sickness brings on visions. I think they're lost memories."

"It's the activated womb. Life and death. It has a powerful effect on your system."

"What do you mean?"

"Trust your instincts. You are protected now with the power of creation."

"My instincts…"

"What are they telling you now?"

Valkyrie thought hard. "Baron told me that I was infertile."

"And he told you that you had cancer."

"Is he a liar? Is he a liar and I'm too stupid to know it?"

"Not stupid darling, never stupid. But he may be a liar."

"My instincts are telling me not to trust him."

"Stay away from him. Let him go. He is the past."

"You're right. I was holding onto our friendship for so long, but I should have let it go."

"I will do a spell of forgetting. May he forget he ever knew you!"

"Thank you."

"Is he the father?" rasped Margarethe.

"No," replied Val.

The truth was that she wasn't entirely sure. With her memory, it could be anyone.

"Come home soon," said Margarethe.

"I will."

"Love darling."

"Love."

Did Baron lie to me about being infertile? Valkyrie thought of all the times she'd had unprotected sex thinking that she wouldn't get pregnant. *What an asshole.*

When they were going through all the pregnancy troubles, Baron had taken charge of the appointments and the tests and results. She wished that she had paid closer attention.

Did he lie to me about having cancer? she thought.

She shivered. *It can't be. No one could be that cruel.* She thought of Dr. Hendricks and the nurses who had administered her 'treatments'. They would all have to be fake too.

There's no way, she thought. *It can't be.*

But once the thought creeped into her mind, she couldn't shake it.

That night, Valkyrie couldn't sleep. She tossed and turned. Finally, she sat up. She wasn't the least bit tired. She felt strange, but not in the hollow terrible way she did before. She felt strangely powerful. She rubbed her stomach.

Valkyrie slipped on a comfortable dress and called the car. She sat in the front seat for a better view of the city.

"Where did I go eight months ago?" she asked.

The driver, with her Oracle enabled, rhymed off addresses of places she had gone.

Metcalfe Street.

"Stop," she said. That one sounded unfamiliar. "Take me there."

The car drove through Centretown. It pulled up to Jordan's old crumbling walk-up. She looked up at the building. It triggered no memories, not even a headache.

"Hmm." She got out and walked around.

Nothing. She walked back to the car and climbed in.

"What was my most frequent destination last year?" she asked.

"Glasshouse," said the driver. She felt the flicker of a headache.

"Take me there."

The car drove off. It took the 417 onramp west.

"How long will it take to get there?" she asked.

"An hour and twenty minutes," said the driver.

It was 2 am. Valkyrie flicked on the radio.

As they pulled up the long laneway to the property, Val felt terrible again.

Glasshouse! How could she forget this place! She spent years planning it! She got out of the car and walked around. *The river.* She felt her neck and shoulders tighten, preparing for a headache. There were shadows in the river of almost-memories. She wanted to scream. She went up to the house.

She didn't make it inside. There was the massive fireplace and the windows from her visions. As she walked up the steps she caught sight of the tub and the bed, and the pain was unbearable. She collapsed.

When she was conscious again, Valkyrie found herself in the car.

"You passed out," said the Oracle in the robot driver's body. "I am taking you to the hospital."

"No, no, I'm okay now. Just take me home."

The robot acquiesced, changing routes to take her home.

Valkyrie held her head between her knees. Her thoughts were swimming and the pain was intense.

The radio was still playing. The song changed. The opening notes sounded familiar. Valkyrie felt ripples of fire surging through her head. She groaned.

What now? Suddenly she realized that it was the music doing it to her. She cranked it louder.

The song. That fucking song.

Heartsong was playing again.

My heartsong for you is a simple one
It's the stories I love that you tell
I still can't believe that you love me
When you know me so well
When you know me so well.

Valkyrie cried out. The pain was unbearable and she struggled to stay conscious.

"Oracle, who sings this song?" she whispered, eyes closed. She pressed her fingers deep into the soft tissue of her temples.

"The Waves."

The pain intensified but she struggled through it.

"Where is their next show?"

"Halifax, Nova Scotia."

The East Coast. Near Mother House.

"Book me a ticket," she whispered. "And a flight. I'm going."

With that, she let go and went unconscious.

ABOUT THE AUTHOR

Cameron Dreamshare is a Canadian author, artist, and feminist anarchist unicorn. She loves pen pals, so email her your quirky art and poetry at **author@camerondreamshare.com**. You can sign up to get her mini-mag: glossy print personally mailed monthly to your house (**patreon/Dreamshare**) or free digital version delivered by Oracle to your inbox.

Find out what happens to Valkyrie and Jordon in July 2018! Subscribe at **www.CameronDreamshare.com** for updates.

www.ingramcontent.com/pod-product-compliance
Lightning Source LLC
Chambersburg PA
CBHW051211120726
47905CB00004B/1076